How to
a Successful

Owner Builder & Renovator

Pinedale Press

Other Books by the Same Author:
Take Me Back to the Eighties
(A Pen and Ink Sketch Book of 19th Century Australian Homes & Buildings)
The Australian House Building Manual
The Australian Owner Builders Manual
The Australian Renovators Manual
The Australian Roof Building Manual
(Hiddle & Staines)
House Building the Easy Hebel Way
Australian Decks & Pergolas Construction Manual
The New Zealand Owner Builders Manual

Published by Pinedale Press

National Library of Australia
Cataloguing-in-publication data

Staines, Allan 1942
National Library of Australia card number and
ISBN: 978-1-875217-31-1

Holder of Copyright
Pinedale Press
2 Lethbridge Court
CALOUNDRA QLD 4551
AUSTRALIA
For Orders, please fax (07) 54 919 219

Ist Edition	September	1986
Reprint	January	1987
Reprint	May	1987
Reprint	May	1988
Reprint	November	1988
Reprint	May	1989
2nd Edition	December	1989
Reprint	January	1991
3rd Edition	March	1993
Reprint	June	1994
Reprint	February	1996
4th Edition	April	1998
Reprint	July	1999
Reprint	November	2000
5th Edition	March	2002
Reprint	June	2003
Reprint	February	2004
6th Edition	March	2005
Reprint	April	2006
7th Edition	June	2007
Reprint	February	2008

Acknowledgements
The Author and Publisher wish to express appreciation to the following organisations and individuals for their product information or proof reading, input, comments and constructive criticism: Brian Peach (Peach Institute), Buildex screws, Selleys Aust., CSR Building Products and Ramset Aust., Cement, Concrete and Aggregates Aust. for material on concrete and traditional cement rendering, and Scott Squire (national trainer to the Thin Section Rendered Coatings Industry).

Also acknowledgement and appreciation is made to: TAFE NSW MECAT curriculum centre for the utilisation of material on the use of tools from 'Course 5158 - Carpentry & Joinery' — Pages 108, 111, 112, 130-131 and to Commonwealth Copyright Administration for the use of material on tools, from the 'Commonwealth Basic Training Manuals' — Pages 102, 106-108, 111, 112, 117, 125-134.

To Lloyd Hiddle for the use of his material on 'Using the Scientific Calculator in Building' Pages 103-105. Also for the use of the adjustable tool — fig 1, Page 110.

To Noela Ollenburg for her computer skills in preparing this material and to Paul Cooper for his penmanship over the author's drawings.

To Tina Homer for her colour rendering over the Author's cover design and for ink drawings of models in the text.

Author's Notes & Instructions

Purpose of this Manual

This manual is intended to give a panoramic view of house construction, how to manage a house building site and perform some common trade skills.

Companion Manual

The Australian House Building manual (HBM) is the companion manual and covers on-site construction procedures in detail. From foundations through to roof framing and internal fit-out and finishing. Overlapping information has been limited to areas which were necessary for each book to retain its integrity should a reader *not* have access to both manuals.

These manuals are intended to be a guide only and are *not* a statutory building code or form part of any code. National and Local Building by-laws and also any specialised or Engineer's design must take precedence over all information in the manuals.

The Key to being Successful in Owner Builder

The key is to gain as much knowledge on the subject as possible before commencement.
It is far better to begin negotiations with the subcontractors and manufacturers on an informed basis. Take care to familarise yourself with 'Concrete, Timber & Brickwork' (read Chapter 5 thoroughly). More information on brickwork can be found in the pages dealing with the particular house type chosen.

> *Note:* Home renovations over a certain value must be carried out by a licenced tradesperson or on an Owner Builder Licence. Check your local gov't building authority for details on obtaining a licence.

Other Information Sources

After the house plans have been drafted, study them until any areas of uncertainty are resolved. Request the Draftsperson or Architect to provide a large scale sectional drawing of a typical wall taken from footings through a window and through to the roof. While this is not common on house plans, it should be; especially for owner builders. It will help avoid any disputes with subcontractors.

Obtain relevant manufacturers' specification literature. A wealth of information can be found in these. Sometimes manufacturer's warranties depend on adherence to their specifications.

Don't be Afraid to Have a Go

Most house carpentry and bricklaying operations are straight forward commonsense exercises not beyond those who are semi-skilled to attempt. There is nothing to compare with the satisfaction of laying your first bricks or blocks straight and level, let alone the thrill of surveying a complete wall built by one's own hands. Even though you may not be as fast as a tradesperson. Identify your limitations and employ a tradesperson where necessary. It will reduce construction time and that alone will save money.

Building & Other Abbreviations

AC	Asbestos Cement
accord.	according
AL	Aluminium
Approx.	Approximately
A.S.	Australian Standard
BCA	Building Code of Australia
BK	Brick
BWK	Brickwork
BV	Brick Veneer
¢	centre to centre
CCA	Copper Chrome Arsenate
c/s	countersunk
CANT	Cantilever
CP	Chrome Plated
CORR I	Corrugated Iron
CPB	Cupboard
Dia.	Diagonal
DPC	Damp Proof Course
DW	Dishwasher
EML	Expanded Metal Lath
EJ	Expansion Joint
FC	Fibre Cement
FH	Flat Head
FFL	Finished Floor Level
FLR	Floor
FW	Floor Waste
g	gauge (bolts/screws)
GAL	Hot Dip Galvanising
G/L	Ground Level
H1, H2, H3, H4, H5	Levels of treatment in timber. 'H' = abbreviation for 'Hazard'.
HBD	Hardboard
HBM	The Australian House Building Manual
Hex.	Hexagonal (Bolt)
HSOB	How to be a Successful Owner Builder & Renovator Manual
HT	Height
HW	Hot Water
HWD	Hardwood
INSUL	Insulation
kN	kilo Newtons force
kPa	kilo Pascal pressure
Lam.	Laminated
LVL	Laminated Veneered Lumber
LVR	Louvre
M	Metre
mm	Millimetres
MANUF	Manufacturer
MAX.	Maximum
MIN.	Minimum
MPa	Mega Pascal
MS	Mild Steel
MSB	Main Switch Board
N	North
NGL	Natural Ground Level
O	Oven
OB	Owner Builder
OG	Obscure Glass
PERP	Perpends or vertical block or brick joint
PVC	Polyvinyl Chloride
QUAD	Quadrant Moulding
REINF	Reinforcing
REFRIG	Refrigerator
RPD	Real Property Description
RHS	Rolled Hollow Section
RSJ	Rolled Steel Joist
SAA	Standard Assoc. of Australia
SD	Sliding Door
SHR	Shower
SP	Stand Pipe
SPEC	Specification
Sq.	Square
SWD	Softwood
T & G	Tongue & Groove
TEL	Telephone
VB	Vapour Barrier
VP	Vent Pipe
VENT	Ventilator
WBD	Wallboard
WR	Wardrobe
WM	Washing Machine
WPM	Waterproof Membrane
WI	Wrought Iron

Drainage Abbreviations

BV	Back Vent
CIP	Cast Iron Pipe
EV	Educt Vent
EW	Earthenware
GEW	Glazed Earthenware
GIT	Grease Inspection Trap
GT	Gully Trap
IC	Inspection Chamber
IO	Inspection Opening
JU	Jump Up
PJC	Plain Junction Cap
P PAN	W.C. outlet through rear wall
RWH	Rain Water Head
S PAN	W.C. outlet through floor.
SC	Stopcock
SD	Sewer Drain
SP	Soil Pipe and Stand Pipe
SV	Stop Valve
SVP	Soil Vent Pipe
SWD	Storm Water Drain
WC	Water Closet

Timber & Concrete Terminology & Abbreviations

See Pages 82—84.

Contents

1 Becoming a Successful Owner Builder

Methods of Owner Building

Several methods of Owner Building are possible to suit the individual. Where uncertain which to adopt, thoroughly cost the options to ensure which will offer the maximum advantage.

Simple & Easy Methods

It is advisable for Owner Builders without experience to select designs that have simple basic shapes without too many offsets and to avoid multi level designs unless a tradesperson is working alongside.

Total Construction by the Owner Builder

Except plumbing, drainage and electrical.

This system is more ideally suited to the person on long service leave, retired or self-employed and who possesses the necessary building skills. Maximum cost savings are possible if the Owner Builder can perform all the workmanship. Factor in financial losses incurred through time lost at the normal place of employment and the delay in moving out of rented accommodation.

Part Constructed by the Owner Builder

This is the most common method adopted. The Owner Builder carries out all the work within his capability and employs subcontractors to perform the remainder.

Methods of Owner Building Part-time

The following methods will suit persons who must continue at their normal job yet desire to construct their own home or at least part of it.

Contract to Lock Up Stage

Employ one or two recommended carpenters on a fixed quote and contract to build the house either with prefabricated walls, or conventionally to lockup stage; complete the remainder of the work yourself.

Subcontract & Supervise Yourself

Employ carpenters on an hourly or contract basis and all other subcontractors on a contract basis. Mornings, evenings and weekends are used to supervise and supply their material requirements. This is the method adopted by most professional builders. Ensure those on an hourly basis provide a close approximation of time and cost prior to commencement. If the house is complicated and difficult to estimate, help them to determine an approximate figure by dividing the house into segments:

a). *Work to floor level;* ***b).*** *Up to wall completion;* ***c).*** *Roof completion; &* ***d).*** *Linings and finishing.*

A detailed full specification should be used in these circumstances, but allow a margin for the unforeseen.

Build in Cavity Brick or Concrete Block?

Construct the foundation and work up to the slab floor level on weekends and spare time.

Cavity Brick (double brick) with brick partitions
When erected by a brick laying gang, this can prove a speedy and practical method of construction on an average sized house.

Within two weeks, the walls can be built ready for the roof, and remember, at the same time, all door and window frames are built into the brickwork, so another task is eliminated.

Concrete Block
Although dismissed in many areas because of its plain appearance, when well proportioned with the use of other materials, this method can have high aesthetic appeal.

A modern finish is to fill the joints, cement bag and paint. The structure is extremely fast to construct by blocklayers. As with cavity brick, it enables a speedy lockup stage.

One downside to cavity brick and concrete block is the difficulty encountered when attaching fitments and decor to walls or in years to come moving walls or making openings in walls.

Kit Home Building

This option is most suitable for the Owner Builder who prefers to have materials supplied, avoiding continual measuring, ordering and fetching. However, while there are many positive aspects to this method there are also many negative ones which should be considered.

Kit Home Options

Some kit home suppliers can provide various options such as:

a). The kit only (you construct).

b). Kit built to lock-up stage by the supplier (you complete).

c). Kit built to completion by supplier.

What to look for in a Kit Home

a. Simplicity of Construction — Ask to see a typical plan specifications and installation instructions. Do numbered parts coincide with numbers marked in the installation instructions?

b. Is the Company Accessible — If the sales people are difficult to communicate with before purchase, is that an indication of future expectations?

c. Request a complete list — Obtain a complete list of what the kit includes and what it does not.

d. Does the kit contain: Prefabricated walls and roof framing and to what stage are they assembled.

Are the wall members joined together as complete wall units in the factory, or do you have to assemble pre-cut members? Are claddings factory attached to walls or not? What else is pre-fabricated?

Check out the Kit Home Provider

1.Does the provider/supplier have a good track record? Ask for references of previous kits supplied to other Owner Builders who have completed their homes.

Contact them to obtain their comments on the following:

a). Was the kit complete or was there a constant shortfall of materials?

b). Was the supplier accommodating when a problem or shortfall was presented?

c). Was the supplier quick to respond to requests or did construction come to a standstill through long delays. If you employ tradespersons, they may leave when delayed and work elsewhere creating further delays.

2. How far in distance is the suppliers headquarters from your site? This can definitely create problems as any delays will only be compounded by extended delivery times.

3. Will the chosen design, actually look like the artist's impression. Check by viewing one already built.

4. Make price comparisons. Firstly, armed with the square metre area of the house. Obtain a current fixed price for a house in a builder's catalogue which has the same square metre area and similar construction design and materials. These will include labour costs and builder's profit. Are the savings in the kit home option worthwhile?

Now if you wish, compare the kit home option with either; 'Total Construction by the Owner Builder' (Page 6) or 'A Quick Building Program' (Page 8).

When making comparisons, be sure that all quotes include everything *(for further guidance, see Pages 86-87).*

Take into consideration all the items which the kit home supplier does not include.

Items not Included

The supplier should provide a list of items included as well as a list of items not included in the total cost.

Items *not* included will most likely be, council and engineer fees, foundation concrete and formwork but may include reinforcing, anchor bolts and other hardware which are required in the footings. Electrical and plumbing materials may *not* be included.

However, prime cost items such as, bath, WC, vanity, shower taps, kitchen sink, HWS, etc could possibly be included. You could make savings by purchasing these locally if you live in a populated area. Check also if delivery is included.

The Kit Home Building Process

The building process in most situations remains similar to say 'A Quick Building Program' (Page 8). You still have to construct the foundations prior to assembling the kit. The foundation stage may be either concrete footings with slab floor or piers with footings ready to receive floor bearers, joists and flooring. *Construction of these is detailed in the 'HBM'.*

It is advisable when the kit home supplier provides the sub-floor piers or stumps, framing and flooring to have these and their relevant fasteners and anchors all supplied in a first stage prior to receiving the next load of materials. This is a particularly good idea if the floor is timber and their is storage space underneath.

Storage on-site

This is a major consideration as you don't want a complete house lot of materials delivered to a site exposed to the public view, then to find it being gradually depleted through theft.

If you intend to build a separate barn, large garage or shed, then do it first so you can lock up much of the materials. If you can afford it, have the materials delivered in stages to reduce the amount of storage required. The only other alternative to lock-up storage is fencing then tarpaulins to protect materials.

A Quick Building Program

This program is designed for those who would like to have the bulk of their house built during their four weeks annual leave. The program is particularly practical for low set brick veneer construction. Where two-storey, split level or complicated designs are envisaged, additional time will be required.

How the Program Works

The house is divided into three stages:

Stage One

This includes footings, base and floor and is constructed during spare time at weekends etc, prior to taking the annual leave.

Stage Two

This includes walls, roof framing and roof claddings. All external and internal wall linings, windows, doors, cupboards, mouldings, plumbing, drainage and electrical. This work is carried out during four weeks annual leave.

To achieve this goal, there are five essential requirements:

a). A carpenter must be employed for the four weeks with the Owner Builder being his offsider unless the Owner Builder is a carpenter. In which case an offsider is needed.

b). A pre-cut and pre-nailed frame and prefabricated truss roof must be used.

c). All wall linings will need to be fixed by a wallboard contractor.

d). Thorough planning, organisation and co-operation between the Owner Builder and his suppliers and subcontractors prior to taking the annual leave.

e). The exterior, if brick, is laid by a bricklayer. If weatherboard, an extra four to five days must be added to this schedule.

The program works like this:

A pre-nailed frame arrives by truck and is erected, straightened and plumbed in one to two days. The truss roof is then erected with braces, fascias and barge boards fixed ready for roof covering in three days. This means that a house can have its roof covered-in within seven days. Following this the Plumber, Electrician and Wallboard Fixer are organised to carry out their work.

This leaves three weeks for the Carpenter and Owner Builder to install windows, doors, bath, shower, cupboards and mouldings. Windows should have pre-fitted reveals. If the outside is brick veneer and is carried out by a bricklayer, then the remaining three weeks can be totally devoted to completing the inside.

It is very possible the house could be ready for occupancy at the end of four weeks. The extra cost of the pre-nail frame and a carpenter are minimal considering the savings referred to in 'Speedy Completion', Page 89 . Further speed can be achieved through the use of pre-hung doors. Plumbing, drainage and electrical work is performed by those tradespersons whilst the Owner Builder and the carpenter are concentrating on internal finishing.

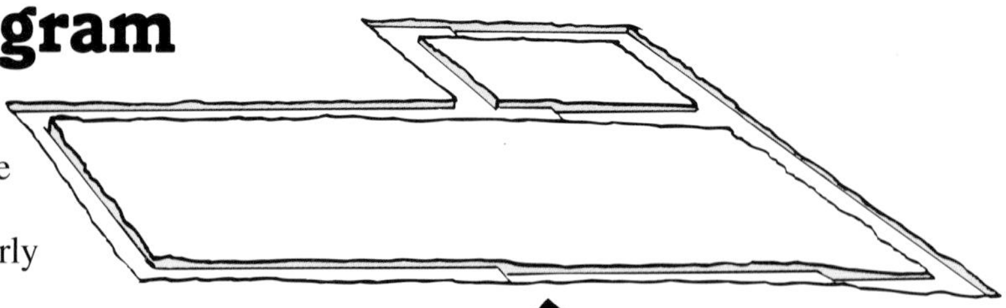

Stage 1

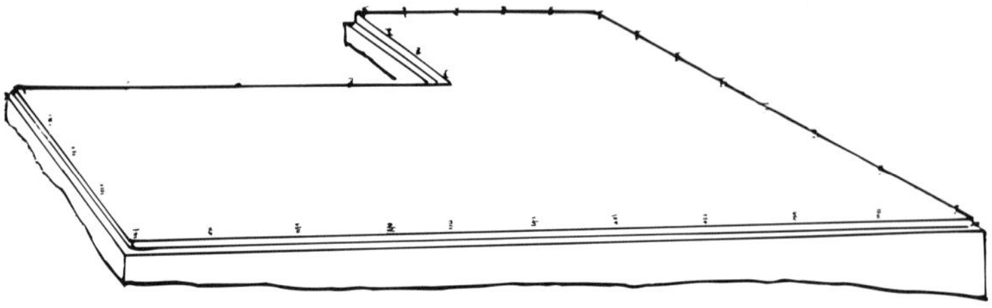

Stage 2

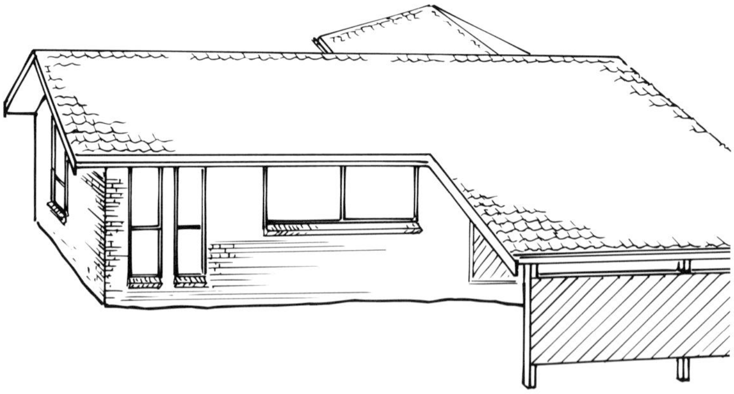

Stage 3

This includes any work remaining, such as any unfinished internal mouldings and decorating, outside soffits, concrete drives and paths etc, all of which can be completed after moving in if permitted by local gov't authorities.

What is Involved in Being an Owner Builder

You become the legal builder and subject to obligations such as: workplace, health and safety, insurances and oversight of the job. The construction process should be treated as a series of tasks linked together in a planned sequence starting with arranging finance, to moving your furniture in on completion.

What do Owner Builders Gain?

On completion:

1. There must have been a cost saving.

One must take into consideration these angles:

a). Either money saved, thus a lower mortgage; or

b). A larger home for the same cost as a professionally built smaller home.

To establish this criteria, one should obtain prices for the house of choice to be built professionally, or establish the price of the home one could afford to buy versus the larger owner built home.

2. *Moving out of the 'Renting Roundabout'.* Often doing it yourself can mean having your own home years ahead of time.

Pressures Incurred by Owner Building

With any longish project, it is possible that the initial vigour wanes and the Owner Builder moves in with incomplete elements. This often remains the case infinitum and adds pressure to occupants and incurs the displeasure of the lending institution. It is wise to have a built-in safety margin to prevent such a situation.

Why Do some Owner Builders Lose Money?

Lack of Preparation

In most cases, this is caused by a lack of pre-construction planning and preparation. It is in your interest to learn how to oversee the construction of your house. This manual and its companion 'The Australian House Building Manual' have been prepared to supply this information as well as simple guidelines to follow.

Where Owner Builders Strike Trouble

It is good to know before you start some of the pitfalls that can be encountered. It's nicer still to be shown how to avoid them.

All Brawn & Little Brain

To undertake any 'do-it-yourself' project is indicative that one has a liberal dose of 'get up & go'. Often what happens is that the brawn grows a little tired and wishes the brain had advised to build only 200 sq. metres instead of the 300 sq. metres undertaken. Understanding your labour capabilities and time limits should cause you to build only the size house that can be comfortably managed.

Lack of Time Control

If building during time taken off from regular employment, it is important to build quickly. This takes organisation and discipline. It is important to be on the job as you would if at your regular job and more important to see what is going on there and by whom.

Selling the Owner Built House

Some states require you to state to prospective buyers that the house is owner built. This may cause suspicion in some buyers especially in states where the State Government has *not* made provision for Owner Builders to have a structural insurance cover within the 'State Building Authority'. This problem can be overcome in a number of ways:
1). purchasing a private cover; **2).** engage an engineer to design and inspect the footings and any concrete slab floors and the frame prior to cladding and issue certificates for these; **3).** Keep all documentation as proof that the building has been constructed to standard including:

a). Ready mixed concrete dockets stating the MPa strength of concrete footings and any slab floors.

b). Termite control certificates.

c). A copy of local gov't approved plans.

d). Building Inspector's or Certifier's signed inspection tickets or dockets.

Take photographs during construction of the following:
a). Footings with steel reinforcing included; **b).** The slab floor before the concrete pour showing the reinforcing, bar chairs and plastic moisture membrane; & **c).** Walls and roof framing with all wind braces and anchor bolts included prior to installation of roof and wall claddings. These photographs should be taken of each side and section of the building as well as close-up.

Those States issuing an Owner Builder's Permit which is subject to the house *not* being sold for a certain number of years, generally have a clause that permits an earlier sale in particular circumstances on approval by the 'Builders Licencing Authority'.

2

Successful Planning

Selecting a Building Site

Points to Consider:

a). Proximity to services.

b). Proposed public development which could adversely affect resale value.

c). It is foolish to put an expensive house on cheap land or a very cheap house on expensive land.

d). Will yearly rates prove prohibitive.

e). Is the title available on purchase? It is almost impossible to raise a mortgage without this piece of paper. It is not always readily available on new subdivisions.

f). Are there any legal restrictive convenants. Check this item before you sign.

g). Check with your local gov't regarding position of sewer lines etc. These could have to be redirected at your expense.

h). Ensure boundary pegs are in position and are actually the pegs of your property. This is of utmost importance. Each peg will have the 'lot number' carved into it. Missing pegs are costly to replace.

i). Has the site been subject to flooding or tidal surge in the past?

j). Could the land be resumed by a Government body? Check with Local Authority.

k). Is the land beneath an air flight path?

Look for:

a). Springs or presence of water courses.

b). Slope of land is always greater than the eye estimates. This increases the cost of the sub-floor structure. When this cost is added to initial outlay for land it may prove too expensive.

Note: Fill on house sites can sometimes be many metres deep and this in turn, can incur a great increase on foundation and footing costs. If in doubt, have a Soil Engineer carry out pre-purchase test bores. The purchase contract can be made conditional on the results of a Soil Engineer's report. Alternatively, ask the land owner if he/she will provide this service.

Medium Density Estates

These estates don't offer sufficient space to ensure privacy from noise such as generated from normal domestic living, domestic disputes, musical instruments, parties, dogs, swimming pool activity etc. They also deprive the lots of sufficient street parking.

Which Lots offer the best Value

Keep in mind aspect, views and breezes. With the privacy/space factor so important, select from the larger blocks. The odd shape cul-de-sac blocks often offer more privacy. If your buying into a medium density estate vacant of houses, you can't be sure what will be built on the adjoining lots that could cause loss of breezes, view and privacy. Whereas on estates with larger blocks you may lose your view and some breeze but you can retain privacy.

Advantages & Disadvantages of Typical Building Sites

When selecting a building site, it is good to have a rough idea of your house floor plan. This will help you to know how well the design will orient on the site in relation to views, breezes and sunshine. The following can only provide some guidelines as to advantages and disadvantages of allotments in a typical estate apart from the elements of view, breezes, the sun's path, or existing buildings which will also determine orientation. The latter is extremely important on medium density estates.

Cul-de-sac lots

11-18 in short streets are quieter (road wise). Boundaries are odd shape but may offer better privacy. Road parking is a problem.

Easement lots (see fig 1)

8,9, 26&27 offer total privacy from the road but have longer driveways to construct and maintain and further to walk for rubbish bins, mail etc. 26 has too many neighbours for comfort.

Other lots (see fig 1)

Lots 7,10,24&25 have additional loss of privacy and quiet from the adjoining easements. But are compensated by not having a neighbouring house too close on the easement side.

Lots 23&28 are corner lots. Good for showing a beautiful home or garden to advantage but will experience traffic and loss of privacy along two boundaries.

Lots 3 and 33 (see fig 1) experience traffic headlights directed into their windows at night. 'School Road' being a larger straight thoroughfare will experience greater traffic flow and noise with the odd high speedster.

Lots 21, 22, 24, 25, 30 and 31 have desirable wider frontages offering greater space as well as the opportunity to have circular driveways enabling more off street parking and avoiding any need to back onto the street.

Pinedale Parade (see fig 2)

Sites 1,2,&3 are preferred over 4-8 as they present longer boundaries facing north. This enables more rooms to take advantage of the more desirable northern aspect.

Fig 1

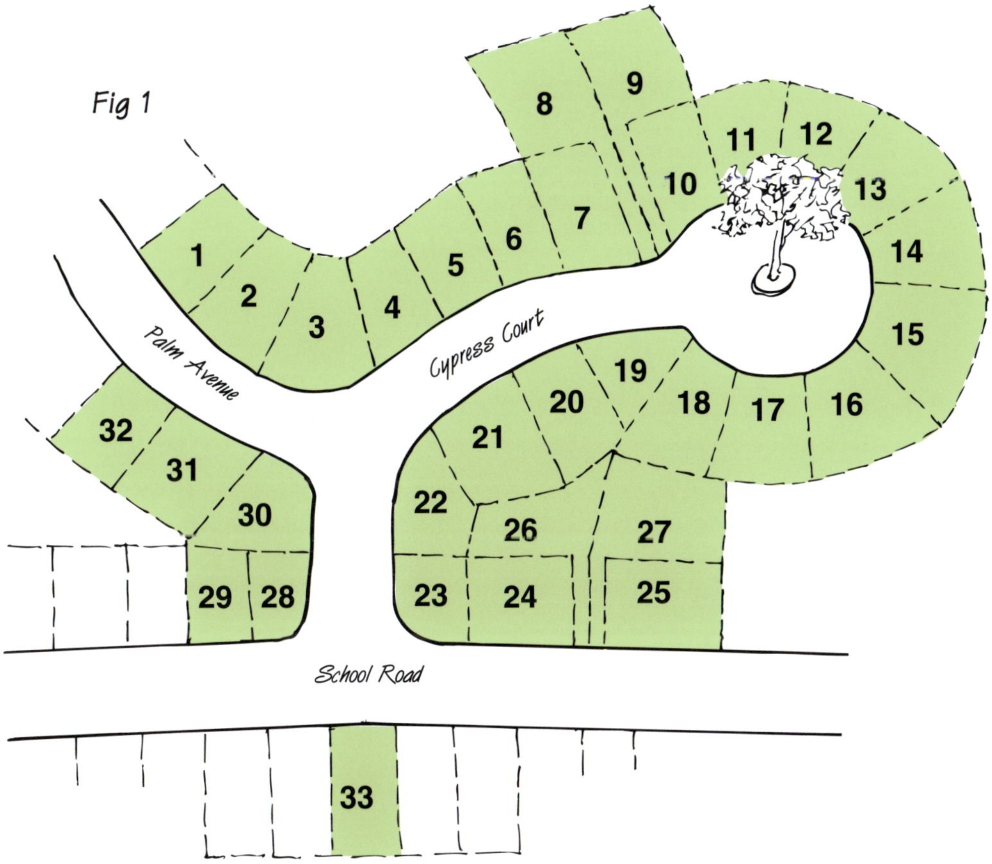

Fig 2

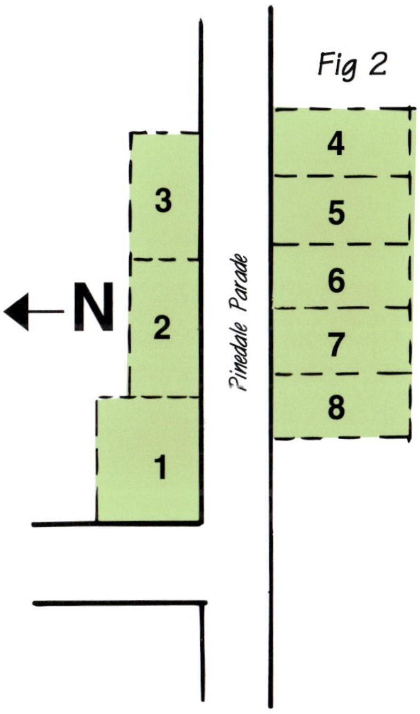

Measuring the Fall in Land

Peg the proposed corners of the house. Attach a string line at the high end and stretch it out to the lowest end of the proposed house site onto a stick. Attach a line level to the centre of the string line. Raise the lower end until the levelling bubble is centralised. The level is checked by an assistant. Mark the level line then reverse the level and mark the new level line again. Accept a point between the two level marks as the level.

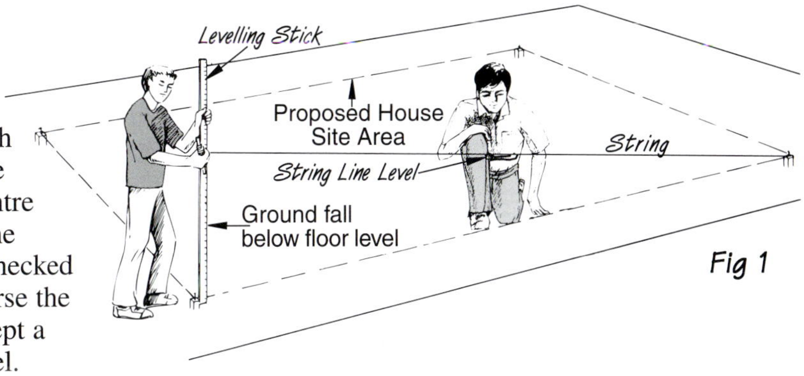

Fig 1

On steep sites, the string line may have to be attached to a batten to gain sufficient height. The height required to bring the string line into level will be the amount of fall in the length of the house site. This procedure should be carried out for each corner of the house and the falls recorded in a sketch plan.

Design the House to Suit the Site

The following two pages contain suggested house styles to suit the three slope types. The designs presented are silhouettes of common architectural shapes and lines. These can be adopted to accommodate individual requirements by lengthening or shortening the horizontal or vertical lines. Roof pitches can also be raised or lowered. *Don't* underestimate the value of roof design. *Roof style and pitch can make or break the character of the house design.* Try to imagine these designs with various exterior wall surfaces.
Such as: Brick, render coatings, weatherboard, timber or fibreglass planking, or a combination of two wall surface materials.

Observe the following rules to contain costs:

a). Level sites *suit* slab floors and single or two storey construction.

b). Sloping sites (5-15°) *suit* split level construction with timber floors or a combination of timber and concrete.

c). Steep slopes (more than 15°) *suit* pole or post and beam construction. Sometimes a very steep site is available at a reasonable price. This may compensate for increased building costs.

House Styles for Level Sites

1

Conventional 'L' shape with attic and dormer windows. These usually require steep pitch roofs in order to gain sufficient attic space.

2

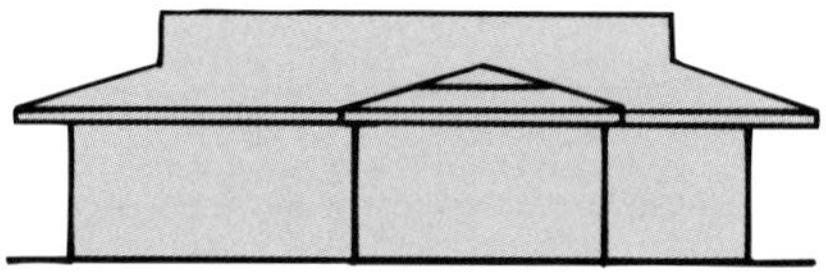

Conventional low cost design with dutch gables will suit brick, weatherboard or render coatings construction.

3

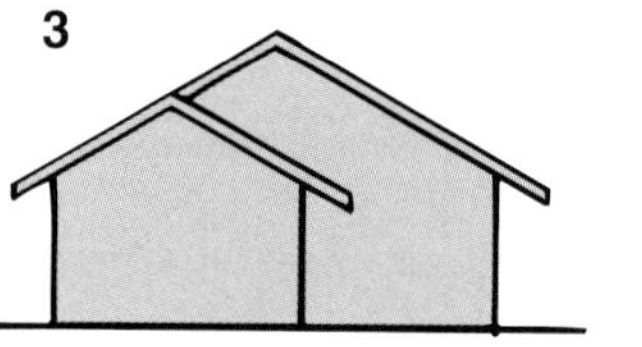

Conventional low set or single storey with open gables. Suits exposed or cathedral ceilings.

4

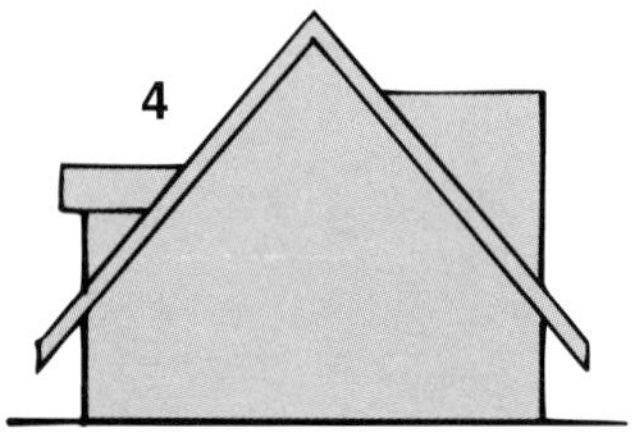

'A' frame with steep pitch enabling a liveable attic space.

5

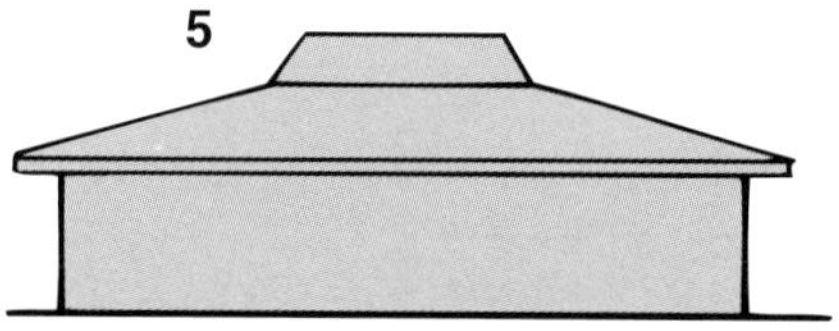

Simple conventional single storey is cost effective to construct in brick masonry or weatherboard.

6

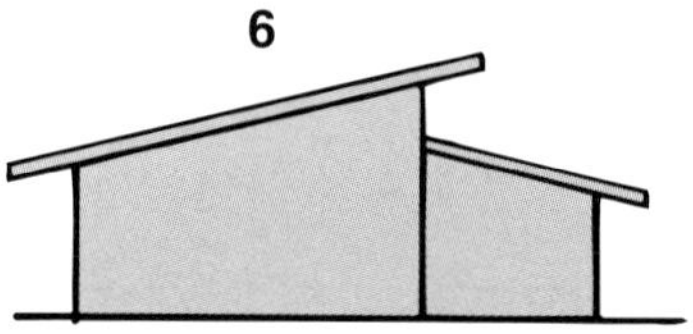

Low pitched skillion or shed roof design has walls constructed on the rake with studs all varying in length. Suits long run roofing profiles.

7

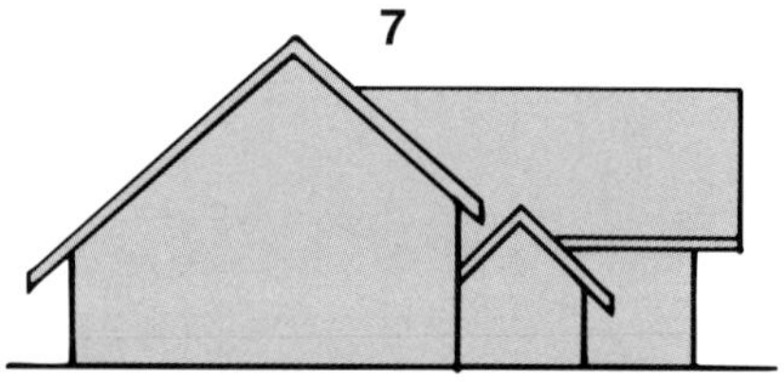

Could also have 1½ stories with mezzanine floor.

8

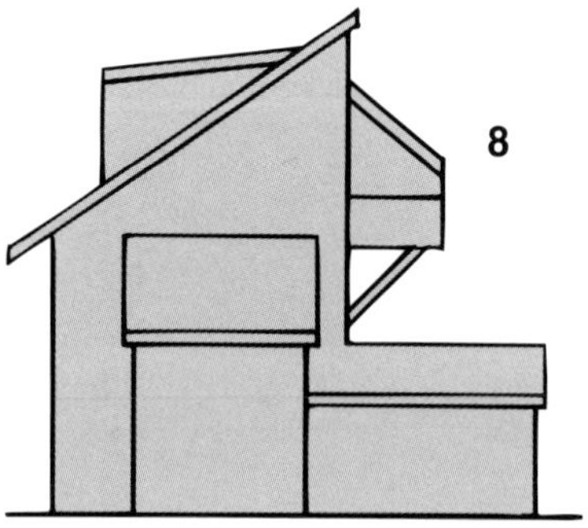

Modern multi shape with varying roof pitches.

9

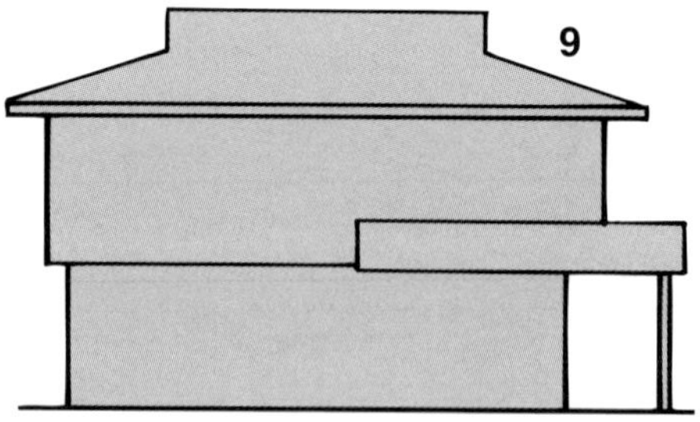

Conventional upper storey in light cladding cantilevered over a base of either brick, or block masonry.

10

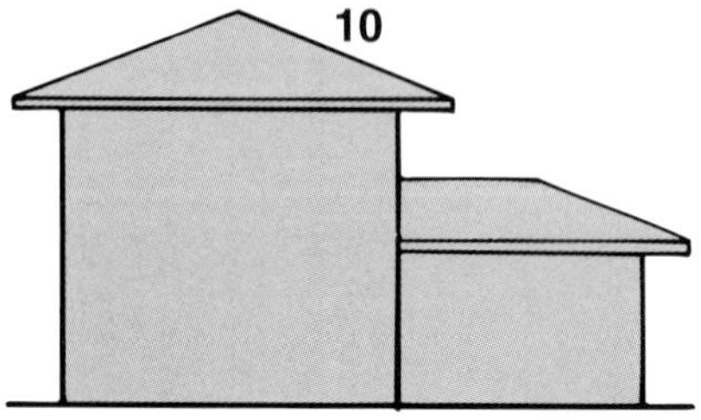

Two storeys conventional. These usually contain garaging under the second storey and living areas on the lower storey.

11

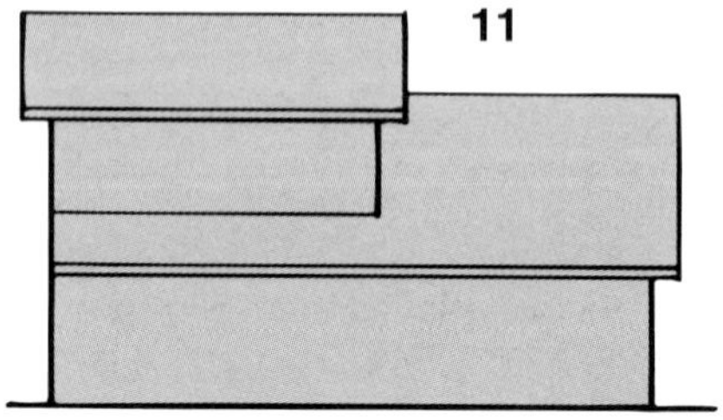

Conventional first floor with a second storey sleeping area.

12

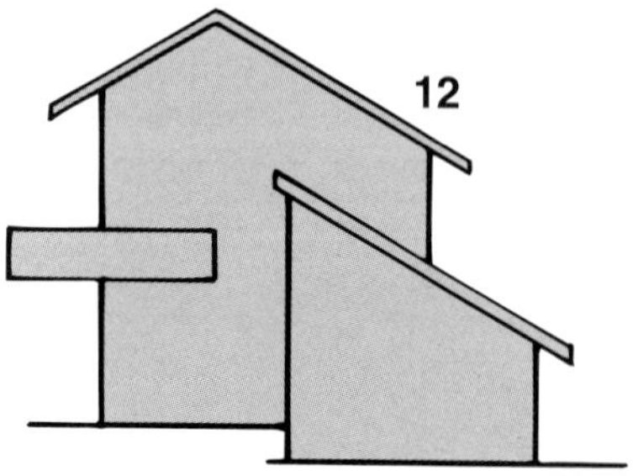

Repeating angular shapes.

House Styles for Moderately Sloping Sites (5-15°)

If ground falls dicate a basement height at one end of approx. 1500mm, it would be practical to excavate that end in order to increase the basement to 2400mm to create living space.

1

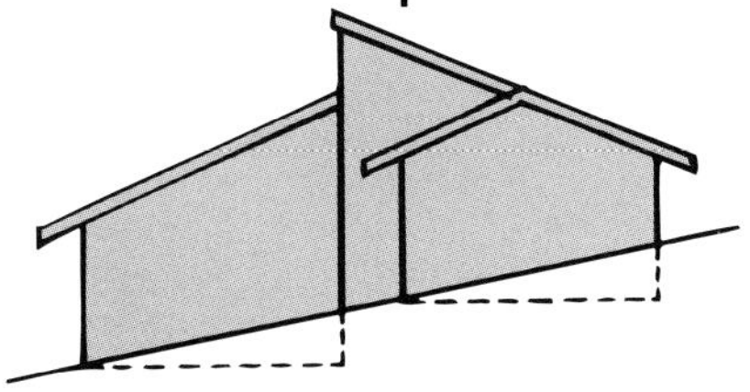

Split level with a mixture of shed or skillion roofing with an open gable end.

2

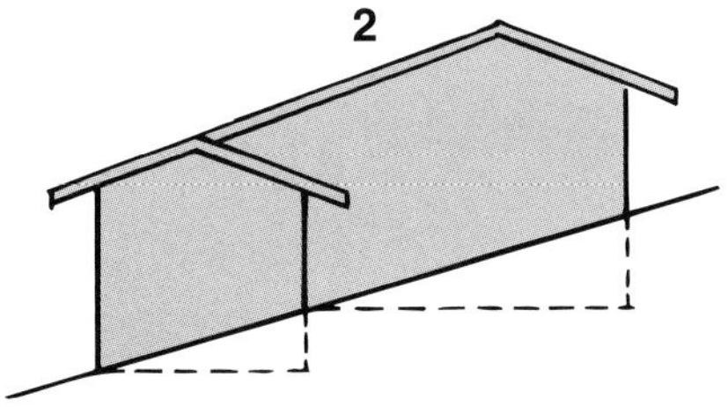

Split level containing some equal height walls and some raked walls. Ceilings are usually raked through a portion of the house.

3

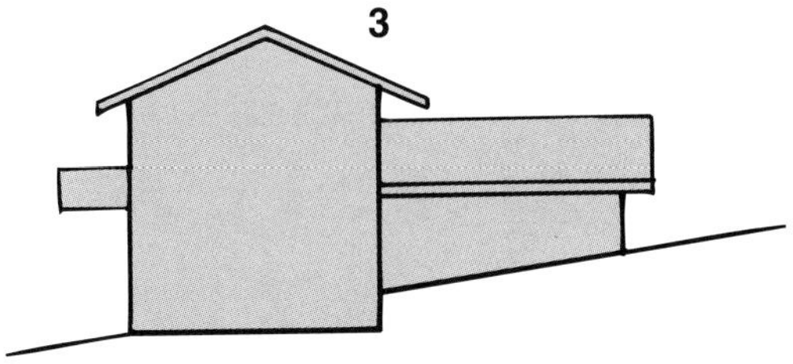

Conventional split three level usually contains garaging on the lowest level.

4

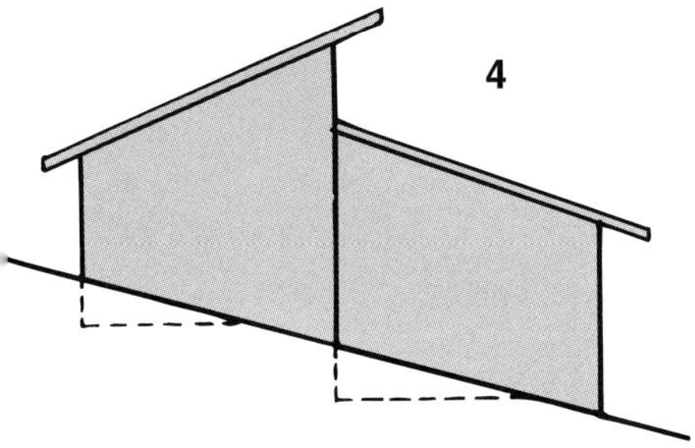

Split level design with raking walls. Space between the upper and lower roof enables installation of clerestory windows.

5

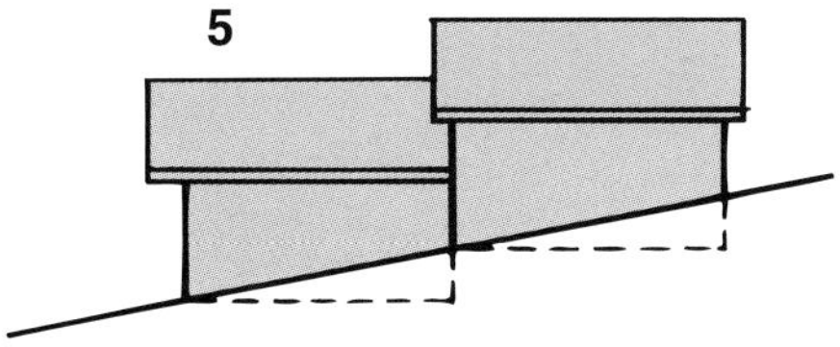

Conventional split level gable ended design is simple to construct with either concrete or timber flooring.

6

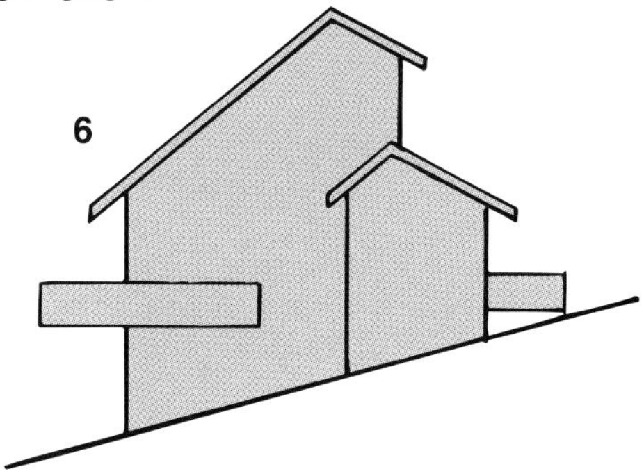

Modern split and multi-level design to suit cantilevered balconies and varying pitch or length of roof shapes.

House Styles for Steep Sites (over 15°)

1

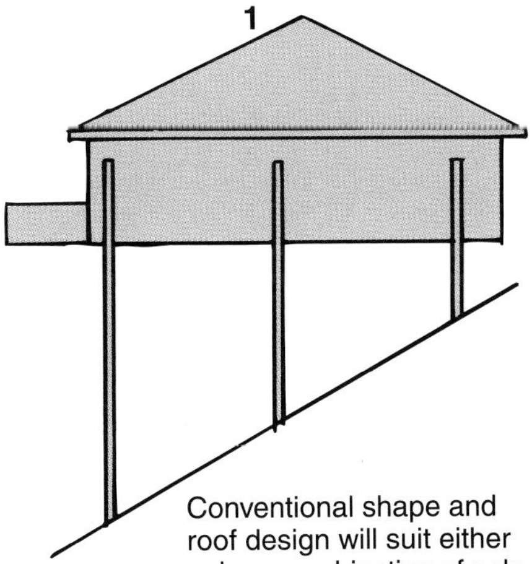

Conventional shape and roof design will suit either pole or combination of pole and conventional framing.

2

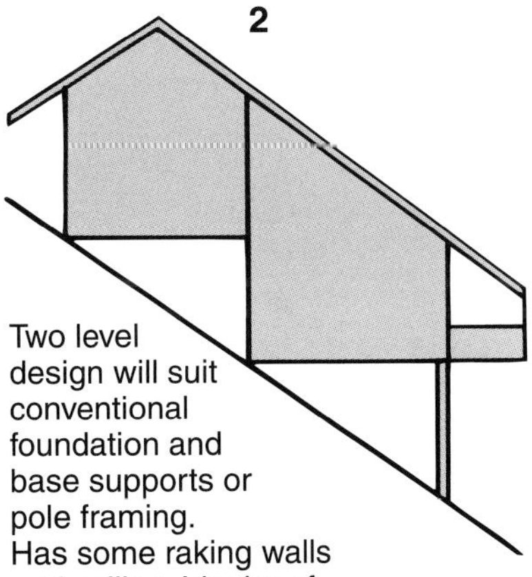

Two level design will suit conventional foundation and base supports or pole framing. Has some raking walls and ceiling. Ideal roof design to resist high winds.

3

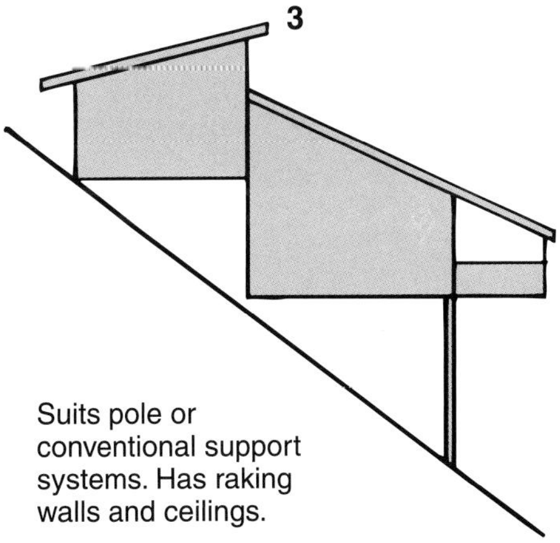

Suits pole or conventional support systems. Has raking walls and ceilings.

4

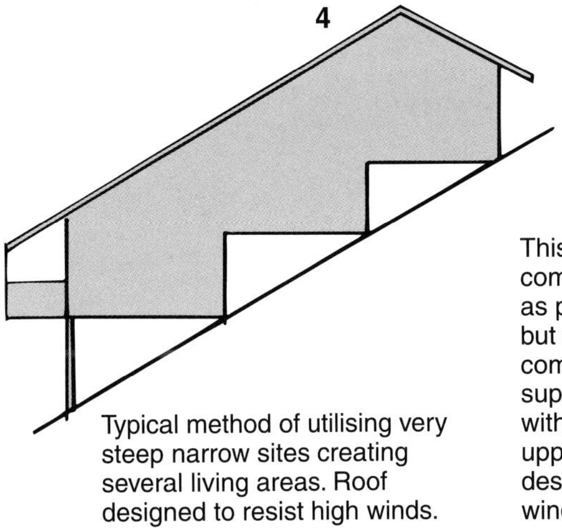

Typical method of utilising very steep narrow sites creating several living areas. Roof designed to resist high winds.

5

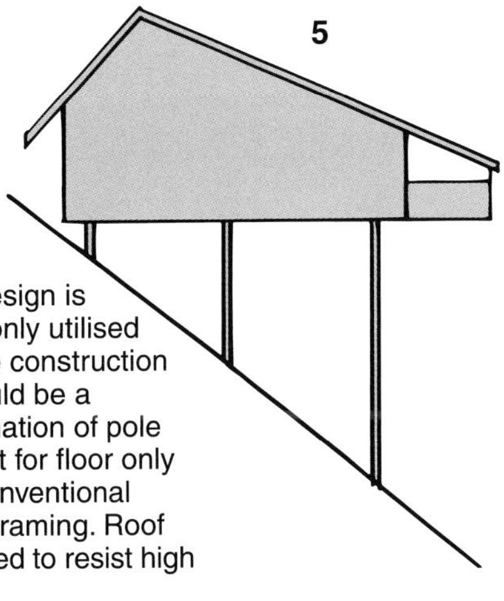

This design is commonly utilised as pole construction but could be a combination of pole support for floor only with conventional upper framing. Roof designed to resist high winds.

6

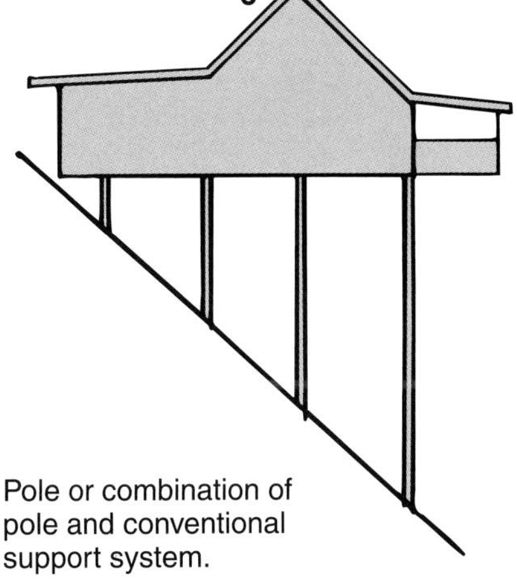

Pole or combination of pole and conventional support system.

Build Single Storey or 2-Storeys?

This will often be determined by the land contour.
However, consider the following:
A single storey house of say, 224sq.metres (size is irrelevant) when redesigned into two storeys of 112sq.metres each, can reduce the foundations and footings by more than a third and the roof area by a little under half.

These cost savings will more than pay for the penalty of having to work using ladders and scaffolding. (The savings on the ground floor will be spent on building the second storey timber floor). 2-Storey affords the benefit of gaining extra land area, better security upstairs from burglars and an improvement in outlook, views and breezes.

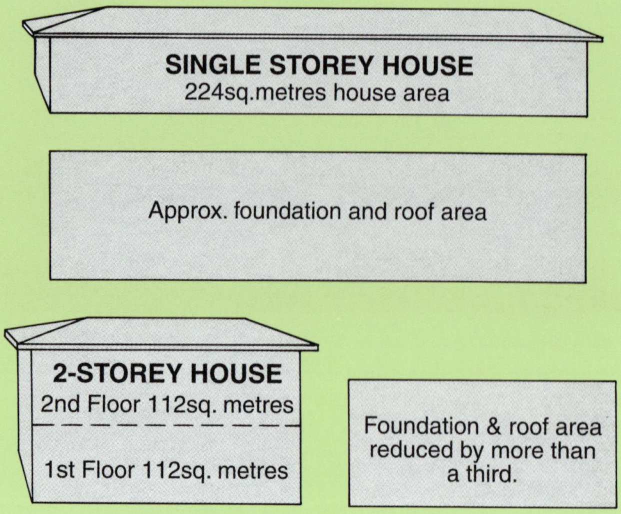

Designing the House

Designing for Aspect

Sunshine and breezes are free so be sure to take maximum advantage of them.

Note the following points when planning walls & windows:

a). Rooms facing North are ideal all year round. Take advantage of this aspect by placing as many rooms as possible at this side especially (1) dining and lounge and (2) main bedroom. Use large glass areas on this side.

b). Rooms facing South will be cold during the Winter. To prevent loss of warm air keep glass areas to a minimum.

c). Rooms facing East will only receive morning sunshine but this aspect is preferred before southern or western aspects.

d). Rooms facing West are hot in the afternoons (very nice in Winter but unbearable in Summer). If windows must be used at all, use narrow horizontal highlights or narrow vertical windows.
Never locate kitchens on this aspect.

Sites with north and easterly aspects are the most sought after. These sites provide maximum sunlight in Winter and breezes in Summer. A steep site may be more expensive to build on but may be cheaper to purchase or may have good views or a desirable north-east aspect.

Position the House for Aspect

Decide which rooms should receive maximum sunlight in Winter and cool breezes in Summer. The ideal is to place kitchen and breakfast rooms at the eastern end to receive morning sun, then family, lounge and if possible, main bedroom facing north. The North-East corner is a perfect location for the dining room or kitchen, as in fig 1. Design remaining living and sleeping rooms to receive as much northern and eastern aspect as possible.

It's ideal for views to be on the northern or eastern sides. If they are on the southern or western sides, the larger glazed areas will require special attention. To protect the southern side from cold - double glazing etc, and the western side from heat - pergolas etc but late in the afternoon there is no way to retain the view as well as prevent the direct sun.

Using Figure 1 as an example, establish a string line along the East-West (or winter sunpath line) across your land. Then peg the four corners of the house parallel to that line. If a site receives or requires a more easterly aspect, adjust the four corners of the house accordingly.

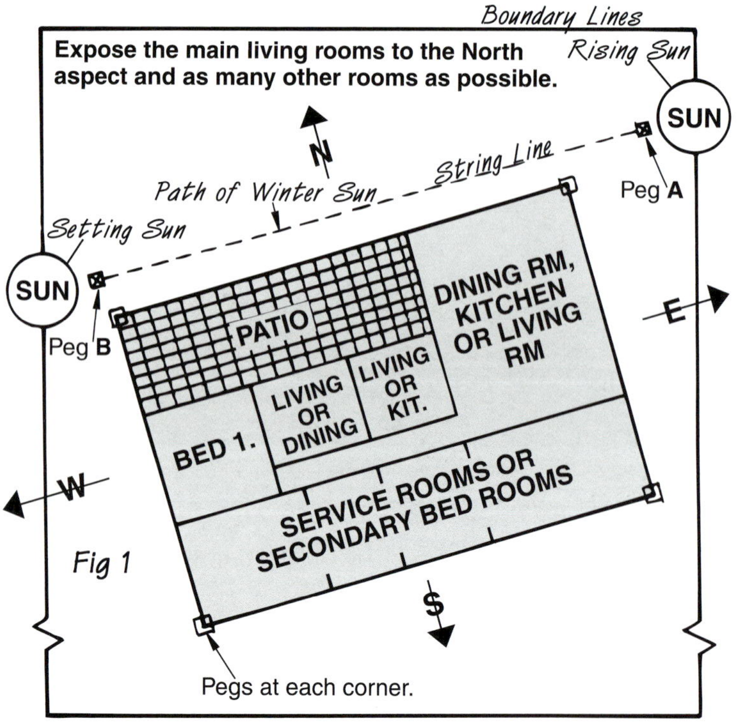

Fig 1

Designing Rooms

Kitchens

Minimum Size: 8.36 sq metres or 3.0x2.7 metres. The eastern end is ideal for kitchens. Kitchens *should not* be positioned on the western end. If unavoidable a window *should not* be fitted to that western wall. The solar heat will further heat an already hot room. To minimise unnecessary walking position the fridge, stove and sink as in fig 1.

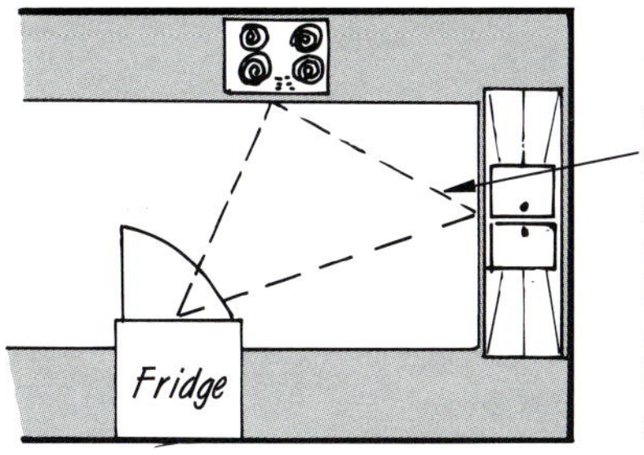

The ideal walking distance between these three appliances in an unbroken triangle is 3.6m. A triangle of 4.8m is acceptable but 6.0m is poor designing.

Steps to Designing a Kitchen Layout

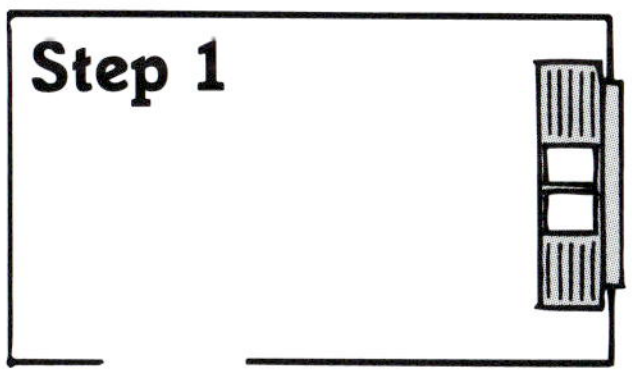

Sink & Window: It is preferable to place the sink under a window. Place these first. Sinks should *never* face a blank wall and are *not* always successful over-looking dining and living areas.

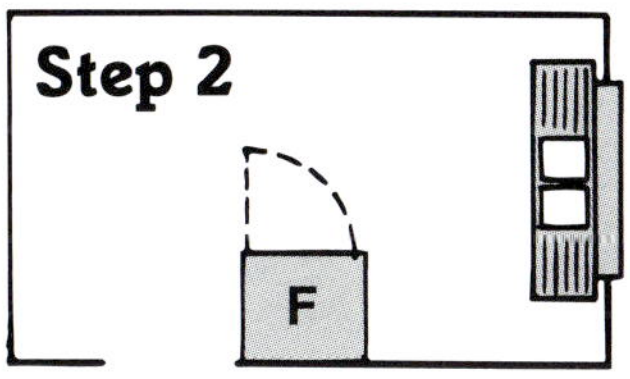

Fridges: Then position the fridge, as it is the bulkiest item in the room. Check its position will suit your fridge door preferred opening side (left or right hand). Avoid placing by a passage or doorway.

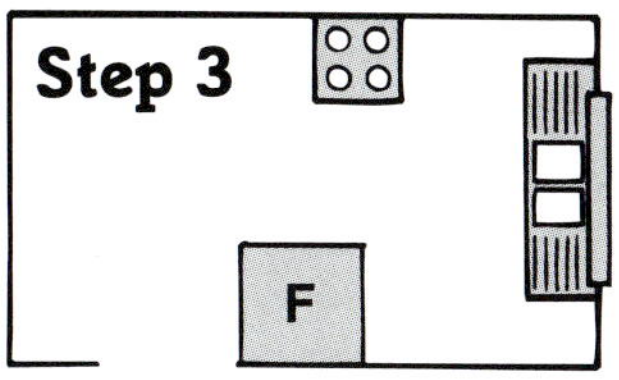

Stove & Oven: Determine the cooking area. Ideally it should *not* be more that 1.2m from the sink (closer if possible). A bench should be provided beside the stove and oven to accept hot dishes.

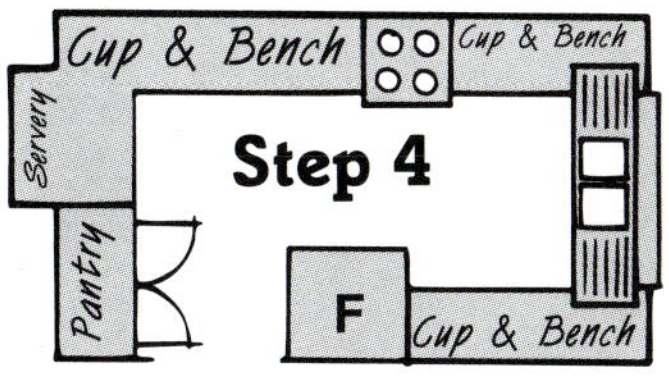

Pantries: Walk-in pantries are *not* always practical creating additional walking. The shallow depth wall pantry is quicker to access and with good design holds nearly as much. Ideal sizes range between 600-900mm wide and *not* more than 500mm deep.

Additional Hints:

a). Position lights above the sink and in the centre of the room or around the perimeter.

b). Power points should be distributed to give access to other users rather than be all at one end.

Typical Kitchen Layouts

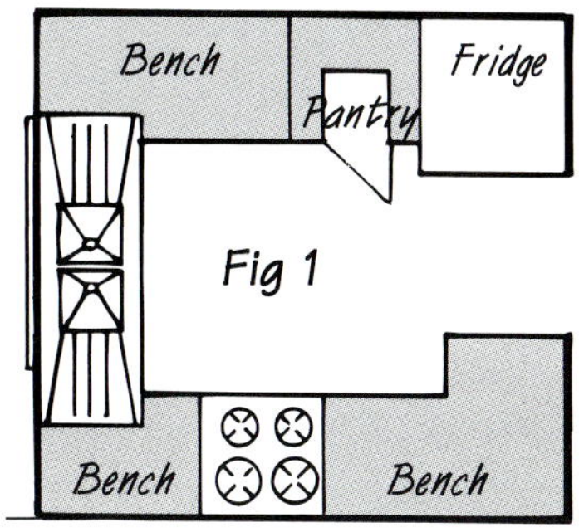

Enclosed Kitchens

This is the most space efficient. Ample bench space, adequate storage and minimum exertion required to reach essential points.

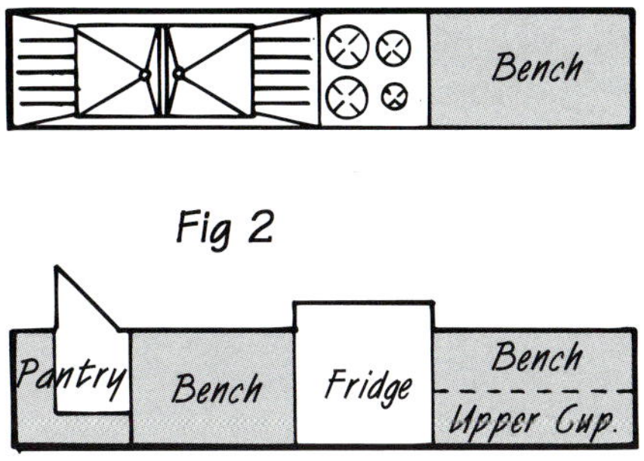

Corridor Kitchens

Ideal where space is limited. Everything is handy but the kitchen tends to become a thoroughfare.

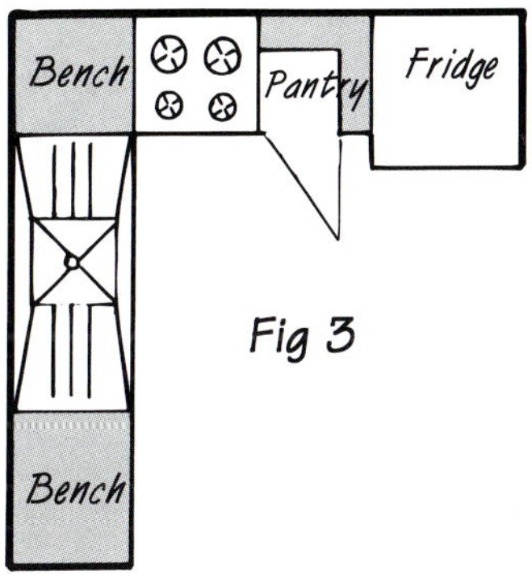

'L' Shape Kitchens

Whilst everything is handy, the lack of bench space is a drawback.

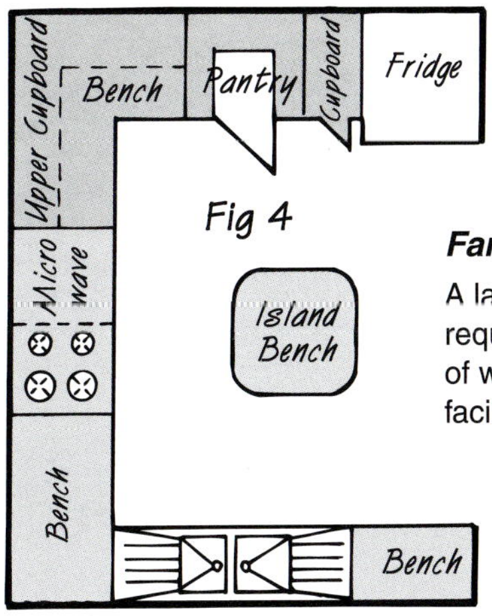

Farmhouse Kitchens

A large amount of space is required necessitating a lot of walking to reach each facility.

When Buying a Kitchen, check:

a). Drawer fronts should be screwed. Cheaper brands are commonly only stapled and easily come adrift.

b). Laminate joins should be tight fitting.

c). Spaces between doors and drawers should be parallel and *not* showing wider gaps at one end.

d). A good hinge is expensive but superior.

e). Drawers should roll out freely.
Drawer slides come in differing qualities and price tags.

f). Door handles are an important design element.

g). Splashbacks will cost extra.

h). Wider than average benchtops can be more convenient, but do cost extra.

i). Solid wood doors are expensive. Would a wood laminate create the mood at a cheaper price?

Bathrooms

Minimum Size: 4.32 sq metres or 2.4x1.8m.
Baths are usually 1.525 &1.67m long. Shower bases should be a minimum of 900x900mm.

In single bathroom homes it is good sense to keep the bathroom near the main bedroom. Alternatively, keep the bathroom size to a minimum standard size of (4.32sq metres) and include an ensuite off the main bedroom.

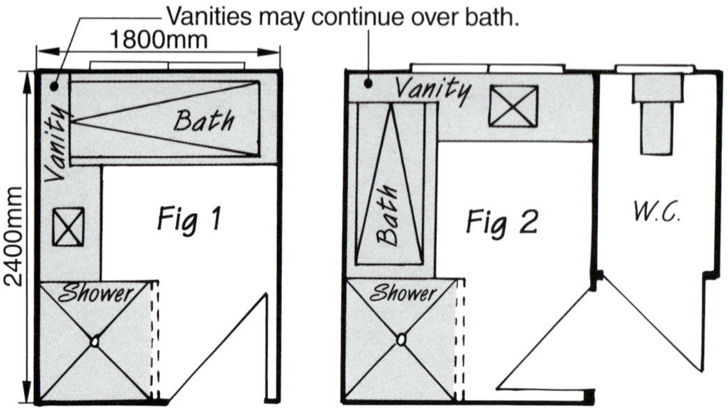

Typical Standard 2400x1800mm Layout

Alternative Standard Layout with W.C. adjoining

> ***Additional Hints:***
>
> ***a).*** Avoid vanity units under windows as a mirror can't be positioned above the unit.
>
> ***b).*** Install a power point for shavers and hairdryers.
>
> ***c).*** Showers over baths are a disadvantage as a resale feature.

A typical bathroom has a dimension of 1800x2400mm. This allows a separate bath and shower to be comfortably positioned. If space permits, a four-way bathroom is excellent for families permitting all facilities to be used at the one time (see fig 3). Obscure glass panels are required above 2050mm height up to the ceiling to permit illumination to pass to the shower and vanity areas.

Fig 3

4-way Bathroom

A 4-way bathroom offers access and privacy to four facilities at the same time.

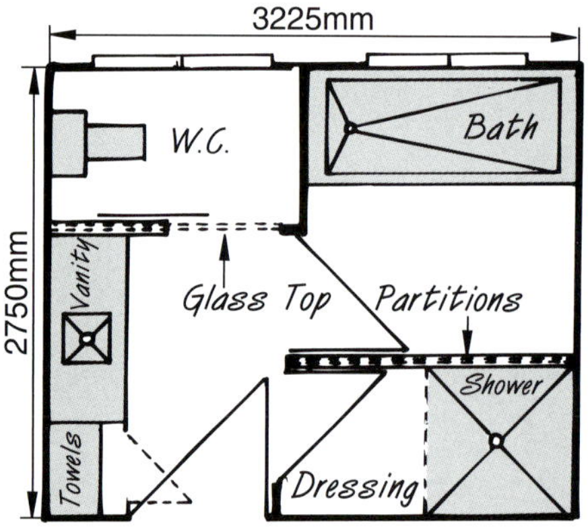

Dining & Family Rooms

Minimum Size: 9.0 sq metres or 3.0x3.0m if two separate rooms are planned. For a large combined family/dining room about 14.4 sq metres or 3.6x4.0m MIN. The family/dining room should have close access to the kitchen and, being a most used living area, ideally it should be placed on the north-east corner to take advantage of early morning and day time sunlight.

Lounge Room

Minimum Size: 21.6 sq metres or 6.0x3.6m.
Front doors opening directly into the lounge should be avoided. If a large family room is planned, the lounge size may be reduced.

Master Bedroom

Minimum Size: 12.96 sq metres or 3.6x3.6m (this is including built-in wardrobe space).

Additional Bedrooms

Minimum Size: 8.0 sq metres or 3.0x2.7m.
If two single beds are planned for these rooms, the size is increased to 3.0x3.6m (including wardrobes) and positioning of the windows and doors *should not* prevent the placement of two beds.

Toilets (WC - Water Closets)

Minimum Size: 1.8x1.0m.
The door should open out or have hinges detachable from the outside. This is to extricate people who have vomited and fainted - a common occurrence. All toilets should have a small hand basin if possible. Avoid placing toilets at the end of passageways or in view of the front door.

Laundry

Minimum Size: 5.6 sq metres or 2.7x2.1m.
This room should have a window and outside exit door, be capable of containing washing machine, tub, dryer, storage cabinet, and maybe the hot water system.

For damp and/or cold localities, incorporate the hot water system into a cupboard with drying shelves. Damp clothes can then be dried around the system. This dual purpose is lost if the system is placed externally. If ironing is carried out in the laundry, the width of the room may require increasing.

Deciding Which Materials to Use

Concrete or Timber Floors

Concrete

Advantages —
Easier and quicker to construct. Cheaper than timber on level or near level sites. Warmer in Winter as insulation qualities are higher. When covered with wood or carpet are quieter to walk on than timber.

Disadvantages —
Requires a floor covering such as carpet, tiles, vinyl or timber. Misplacement of wastes, shower recesses and bolts are difficult to rectify. Due to setting qualities of concrete, absolute preparedness is essential to ensure floor is poured and finished off at one time under good weather conditions.

Timber (on joists)

Advantages —
It is cheaper when used for upper storey levels or sloping sites. Floor coverings are *not* essential.

Disadvantages —
Colder in Winter. More expensive on level or near level sites. Noisier than covered concrete.

House Framing

Pine (Radiata, Slash or Caribbean)

Advantages —
Easier to handle, usually lighter and relatively splinter free. Easier to nail. Can be treated to rot and termite proof. Overlogging is not a problem.

Disadvantages —
Unless treated, is *not* termite resistant.
Some structural members require a larger sectional size to obtain the equivalent 'F' rating of hardwood.

Cyprus Pine

Advantages —
Naturally termite resistant. This could save the use of other termite control measures if the slab or sub floor is constructed as a termite barrier see 'HBM' and the 'BCA'.

Disadvantages —
The timber has a strong odour which some carpenters dislike. Must be used in a green state otherwise it can become brittle and easy to split fairly quickly.

Hardwood

Advantages —
Smaller sectional sizes may be used to obtain the required 'F' rating thus reducing costs. Some species are naturally rot resistant for inground use for a limited number of years depending on the soil type. Classified as 'durable hardwood' and termed Durability Class 1 & 2, one being the most durable.

Disadvantages —
Most species are heavier to handle and splinter the hands. Drilling often required to prevent splitting. Many species will bleed during rain causing staining of other building materials. Overlogging can occur with some species.

Manufactured Roof Trusses or Conventional Framing

Manuf. Trusses

Advantages —
Cheaper labour costs to erect. Easier and quicker to construct. Smaller timber sections required. Are lighter and of equal strength to conventional framing.

Disadvantages —
Slightly more expensive to purchase.

Conventional Roof Framing

Advantages —
Slightly cheaper overall.

Disadvantages —
Higher labour costs for erection. Takes longer to construct. Requires more carpentry skills. More timber wastage.

Roofing Materials

Concrete or Clay Tiles

Advantages —
Wide range of colours. Good sound insulation against rain. Weight helps to resist uplift in high winds, though individual tiles may lift if *not* tied down.

Disadvantages —
Tiles can crack through misplaced footsteps. Can be damaged by hail. Require specialist tradespeople to fix. *Can't* be used on pitches lower than 15° although verandahs *not* wider than 2m may be pitched at 12½°. As they are a heavy weight roofing material, in some instances, they will require a higher strength roof framing.

Metal Tiles Coated with Stone Chips (Decrabond)

Advantages —
Good range of colours. Good sound insulation against rain, better appearance than iron sheeting but *not* as good as concrete or clay tiles. Lightweight. Edges cut with snips are self healing. Can be made extremely hail and cyclone safe.

Disadvantages —
Care must be taken when working to avoid denting through misplaced footsteps. Require specialist tradespersons to fix. *Can't* be used on pitches lower than 12º. Uninsulated areas underneath are hotter during sunshine.

Corrugated & Profile Metal Sheeting

Advantages —
Semi-skilled labour can fix (state or local laws permitting). Light weight. Cheaper than most other materials. Some profiles can be fixed at very low pitches. Will withstand large hail stones.

Disadvantages —
Is noisy during rain. Most types become very hot on the underside in Summer heat. Check for the coating which provides the coolest cladding.

Flooring Materials

T & G Flooring (on joists)

Advantages —
Good natural appearance. Cool in Summer *not* as cold as ceramic tiles in Winter. *Doesn't* have to be laid in a single operation as does concrete.

Disadvantages —
Low insulation qualities. Is noisy and requires resurfacing with wear in the long term.

Ceramic Tiles & Slate

Advantages —
Can help keep the house cool in Summer.
Good visual appeal.

Disadvantages —
Can be cold underfoot in Winter, hard on china and babies. Tile joints can become difficult to keep clean especially in service areas. *Not* possible to guarantee cracking will *not* occur.

Sheet Vinyl on Concrete Slab

Advantages —
Cushioned and continuous. Easy to clean, soft under floor.

Disadvantages —
Can be marked by sharp objects, stiletto heels etc. Needs to be laid by professionals.

Cork

Advantages —
A natural product. It is soft and warm underfoot in Winter.

Disadvantages —
The surface will eventually require resurfacing. 4.5 or 6mm thickness cork. For future resurfacing it is preferable to use 6mm cork. For maximum resistance to wear, three coats of polyurethane is recommended.

Carpet on Concrete Slab

Advantages —
Warm and soft especially if higher quality underlay is used. Carpets maintain a quiet floor when compared to walking in shoes on wood floors.

Disadvantages —
Requires additional cleaning to control dust mite etc. Needs to be laid by professionals

Selecting Windows

When designing the windows for a room, 3 factors must be considered:

a). ***Shape.***

b). ***Size.***

c). ***Position.***

These factors in turn will be based on 3 requirements:

a). ***Light.***

b). ***Ventilation.***

c). ***View.***

As a general rule, keep broad expanses of light and ventilation on the North and East aspect and reduce window areas on the West and South aspects.

If your view is southerly, you will want to take full advantage of it but heat loss will be greater in Winter. You could install double glazed windows.

In Summer, windows on the western aspect can make those rooms extremely hot. Where this is unavoidable, pergolas and awnings etc can be provided over those windows.

Points to Consider when Designing Windows:

A. Where possible, avoid placing the ventilation portion of windows high in the frame. Over head ventilation in summer is *not* beneficial.

B. For maximum ventilation where possible, use cross ventilation by placing windows in two walls well back from the corners. Avoid corner windows unless the design demands it.

C. Allow sufficient space at either side of windows to permit drapes to be pulled back past the windows.

D. To maximise light, ventilation and view (as well as for other factors) more than one type of window design may need to be considered.

Aluminium versus Wooden Joinery

Timber windows require a higher maintenance level than their aluminium counterparts. Also, timber joinery can *not* obtain the air tight fitting which vinyl sealed aluminium joinery can achieve. Aluminium windows are usually powder coated or anodised. This coating should have a minimum thickness of 10 microns. When exposed to salt air or industrial pollution,

Cont.

it should be increased to 15-20 microns. In these conditions, aluminium joinery should be washed down regularly with water and detergent to prevent corrosion commencing.

Quality between Brands

There remains a difference in quality between brands. Some utilise larger aluminium sections and different locking mechanisms. Also some manufacturers have a better quality in their commercial range.

Advantages & Disadvantages

Sliding Windows

Advantages —
Fit most building situations and are easy to install. Economical to purchase. Easy to clean. Easy to install window locks. Fly screens can be fitted externally.

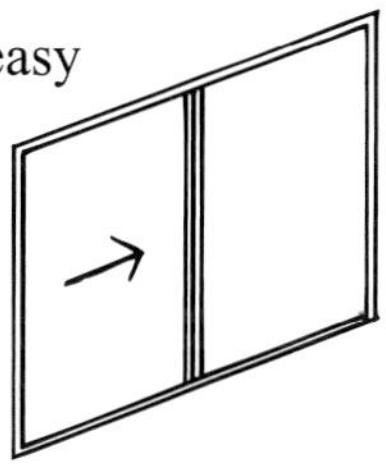

Disadvantages —
Opening area limited to half the glass area. Rain penetrates when opened even partially. Curtains will blow through open windows unless screened.

Awning Windows

Advantages —
The whole glass area can be opened, though may inhibit some breezes. Can be partially opened during rain. Curtains can be displayed with little disturbance. Fairly easy to clean.

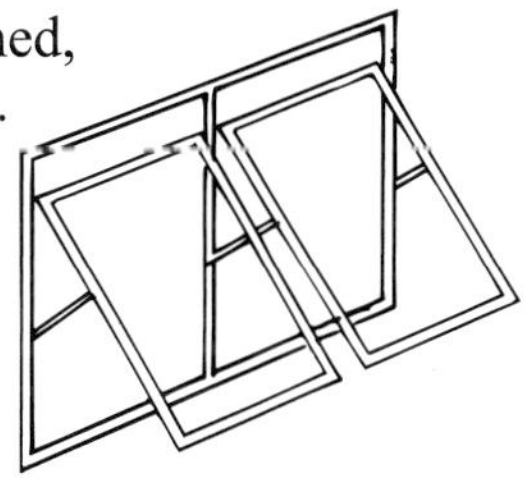

Disadvantages —
When open will collect dirt more easily. Protruding corners are dangerous on low set houses or verandahs. Fly screens must be fitted on the inside which can be a nuisance. Normal friction stays will rust. Use brass or stainless steel.

Casement Windows

Advantages
The whole glass area can be opened. Allows directional control of ventilation. Easy to clean from inside.

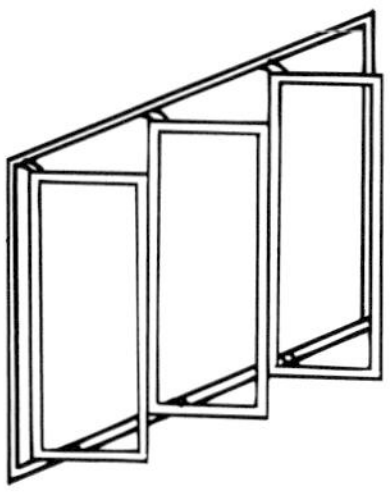

Disadvantages
Protruding corners are dangerous on low set homes or on verandahs. Fly screens must be fitted on the inside. May inhibit some breezes.

Double Hung Windows

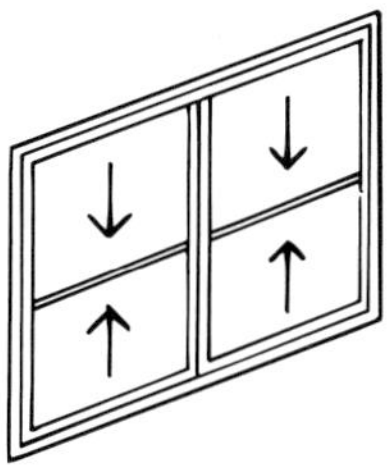

Advantages
Even breeze flow top and bottom and better selection of aperature.

Disadvantages
Opening area limited to half the glass area. In high set houses, the sliding sash can be difficult to clean. The cross members can interfere with views. Spiral mechanism gives trouble, the spring type are best.

Lourved Windows

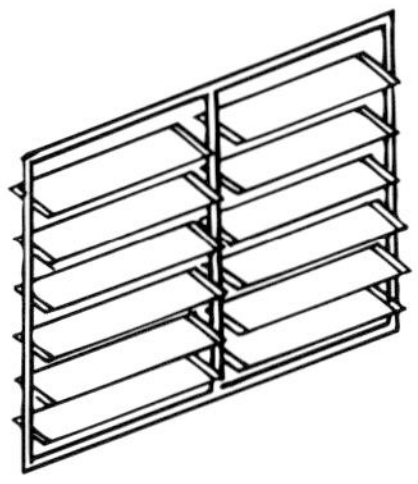

Advantages
Allow full ventilation flow and can be tilted to desired angle.

Disadvantages
Some brands leak with heavy rains and rattle in the wind. Cleaning is more effort. Can be easier to burgle.

External Surfaces

Brick Veneer

Advantages —
No maintenance. Excellent waterproofing when properly installed. Offers a measure of wind bracing. Hard surface. Has good energy efficiency value.

Disadvantages —
Some colours or patterns date. May cost more. May require tradespeople to install.

Thin Section Render

Advantages —
In trend. Surface colours can be altered.

Disadvantages —
Requires repainting every eight to ten years, may cost more than fibre cement claddings and timber weatherboard but when properly installed may not be cheaper than brick. Substrates such as fibre cement sheet and polystyrene, if *not* installed strictly according to manufacturers requirements, can cause future problems which are expensive to rectify. Hail or hard objects can damage walls with too thin coatings over polystyrene. Offers no wind bracing when using polystyrene as a substrate.

Fibre Cement Claddings, Planks etc

Advantages —
Can be in-trend depending on profile. Hard surface. Offers a measure of wind bracing. Could be installed by the DIY'er. Can have a colour change in future. Is resistant to rot and termites.

Disadvantages —
Requires repainting every eight to ten years.

3 Understanding House Construction

House Construction Types (systems)

***Important:** The timber framing of houses has been more fully covered in the 'HBM'.*

There are basically four types or systems of house construction used in Australia.

1. Brick Veneer
2. Cavity Brick
3. Weatherboard
4. Concrete Block

The purpose of this chapter is to provide a bird's eye view of how these four house types are built.

Each construction type has its own advantages and disadvantages which should be carefully considered. Having a knowledge of how the house is built will enable a close estimate of costs and help identify faulty building practices.

An understanding of how the chosen house type is built will become clearer once the house plans are prepared. These provide the correct dimensions, positioning and spacings for timber, bolts, straps and reinforcing etc. Most of the relevant building code requirements should be found either on your plans or specifications.

Where to Start

To gain an overall knowledge of how the house will go together stage-by-stage, mentally divide the house into the stages as illustrated opposite. Add a final stage called cladding, lining and finishing. This will also include installation of joinery, kitchens, PC items, plumbing, mouldings, and painting etc.

Stage-by-Stage

Commencing with footings obtain an understanding of how that particular stage is constructed. Check what is specified in the house plans for that stage. Note all the materials that will be required to complete the stage.

This will enable the Owner Builder to properly co-ordinate supplies and tradespersons, and not be overwhelmed by the size of the task. This exercise should be repeated for each of the stages. The effort involved will make greater cost savings possible.

Fig 1

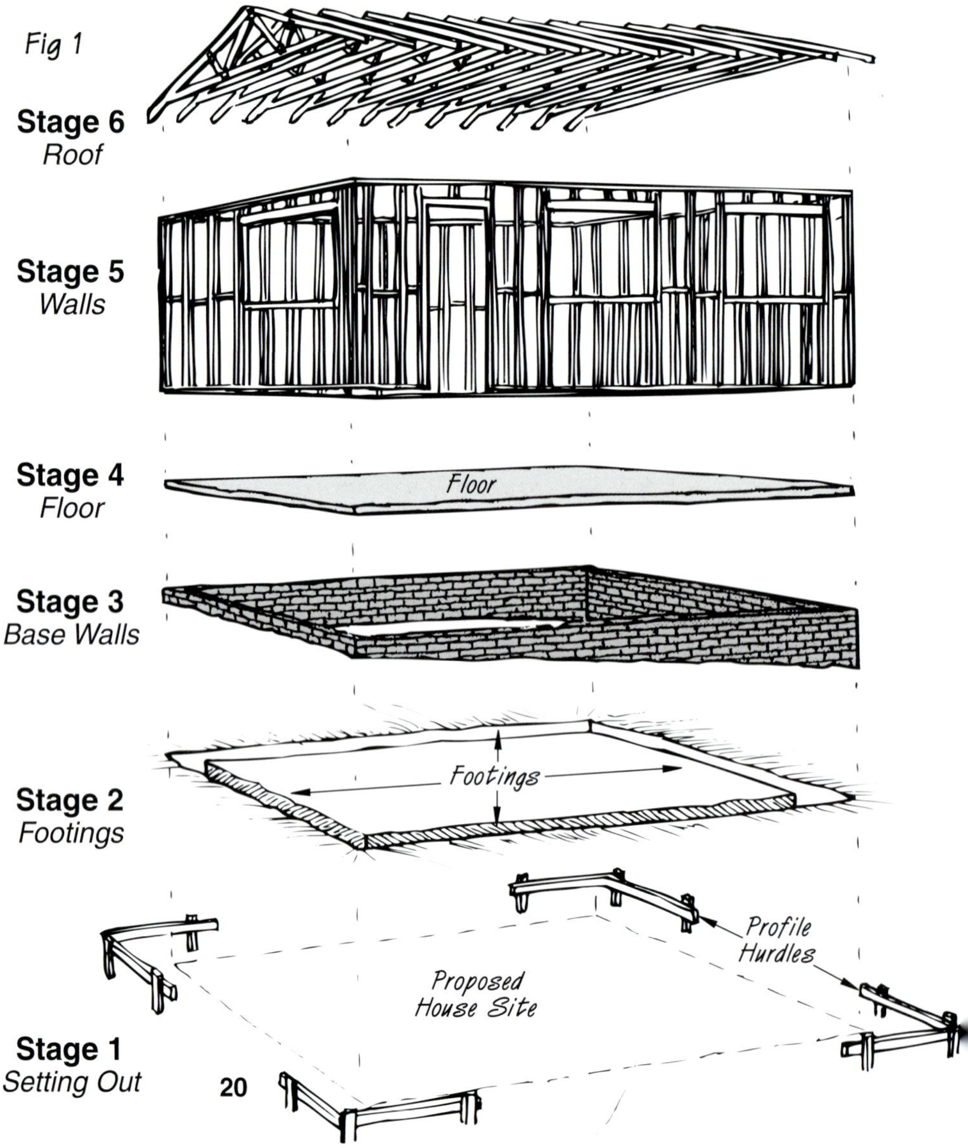

Understanding Foundations & Footings

Poorly constructed footings can result in wall corners sinking and cracking of walls at corners and around openings.

Causes of Footing Failure

Faults are caused by the foundation's inability to support loads whilst being under pressure through movements in the subsoil. Particularly in organic soils, plastic clays or soils with a high clay content.

Three points must be adhered to:

1. *Footings are Properly **Designed***
2. *Footings are Properly **Prepared***
3. *Footings are Properly **Concreted***

Footings are Properly Designed

All subsoils can be classified to fall somewhere between non expansive and expansive. Expansive simply means the subsoil has the ability to increase or decrease its volume during wet or dry seasons. Cracks in adjacent houses or buildings may be an indication of expansive subsoils. Particular care must be taken in designing foundations for expansive subsoils.

Footings should be designed, inspected and certified by an engineer. particularly in expansive subsoils. Some Local Councils require an engineer's design of prospective footings to be submitted with the plans. It will certainly help the sale of an owner built house if the buyer is informed that an Engineer designed and inspected the foundations and the relevant certificates are produced. It will cost a little more money but will increase the value of the house.

Footings are Properly Prepared

When the excavator has finished, the footings should be checked for level and alignment. Stretch the string lines through the footing width marks as shown on the profiles. The sides of footings may require straightening by hand spade and the bottoms may require levelling. On sloping ground steps are necessary (see fig 4, Page 22). These are levelled and the risers cut square. Soft patches in footing bottoms are removed, taking the area down until a firm bottom is obtained and leaving nice square, clean steps at each end of the area. If rain occurs prior to pouring concrete, check the footing bottoms for soft spots and remove. Concrete height pegs are then installed unless a laser level is to be used during the concrete pour.

Placing the Reinforcing

The correct reinforcing and stirrup spacing is indicated on the plan. Reinforcing should then be lowered into footings and correct overlaps made at joins and steps (see the 'HBM' for details). It is important to ensure that reinforcing *will not* be forced into contact with the trench when readymix concrete is being poured. A 40mm concrete cover must be maintained on all sides of the steel.

It is important to wait until the inspection and certificate has been issued by the relevant authority prior to ordering concrete.

Footings are Properly Concreted

Before pouring concrete, ensure that where clay has adhered to the reinforcing, it has been removed with a wire brush.

The pressure of the flowing readymix will tend to force the reinforcing out of central position. A man should be stationed to steady the reinforcing whilst the concrete is being poured to ensure the 40mm MIN. concrete cover will be maintained.

Concrete should then be mechanically vibrated to ensure maximum compaction and removal of air around reinforcing. Vibrators can be hired. However, if a vibrator is available, the concrete should be thoroughly tamped using a tamping rod or a spade.

All footings should be poured at the same time to ensure that they are one integral entity without joins. Intervals between concrete trucks *should not* be more than half an hour and joins should be prevented from drying out by covering with plastic or wet sacks. Footings should also be continuous below all openings including garage doorways etc. The footing surface is then screeded off with a straightedge.

Footing Types

Foundations are designed by a Geotechnical Engineer to suit the house style and subsoil type. Owing to the variations in subsoil types from one site to the next, test holes should be drilled. This is usually arranged and supervised by the Engineer. Obtain two or three quotes before engaging one.

There are basically four types of footings used with slab floors:

1. *Strip*
2. *Beam*
3. *Raft*
4. *Pier and Beam (see 'HBM')*

Strip Type Footings

These are wider than their depth. They are used on non expansive subsoils on level or sloping ground (see fig 1).

Beam Type Footings

A beam footing is one that is deeper than its width (see fig 2). Plans and specifications will stipulate the reinforcement requirements.

Steps in Footings

On sloping sites, footings require steps as in fig 4. The steps should be brick or block module height and length.

Where foundations have to be taken into solid rock, the footings are usually only a shallow strip as in fig 5. The rock is scabbed or (made rough) and is sometimes required to be trenched out up to 150mm deep.

Raft Type Slabs & Footings

On level sites, the raft type design is frequently used. In this case, the slab and footings are concreted at the one time (see fig 6).

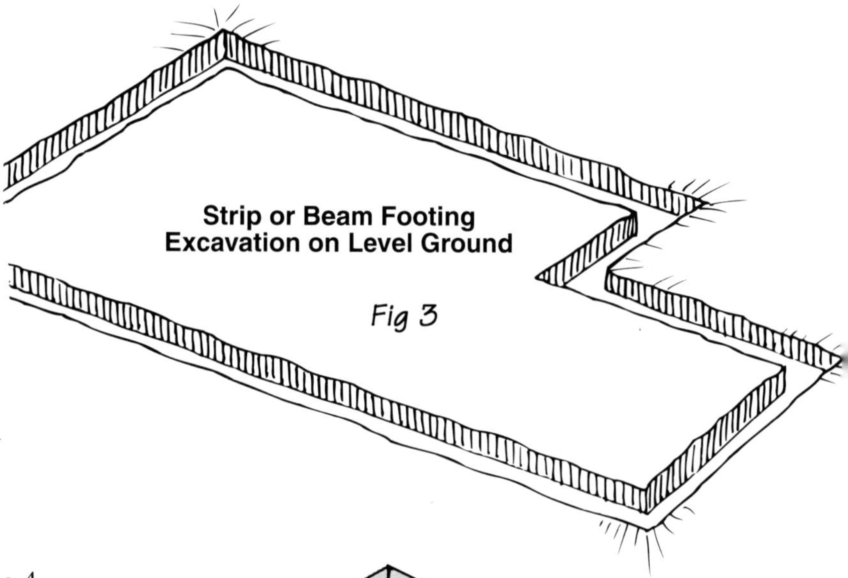

Strip or Beam Footing Excavation on Level Ground

Fig 3

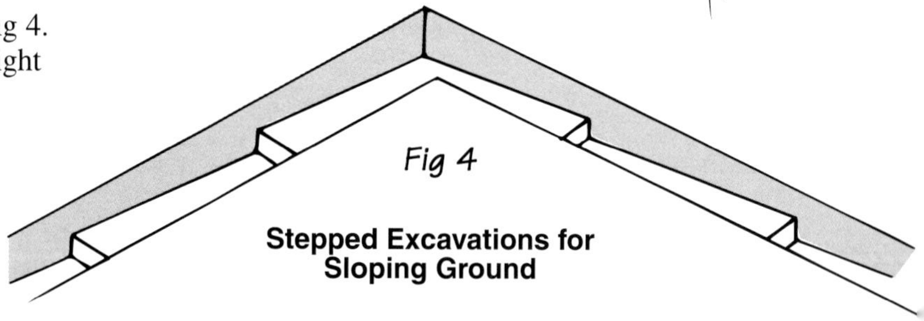

Fig 4

Stepped Excavations for Sloping Ground

Fig 1

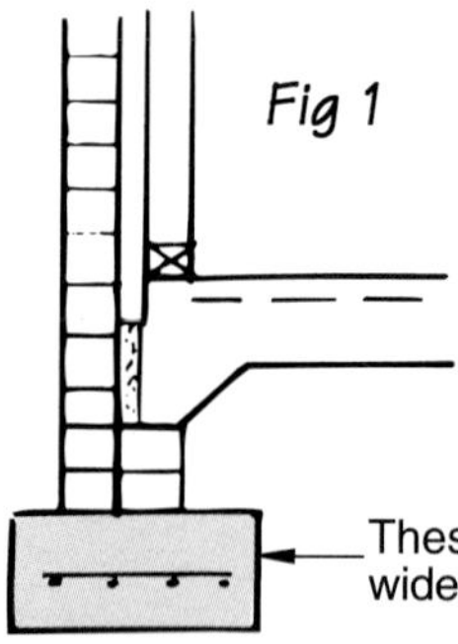

Strip Footings

Fig 5

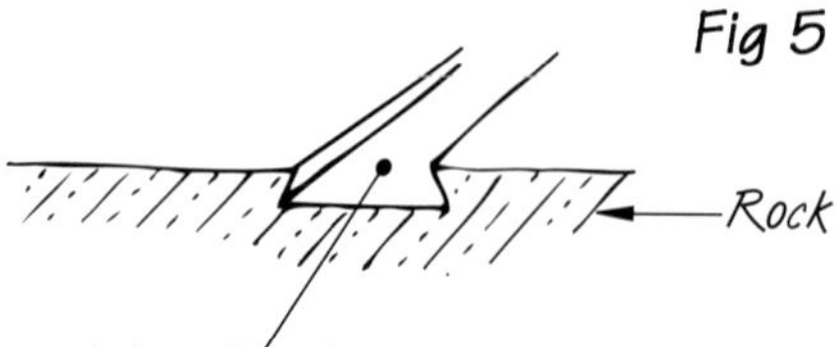

Foundations in solid rock require only shallow excavations.

To level the surface and make steps where slopes occur, pneumatic tools and machinery are available.

Fig 2 **Reinforced Beam Type Footings**

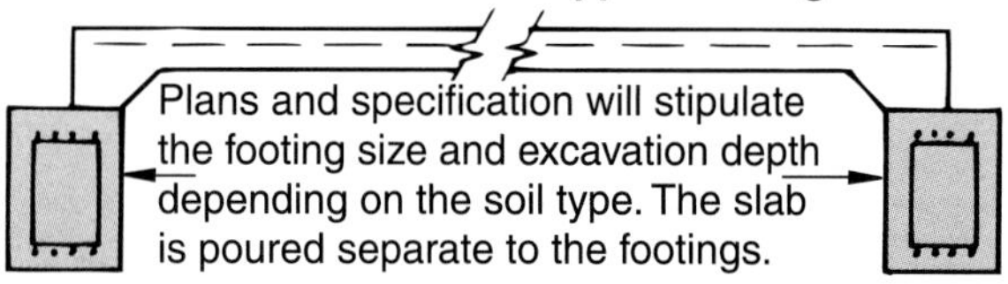

Fig 6

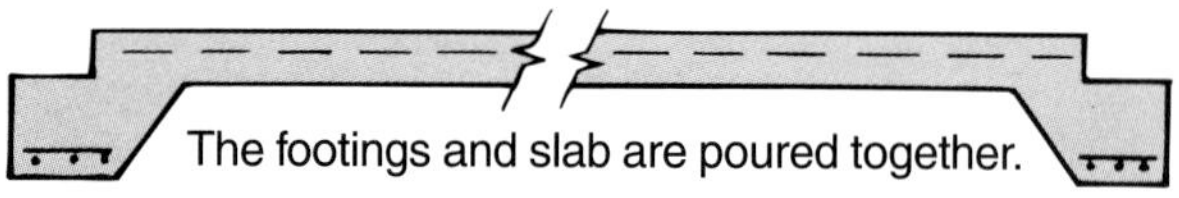

Raft Type Slab & Footing

Weatherboard Houses & Timber Framing

Wall Framing Members

For the specific sizes and spacings, refer to the house plan and specification.

Top Plates

These hold the top ends of the studs in place and may also support roof framing. On load bearing walls, they may need to be increased in thickness.

Bottom Plates

These hold the bottom ends of studs in place. The wall is fastened to the floor through the bottom plates.

Studs (common)

These provide support for internal linings and external claddings. Usually spaced at either 450mm or 600mm centres and may be between 70x35mm and 90x45mm depending on the specifications.

Nogging

These are fitted between studs *not* more than 1350mm apart in height. They can be the same thickness as the studs or 35mm MIN. They are easier to nail in position when fixed in a staggered pattern. When plasterboard is used, they must be kept away from the horizontal plasterboard join.

Sill Framing

These are usually the same size as studs.

Lintels

Lintels are used to support loads such as the roof or upper floors above openings and normally constructed using timber.

Roof Framing

For truss roof framing instructions see the 'HBM'. For conventional cut-out-and-erect-on-site roofs see 'The Australian Roof Building Manual'.

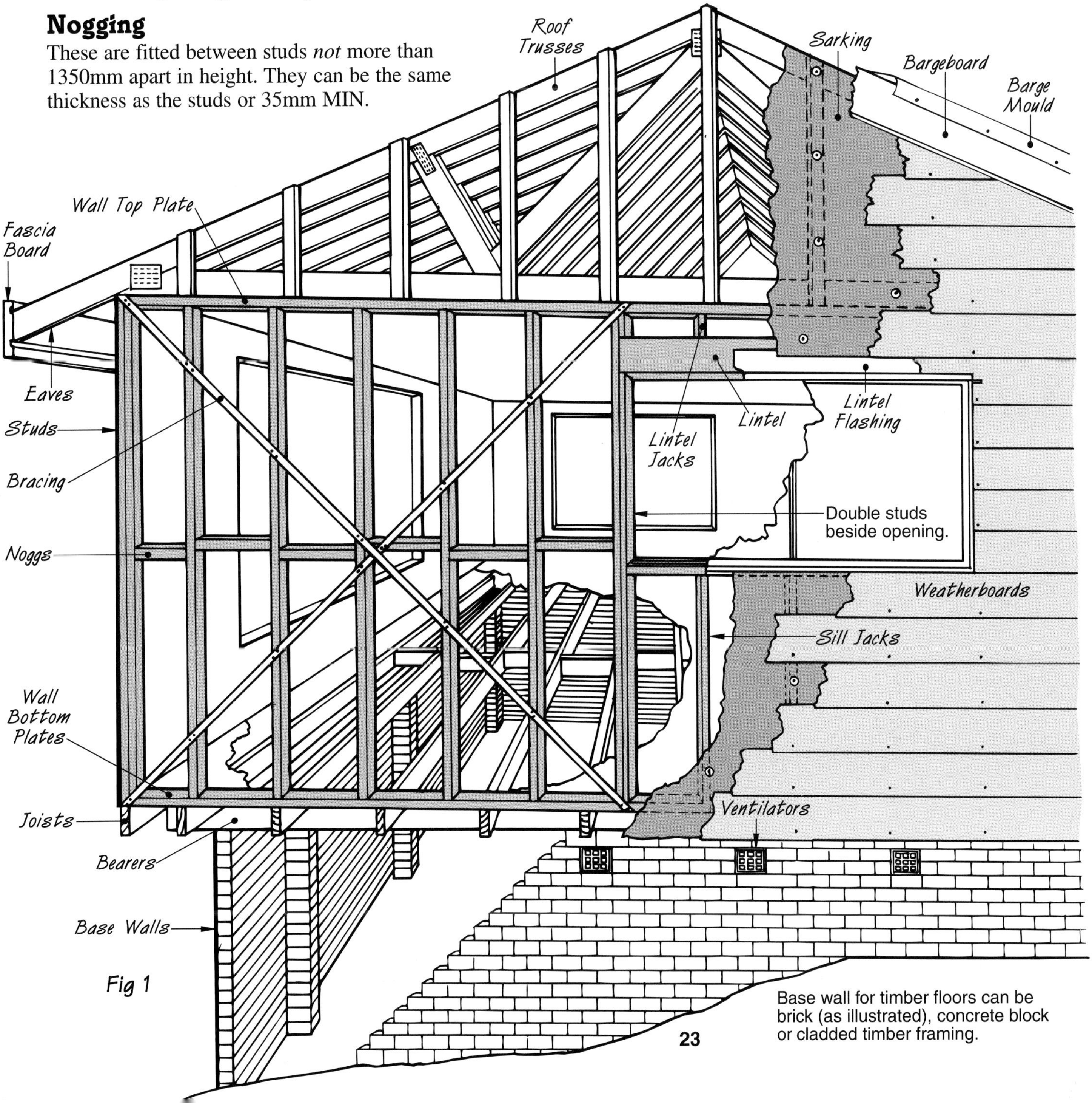

Fig 1

Base wall for timber floors can be brick (as illustrated), concrete block or cladded timber framing.

Timber Floor Systems

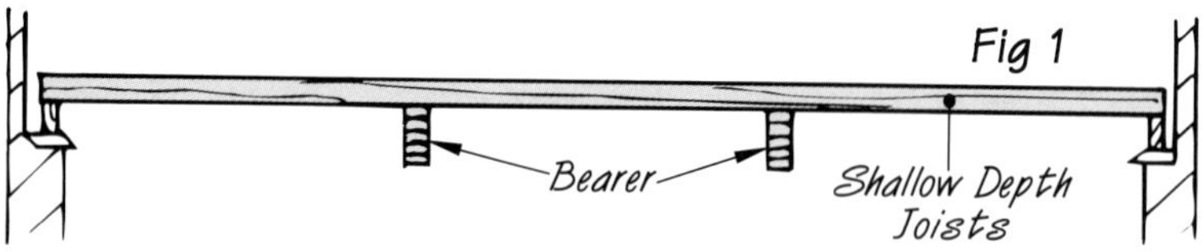

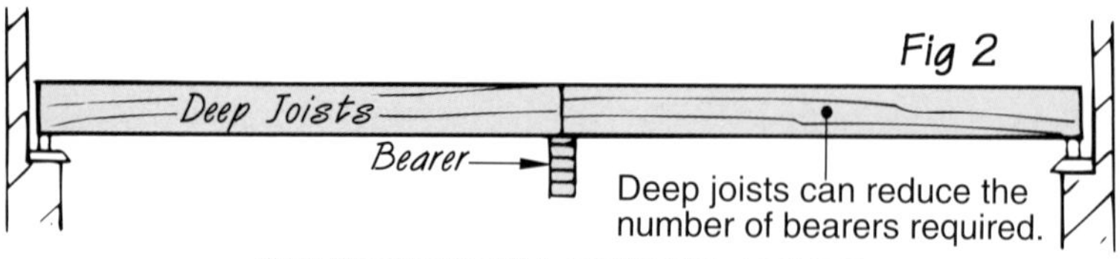

CONVENTIONAL TIMBER JOINTS

Timber floors consist of a flooring material attached to floor joists usually spaced at 450mm ¢ and are in turn supported by bearers.

When constructing timber floors, it is often desirable to have as few supporting posts beneath the floor as is necessary. This requirement can be met by the application of one of the following floor supporting methods. Each has its own inherent advantages and disadvantages. *See fig 9, Page 25 for the method recommended by the Author for floors which are elevated sufficiently to become a basement area.*

Conventional Timber Joists (figs 1 & 2)

All solid timber joists should be seasoned (dried), especially deep joists, otherwise excessive shrinkage will occur. However, Cyprus Pine is one species which experiences a low shrinkage factor.

Where average sized joists on a normal house may require two or three supporting bearers, deep joists may make it possible to eliminate one supporting bearer and one row of posts as in fig 2. However, should deep joists be necessary, most of the alternatives will out-perform solid timber as far as economy of on-site installation and use of the natural resource is concerned.

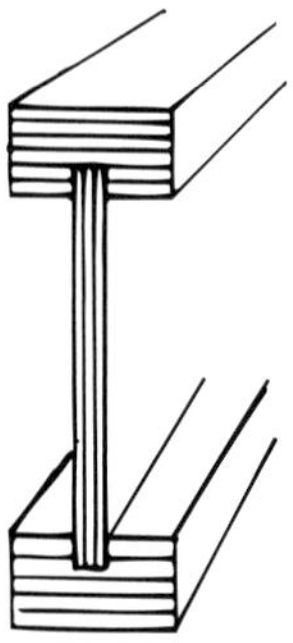

Fig 3

hyJOISTS or 'I' Joists
'I' joists are available in various sizes to suit the spans.

The hyJOIST System (fig 3)

hyJOISTS are a ply laminated ('I' joist). These are lightweight and quick to erect joist. They arrive on-site true and straight so save on-site straightening. They provide a truly economical utilization of the timber when compared with solid timber. *See the 'HBM' and manufacturers' instructions for installation.*

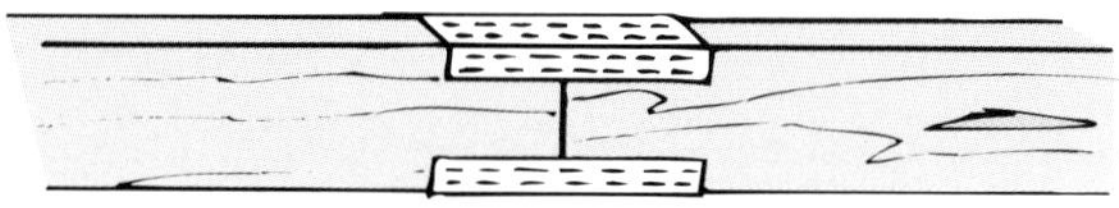

Fig 4 EASY JOIN JOISTS BY PRYDA

Nail Plate Joists & Beams (fig 4)

A variety of these systems are available. All have their own advantages. Obtain the manufacturers literature and costings for the following:

Mussel Beam (Ezijoin or Pryda Joists)

These are available either laminated or butt jointed. The butt jointed system uses nail plates to connect adjoining members and glue is *not* employed. These joists are an excellent alternative to conventional joists because they come in lengths up to 12 metres and are reliably straight which saves time on-site (see fig 4).

Longreach Floor Trusses (Joists)

These are webbed trusses available in lengths up to 8 metres. They enable easy installation of plumbing and electrical cabling through them. The system provides a stiff floor free of bounce and with a lower shrinkage factor.

Glue Laminated Timber Beams (fig 5)

Glue laminated timber beams use glue only to build up each additional timber strip. They have largely replaced the steel beam because of their aesthetic appearance and ease of handling.

They are capable of spanning most areas in a housing situation. Keep in mind the higher the 'F' rating of the timber used, the shallower will be the depth requirement of the beam. This is important when considering head room.

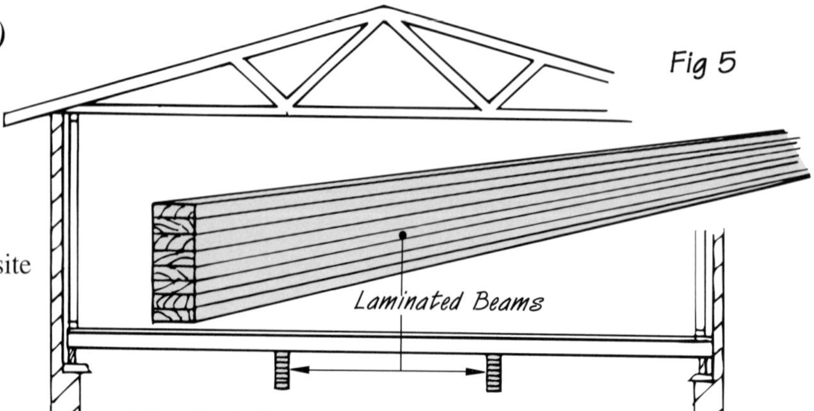

Joists fixed directly to glue laminated timber beam.

GLUE LAMINATED TIMBER BEAMS

Cont.

Steel Universal Beams (fig 6, 7, & 8)

Steel universal beams have the advantage of being capable of supporting a greater span using a shallower depth beam than laminated timber.

However, steel beams are more difficult to work with and attract rust. Refer to fig 8 for one method of cladding over steel beams.

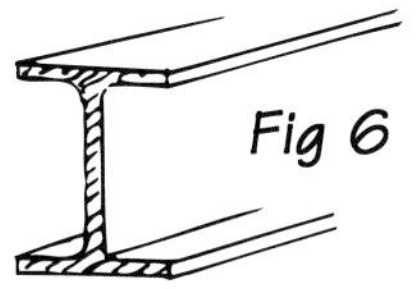

Fig 6

UNIVERSAL STEEL BEAMS

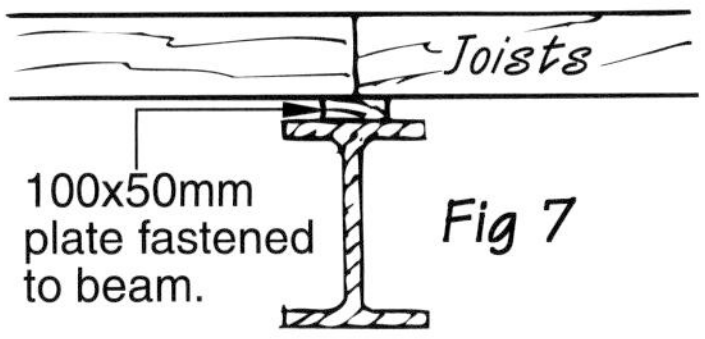

Fig 7

Steel beam with joists in place.

STEEL BEAMS

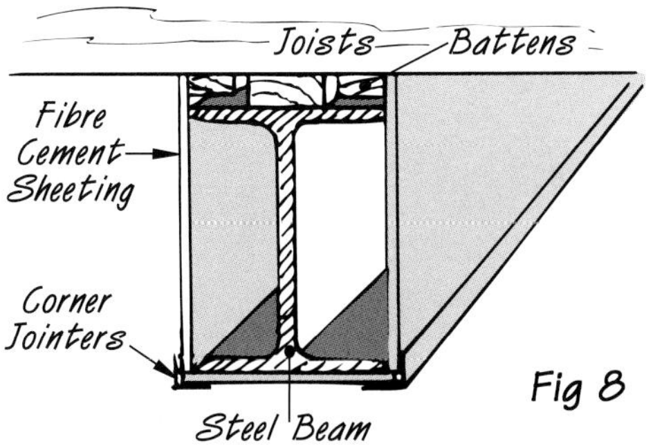

Fig 8

A simple method of cladding steel beams is to use fibre cement flat sheet or similar with plastic external corner moulds and a little adhesive or perforated corners ready to receive thin section render or textured coatings.

An Ideal System

For the average situation this system provides a low cost alternative with a minimum of post supports obstructing the floor area. Glue laminated beams are used with only one or two supporting posts or walls along their length and conventional joists of seasoned or kiln dried timber dressed on both edges to provide same depth joists throughout.

Alternatively, and even better if the extra cash is available, use hyJOISTS or Ezijoin joists instead of conventional joists. They will save a lot of time on joist and sheet flooring installation. With hyJOISTS you may even be able to elliminate one supporting beam and row of posts.

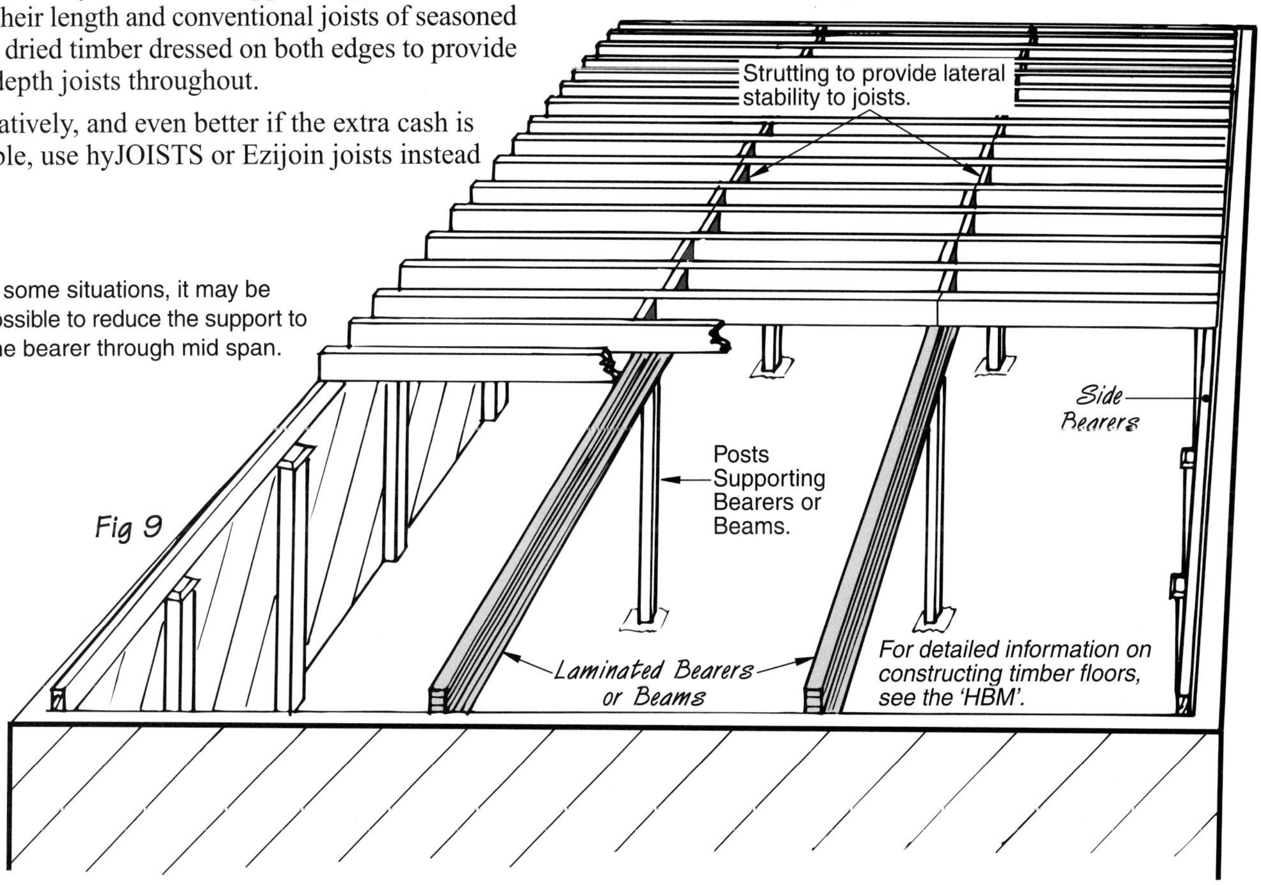

Fig 9

Restricted Head Room under Bearers

Figs 10 & 11 are two methods of increasing head room under bearers.

In fig 10 the bearer is raised and the joists are notched around the bearer.

In fig 11 the bearer is raised to the level of the joist tops.

Fig 10

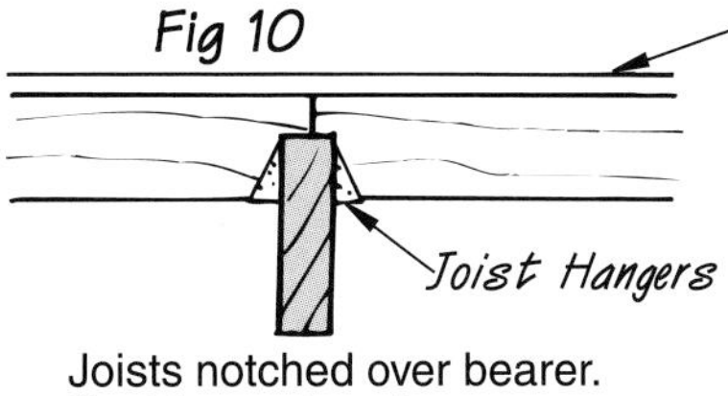

Joists notched over bearer. Best to use lam. beam.

Fig 11

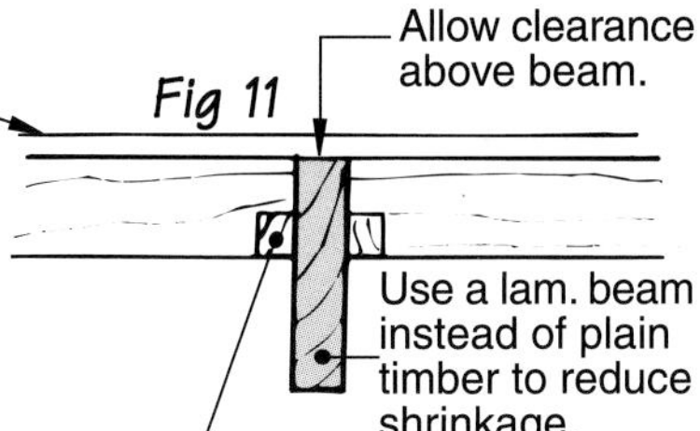

Bearer raised up to underside of flooring and joists supported with either 50x50mm ribbon battens or by Pryda joist hanger brackets. A shrinkage variation can occur with this method causing a hump in the floor. So allow a clearance above the beam itself.

Windows in Weatherboard Walls

Installation Details

When installing aluminium windows, it is best to have the reveals factory fitted. When requesting the factory to fit timber reveals, provide the thickness of the walls, internal linings and external claddings. Aluminium windows are fitted prior to attaching the external sidings to enable the sidings to be inserted well inside the frames.

The sarking should be attached before installing windows. Flashings should be fitted to the perimeter of the frame (these can also be factory fitted) *(see fig 1, Page 97)*. Flashings are fitted above the head unless eaves offer sufficient protection.

Sidings at the sides and sill should be taken to butt inside aluminium frames. The remaining tapered gaps between sidings and frame should be filled with long life paintable sealant. The sealant should be smoothed off so that a good bond is maintained between the aluminium and the siding and that *no* gaps remain.

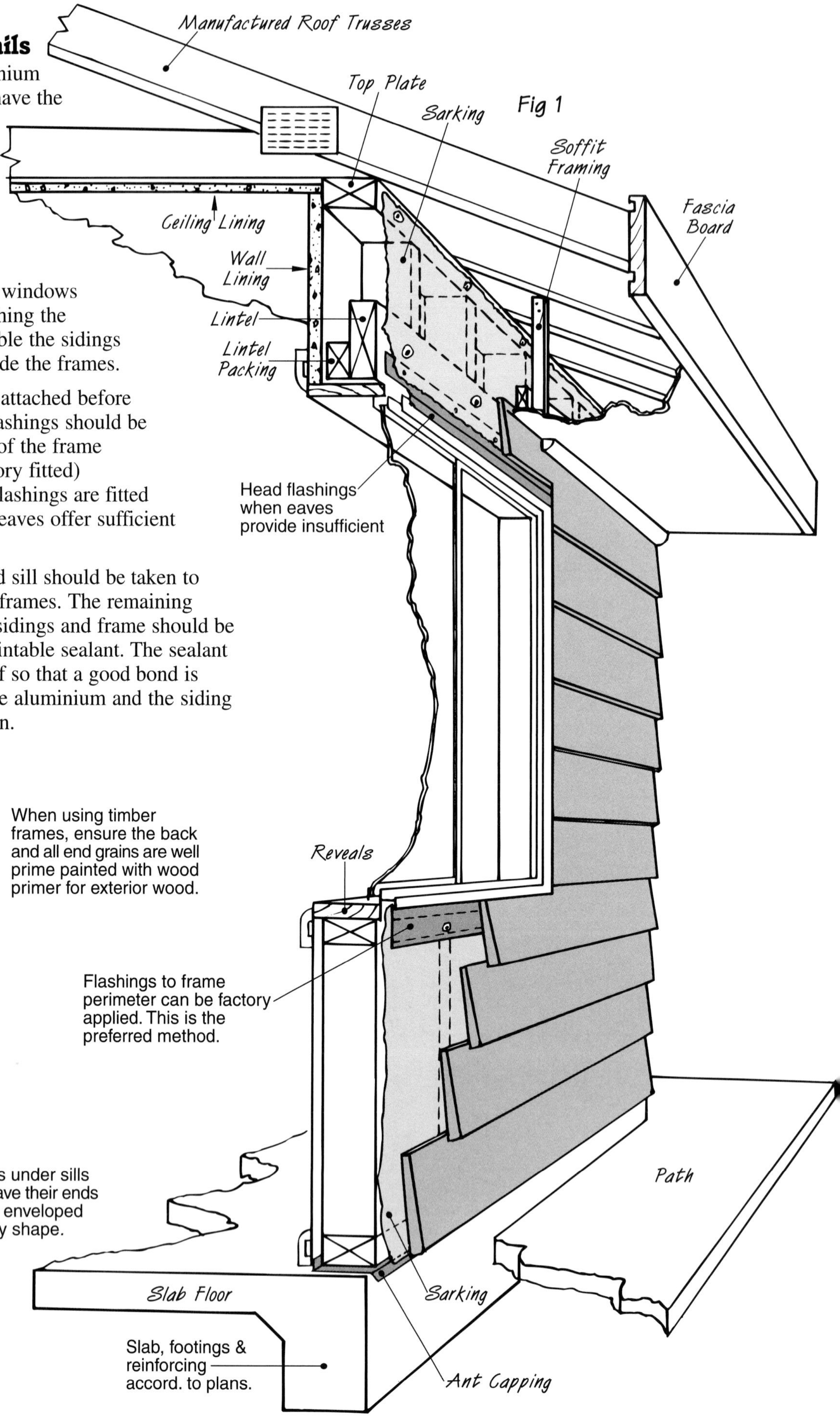

Fig 1

When using timber frames, ensure the back and all end grains are well prime painted with wood primer for exterior wood.

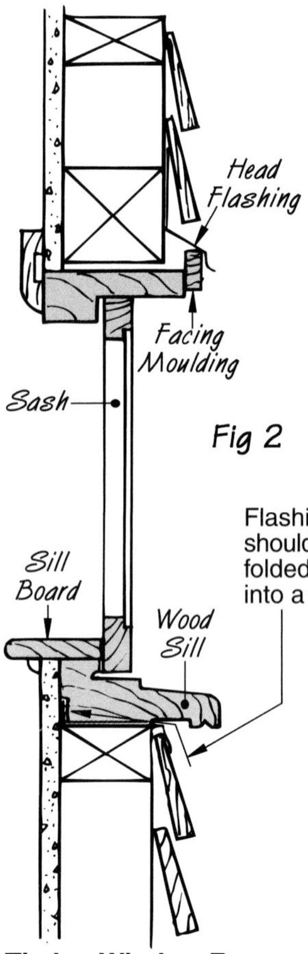

Fig 2

Flashings under sills should have their ends folded or enveloped into a tray shape.

Timber Window Frame

Bay Window Construction

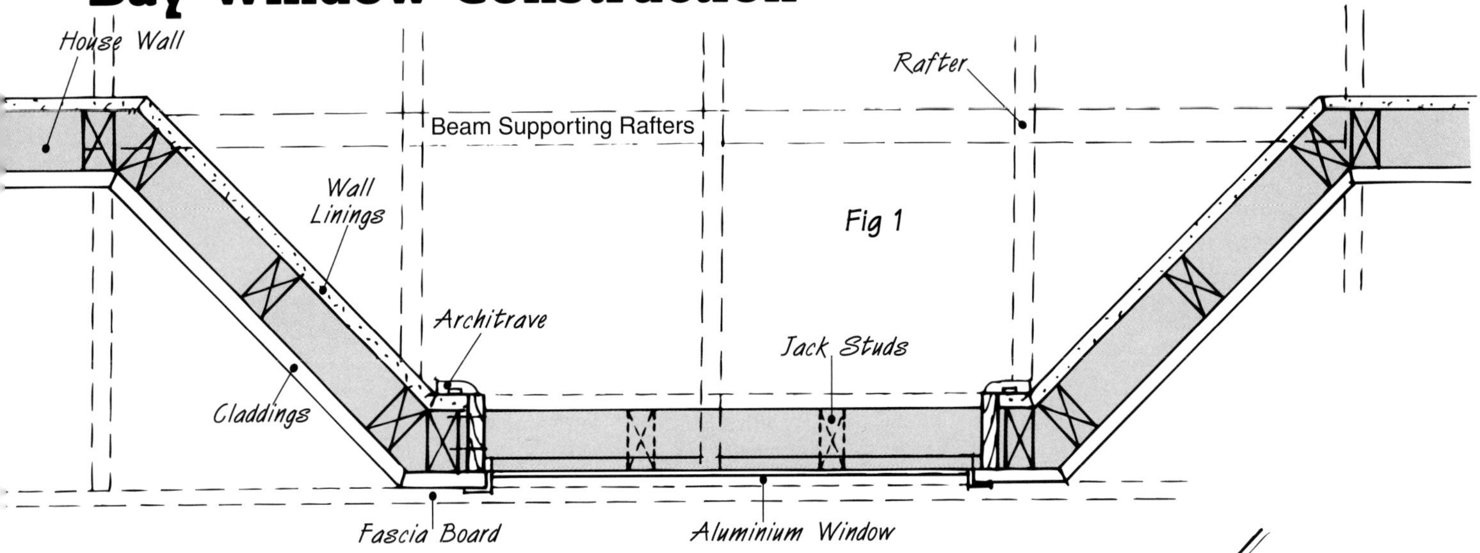

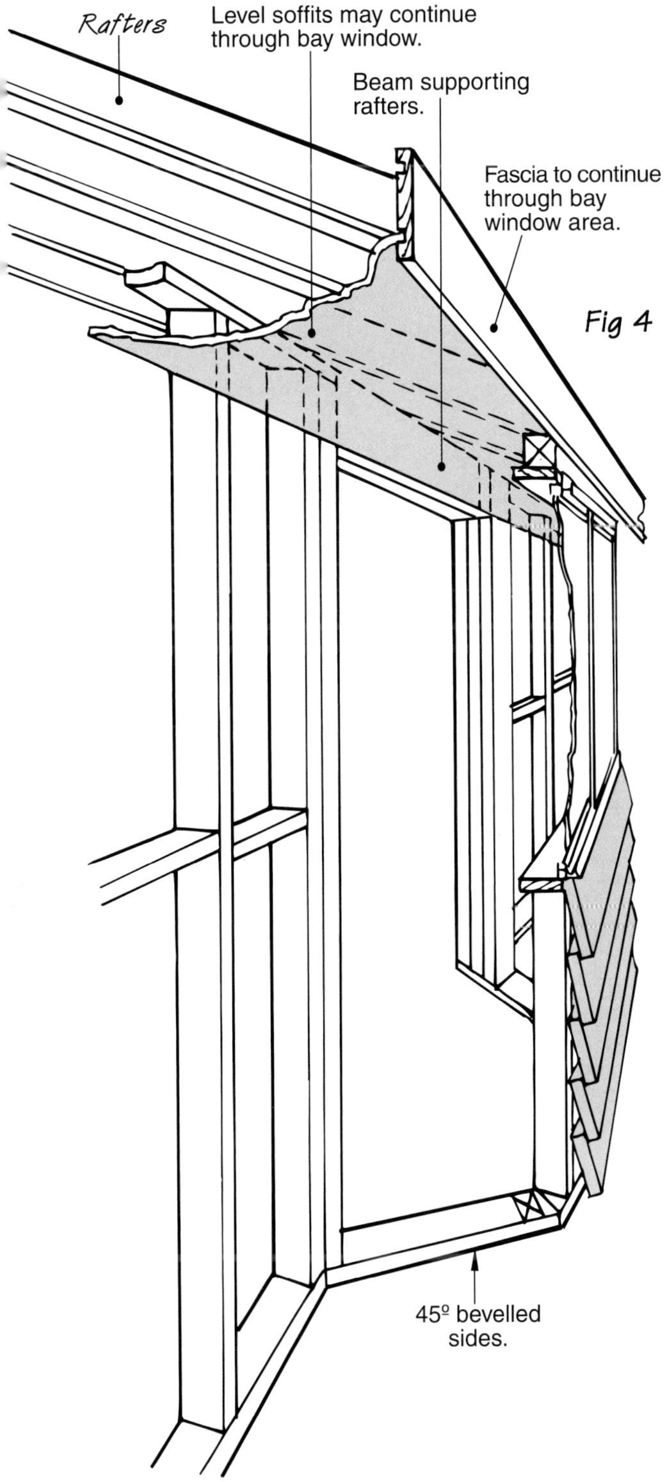

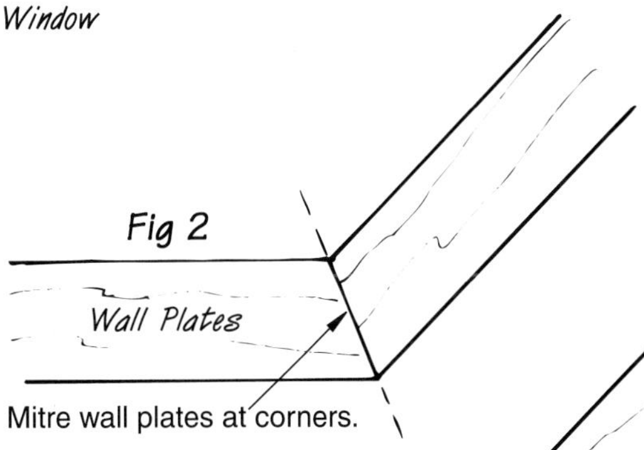

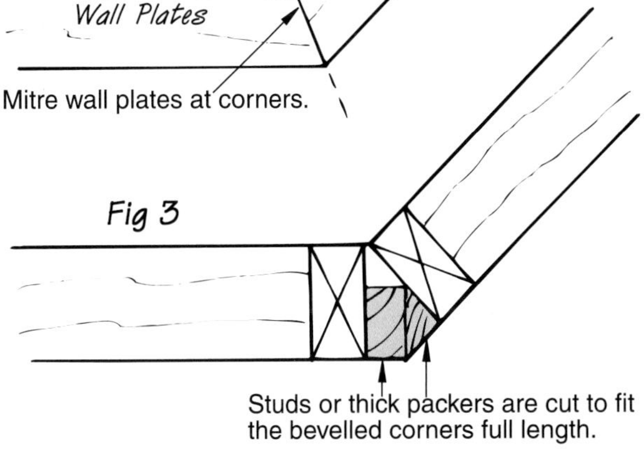

Bay window construction is simplified when the bay depth is confined to the width of the eaves thereby avoiding the need for extending the roof. The soffit line on the house (where level or sloping) may continue through the bay window area. Where bay windows have bevelled sides, it is easier to construct if the bevel is at 45º.

The corner space between the studs at internal and external corners is filled with studs or thick battens sawn or planed to fit the bevelled shape. This provides continuous support for attaching wall linings (see fig 3). If windows are being installed in the sides of the bay window, aluminium window manufacturers can provide windows to continue around the corners. Where corners are required to support a roof load, then aluminium load bearing corner sections are installed. It is preferable to continue to support the roof along the house wall line by installing a beam across a bay window opening as illustrated. It is easier to use sized wall framing and 70x35mm timber is adequate for non loading bearing walls in the bay framing.

Constructing Dormer Windows

Fig 1

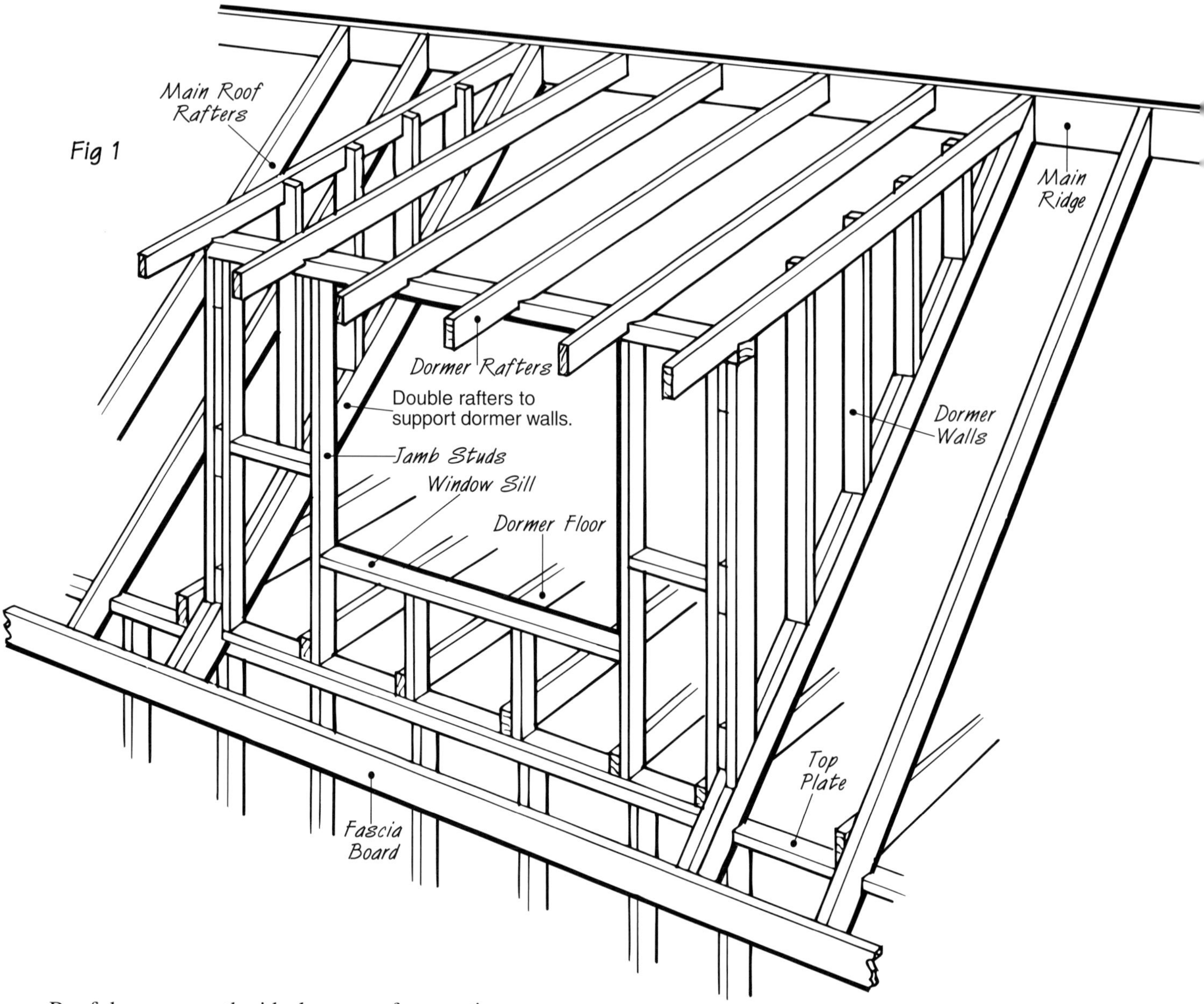

Roof dormers are the ideal means of converting an otherwise wasted roof space into usable living or sleeping areas. Skillion, or near flat, roof dormers enable head height to be maintained over most (if not all) of the area.

The pitched or gable ended dormer may restrict usable head height to the area close to the ridge. Their main function is to provide light and ventilation.

Head Heights

Check with the Local Authority regarding minimum head height requirements for the designated room.

Roof Design

The design, position and pitch of dormer roofs is critical if they are to enhance and be in keeping with the overall house design.

Load Bearing Factor

Ensure that the proposed weight of the dormer will be adequately supported by the walls and roof of the main structure.

Flashings

Long life flashings should be used at the joint between the main roof and the walls of the dormer on all three sides and care taken to lap flashing joins at the corners.

Insulation

In hot climates, rooms inside roof spaces can prove to be difficult to keep cool. Most, if not all, of the following methods should be used:

a). Double sided aluminium foil under roofing material and any walls.

b). Insulating batts to every ceiling and wall space.

c). Windows permitting cross room ventilation.

d). Roofing material of a light colour. White should be considered. Check with local authorities as some prohibit the use of white or silver or colours which create a nuisance reflection to neighbours.

Gable Dormers

The gable roof dormer is used mainly to provide light and ventilation. The method of construction is similar to the skillion roof dormer except that its roof rafters are supported on the side walls of the dormer instead of the front. A short valley on either side is also necessary.

Stage 1

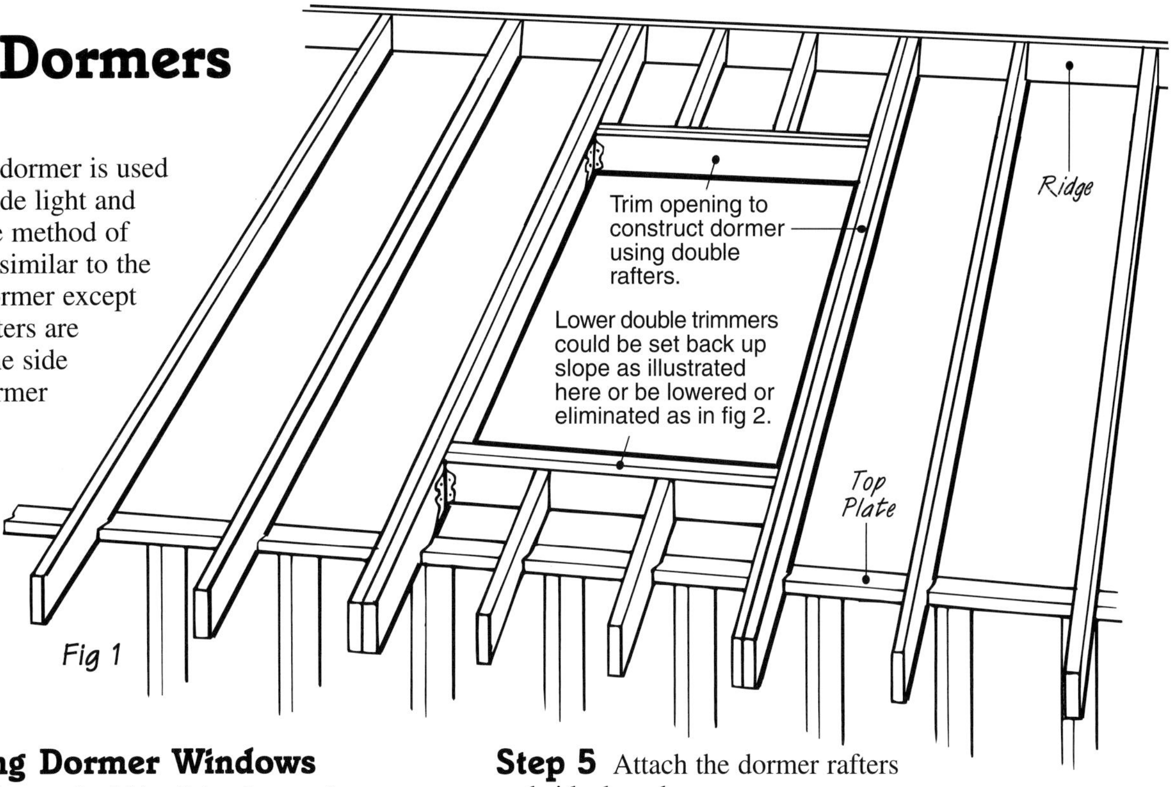

Fig 1

Constructing Dormer Windows

Step 1 The internal width of the dormer is marked out on the ridge board and house wall top plate.

Step 2 Double rafters are positioned directly underneath the proposed dormer walls.

Step 3 The floor joists and flooring of the dormer is then laid, or this work could become Step 1. It is generally easier to construct dormers with the floor as a working surface.

Step 4 Construct the dormer walls.

Step 5 Attach the dormer rafters and ridgeboard.

Step 6 Attach fascias, bargeboards and guttering then roof cladding.

Step 7 Fit windows and external cladding.

Step 8 Attach and finish internal linings and mouldings.

Stage 2

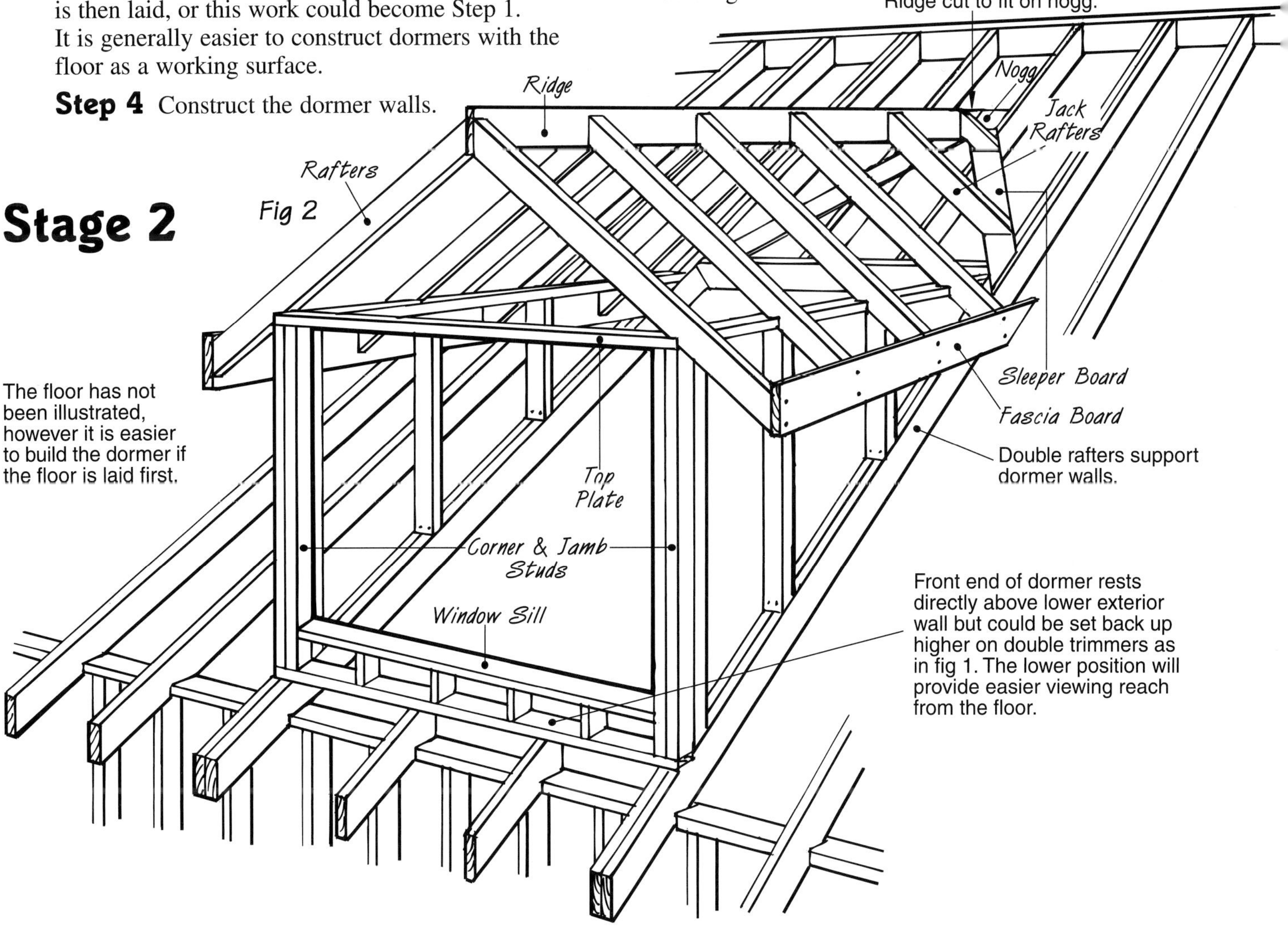

Fig 2

Opening-in Exterior Door Details

Where opening-in door sills are exposed to driving rain, they will inevitably leak, even when beneath wide eaves. Storm moulds are fitted to reduce this problem.

Opening-out door sills will provide a watertight sill but *should not* be used for front entrance doors. *Refer to 'HBM' for further information on door sills and door installation.*

Fig 1

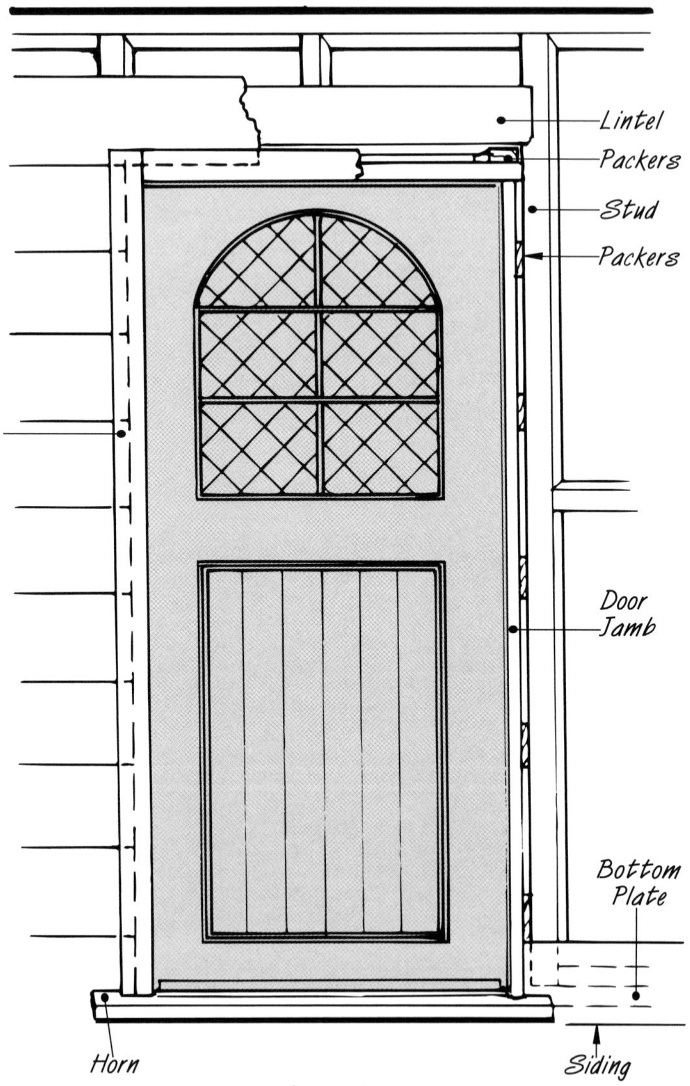

Fig 2

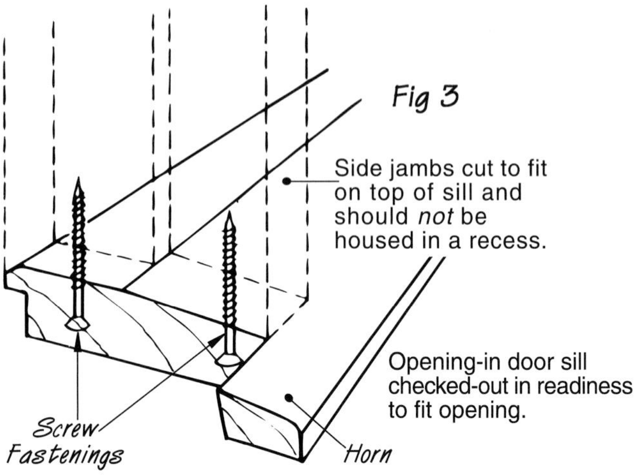

Fig 3

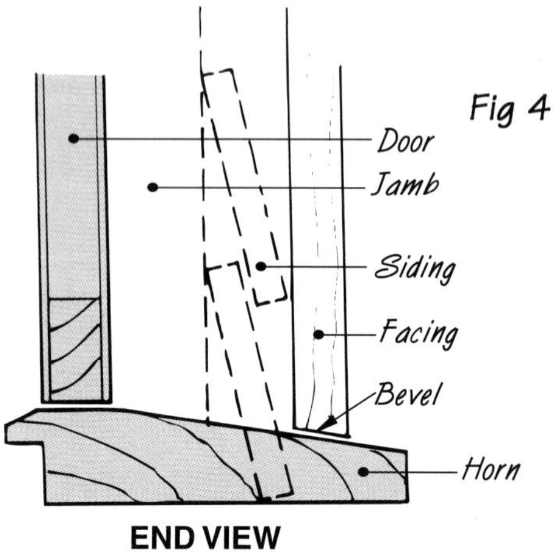

Fig 4

END VIEW

Brick Veneer Low Set (Slab Floor)

Brick veneer construction is a popular form of house construction. It can be applied to high or low set dwellings. It requires no maintenance.

The advantage of brick veneer for Owner Builders is that when a bricklayer is employed to build the brick walls, the builder is almost totally relieved of external work apart from eaves and painting trim.

Fig 1

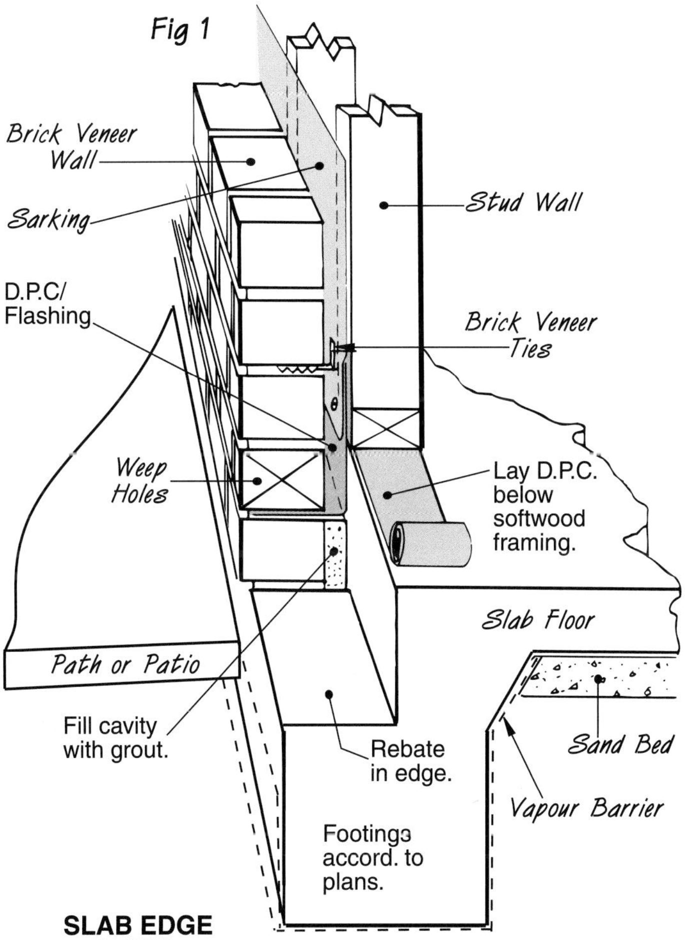

SLAB EDGE DETAIL

Fig 2

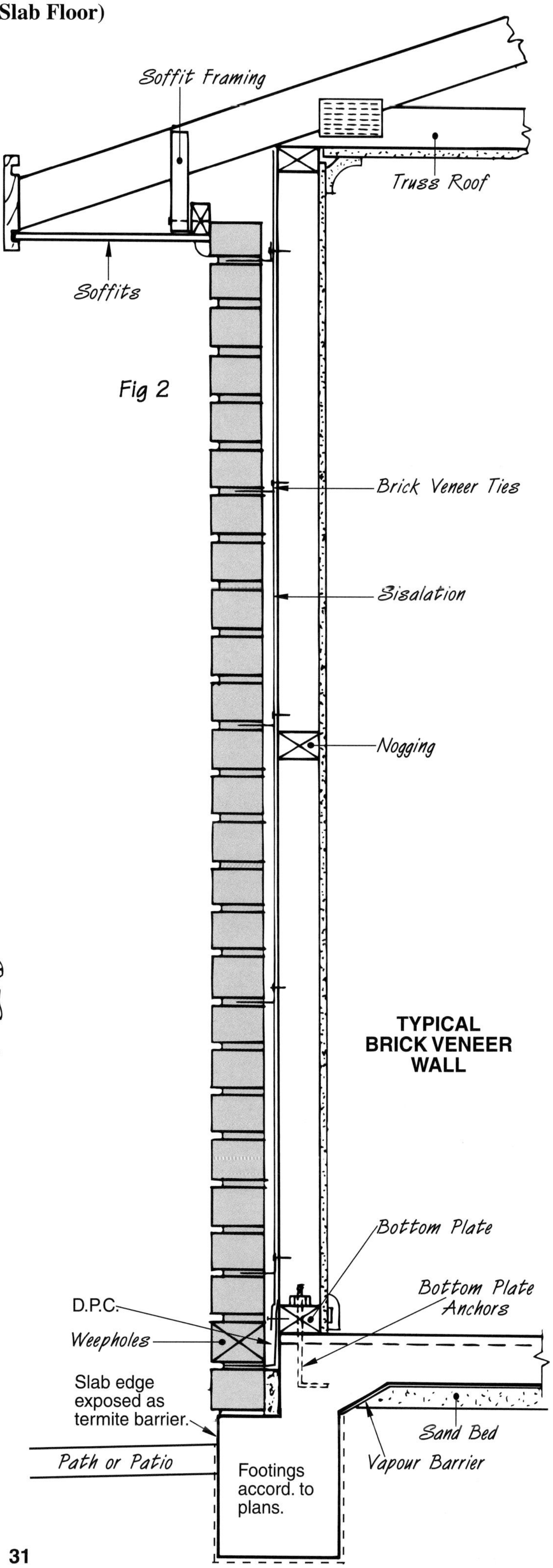

TYPICAL BRICK VENEER WALL

The Slab Edge

The slab edge perimeter is provided with a set down rebate. This can be constructed in several ways. The slab footing edge can be utilised as a termite barrier; the best method or footings can be stepped as is necessary on sloping sites (see the 'HBM' for details).

Cont.

The brick veneer house is in all respects identical to a timber framed weatherboard house, except that a brick wall is attached to the timber framed wall instead of weatherboards.

The following extra details are necessary:

a). A step or rebate around the perimeter of the slab floor edge as in fig 1, Page 31.

b). A damp proof course is laid along that rebate with weep holes.

c). Brick veneer ties at specific spacings to hold the brick veneer to the timber frame. The spacings will vary with the locality *(see plans and specifications, also 'HBM').*

d). A gap should be provided between the brick sills and the window frame sills to prevent damage caused from house frame shrinkage *(see 'HBM' for details).*

Further basic construction requirements are explained in this section.

For further detailed step-by-step instructions refer to the 'HBM'.

Fig 1

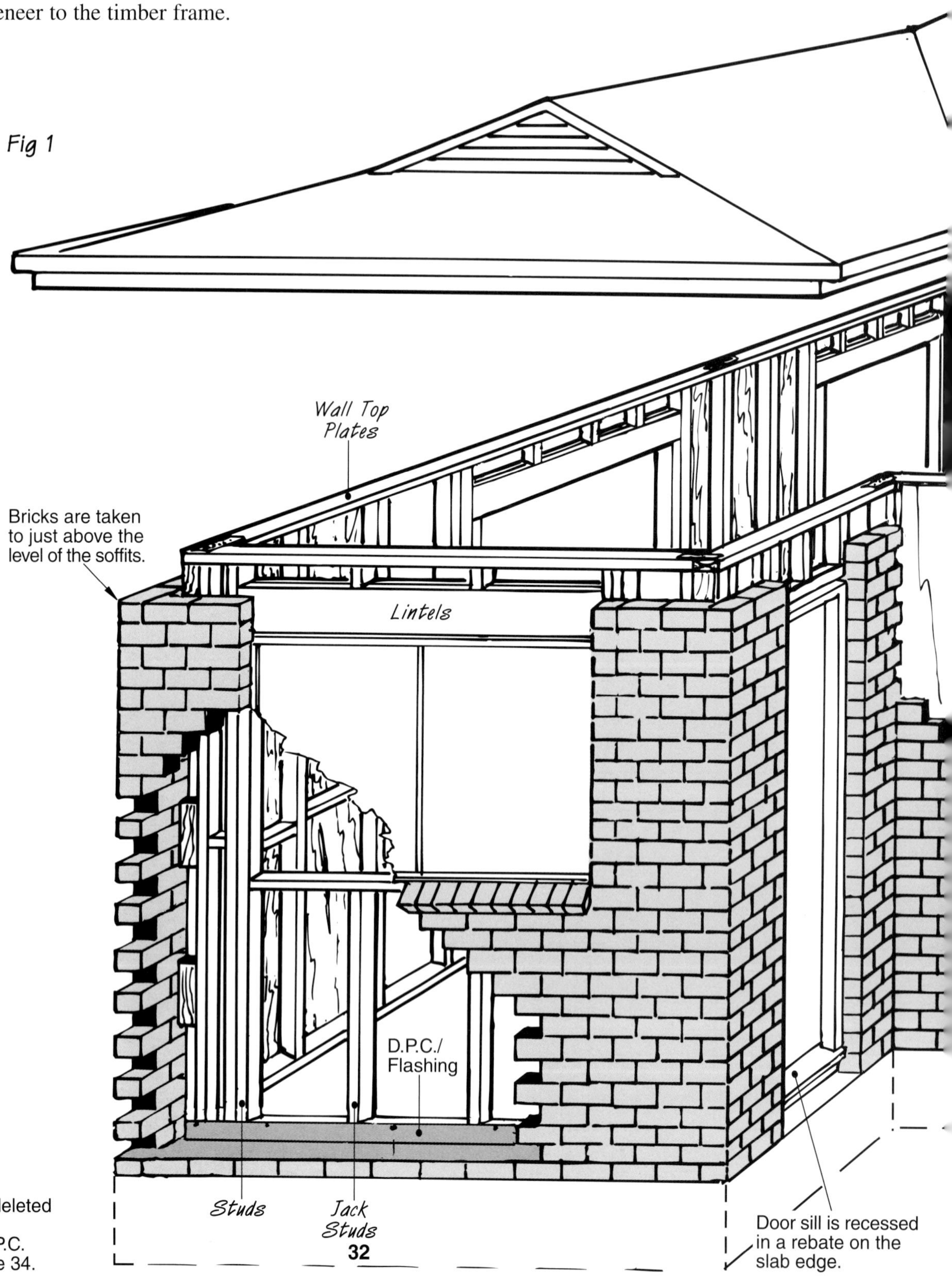

Wall sarking has been deleted for illustration but would normally overlap the D.P.C. flashing as in fig 1, Page 34.

Windows, door frames and electrical meter box are installed prior to commencing brickwork. This ensures the bricks will fit tightly up against the frames. Interior linings and finishing can be carried out while the bricklayer is erecting the brick walls. However, be sure to have all brickwork accessories such as D.P.C. and brick ties on-site before the bricklayer arrives.

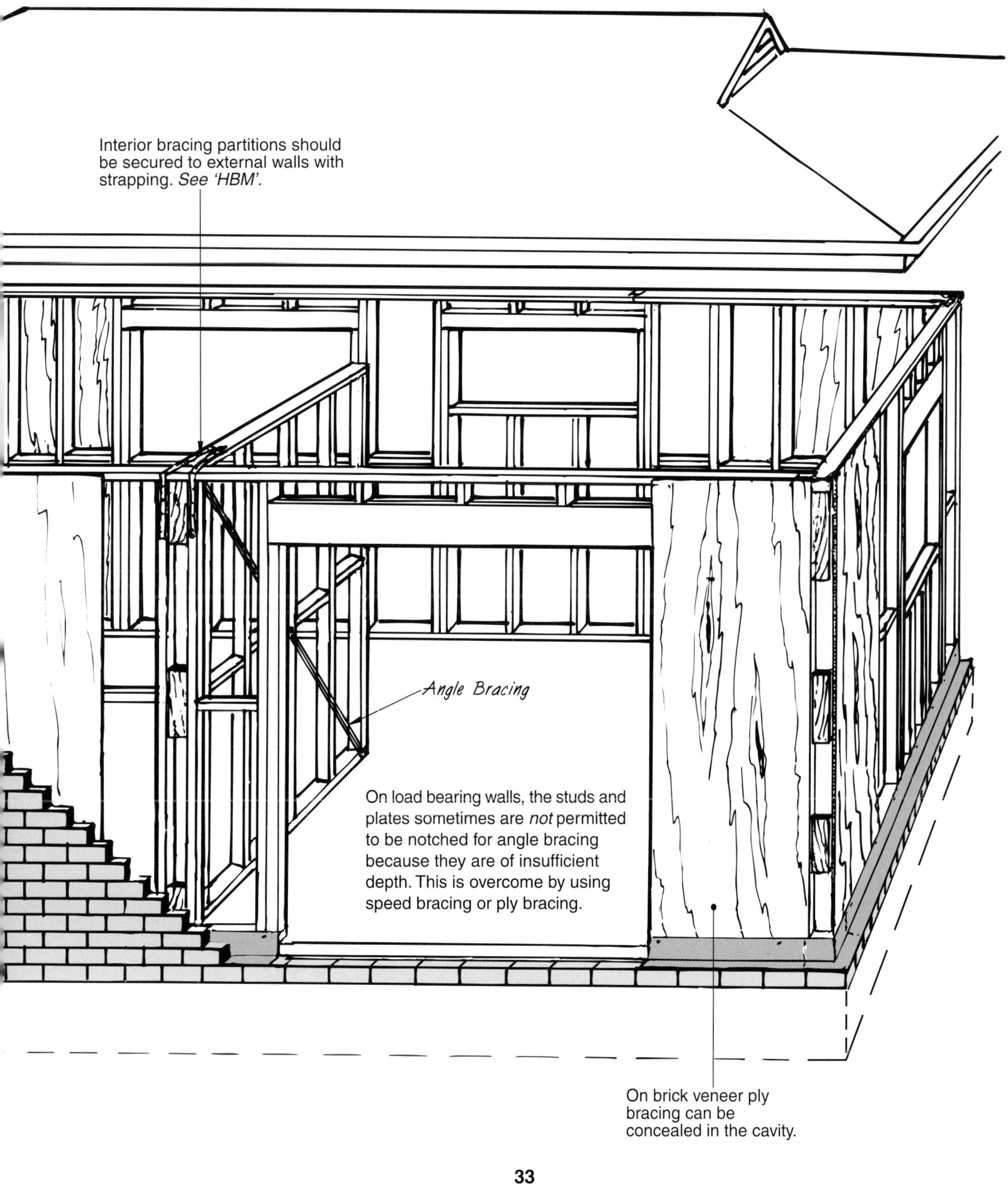

Installing Windows in Brick Veneer

Installation Details

Installation of aluminium windows in brick veneer is simplified if the timber reveals have been factory fitted to the aluminium frames. Windows are always installed before brickwork commences. Reveal and sill flashings should always be installed *(see fig 1, Page 97)*.

Note: Provide a space allowance of 5mm between brick sills and window frames on the lower storey or single storey houses and 10mm on the second storey. Double these clearances when using unseasoned hardwood.

For other space allowances for timber frame shrinkage on brick veneer dwellings, see 'The Australian House Building Manual'.

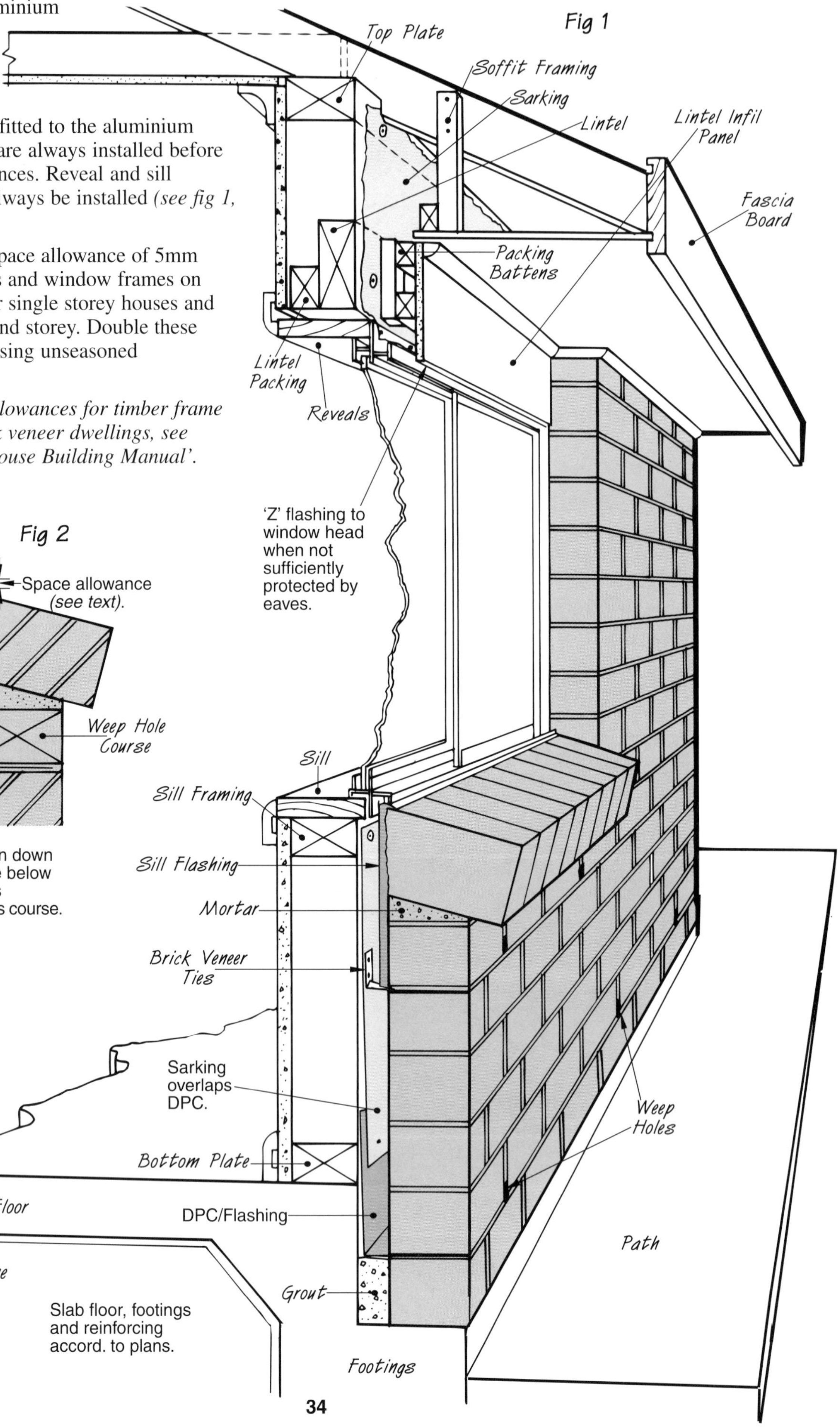

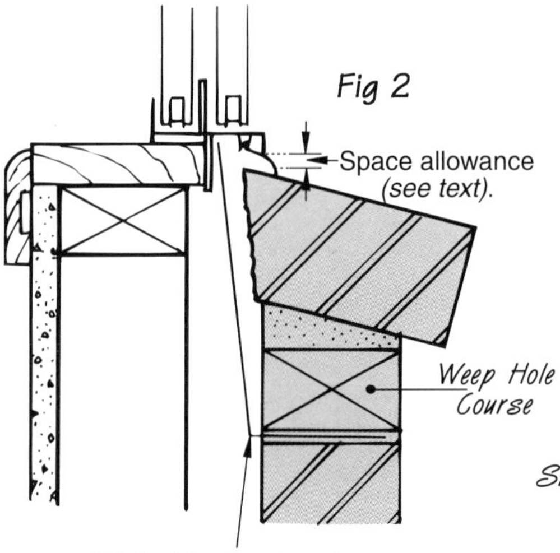

Sill flashing is taken down to one brick course below sill and weep holes positioned along this course.

Brick Veneer Low Set (Timber Floor)

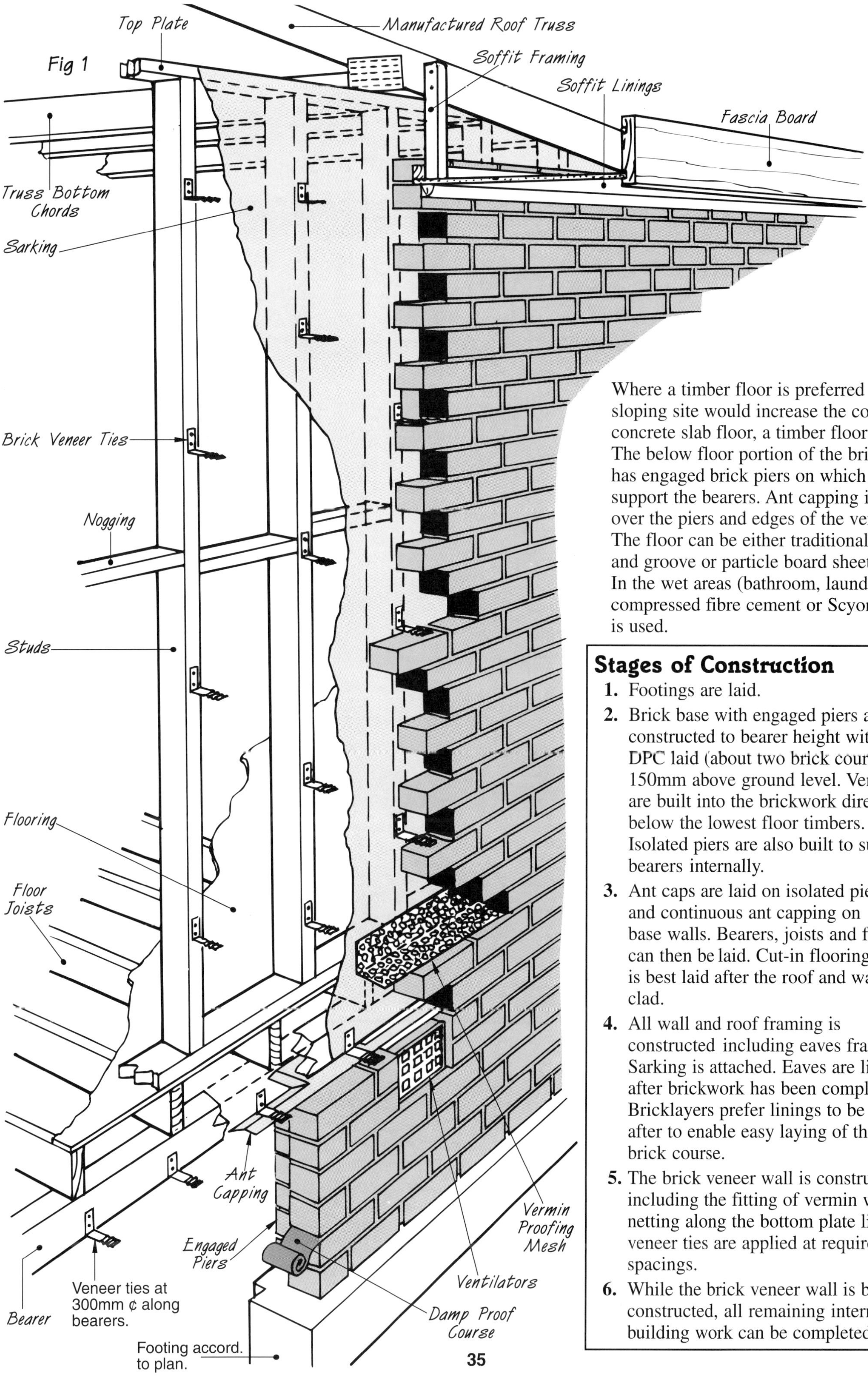

Where a timber floor is preferred or a sloping site would increase the cost of a concrete slab floor, a timber floor is used. The below floor portion of the brick veneer has engaged brick piers on which to support the bearers. Ant capping is applied over the piers and edges of the veneer wall. The floor can be either traditional tongue and groove or particle board sheet flooring. In the wet areas (bathroom, laundry etc) compressed fibre cement or Scyon flooring is used.

Stages of Construction

1. Footings are laid.
2. Brick base with engaged piers are constructed to bearer height with a DPC laid (about two brick courses) 150mm above ground level. Ventilators are built into the brickwork directly below the lowest floor timbers. Isolated piers are also built to support bearers internally.
3. Ant caps are laid on isolated piers and continuous ant capping on base walls. Bearers, joists and flooring can then be laid. Cut-in flooring (T & G) is best laid after the roof and walls are clad.
4. All wall and roof framing is constructed including eaves framing. Sarking is attached. Eaves are lined after brickwork has been completed. Bricklayers prefer linings to be fitted after to enable easy laying of the top brick course.
5. The brick veneer wall is constructed including the fitting of vermin wire netting along the bottom plate line and veneer ties are applied at required spacings.
6. While the brick veneer wall is being constructed, all remaining internal building work can be completed.

High Set Brick Veneer Houses

The high set brick veneer house has largely been replaced with low set or two storey housing. On sloping sites this form of construction enables garaging and laundries to be sited underneath the elevated portion of the house. This saves the cost of constructing a separate garage. Builders have replaced this method of building with slab on-ground construction to avoid scaffolding and having to construct timber joisted floors.

Advantages of High Set Houses

These advantages also apply to two-storey houses.

They are:

1. The floor area can be doubled with just the added cost of the brick base walls and the floor. as foundations and roof are already provided. Also the space can be developed at a later date when funds permit.

2. Being high set provides extra security.

3. Provides extra living space without reducing the land area.

4. Enables better reception of land breezes and access to views.

Employing Bricklayers on High Set & Two-Storey Houses

Brick walls on high set houses are constructed in two stages sometimes weeks apart. Bricklayers are usually co-operative in erecting the base walls. but not always so keen to return to build the upper walls because of the difficulties involved with scaffolding and transporting bricks and mortar to the upper level. Some expect a higher rate per thousand bricks to work on the upper level.

Important Note:
It is customary to withhold 10% deposit on completion of the brick base walls to ensure the bricklayer returns to complete the upper portion.

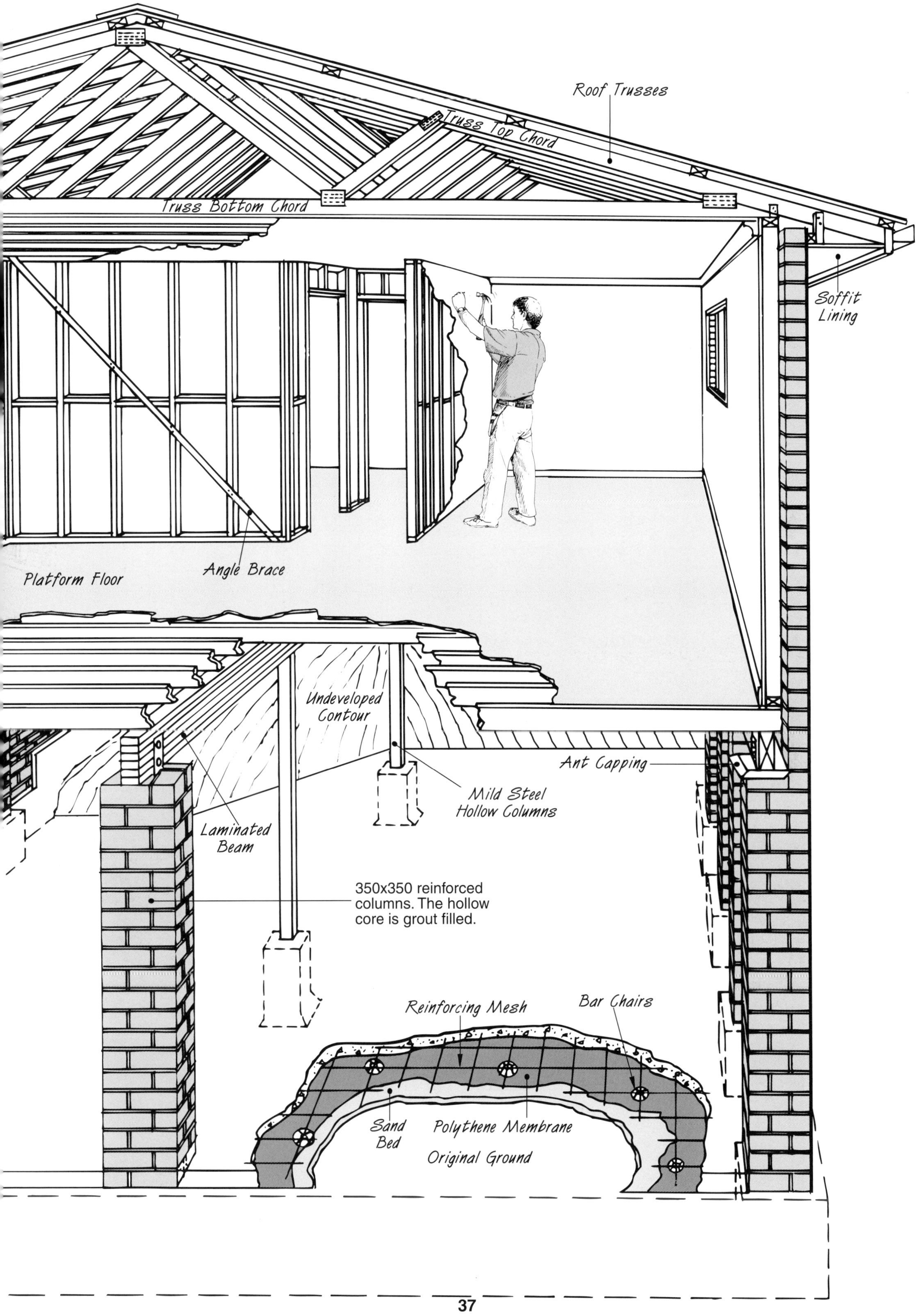
Roof Trusses
Truss Top Chord
Truss Bottom Chord
Soffit Lining
Platform Floor
Angle Brace
Undeveloped Contour
Ant Capping
Mild Steel Hollow Columns
Laminated Beam
350x350 reinforced columns. The hollow core is grout filled.
Reinforcing Mesh
Bar Chairs
Sand Bed
Polythene Membrane
Original Ground

Two-Storey Brick Veneer & Weatherboard

When a brick veneer base is to have a weatherboards or thin section render upper storey, the floor joists are usually cantilevered over the brick veneer wall in order for the siding to lap the brick veneer (see fig 2). A gap of 15-20mm should be left between the top brick and the joist to allow for shrinkage of the bottom storey timber frame. The brick veneer is *not* load bearing. Should the weight of the upper storey rest on the veneer, damage is likely to occur.

Fig 1

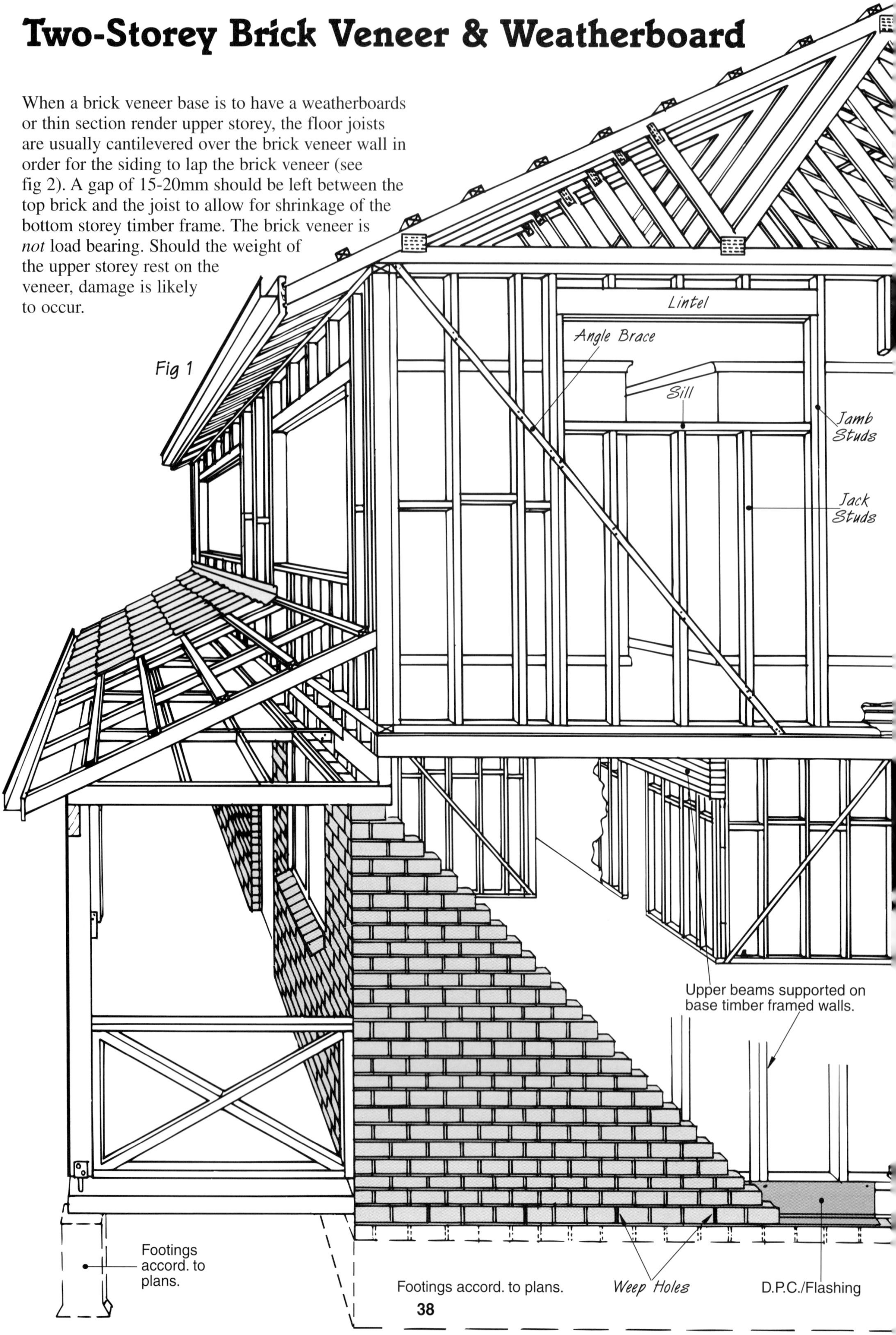

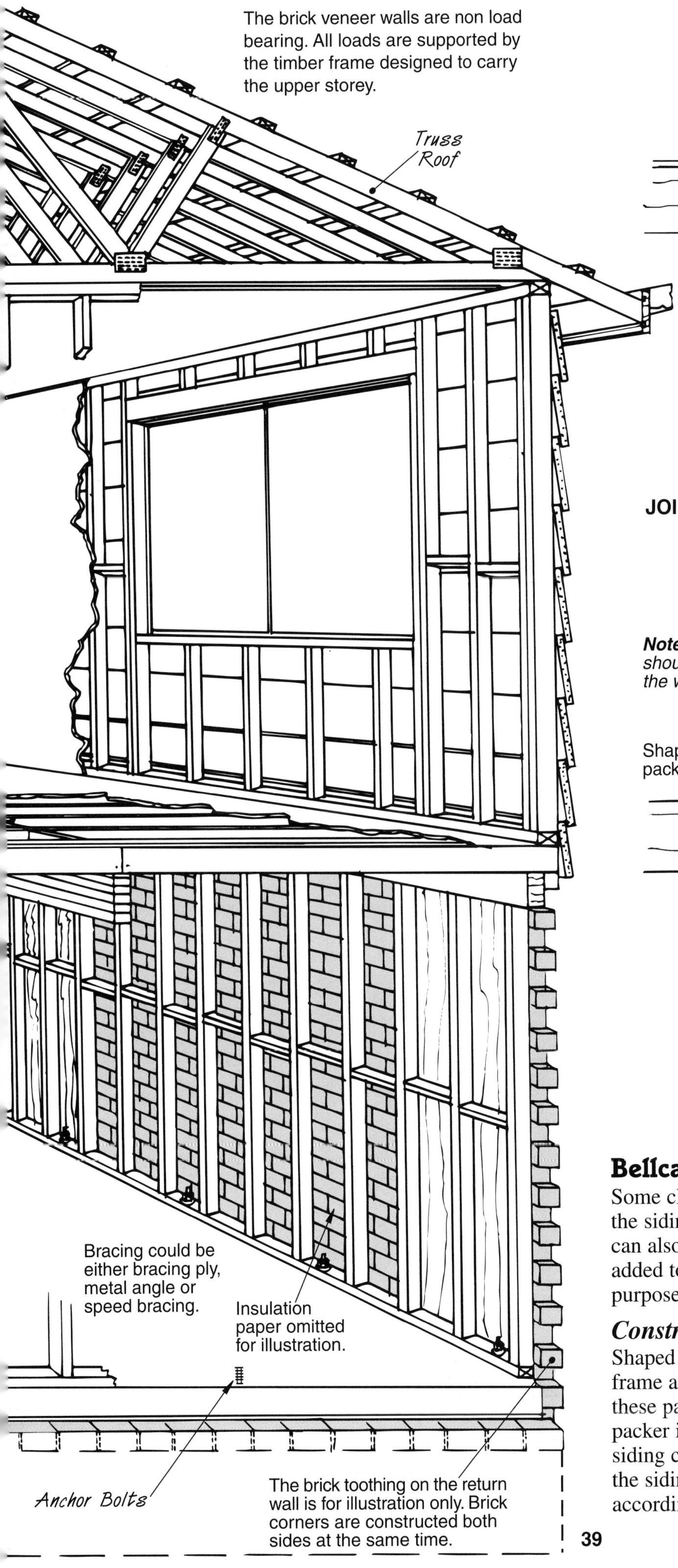

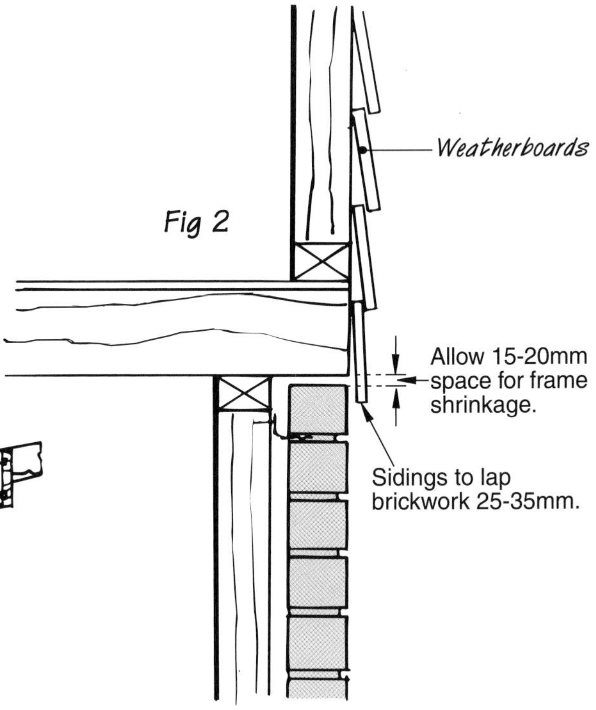

JOISTS CANTILEVERED OVER BRICK VENEER

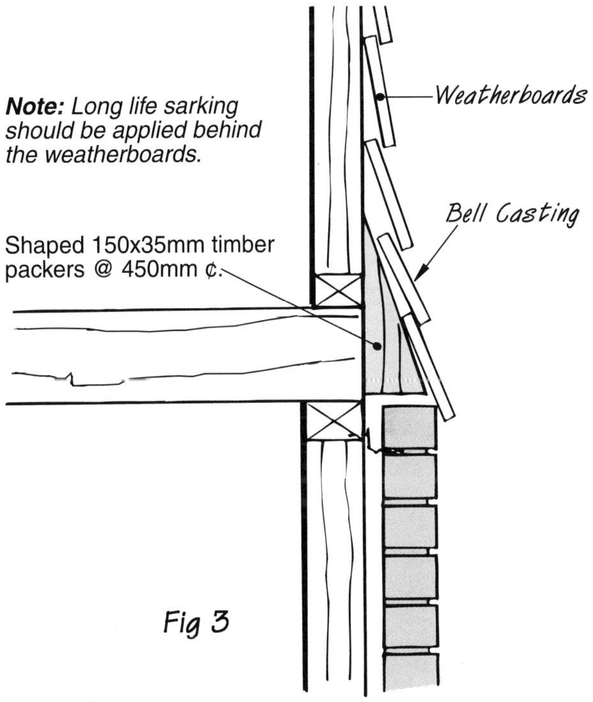

BELLCAST SIDING

Bellcasting

Some classical designs require a bell cast where the siding and brick surfaces meet. The bell cast can also be applied where brick veneer is to be added to an existing house for renovating purposes.

Constructing Bell Casting

Shaped supports 150x35mm thick are fixed to the frame at 450mm centres. The siding is attached to these packing supports. Tack the first shaped packer in position and with a few samples of siding check that the shape of the bevel will allow the siding to fit nicely. If not, adjust the shape accordingly.

Split Level Houses

The split level house illustrated in fig 1 is typical, with the lower floor supported on engaged piers attached to single leaf brick walls as well as isolated piers to support bearers. The upper walls are weatherboard clad but could also be brick veneer being simply a continuation of the base walls.

Head Heights above Staircases

In split level houses where one level is 300mm or more below the upper level, the ceiling of the lower level or the ceiling directly above the connecting staircase will of necessity require a higher ceiling or sloping ceiling to enable normal head height access over the stairs. Alternatively, the staircase can be cut into the upper level floor.

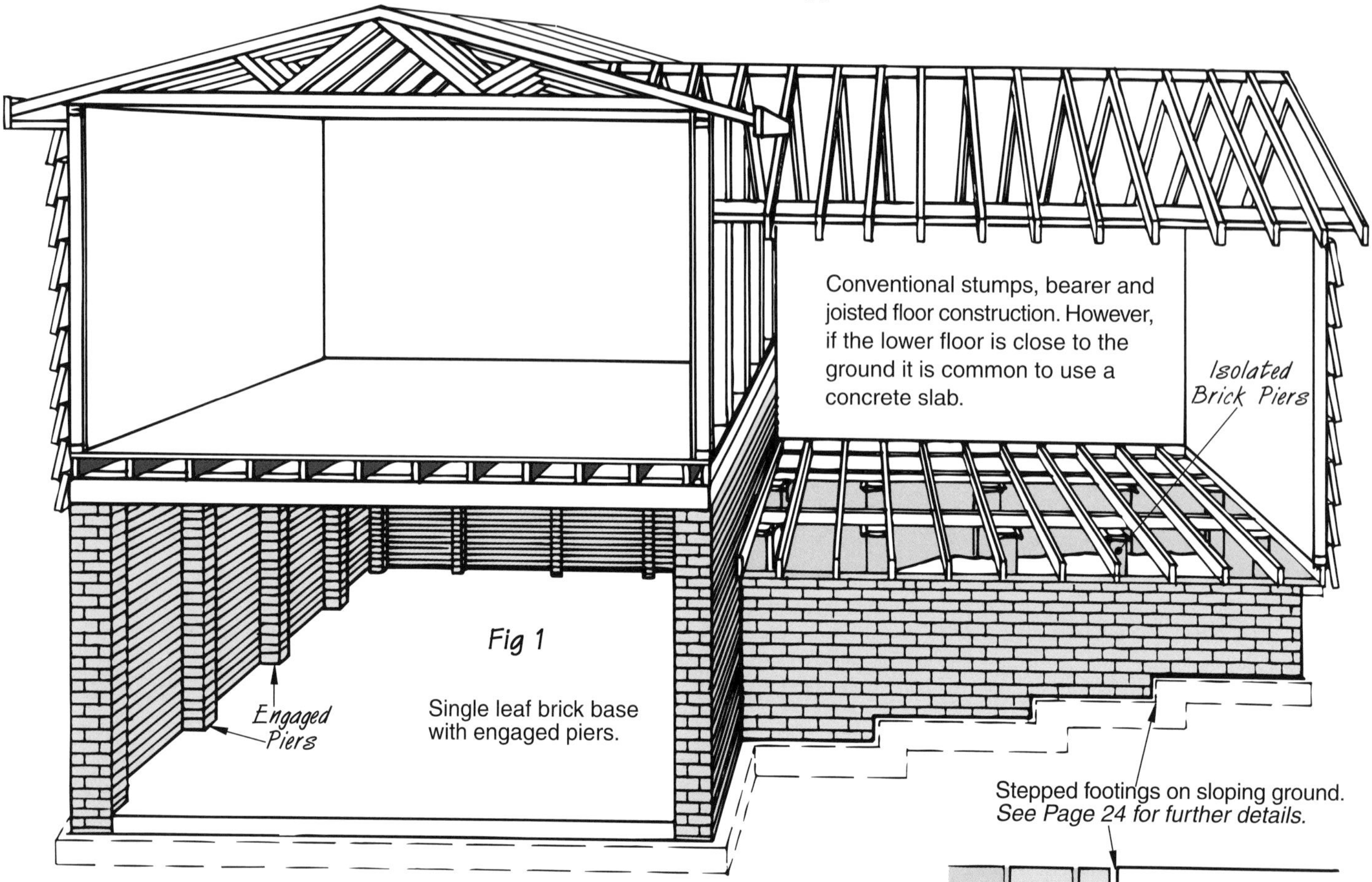

Fig 1

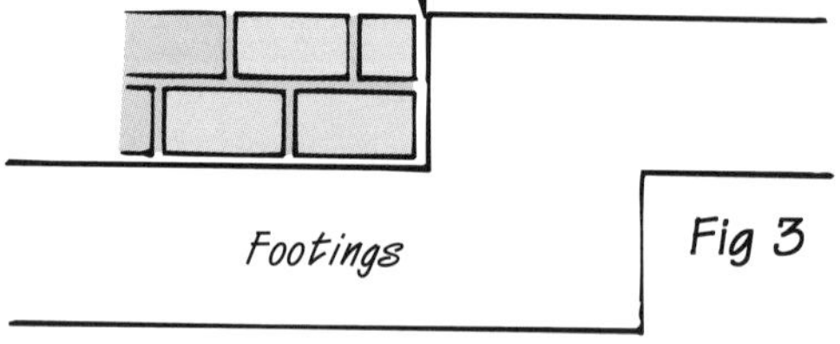

Fig 3

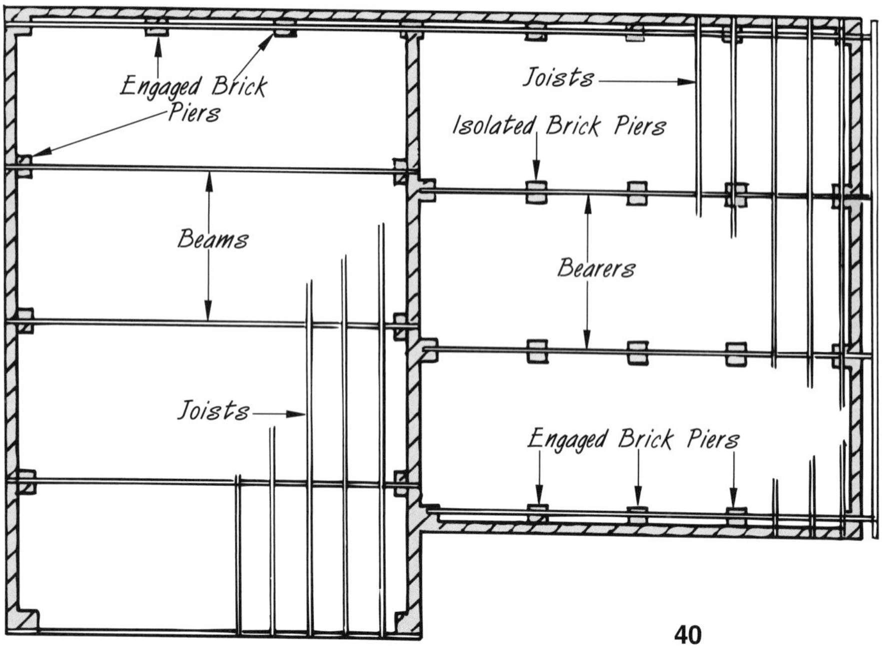

SUB FLOOR PLAN VIEW

Fig 2

Cavity Brick (Double Brick) Construction

Cavity brick is a good method for Owner Builders to adopt, particularly if the brickwork is to be constructed by a bricklayer. Major construction work performed by the Owner Builder is reduced markedly especially if the internal walls are brick also. Skirting boards can also be deleted on brick walls. Alternatively it is quite acceptable to use double brick for exterior walls only, and use timber partitions internally.

Purchase the total brick requirement at one time to avoid a colour variation. If you end up with pallet of bricks with a colour variation, lay them either below ground level, or on an inconspicuous wall. If there are too many, mix throughout the walls evenly or have them replaced.

Disadvantages of Cavity Brick

a). In most States construction costs are much higher than for other systems, except WA.

b). Can *not* be used economically on steep sites.

c). Should *not* be used where the subsoil has a poor bearing capability.

d). Where internal walls are left as a brick finish, the occupants may tire of the finish in time.

Internal Surface Finishes

Internal brick walls can be:

a). Left as a natural brick surface. This is a most economical finish.

b). Bagged surface. Again use a cheaper brick. This method eliminates joint finishing. Bagging can be performed by the Owner Builder.

c). Cement render and finish with various surfaces e.g. smooth solid plaster for painting or wall papering and stucco finishes. These surfaces require a Solid Plasterer. Cheaper bricks or 100mm thick concrete blocks can be used. In some areas, Speed Brick is available.

d). Plasterboard can be glued directly to the brickwall when dry. Surfaced, then decorated.

Internal partitions can be single brick finished as above or timber framed with plasterboard linings.

Buying or Renovating a Cavity Brick House

Some older style cavity brick houses are badly designed internally and require extensive renovations.

The following points should be considered:

1. Existing internal partitions are *not* as easily or as cheaply removed as timber walls.
2. Often electrical wiring and plumbing is concealed within the brick partitions and may need replacing if a wall is substantially altered.
3. Demolishing a brick partition in an existing house can be noisy and dusty. Rubble will have to be removed often barrowed through existing rooms.

Check for Foundation Movement

In years past, little consideration was given to foundation design, in many instances. It is important for the prospective buyer to look for signs of footing movement. This will be evidenced by significant cracking or signs of recent filling and concealment of cracks. They may also appear in a stepped pattern at wall corners, beside doors and window sills and lintels. Although cracks may be concealable, they will open up again. The extent to which this may occur is impossible to predict.

Labour Cost Savings

The Owner Builder can save costs when building in cavity brick by assisting the bricklayer in the following areas:

1. Marking out with pencil and straightedge (or chalk line) the position of walls.
2. Installation and temporary bracing of joinery — a simple task if shown how (see Page 43).
3. Installation of anchor bolts and mild steel lintel angles for window and door heads.
4. Carting and stacking of bricks.
5. Mixing of mortar (if shown).
6. Raking or ironing of joints and cleaning of brickwork.
7. Erection of scaffolding.

Constructing a Cavity Brick House

Stages of Construction

Stage 1 Footings and slab floor are constructed with a set down rebate at the edge of the slab as in fig 1. The step is used to ensure a dry floor. The site and soil type will affect the design of the slab and footing. Some sites will be suitable for a raft slab while sloping sites which are not being excavated level may require some brick base walling below the slab. *The 'HBM' will provide more detail on this.*

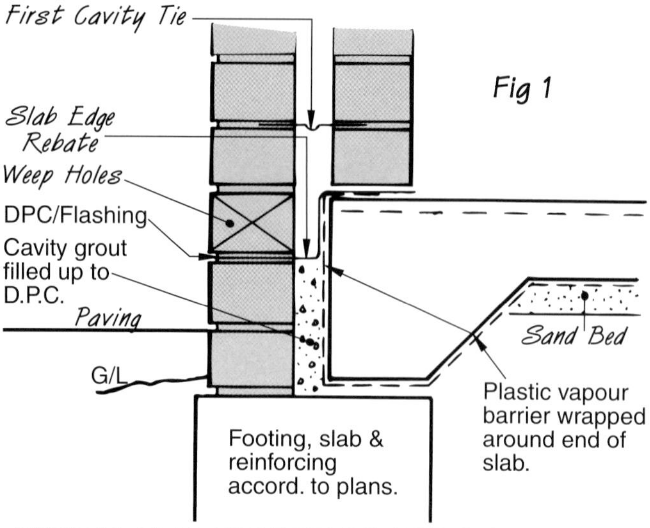

TYPICAL SLAB EDGE DETAIL FOR CAVITY BRICK

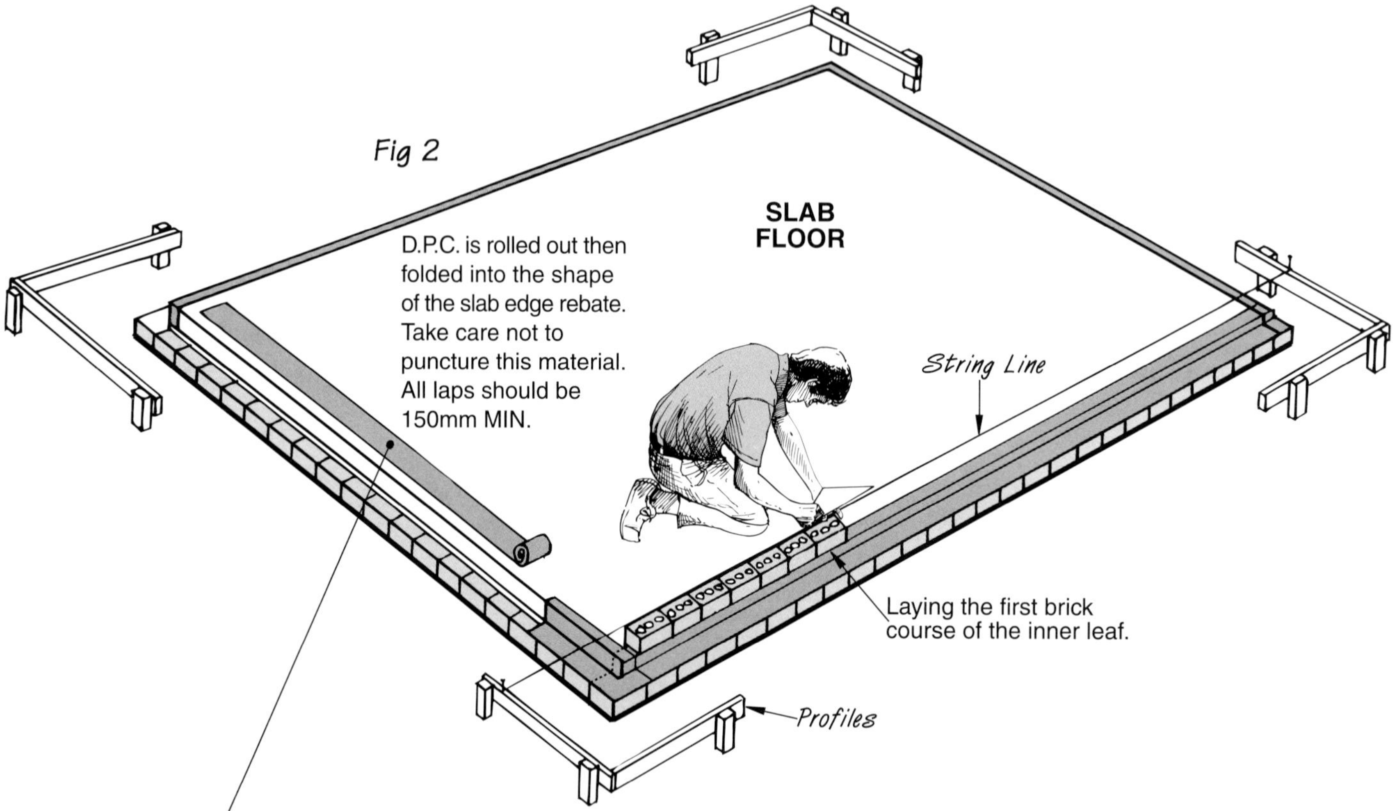

D.P.C. folded to the shape of the slab edge set down. Take the D.P.C. 50mm under the inner brick leaf.

Cavity brick walls must have a set down rebate in the slab edge. This rebate is usually best at a minimum of one brick high.

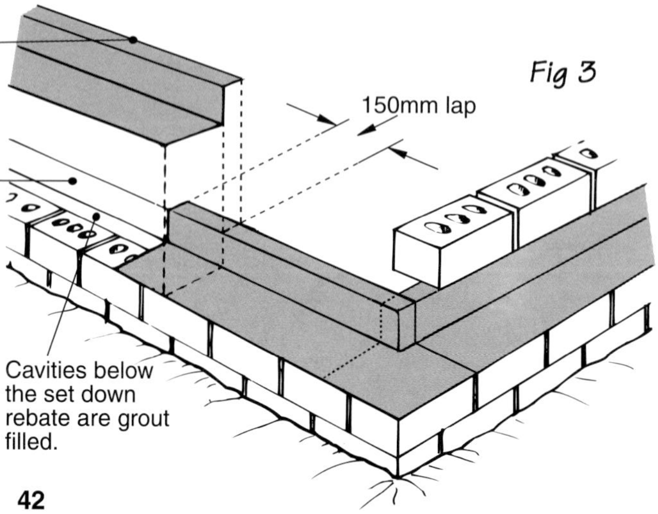

Stage 2 The DPC is laid as in figs 2 & 3 and the inner brick leaf constructed, remembering to install cavity ties as specified vertically and horizontally and 300mm apart around the perimeter of all openings. When brickwork reaches sill height, the windows and doors are braced plumb in position as in fig 4. Flashings are provided to sills and heads of all windows and doors whether timber or aluminium. Head flashings may be deleted where wide eaves provide sufficient weather protection. Remember to install wire ties or bolts on the inner surface for tying in partitions.

Cavity Ties

Cavity ties are very important. They come in different weights. Light duty ones are *not* suitable for cavity brickwork. Check with house plans or specifications. When straps are required to hold down the timber wall top plates, these should be installed in the brick joints at the stipulated distance down from the wall top on the cavity side.

> *Hints:*
>
> ***a).*** Prior to laying bricks, have them stacked close to the work for easy and quick access. Seek advice from the bricklayer on his preferred method.
>
> ***b).*** Before leaving the site each night, check the brickwork for any joints which have *not* been jointed and cement stains on the brickwork or joinery.

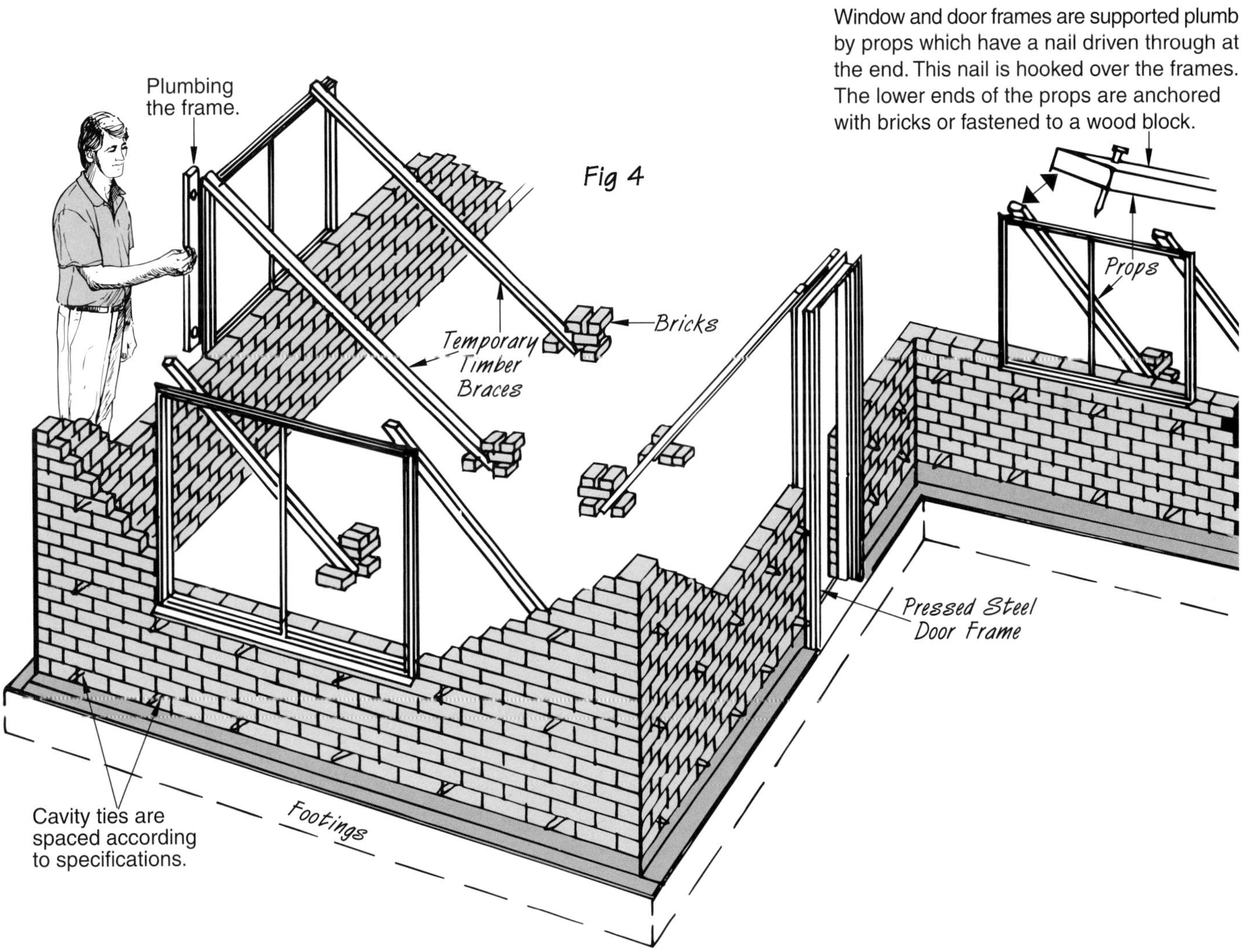

Door Sills

Door sills should be set about 20mm below the slab surface. This will entail forming a rebate prior to pouring the slab.

Cont.

Stage 3 After completion of the inner brick leaf, the outer brick wall or leaf is commenced with the first brick course along the slab edge set-down-rebate. At sill height place sill flashing one brick course below sill (see fig 8) and leave weep holes.

At lintel height if bricks continue above windows, install hot dip galvanised angle or arch bars with the long leg positioned vertically. Ensure these have the required bearing on the brickwork at each end.

See the 'HBM' for bearing allowance and the arch bar size table.

Fig 6

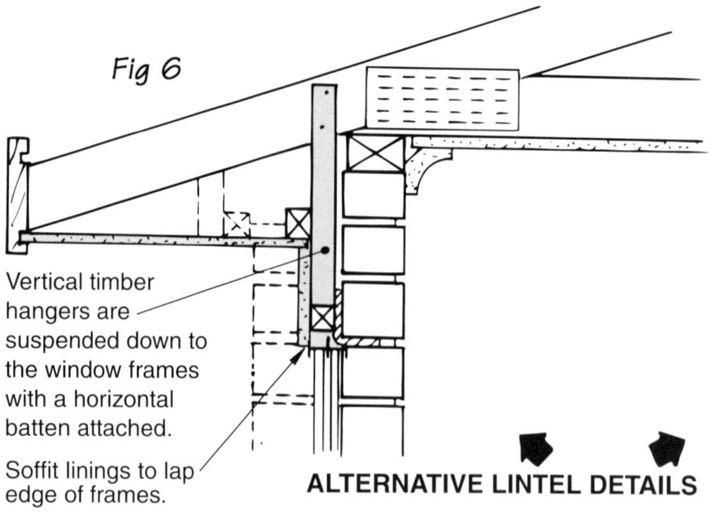

Fig 5

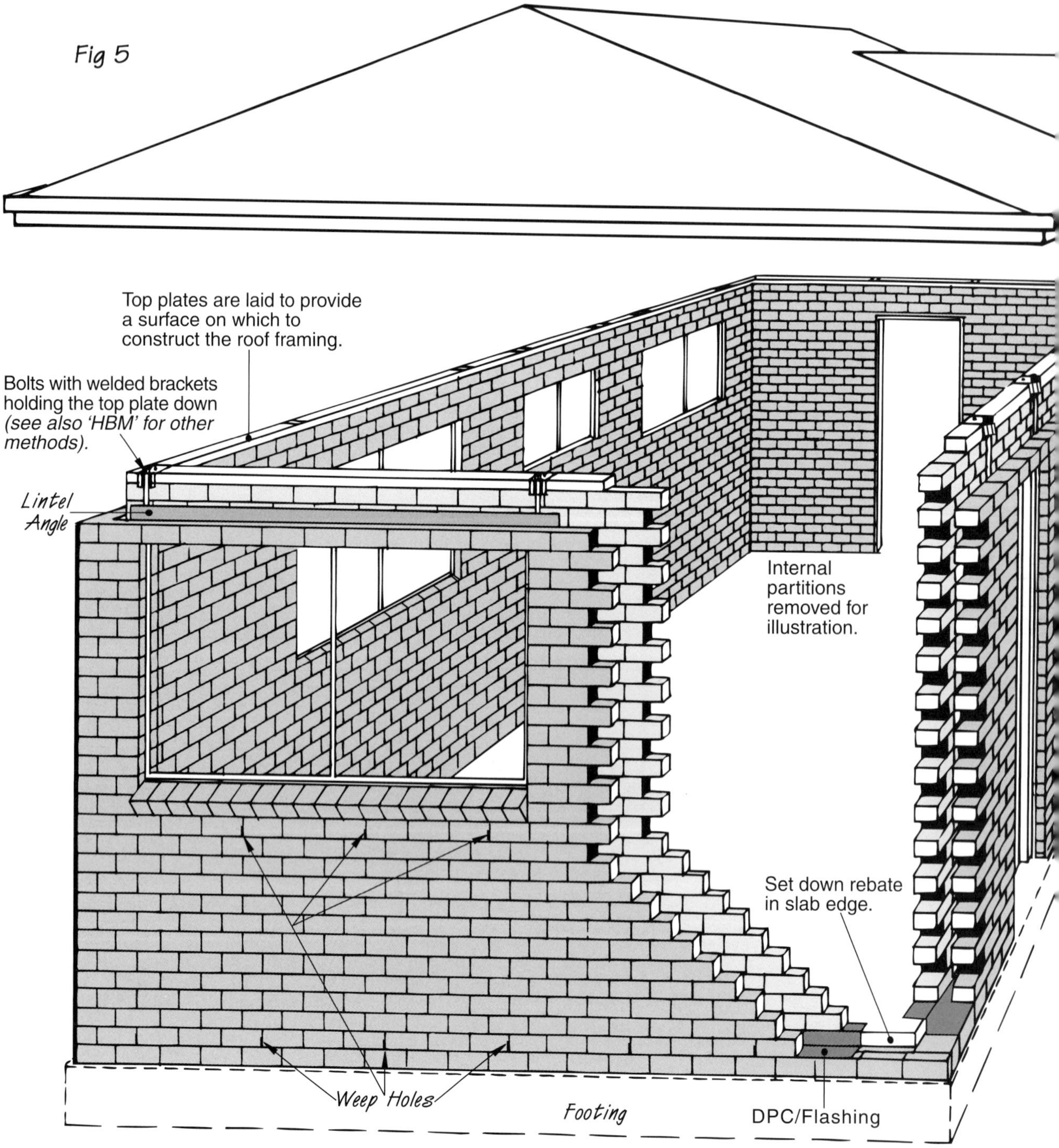

Fig 7

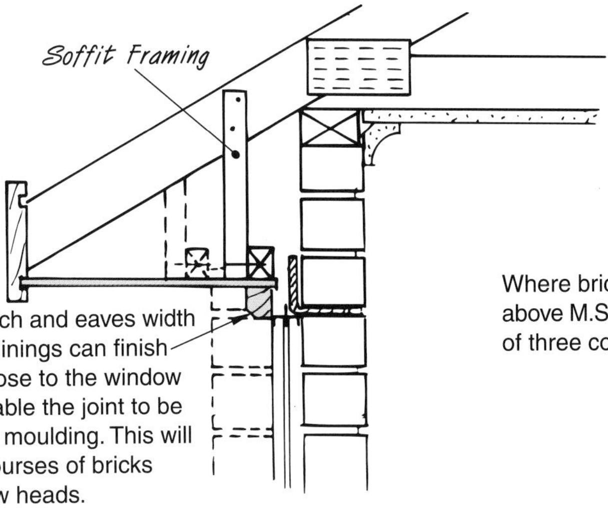

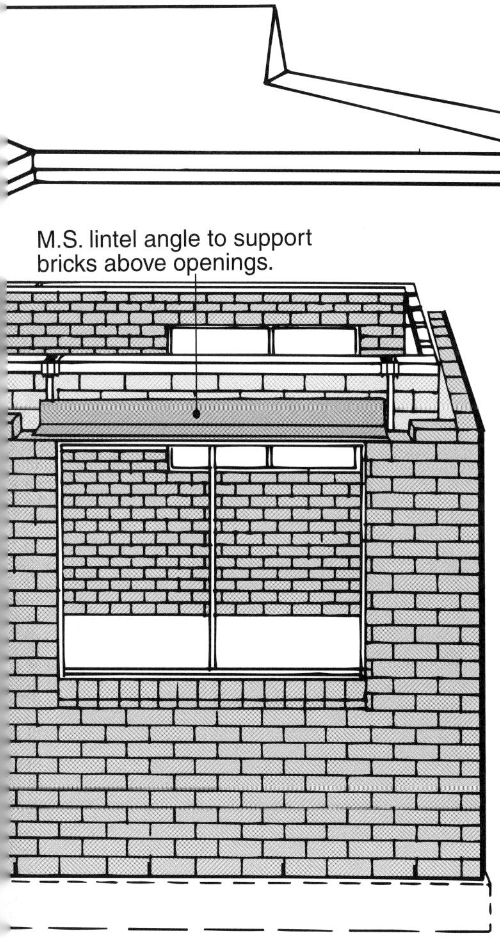

Fig 8

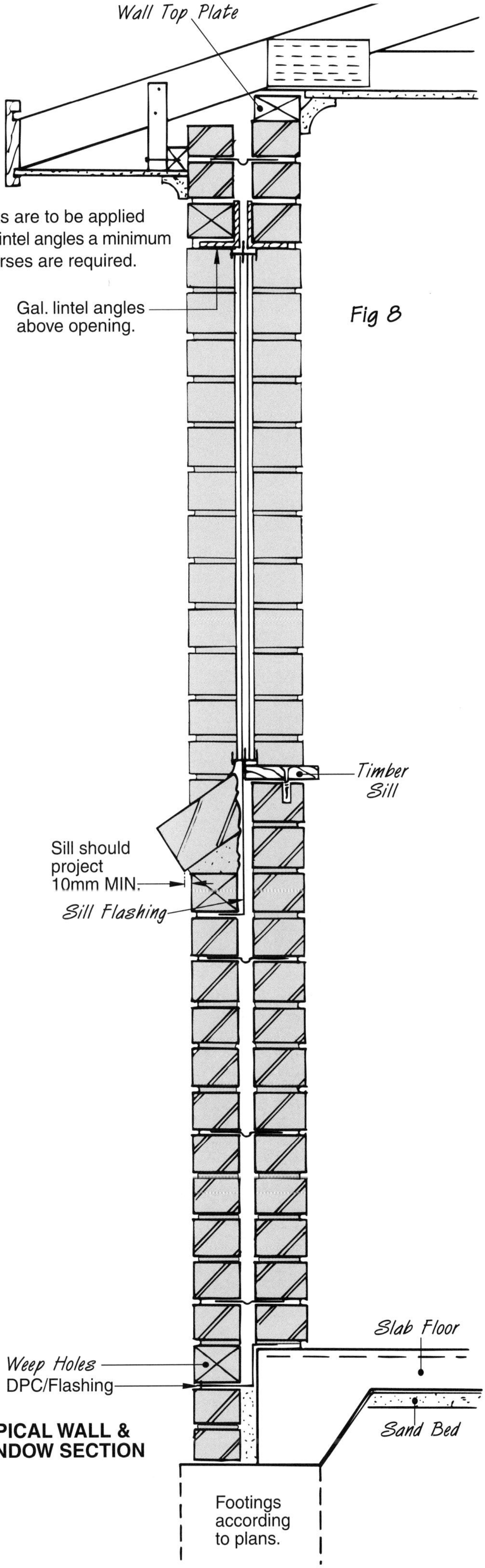

TYPICAL WALL & WINDOW SECTION

Keep Cavities Clean

Mortar should *not* be allowed to gather in the cavity, particularly on ties or the cavity bottom. This will create a bridge for moisture to cross to the inner leaf. To keep the cavity clean, use a batten to block off the cavity and catch any mortar droppings. Two cords attached will enable the batten to be raised as work progresses. The cavity should then be hosed out. For hosing out, port holes may be provided by leaving a brick out at about every 1500mm along the cavity bottom.

Cavity Brick with a Timber Floor

Stage 1 Foundations are laid out and the position of engaged piers pegged. Excavations are carried out and footings reinforced and concreted.

Holding Down Rods

Where holding down rods are required for high wind areas, these are embedded in the footings to the depth required by local authorities.

Anchoring Roofs

For holding down the roof structure, the anchor rods are threaded through the centre of the proposed cavity. Use a string line to align them when embedding them in the footings. Starter bars are used and female couplings attached later for extending the rods.

Anchoring Bearers

Rods for this purpose can either be installed through the centre of a 350x350mm brick pier which is grout filled, or where Local Authorities permit, they can be embedded in the footing beside 110mm engaged piers (see fig 1). The latter is a much simpler method.

Stage 2 The double walls with engaged piers are constructed up to the underside of the bearers. Remember to include the DPC through the second brick course above ground or not more than 150mm above ground. Place ventilators directly below bearers.

Stage 3 The ant capping is laid over engaged piers through the length of the inner leaf wall. The bearers, joists and flooring can then be laid. Keep the ends of bearers, joists and flooring 20mm short of touching brick walls to prevent damage to brickwork should rain swell the floor.

Stage 4 Cavity walls are taken up to full height. Remember to install any nominal holding down straps for wall top plates the minimum requirement down from the top plate (see plans and specifications). In cyclone areas 12mm threaded cyclone rods are used. *For details on 'Anchoring down', consult the 'HBM'.*

Stage 5 The wall top plates are secured and all internal partition framing erected and braced true and plumb.

Stage 6 Roof framing and cladding is secured.

Stage 7 All internal finishing is carried out.

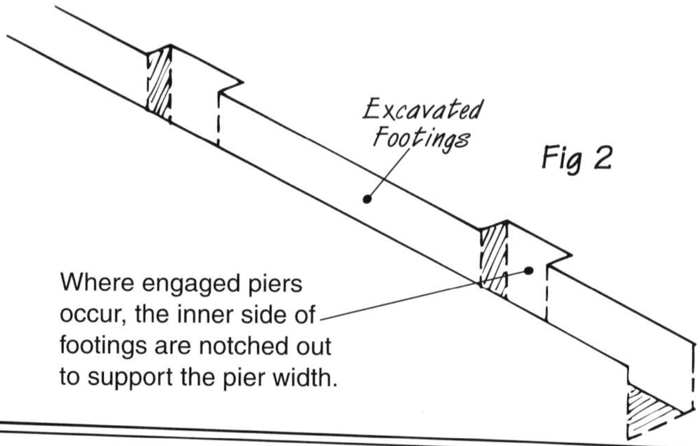

Fig 2

Fig 1

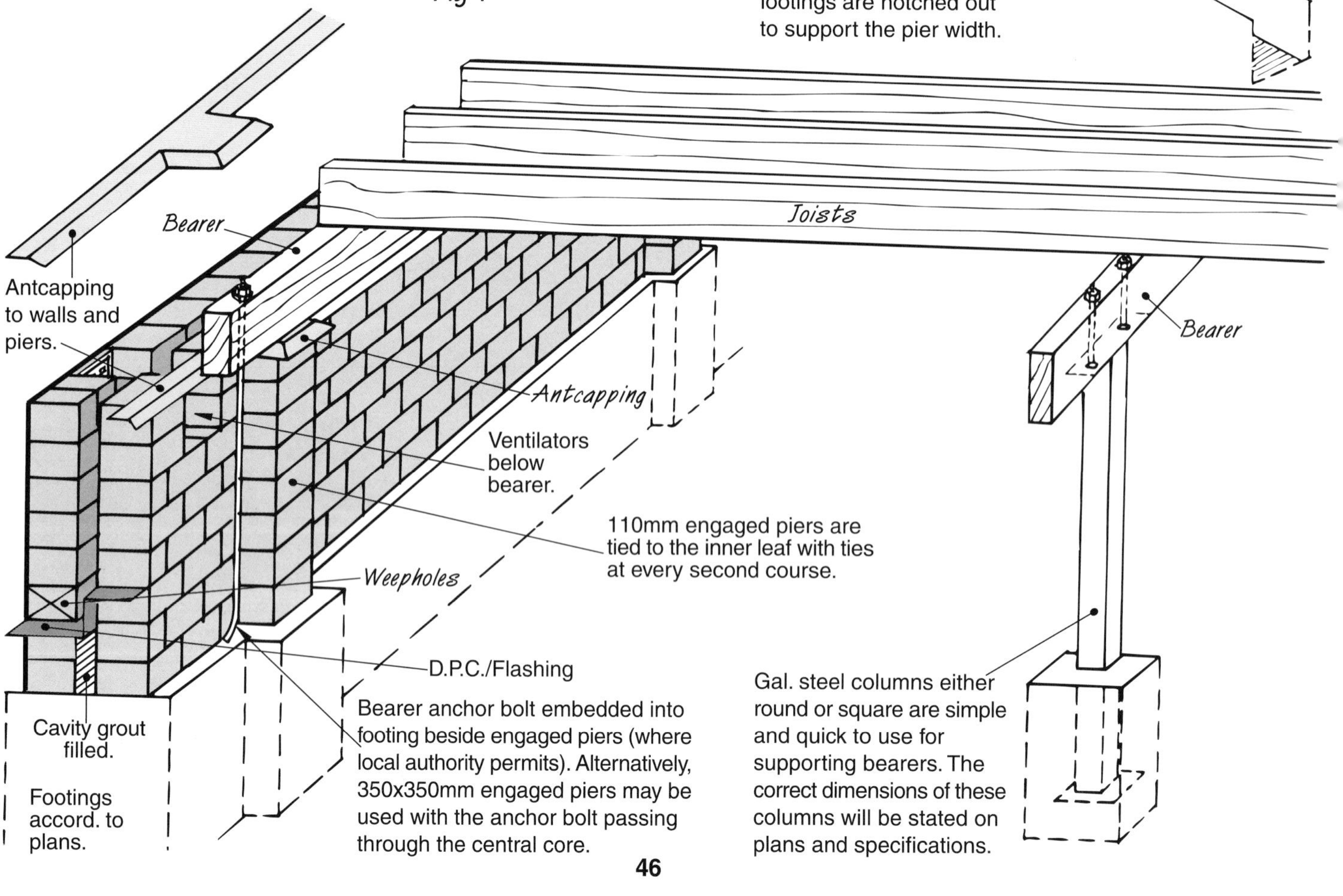

Concrete Block Masonry Construction (with slab floor)

Concrete block construction is a common method of house building in specific localities in Australia, North Queensland in particular.

Choosing a Masonry Block System

There are various options available. Some of the most attractive are those which do not require mortar jointing. The blocks are simply stacked, reinforced and grouted as the walls are being constructed.

This method ideally suits the situation where the wall surfaces are bagged or alternatively cement rendered and textured prior to painting. This is because there are no mortar joints and the joints will not conceal well with paint alone as does conventionally jointed blockwork. This excludes the need for specialised tradespersons.

Another method known as composite masonry utilises a 90mm block wall for the internal leaf or skin of a double or cavity constructed external walling system. The outer leaf or skin can be clay brick or block. Internal walls can be block or timber frame. Request literature from manufacturers on these systems. The system described in the following pages utilises the conventionally mortar jointed system.

The conventional mortar jointed system is quick to construct (but *not* as quick as the non-joint systems above) particularly if professionals lay the blocks and if the walls are simply paint finished.

'The Australian House Building Manual' provides further construction details.

Wall Heights & Lintels

This is the first consideration for the designer. The locality, wind loading, window and door opening widths and wall heights are all factors which determine the lintel, bond beam reinforcing and design. Manufacturers can provide easy to follow literature to help select these designs elements.

Waterproofing

The most important consideration with concrete block construction is waterproofing. Waterproofing is mainly dependent upon the paint coatings applied to the external surface.

These must be meticulously applied with all pin holes filled in the first coat. Following coats must be just as thoroughly applied. All paint coatings are applied prior to joinery installation.

Common approved paint systems are either three coats of 100% quality acrylic paint or a first coat of approved cement based filler paint followed by two coats of 100% acrylic paint.

The Slab Edge

While block walls are often constructed without a slab edge set down rebate, it is a practice not approved by all designers. The 'HBM' provides some alternative footing slab edge designs.

Stages of Construction

Stage 1 Footings are excavated and reinforcing installed including all starter bars for reinforcing vertical block cores. Footing concrete is then poured. Vertical and horizontal steps in the footings are multiples of block module of 200 or 100mm.

Stage 2 Any blocks below slab floor level are laid.

a). Where the slab is *not* to have a set down rebate in the slab edge, '2020' bond beam blocks are laid to the perimeter and utilised to screed off the wet concrete slab.

b). Where a set down is required either full or half blocks can be laid to the perimeter and also utilised as slab edge formwork. Alternatively, formwork could be erected, the slab poured then block walls commenced.

Stage 3 If steel door frames are to be used, these are positioned and supported plumb using temporary props. Windows are installed after all blockwork has been painted inside and outside (see Stage 7).

Cont.

Stage 4 Blockwork is commenced and clean- out blocks (1545 or 2045) are laid at the base of all vertical cores to enable the cores to be cleaned out *(see Page 51)*. The block course below all sills over 1500mm wide is reinforced with the ends of reinforcing returned into the adjacent vertical cores, then grout filled. The sill blocks are laid after all grouting is complete to enable access to the bond-beam below.

The walls are continued to lintel height. Then timber lintel supports are propped into position to support the lintel course *(see fig 2, Page 51)*. These are removed after the grout has cured in lintels and bond beams. Before grout is poured, electrical conduits and plumbing pipelines are installed. Plumbing pipe lines which are embedded in grout should be adequately lagged to prevent temperature changes from cracking joints.

Window Openings

Openings should have an oversize tolerance of approx. 4mm for ease of installation. The gap remaining after installation is filled with polyurethane sealant. *Not Silicone!*

Stage 5 Vertical reinforcing bars are installed and any hard projecting mortar in the cores knocked to the bottom by pushing the bars up and down and the mortar removed from the clean out port holes provided.

Along the bond beams all cores *not* being grouted are sealed off using the knock-out batts from bond beam Block No. 2020.

Horizontal reinforcing is laid in the bond beams. Vertical reinforcing is returned to lap with the bond beam reinforcing.

Wall plate holding-down bolts or roof truss anchor plates are then inserted into the bond beams. See plans or specifications for their size and spacing.

Grout is then poured by pump and flexible pipeline to reinforced cores, bond beams and lintels using readymix grout. This usually takes about two hours.

Stage 6 Where 100x50mm wall top plates are to be applied, these are bolted in place and the roof framing and eaves constructed and cladding is applied.

Stage 7 The exterior surface of the block walls should be filled and painted with approved coatings. Care should be taken to seal the surface thoroughly with each successive coat with *no* pin holes remaining.

Stage 8 Windows are installed and any gaps sealed with a marine grade sealant such as Sikaflex Pro.

Stage 9 All interior ceiling linings, bath installation, tiling, kitchen fittings, cupboard and wardrobe work, door hanging, mouldings, plumbing fixtures and electrical work is finished off.

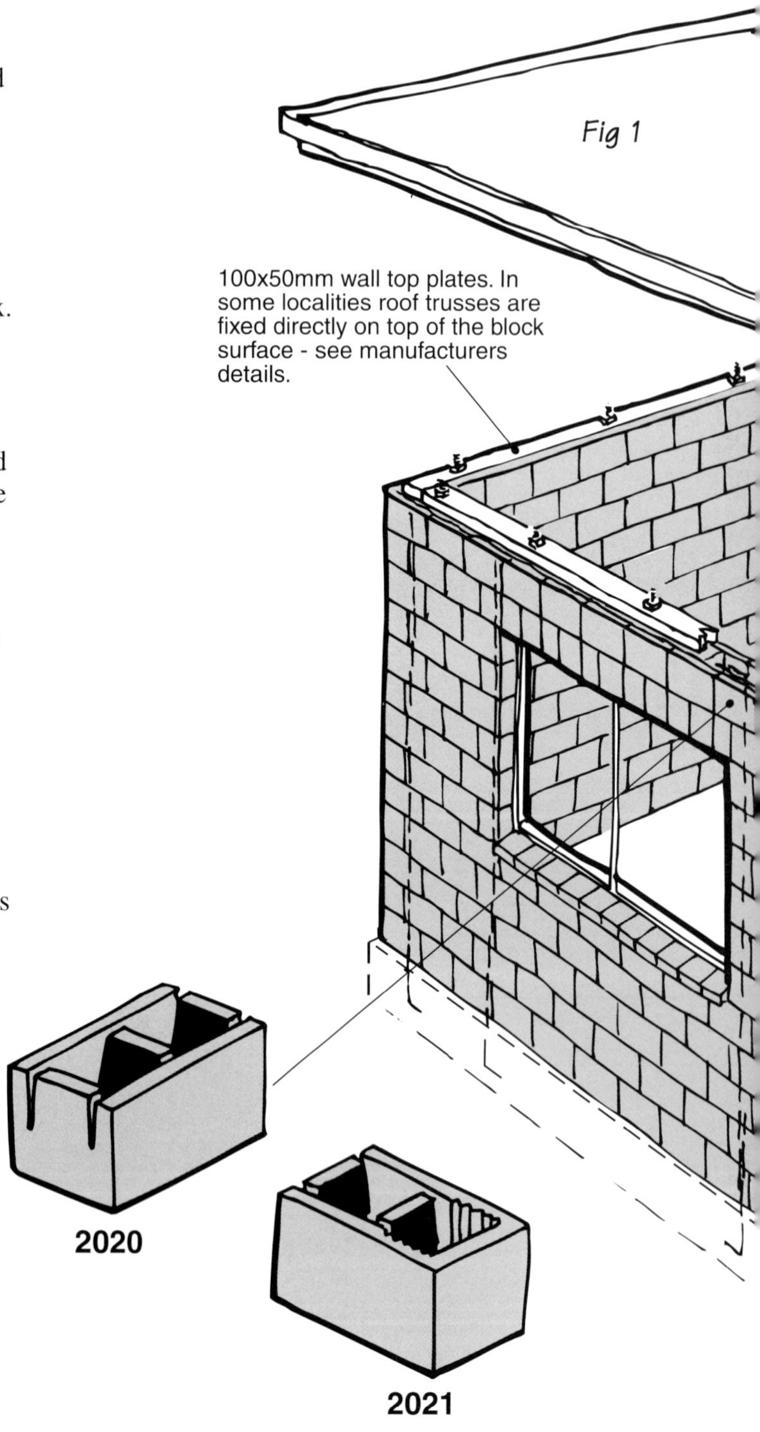

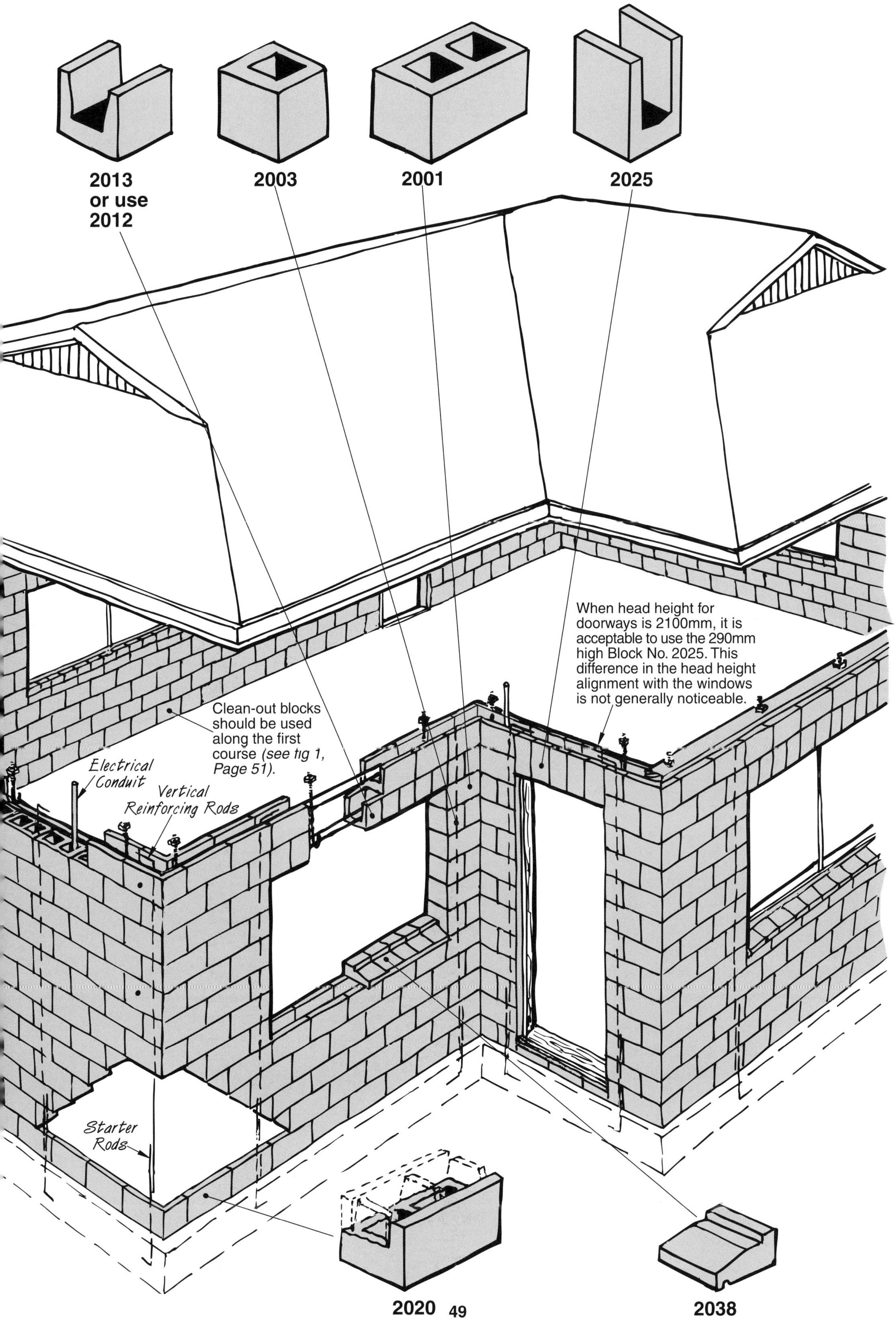
2013
or use
2012
2003
2001
2025
When head height for doorways is 2100mm, it is acceptable to use the 290mm high Block No. 2025. This difference in the head height alignment with the windows is not generally noticeable.
Clean-out blocks should be used along the first course (see fig 1, Page 51).
Electrical Conduit
Vertical Reinforcing Rods
Starter Rods
2020
2038

Block Masonry Footings & Slab Floors

Footings are excavated, reinforced and concrete poured. The vertical starter bars are inserted in the wet concrete and aligned accurately to a string line to the centres of the block cores.

Block work is brought up to slab level and the slab prepared and the concrete poured in one piece and any required expansion joints provided.

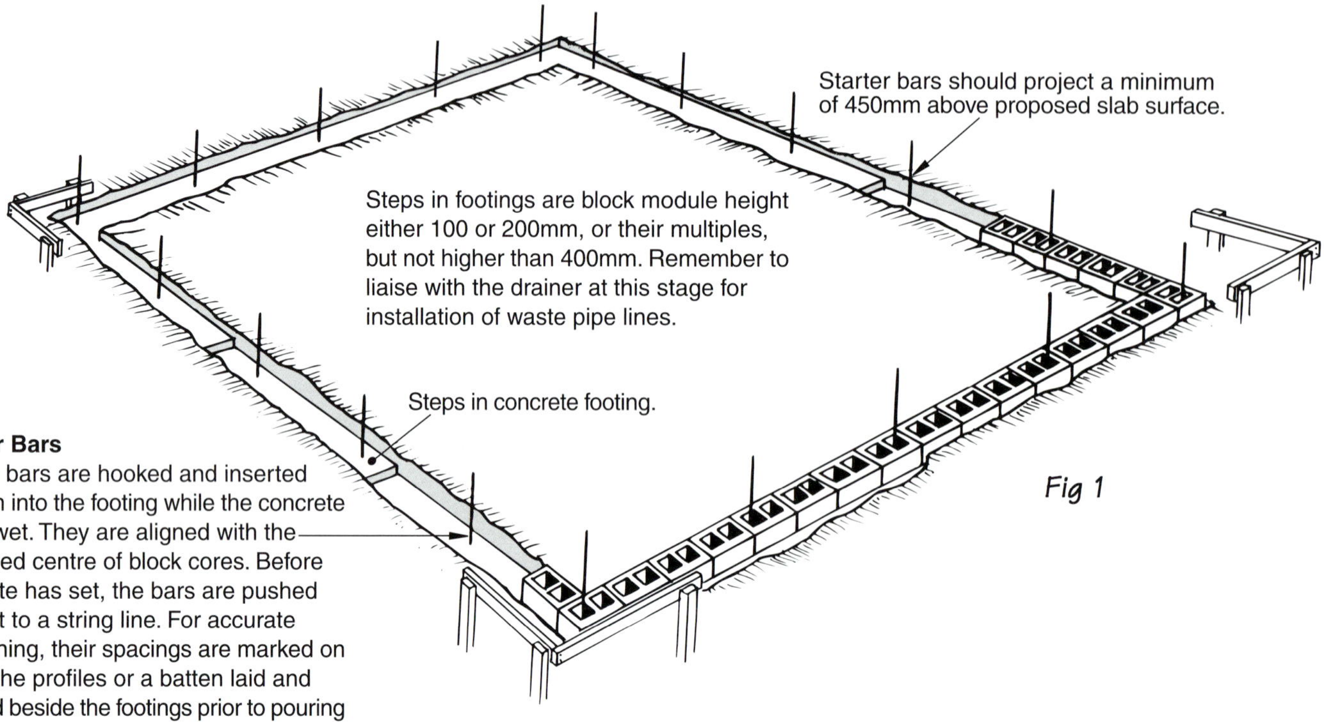

Fig 1

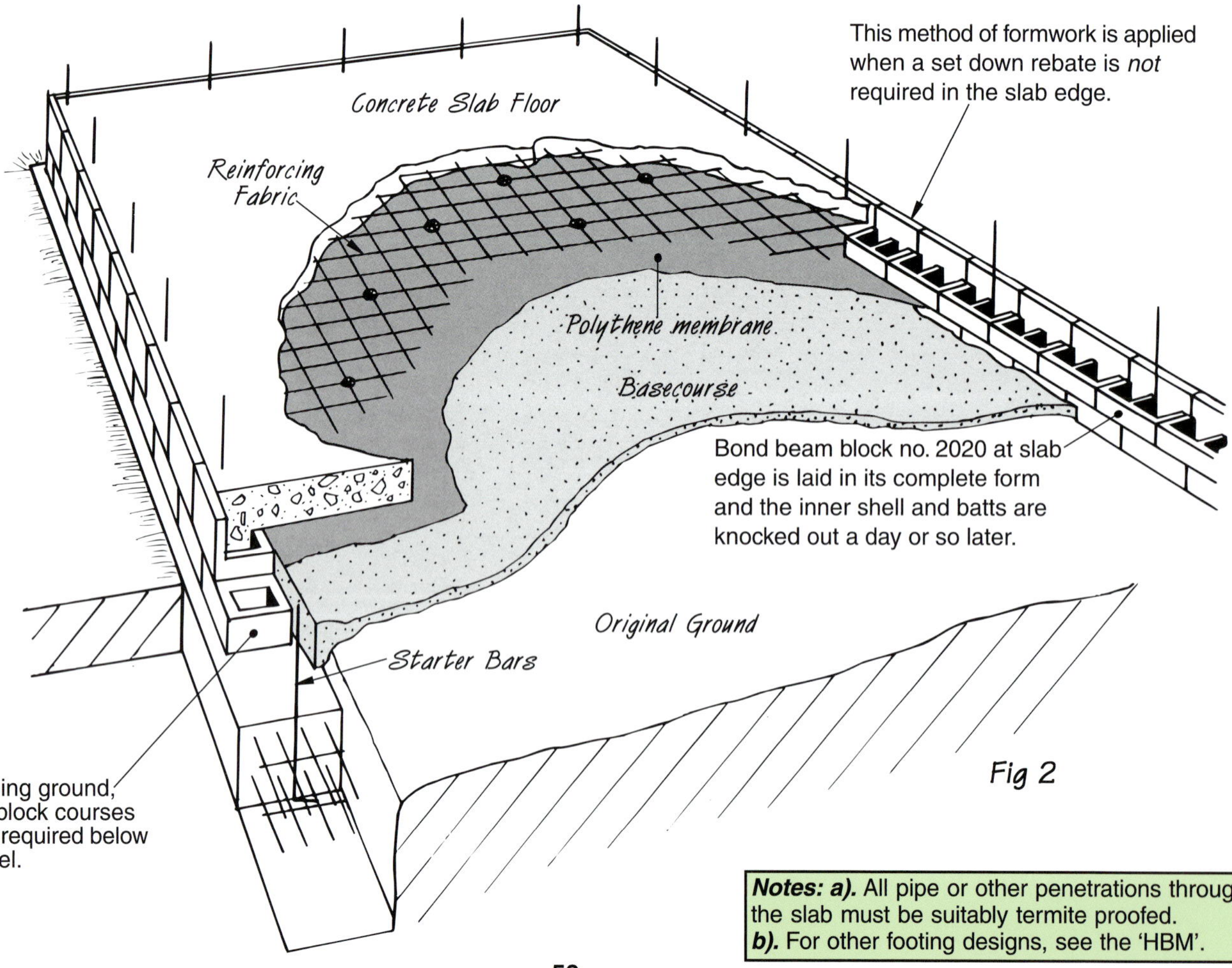

Fig 2

Notes: a). All pipe or other penetrations through the slab must be suitably termite proofed.
b). For other footing designs, see the 'HBM'.

Building Concrete Block Masonry Walls

Starting to Build the Walls

After completion of the slab floor, timber and aluminium door frames are stood in position, and plumbed and braced using available timber. First course above slab is then laid.

Lintels & Bondbeams

Blockwork can then be continued up to head height. To support lintel blocks above all openings, a piece of timber 100x50mm or similar is propped into position (see fig 2). After laying the lintel course, the reinforcing bars are installed in the lintel as it becomes inaccessible after the bond beam course is laid above. The knock-out bond beam course is finally laid and all vertical cores *not* containing reinforcing are blocked off using the knock-out batts in the bond beams. Cores over lintels are left open ready to receive the grout.

Fig 2

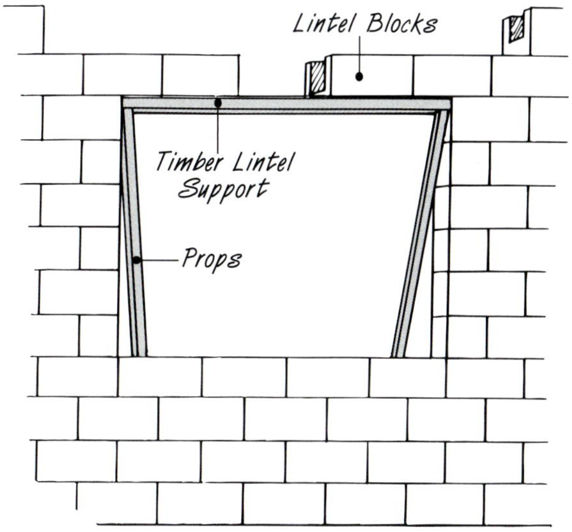

Temporary timber lintel and props are positioned to support the lintel blocks until after the grout is cured.

Important
Keep blocks dry on-site. At the end of each day's work, cover walls to prevent moisture entering the block cores.

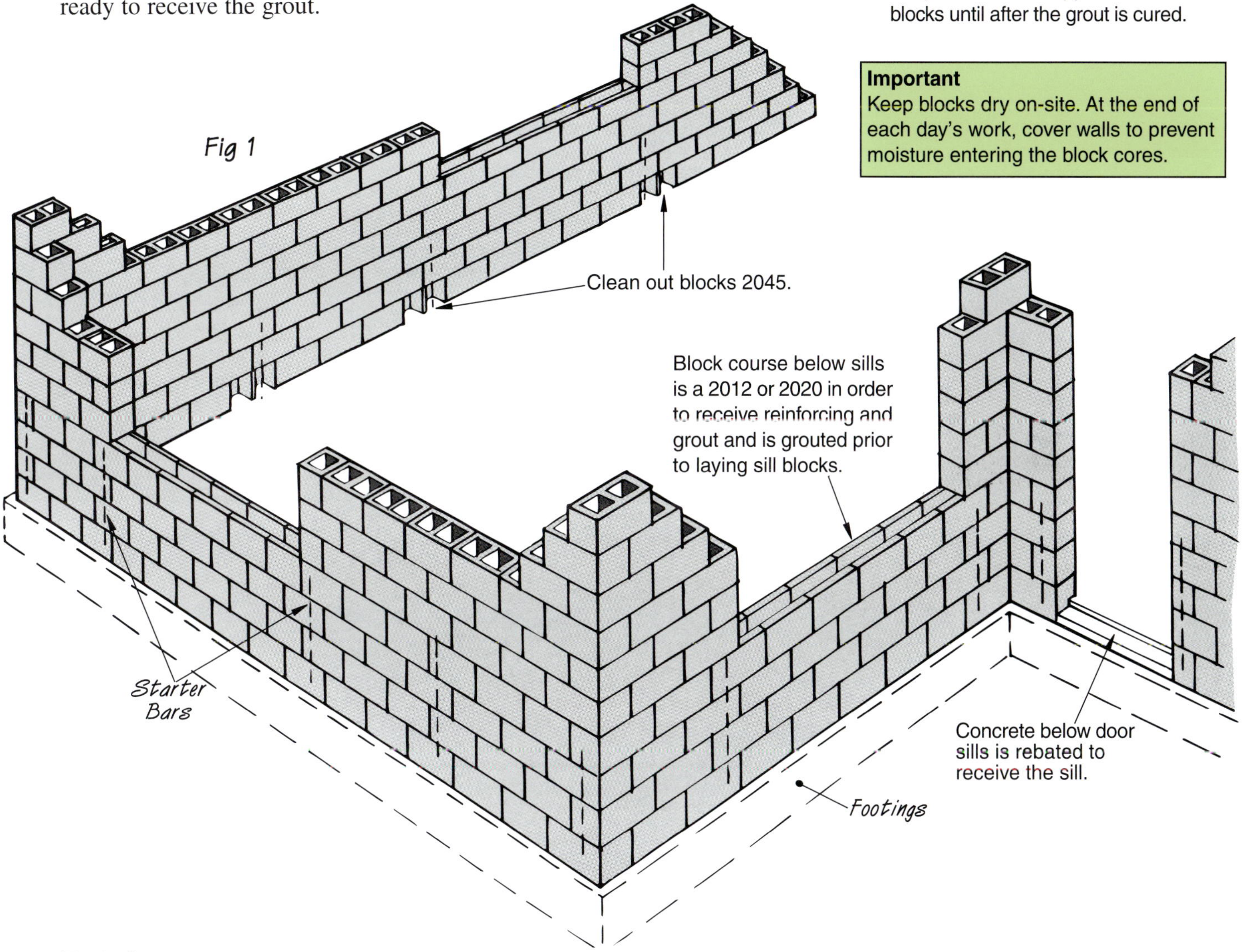

Reinforcement

Plans or specifications will stipulate positions, spacings and size of all block reinforcement. All horizontal reinforcing is placed and tied together at corners and joined with tie wire. For 12mm bars, all laps should be 540mm MIN. for round smooth bars and 450mm for deformed bars. Vertical reinforcing bars are inserted in all cores containing starter bars.

The vertical cores should be cleaned of any projecting lumps of mortar. Grout can then be poured.

Holding Down Bolts

Top wall plate bolts or roof holding down bolts are hooked under the bottom layer of reinforcing at spacings indicated on plans.

Windows & Lintels

Windows are installed after walls are built and all blockwork is painted. Flush-end blocks are used around openings.

The opening is given an extra 4mm tolerance for installing the windows and the gap sealed with long life paintable sealant. Should the frames have a projecting fin, this is to be removed. Request the factory to carry this out.

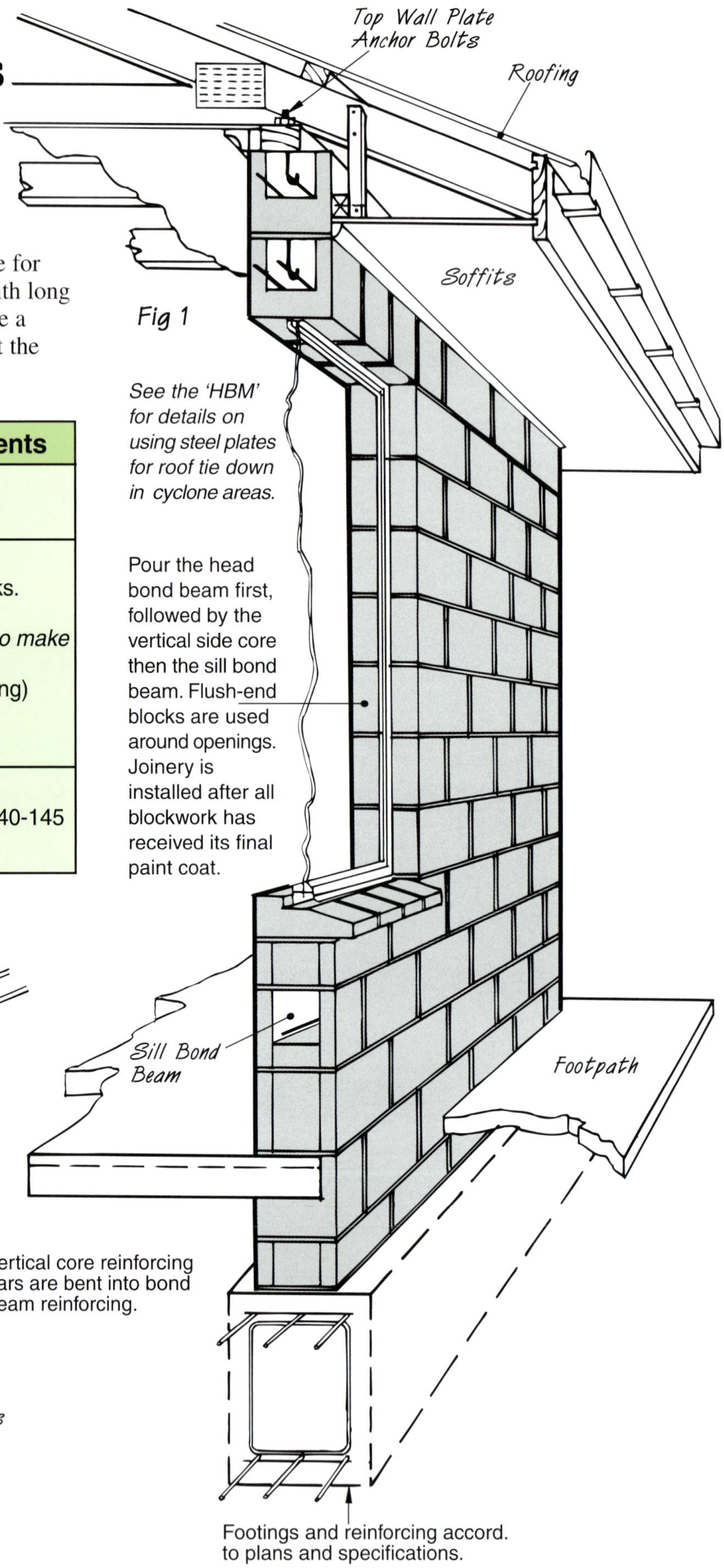

200mm Block Mortar & Fill Requirements
BLOCK QUANTITIES Each square metre of wall contains 12.5 blocks.
MORTAR REQUIREMENT 1 cubic metre of mortar will lay approx. 800 blocks. *Quantities for a mix of 1 cement: 1 lime: 6 sand to make 1 cubic metre:* 1.2m³ of damp sand (allowing 20% bulking) 6 bags of Portland Cement 6 bags of Hydrated Lime
BLOCK FILL (GROUT) REQUIREMENT 1 cubic metre of blockfill grout is required to fill 140-145 blocks.

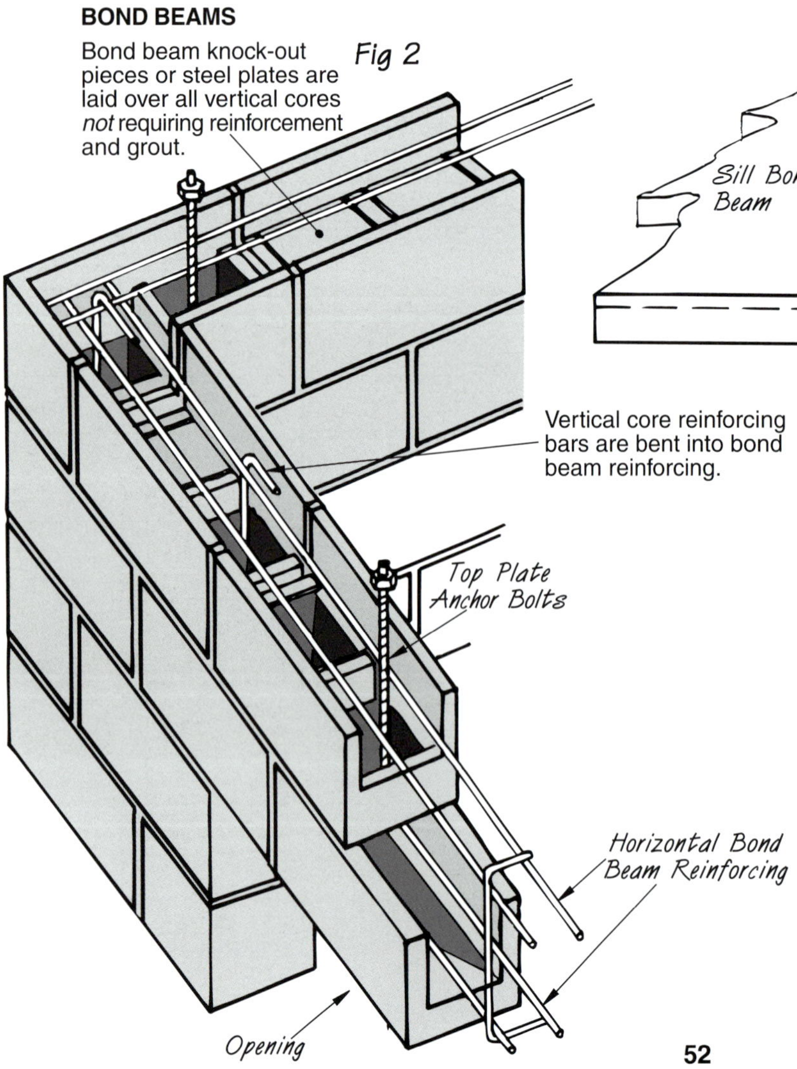

Note: In the above form of construction, the top bond beam is continuous and unbroken by control joints.

Masonry Block Walls with Timber Floors

Stage 1 Construct foundations, including footing pads for the isolated piers. Plans or specifications will indicate correct spacing for vertical reinforcing starter bars.

Stage 2 Build block walls up to top of engaged pier height.

Stage 3 Stretch string lines across the walls each way to indicate the lines of free standing piers. Then construct those piers to the lines.

Stage 4 Place reinforcing in cores and piers specified and pour grout. While grout is still soft, install holding down bolts for bearers or wall plates.

Stage 5 Fit ant capping.

Stage 6 Floor may be constructed then to utilise as scaffolding for building the remaining blockwork.

WALL SECTION

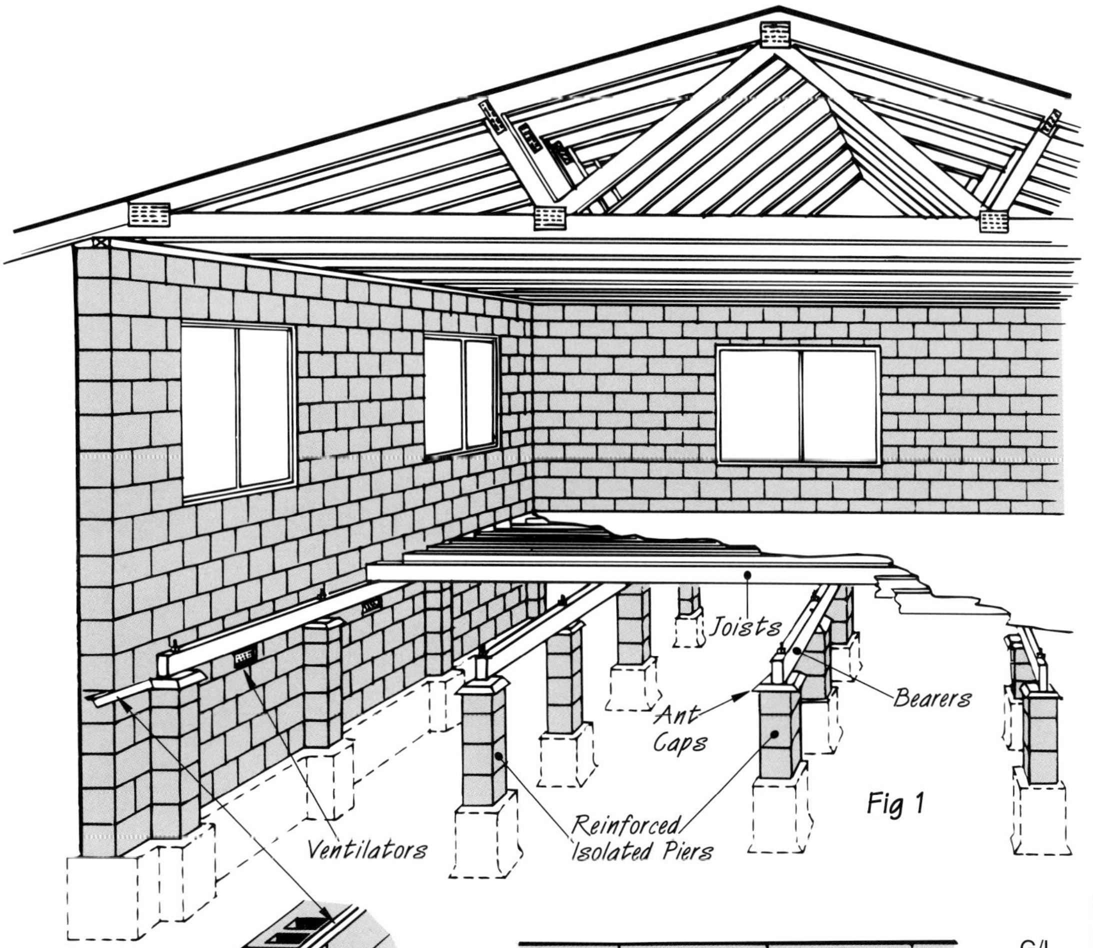

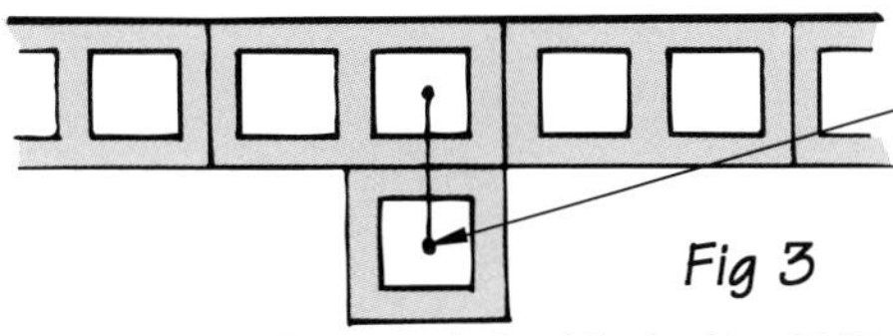

Engaged pier blocks No. 2003 are tied to the main wall with 6mm galv. MS bars or bolts bent into each core at every joint. Both cores are grout filled.

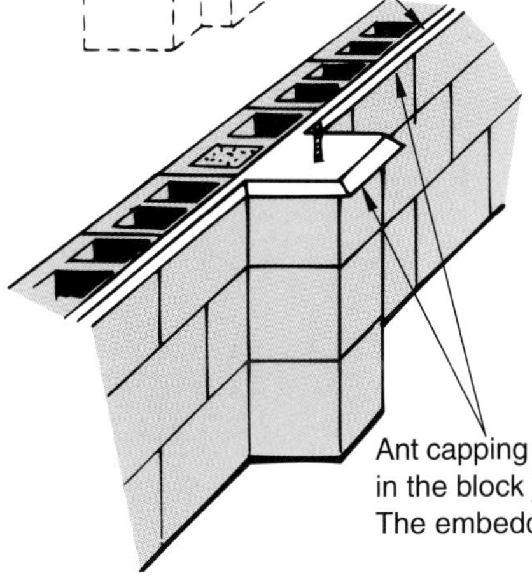

Ant capping must continue along the length of the wall embedded in the block joint and also joined to ant caps on engaged piers. The embedded edge should *not* extend over the cores.

Blocklayers may prefer to complete the walls without having to return at a later date. If construction is well organised, then the floor framing can still be carried out while the blocklayer works from scaffolding on the outside. Lintels, bond beams, reinforcing and pouring of grout is the same as on previous pages.
In this form of construction it may be necessary to install control joints and in some cases articulation joints, refer to engineers details.

Stage 7 Roof is framed and clad, then all walls painted inside and out. Windows and doors are installed followed by remaining interior work.

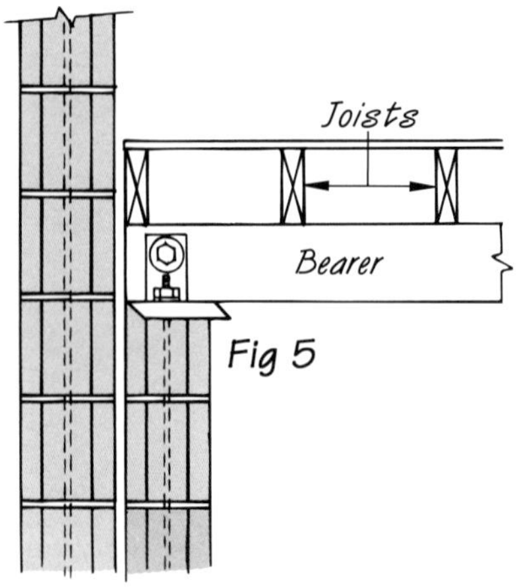

Bearer at Right Angles to Walls

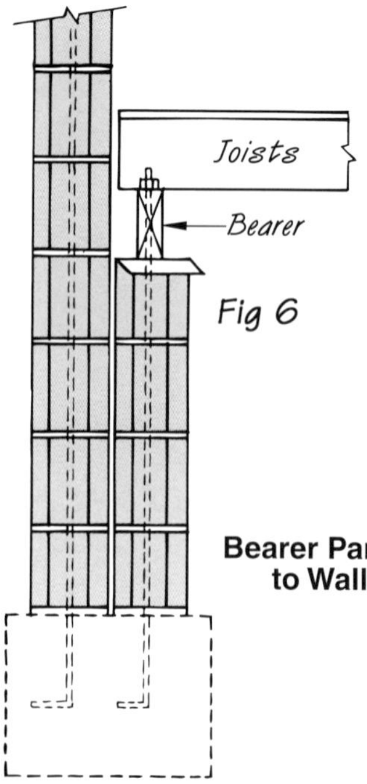

Bearer Parallel to Walls

Installing Joinery into Block Masonry

Window & Door Fixing

Before commencing blockwork, establish opening sizes with window supplier. Windows are attached to blocks by screws through the frames using masonry plugs after the walls and openings have received their final paint coatings.

Alternative method of installing patio doors. Fig 3 has sills embedded in a slab edge rebate, the preferred best practice method while fig 4 has them embedded on the slab surface, *not* as good.

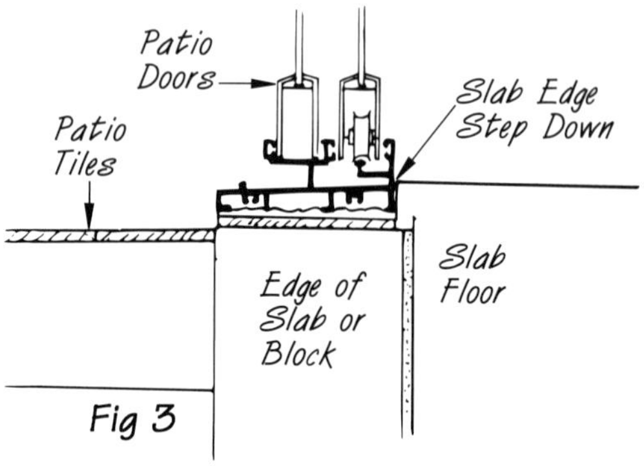

Aluminium sill embedded level in silicone sealant on either a quarry tile or a sand and cement (four sand to one cement) mortar bed in a slab edge rebate.

Opening in Door
Prime paint underside of wood sills and backside of jambs then attach DPC before installation.

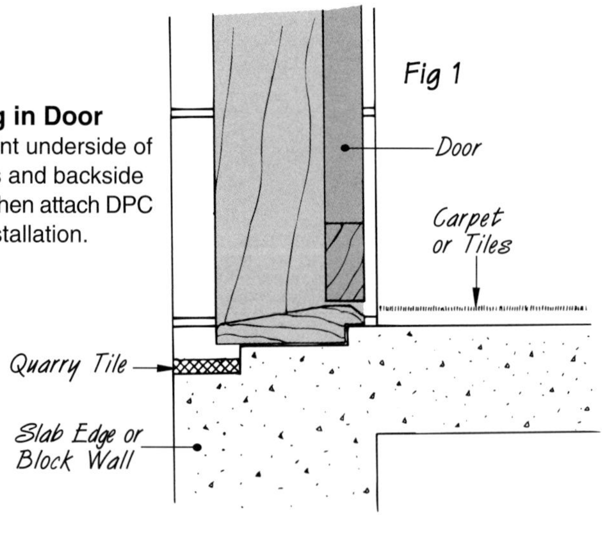

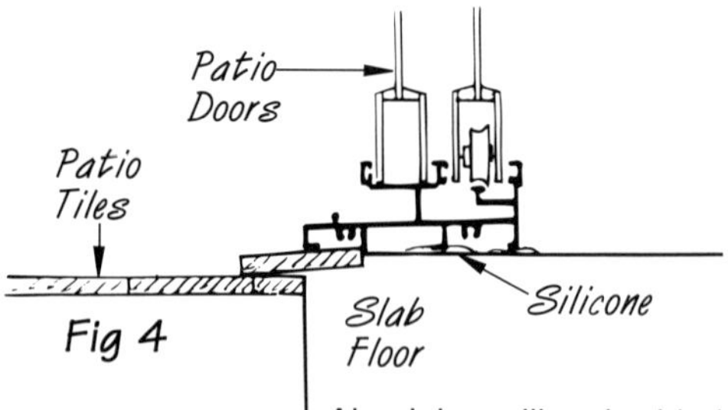

Aluminium sill embedded level in silicone directly onto the slab edge.

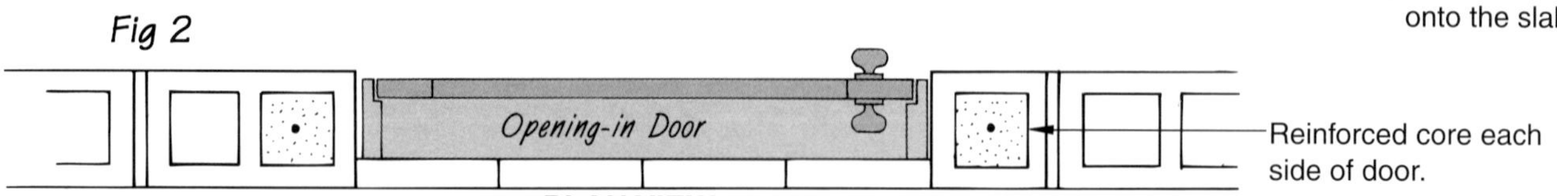

PLAN VIEW

Surface Coatings

Block walls must be waterproofed even if they have been cement rendered. The simplest approved method is the application of three coats of 100% acrylic paint ensuring that each coat is meticulously applied according to manufacturer's instructions.

For this reason, downpipes, mitre boxes, windows and any other wall fixtures should be attached after painting. Paint coatings are applied to both sides of the walls prior to installing windows.

Gyprock® Plasterboard Lining over Masonry Walls

Materials & Tools Required:
- ★ Gyprock® Plasterboard panels
- ★ Gyprock® Masonry Adhesive
- ★ Straightedge and chalk line
- ★ Furring Channels for irregular walls only

Interior brick or block surfaces can be lined with Gyprock® plasterboard. If an exterior wall is damp on the interior surface, correct this before lining.

Where to Begin

Using a straightedge check the wall for irregularities (hollows or high spots) (see fig 1) . Where irregularities exceed 15mm, follow the steps in 'Lining over Irregular Surfaces'.

Lining over True Surfaces

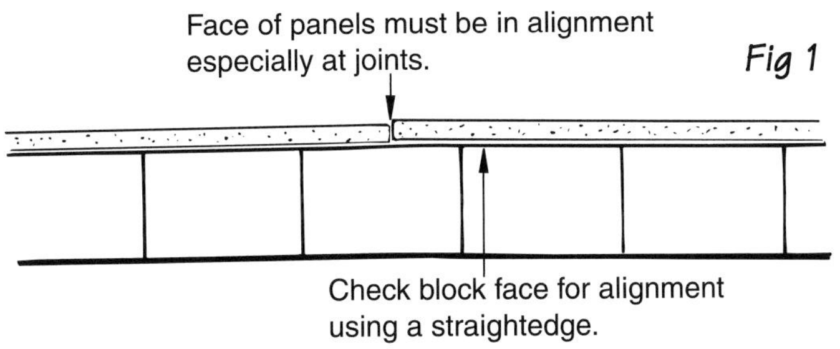

Fig 1

Step 1 The wall should be scrubbed down with a stiff brush to remove all dust. If already painted, the paint must be removed from all points where adhesive is to be applied (see fig 2). For fast paint removal, use a coarse sanding disc in an angle grinder or drill. Wear a dust mask.

Step 2 Spring a chalk line along the ceiling and floor to help align the face edges when bedding the sheet into the adhesive. This in turn will ensure the skirting and cornice moulding are straight. These lines should be a distance out from the wall equal to the plasterboard thicknesses plus the depth of the highest point along the edge area. To perform this hold the straightedge vertically down the wall or better still a panel of plasterboard and mark its edge. Allowing for adhesive.

Step 3 The Gyprock® plasterboard panels are applied horizontally. Apply blobs or daubs of adhesive approx. 50mm in dia. and 15mm thick, 50mm from the edges of the panel and at 450mm MAX. centres vertically and horizontally (see fig 2). Position the first panel and use a straightedge to tamp into alignment, both vertically and horizontally. Support panels in position until adhesive sets by propping or by temporary nailing through sheet edges with masonry nails.

Step 4 Finish the joints, see CSR Gyprock® brochure.

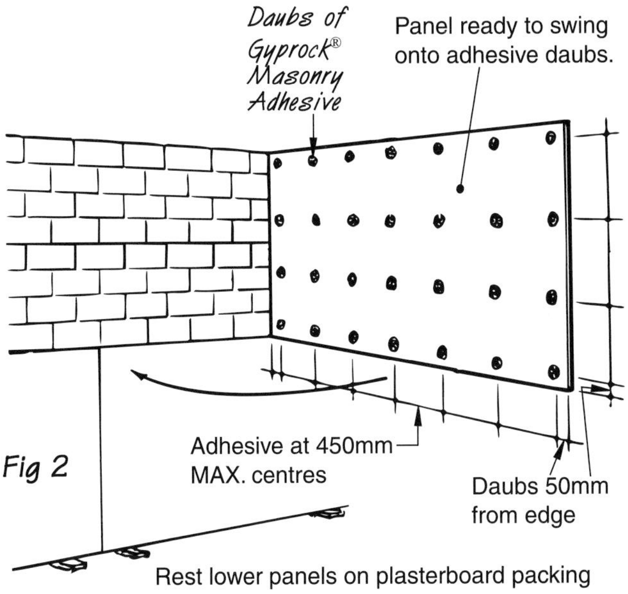

Fig 2

Rest lower panels on plasterboard packing strips. The skirting boards will conceal the gap. Stagger vertical joins so that the upper panel crosses the vertical joint in the lower panels.

Lining over Irregular Surfaces

Step 1 Attach Rondo Furring Channels Part No. 333 to the walls at 600mm spacings. Fasten them with masonry nails spaced at 600mm centres and pack them out where necessary into true alignment. Attach the two end ones, first packing them out to clear the highest spots. Use packers of masonite or DPC material. Attach string lines or use a long straightedge between the two end channels for aligning the remaining channels.

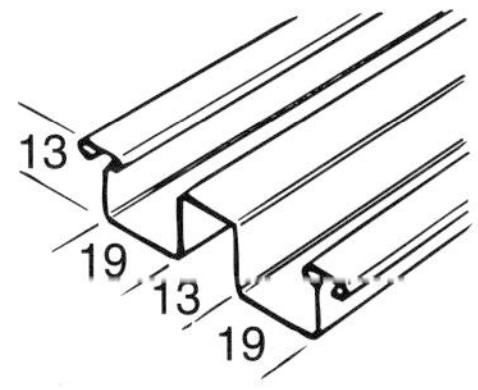

Rondo Furring Channel Part No. 333

Step 2 Fix short lengths of channel along the top and bottom of the wall between the verticals for attaching the sheet edges (see fig 3).

Step 4 Finish the joints. This lining is *not* suitable for tiling over.

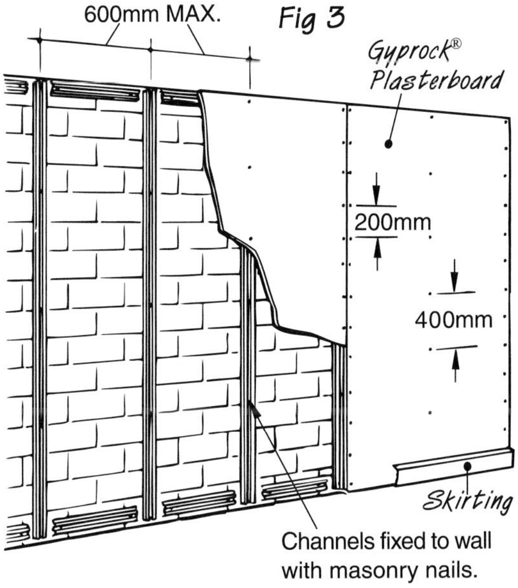

Fig 3

4 Extensions & Renovations

Tackling Renovations & Additions

When planning the ideal place to add more space, the Designer must ignore the present name tags given to rooms for the imagination to be uninhibited.

For example, The owner is extending to gain a family room, why not convert the existing lounge into the family room then extend to create a new lounge.

Suggested Areas to Gain More Space

a). Underneath a high set house.

b). Raise up a low set house creating two-storeys *(see Pages 77 & 78).*

c). Inside an existing roof space: Attic.

d). Extend an existing house.

The key structural factors that keep costs to a minimum when adding on a room are:

1. The sides of the house and roof to which the extensions are anticipated *(see fig 1, Page 57 for further details).*
2. The slope of the land on that side.
   The steeper the slope, the more materials will be required below floor level.
3. The materials chosen and if they marry in with existing materials.

Other Important Considerations

Aspect

This means making the most of sun and breezes. Consider if the extension would interfere with the present path of sunlight and breezes to other rooms. If so, to what extent. Determine by marking on the ground the proposed corners of the extension and bracing a batten upright at each corner, with the top of the batten representing the roof or gutter line.
The sun is high above in Summer and much lower in Winter, so remember the Winter sun will penetrate deeper into interiors.

Aesthetics

Extensions with a 'tacked on' appearance added here and there have a lower resale value. It is preferable to match up building materials as much as possible.

Roof Lines — These should marry together in a pleasing way to retain good resale value. Flat or lean-to roofs may suit a particular design but used where a pitched roof should have been applied can devalue a house.

Hidden Costs

It can be difficult to exactly estimate the cost of extensions because of hidden problems. Often when removing a segment of wall, it will be discovered that deterioration has occurred to the studs or plates etc which will need replacing before new cladding is attached.

Allow 5-10% extra to cover unforeseen expenses. For this reason many tradespersons will only carry out extensions or renovation work on a cost per hour basis. In this situation, the Owner Builder should ask for a time estimate. Divide the work up into stages of say, footings, floor, walls, roof and finishing, and ask the tradesperson for an approximate time estimate for each stage.

Money Saving Tips

Discuss with tradespeople what jobs could be carried out by yourself such as, removing any items such as skirtings, guttering, wall cladding etc. Clearing areas of all impediments such as vegetation, fences, clothes lines etc. Stacking building materials. Removing windows and doors if necessary.

Siting an Extension

When deciding which side of the house is best to extend, the roof line is the major structural consideration. Costs can be increased or reduced depending on the particular part of the roof chosen for alteration.

Fig 1 provides a bird's eye view of where to best cut into an existing roof. The 'L' shaped roof represents typical common roof situations and contains hip ends and one gable end.

Suggested position for additions have been drawn using dotted lines. These represent all possible areas that could be cut into a pitched roof. The comments on each proposed siting gives the advantages and disadvantages of each position.

Although your particular roofline may not be the 'L' shape and may have all hip ends, or all gable ends, or dutch gable ends, the propositions will still apply unless your existing roof line is flat or lean-to.

3. This extension is taken out from a hip end. If the full width of this end is extended, roof altering will not be too difficult. Existing roof timbers can be left in place and the new rafters joined to the hip between the existing rafters.

The existing eaves will have to be removed and rafters sawn off at the wall line. If this extension is not as wide as the existing house end, then a valley will be required. This will then cause a lot more roof work. It is sometimes a better option to take the extension the full width to avoid valleys.

Fig 1

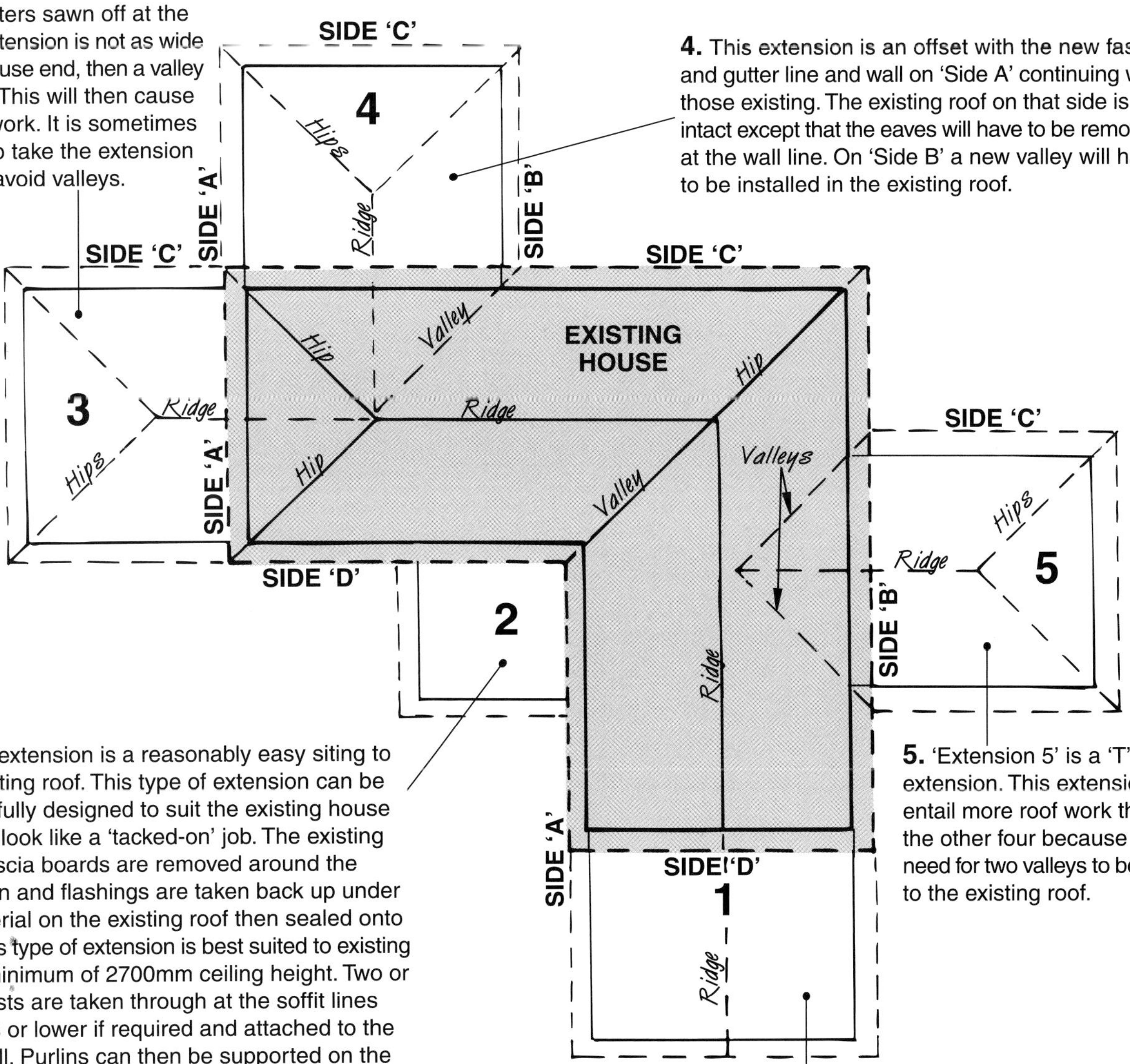

4. This extension is an offset with the new fascia and gutter line and wall on 'Side A' continuing with those existing. The existing roof on that side is left intact except that the eaves will have to be removed at the wall line. On 'Side B' a new valley will have to be installed in the existing roof.

2. This flat roof extension is a reasonably easy siting to join into the existing roof. This type of extension can be attractive if carefully designed to suit the existing house otherwise it can look like a 'tacked-on' job. The existing guttering and fascia boards are removed around the extension portion and flashings are taken back up under the roofing material on the existing roof then sealed onto the new roof. This type of extension is best suited to existing houses with a minimum of 2700mm ceiling height. Two or three header joists are taken through at the soffit lines inside the eaves or lower if required and attached to the existing stud wall. Purlins can then be supported on the header joists.

5. 'Extension 5' is a 'T' extension. This extension will entail more roof work than all the other four because of the need for two valleys to be fitted to the existing roof.

1. This extension is taken out from a gable end. This would normally be the simplest and easiest position to join into an existing roof resulting in little if any disturbance to the existing roof. The existing barge boards and gable materials can be re-used if retrieved in good condition.

Joining New Floors to Old

Bearers Parallel or at Right Angles

In the early planning and design stages, it must be decided whether to run the new floor bearers parallel with the existing ones or at right angles to them. If the new bearers run parallel, then the new joists could be laid beside the existing ones as in figs 1 & 3.

If the new floor joins the old as in the situation in figs 2 & 4, with the bearers at right angles to the existing ones it is most economical if existing stumps can be utilised to support the new bearers if sufficient space remains beside the existing bearer. If this is *not* possible, a separate stump will be required. Steel columns either round or square are ideal for this situation.

Fig 1

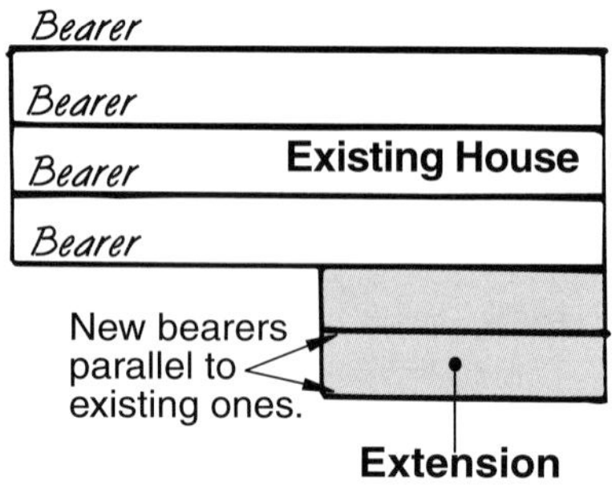

Fig 2

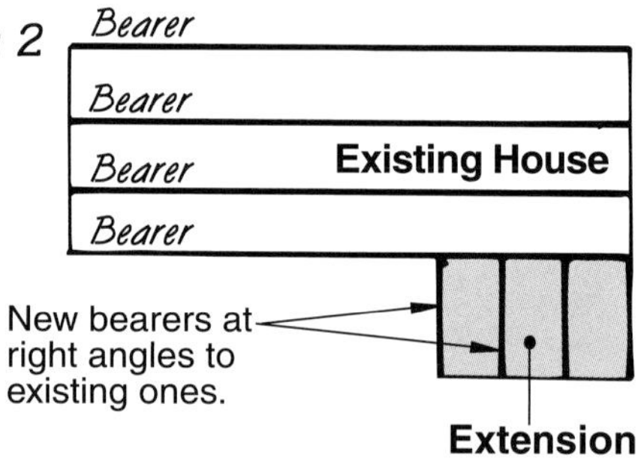

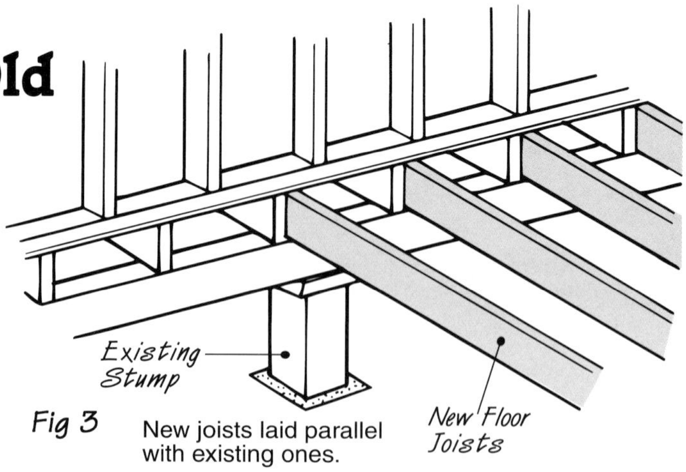

Fig 3 New joists laid parallel with existing ones.

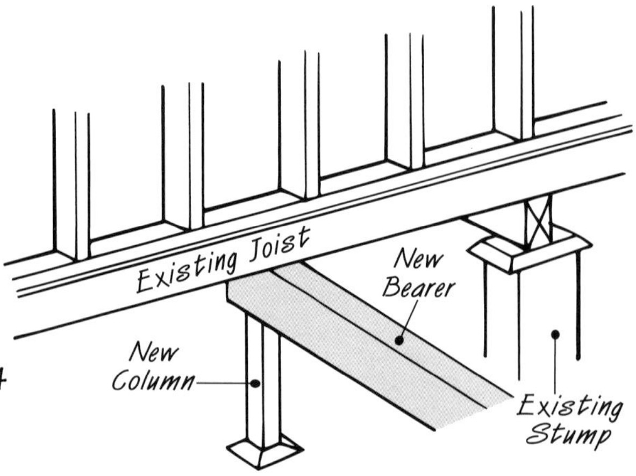

Fig 4

Where new bearer *can't* be seated on the existing stump satisfactorily, a new stump or column support is required.

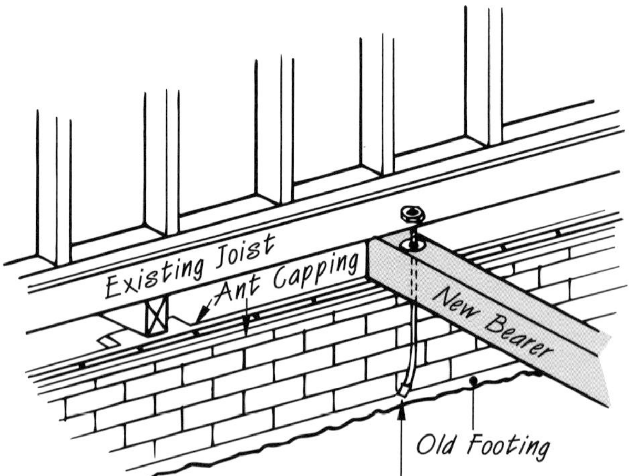

Fig 5 Where acceptable to local authority, new bearers could rest on the existing base wall. If holding down bolts are required, anchor bolts could be installed into existing footings by using a masonry anchor.

Bearers on Existing Brick Bases

Where brick bases already exist, the bearer could be supported on that base with Local Council approval. Ensure ant capping and DPC is laid along the wall and under the bearer. Give the bearer support across the full width of the wall.

Anchoring Down

If the bearer requires anchoring down in high wind areas, a masonry anchor can be installed in the footing beside the wall below the bearer and a female coupling connected. The threaded anchor rod is joined on and then taken up through the bearer (see fig 5).

Where the above method is *not* acceptable, a separate stump will be required. Again steel columns are ideal. These would have to be positioned away from the wall sufficiently to clear the existing concrete footings and to make room for the new column footings (see fig 6).

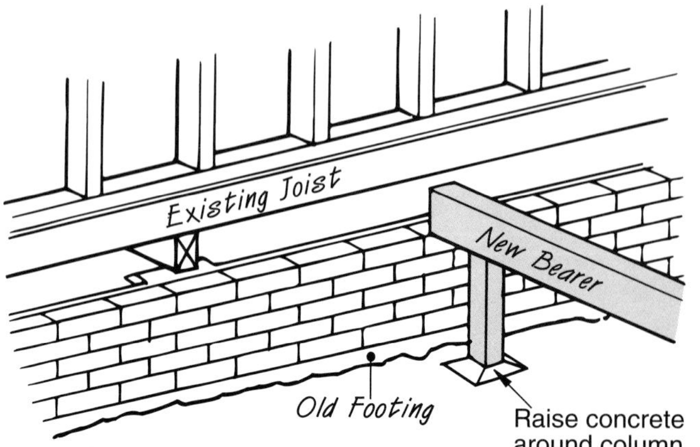

Raise concrete around column to prevent water ponding.

Fig 6 New column support and its footing sited outside of existing footings.

Timber Wall Framing

The wall frame illustrated below is intended to portray a variety of framing situations that could be encountered. Whether the house is brick veneer or weatherboard the timber wall framing construction methods remain the same.

Purpose of Framing Members

Top & Bottom Wall Plates — provide a nailing base to attach all vertical members. The completed wall is attached to the floor through the bottom plate.

Studs — are positioned at either 450 or 600mm centres (as specified in the approved plans).

Double Studs — are used beside openings. Sometimes two or more as required to provide sufficient strength at that point. Plans will usually indicate.

Packing or Spacer Blocks — are used wherever walls or partitions join at corners or 'T' junctions. The studs are nailed together through these blocks. Nail plates are used across the joint over the top plates.

Lintels — are used to support the roof load above openings and are increased in depth with an increase in the opening width. They are cut longer than the opening width in order to rest on the reveal or jamb studs at either side of the opening.

Jack Studs — are centralised above lintels and below sills unless the proposed cladding requires otherwise.

Constructing Wall Frames

Wall frames can be cut out on-site piece-by-piece or factory prefabricated and delivered pre-nailed ready to erect. When using prefab frames for extensions, ensure that the company representative has visited the site and has taken his own measurements of existing heights of top plate surface above floor and the overall length and width of the project. On extensions, these measurements usually differ slightly to those found on the plan.

EXAMPLE WALL FRAMING LAYOUT

Fig 1

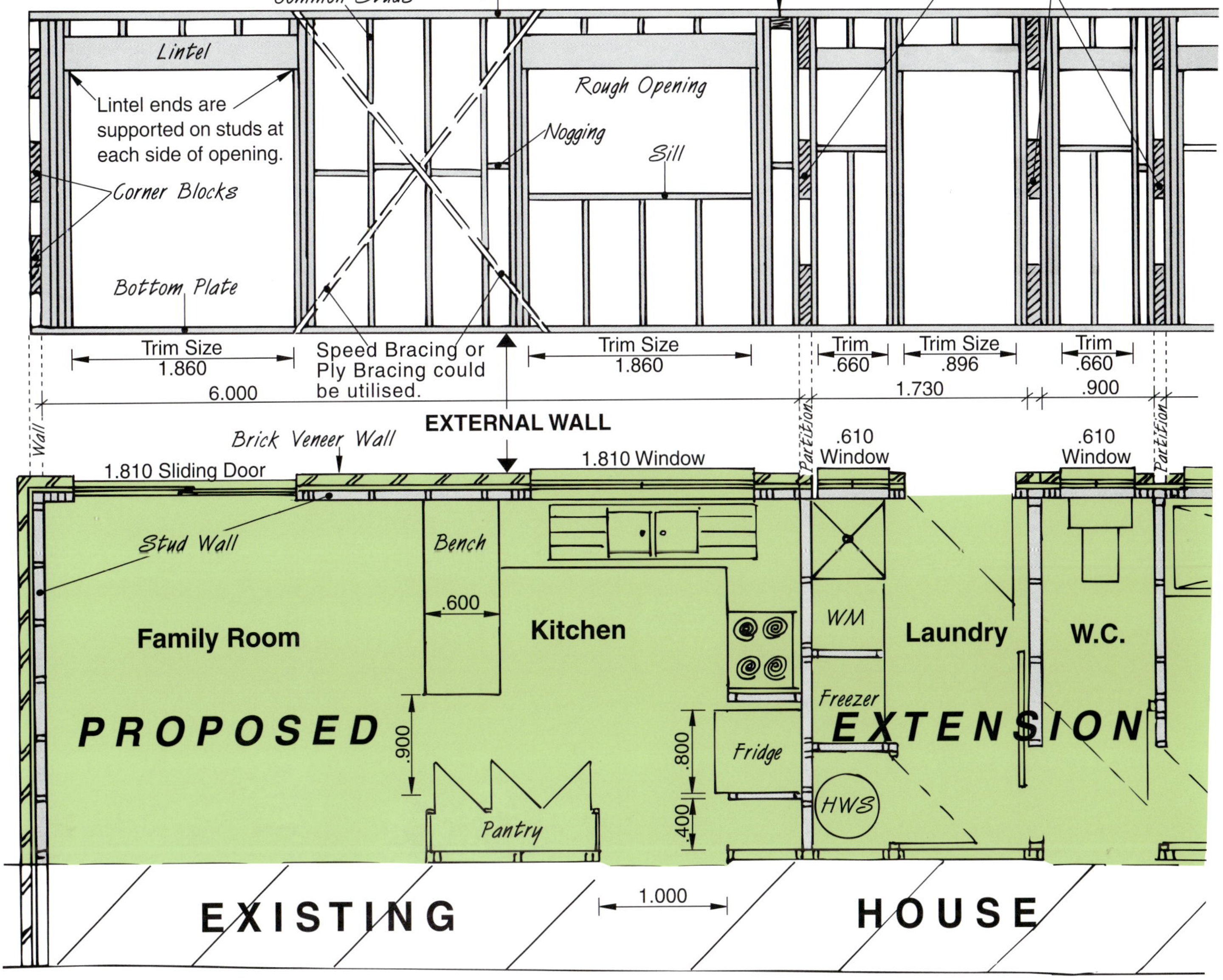

Joining Timber Walls to Brick

Cladded Timber Wall Joining to Brick Veneer at Corners

Fig 1

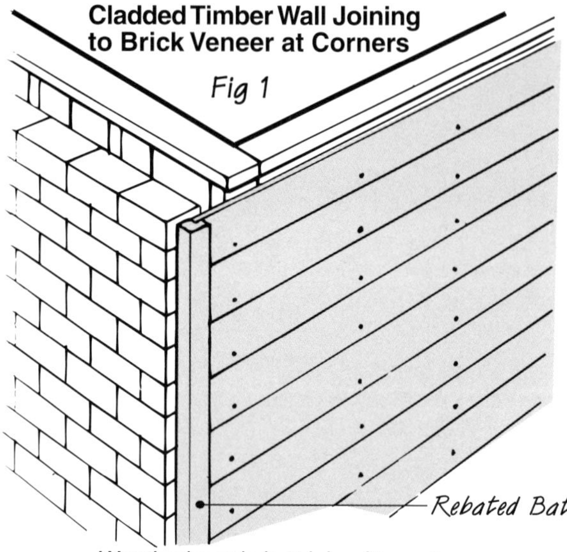

Weatherboards butt joined to a stop-end batten on external corners.

Fig 3

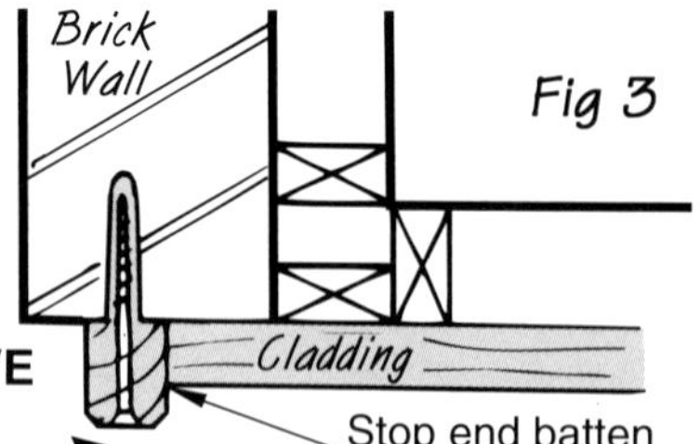

ALTERNATIVE METHOD

Stop end batten without rebate.

PLAN VIEWS

Fig 2

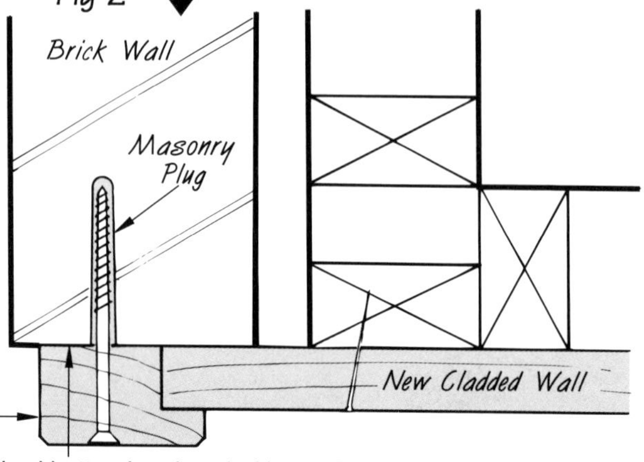

Embed batten in a bead of long life sealant *(not silicone)*.

Fig 4

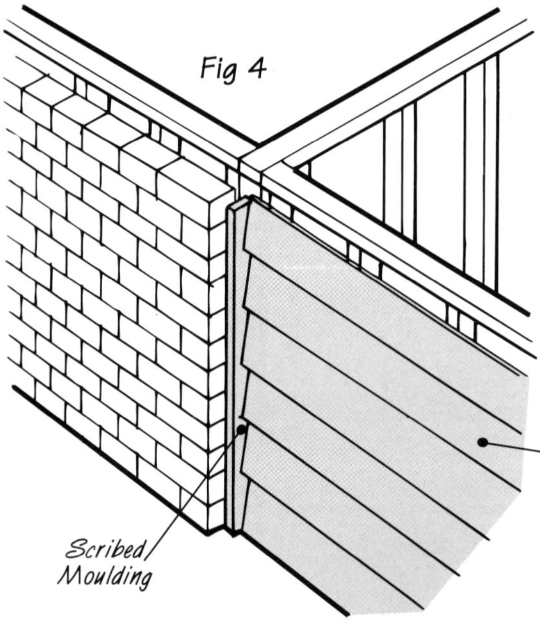

Note: the back of any woodwork touching brickwork should be primed.

Timber and weatherboard wall abutting brick veneer wall.

Fig 5

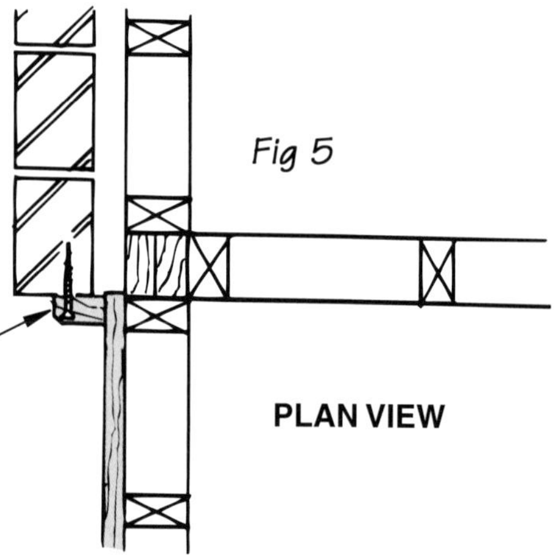

PLAN VIEW

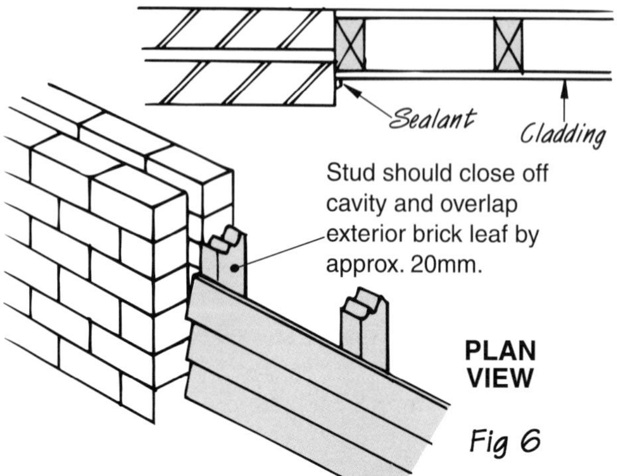

Stud should close off cavity and overlap exterior brick leaf by approx. 20mm.

PLAN VIEW

Fig 6

Timber Wall Abutting Double Brick Wall

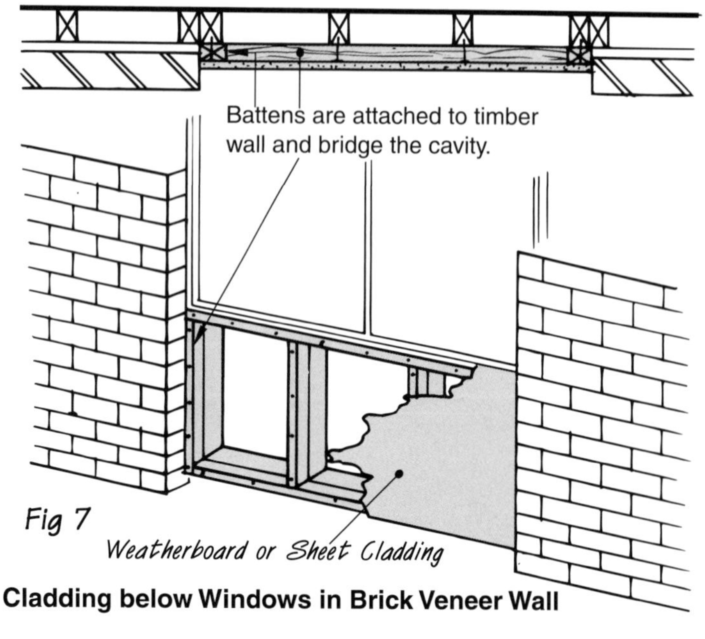

Battens are attached to timber wall and bridge the cavity.

Fig 7

Cladding below Windows in Brick Veneer Wall

Extending a Brick Veneer House (with Slab Floor) Stage 1

Constructing Footings

Step 1 Fix profile hurdles 600-1200mm outside of footing lines to allow machinery working space without bumping them. The exterior faces of the walls are marked on the hurdles, nails are driven at these marks and string lines set up. The area is then squared using either 'Pythagoras Theorem' or the *'3-4-5 method' (see also Page 104 for triangulation and also Page 114&115 for setting out profiles).*

Step 2 The footing widths are marked. These are either centralised beneath the upper walls or recessed 10mm back from the brick face depending on the footing design (refer to the plan). Plans will provide the widths. The outside edge of the footings are marked and indicated with a string line. Lime dust is sprinkled along the line as a guide for excavating machinery to follow.

Step 3 Excavations are carried out usually with a back hoe. On sloping ground, steps are cut into the footings *(see Page 22).*

Step 4 Reinforcing is laid and concrete poured *(see 'HBM').*

Joining New Footings & Walls to Old

Join new footings to old with 2/25mm round reinforcing rods. These should be embedded 450mm into each footing 300mm apart and equally spaced vertically from the top and bottom and centralised across the footing width. The portions embedded into the new footings should be greased and wrapped in paper to allow movement (see figs 2 & 3).

New brick walls should *not* be toothed into the old. A 10mm wide vertical movement control joint should be made between the old and the new. Expanding and contracting brick ties are embedded every fourth course and a strip of polystyrene installed between the two vertical surfaces. The outer 10mm of the joint should be filled with an expansion joint sealant such as Sikaflex Pro or similar (see fig 3).

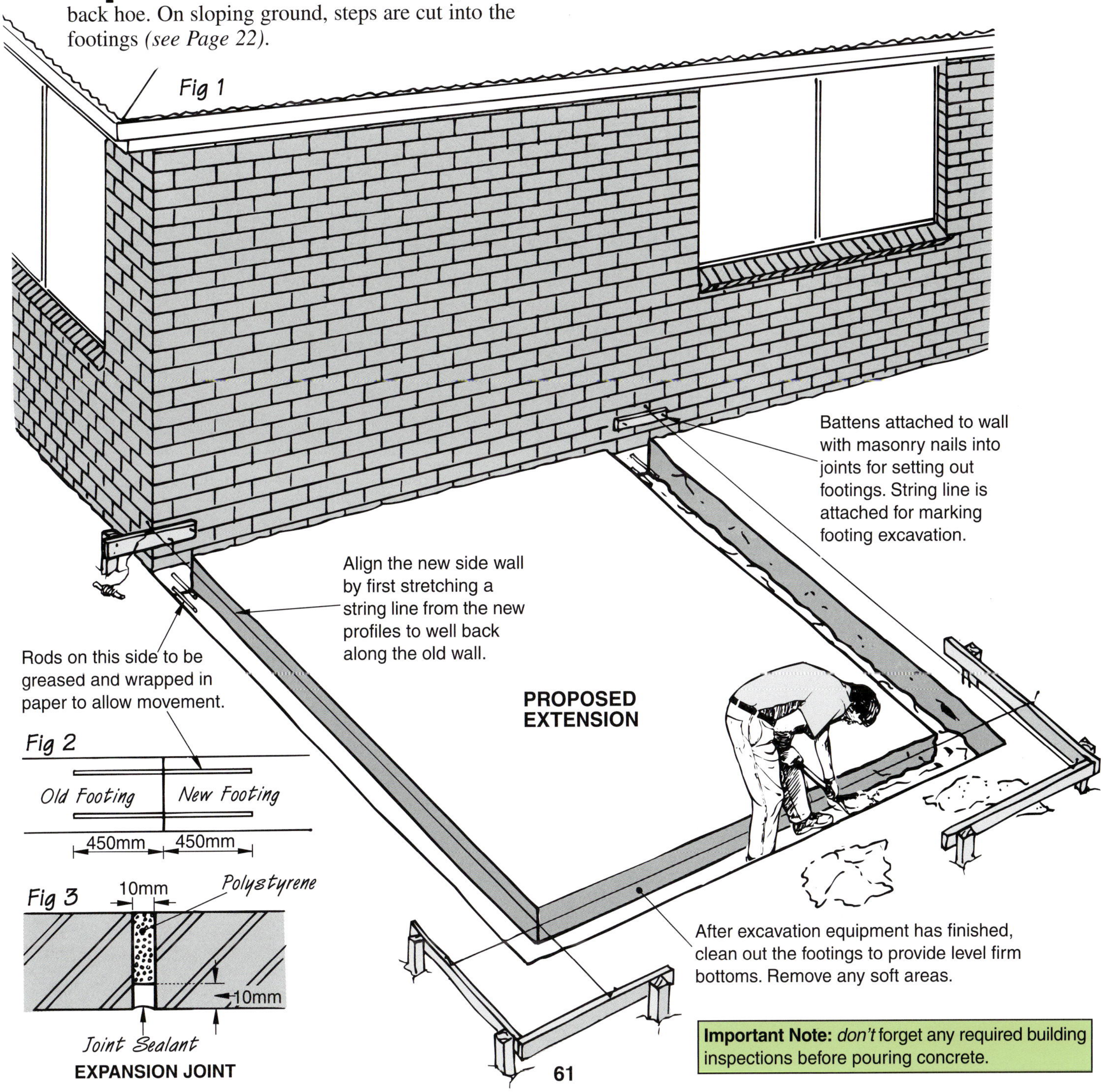

EXPANSION JOINT

Important Note: *don't* forget any required building inspections before pouring concrete.

Stage 2

Constructing the Slab Floor

Step 1 After the footings are completed the slab floor is prepared and poured. Because a doorway will probably be made through from the existing adjoining wall, the new floor should finish flush with the old floor. To perform this, the adjoining doorway should be cut through at this stage or, if desired, the existing brick veneer wall removed. It must be noted that if this brick wall is to be retained, its top will be found to be a few brick courses lower than ceiling height. This can be made up and matched using the bricks that have been removed to make the new doorway.

Step 2 The slab edge on brick veneer construction must have a step or rebate to prevent moisture gaining access to the floor from the veneer wall.

The simplest method of forming this edge step is to request the bricklayer to lay a brick course using weak mortar to enable the bricks to be easily recovered, cleaned and re-used after the slab is poured. The bricks are laid 40mm into the proposed slab area and must have a flush and level surface (see figs 4 & 5).

Step 3 Lay the sand bed. This is levelled off to the specified depth below the slab surface. If termite control is to be Granitguard, this can be substituted for the sand. If Termimesh is to be applied this is laid after the sand bed or alternatively, after the slab is poured but prior to commencing brickwork. This is a specialist job and should be carried out by a certified Applicator who will issue a certificate which your Local Council or lending authority may request.

Step 4 The reinforcing is laid on bar chairs with 225mm laps at joins. *See 'HBM' for further details.*

Step 5 Ensure Local Council or other building inspection is carried out before pouring concrete. Concrete can then be poured. After the pour, the slab should be cured. *See Pages 82 & 83 for more information.*

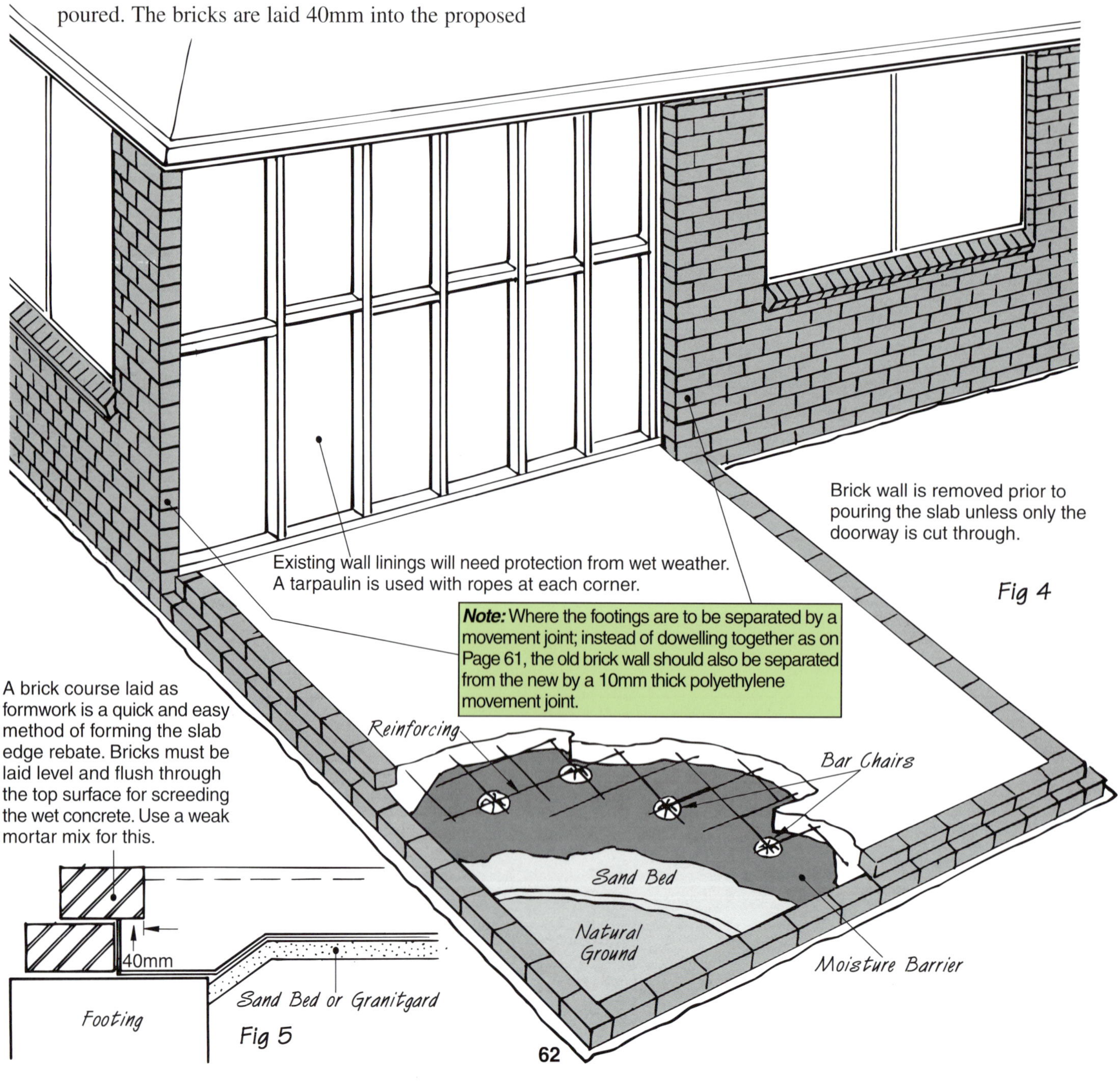

Fig 4

A brick course laid as formwork is a quick and easy method of forming the slab edge rebate. Bricks must be laid level and flush through the top surface for screeding the wet concrete. Use a weak mortar mix for this.

Fig 5

Stage 3

Erecting & Completing the Structure

Step 1 The eaves overhang is now removed and existing rafters sawn off flush with the existing timber wall frame. This is to enable the new wall frames to be erected. Other roof cladding can be left intact until commencing roof framing.

Step 2 Wall frames are erected, straightened, plumbed and braced. Roof framing is then carried out. *See 'HBM' for wall and roof framing.*

Step 3 ***Plumber* —** will be required to install guttering and valley flashing before roof cladding is carried out.

Step 4 ***Eaves* —** these are constructed but lining left off until bricklayer has laid the last brick course.

Step 5 Construct eaves framing, install windows, exterior doors and attach building insulation to walls, the brick veneer walls can then be built.

***Cavity - DPC Flashing* —** must be laid as in fig 6.

***Brick Veneer Ties* —** these should be on-site. *See 'HBM' for details.*

***Weepholes* —** Ensure that weepholes are provided along the cavity step brick course. *See 'HBM' for details.*

Step 6 ***Electrician & Plumber* —** are engaged to install electrical wiring and pipelines.

Step 7 ***Internal Wall Linings* —** Local Council, or other building inspection will be required before lining walls. After all ceiling battens and wall noggs are installed, the interior is lined commencing with ceilings.

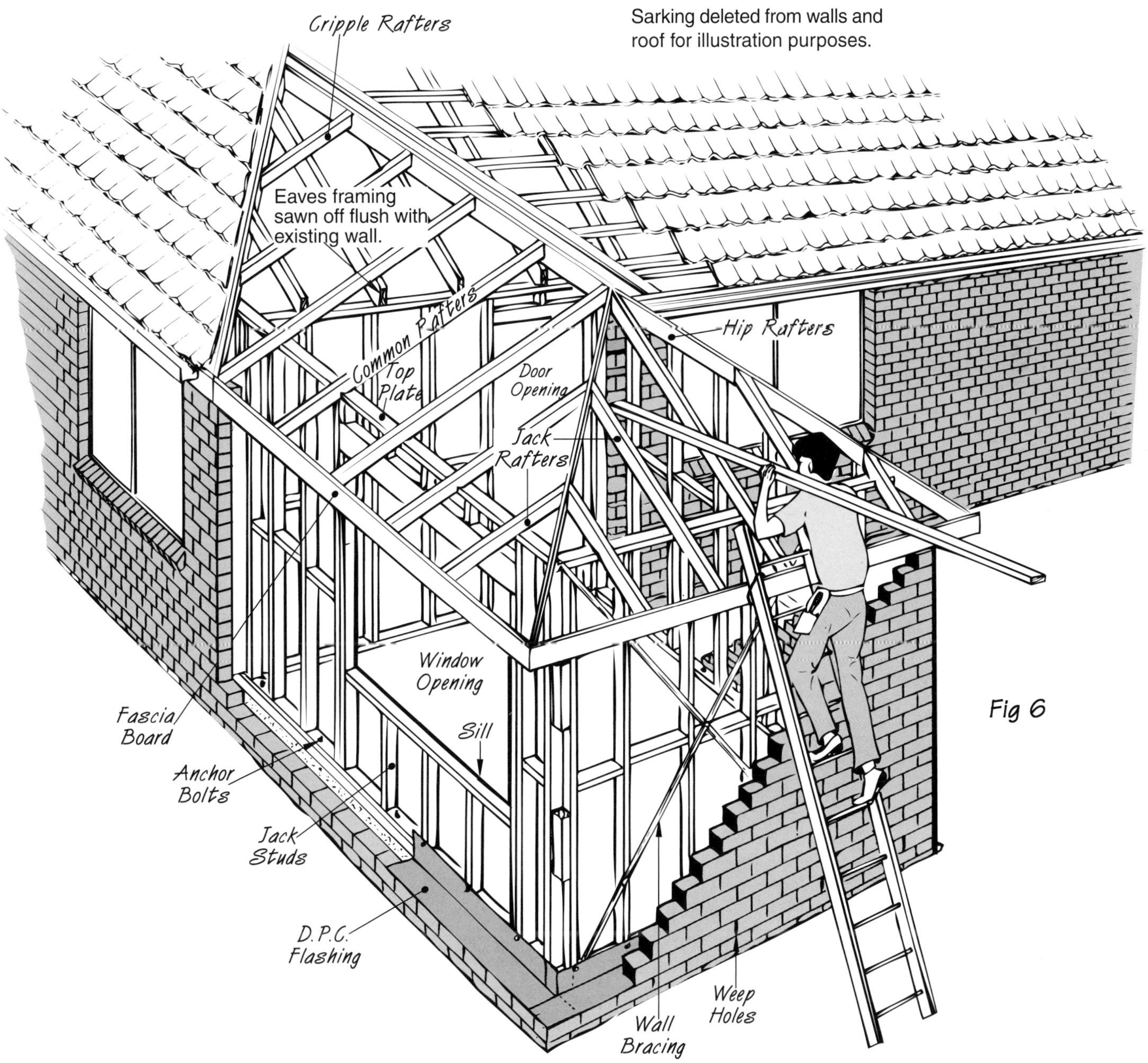

Fig 6

Extending a Brick Veneer House (with Timber Floor)

Constructing the Footings

Step 1 From the plans establish in which direction the bearers lay and construct the profile hurdles leaving space between profiles and footing for machinery to operate. Set out wall positions on hurdles then footing positions; these are sited either centrally beneath both the brick and timber load bearing walls or 10mm back from the brick face. The footing plans should indicate.

Step 2 Excavate footings.

Step 3 Place reinforcing *(see 'HBM' for more information)*. If the free standing piers are to be of masonry blocks which permit holding down rods to be taken from the footings, then install these rods at this stage. If steel or treated timber columns are required, have them on-site.

Step 4 Have any required building inspections carried out. Then order and pour concrete. Footings should be poured in one piece.

Step 5 Because a doorway will probably be made through from the existing adjoining wall, the new floor should finish flush with the old floor. To perform this the proposed doorway should be cut through at this stage or if desired the existing brick veneer wall removed. It must be noted that if this brick wall is to be retained, its top will be found to be a few brick courses lower than the ceiling height. This can be made up and matched using the bricks that have been removed to make the new doorway.

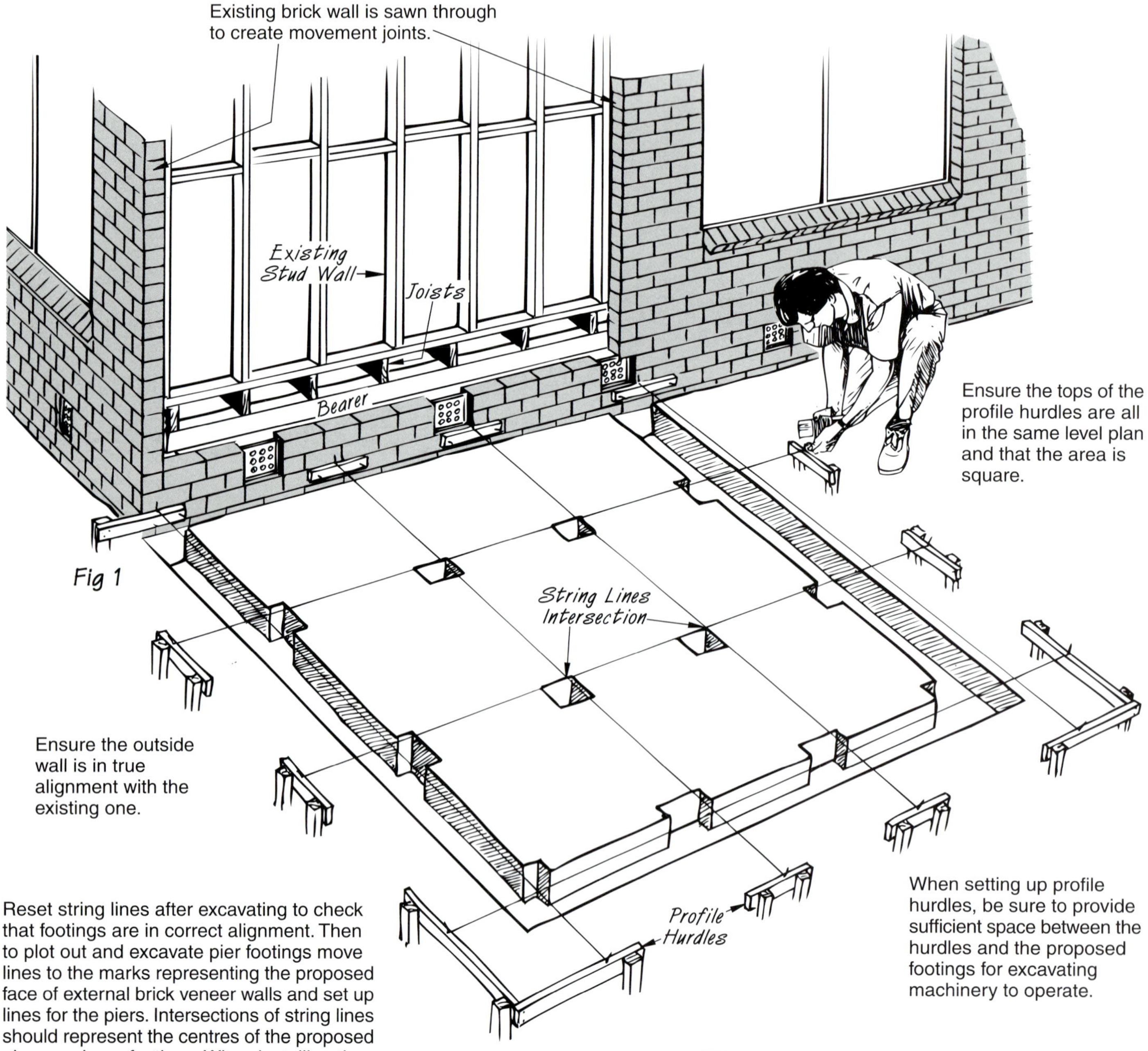

Fig 1

Reset string lines after excavating to check that footings are in correct alignment. Then to plot out and excavate pier footings move lines to the marks representing the proposed face of external brick veneer walls and set up lines for the piers. Intersections of string lines should represent the centres of the proposed pier or column footings. When installing the piers or columns, the strings are adjusted to align with one side of the piers or columns.

Note: *See notes on Page 61 regarding the joining of the new footings and walls to the slab.*

Cont.

Constructing Floor Framing

For detailed floor construction see the 'HBM' Chapter 3.

Step 1 Have bricklayer construct base walls and piers with DPC laid at 150mm above ground height (this is usually the second course) and ventilators at specified spacings.

It is important that piers supporting bearers, arrive at the exact height. Mark this height on the back of the brickwork, measuring down from the existing floor surface. It is a good idea to have the bearers, joists and flooring on-site so these thicknesses and depths can be measured accurately. Transfer these marks around the brickwork at pier positions to ensure they all arrive at the same height.

Step 2 Lay ant capping.

Step 3 Cut and lay bearers, keeping them 40mm short of brick walls to allow for the cavity. Older homes will have cut-in floors (that is the bottom wall plates rest directly on the joists). However, the new floor can be either cut-in or platform (the latter has the floor laid before erecting the walls). This is the simplest method. However, it should only be applied when using sheet flooring *not* tongue and groove strip flooring.

Step 4 Cut and lay joists allowing for the new flooring surface to fit flush with the old to ensure a tight flush fit at doorways between the old and the new floor.

Step 5 Lay flooring commencing with 'Sheet 1'. Manufactures supply fixing instructions with their flooring. *For installing tongue and groove strip flooring see the 'HBM'.*

Remaining Construction Work

For steps to remaining construction work, see brick veneer extensions Stage 3, Page 63 & for Roof Extensions, Page 69. Refer also to 'HBM'.

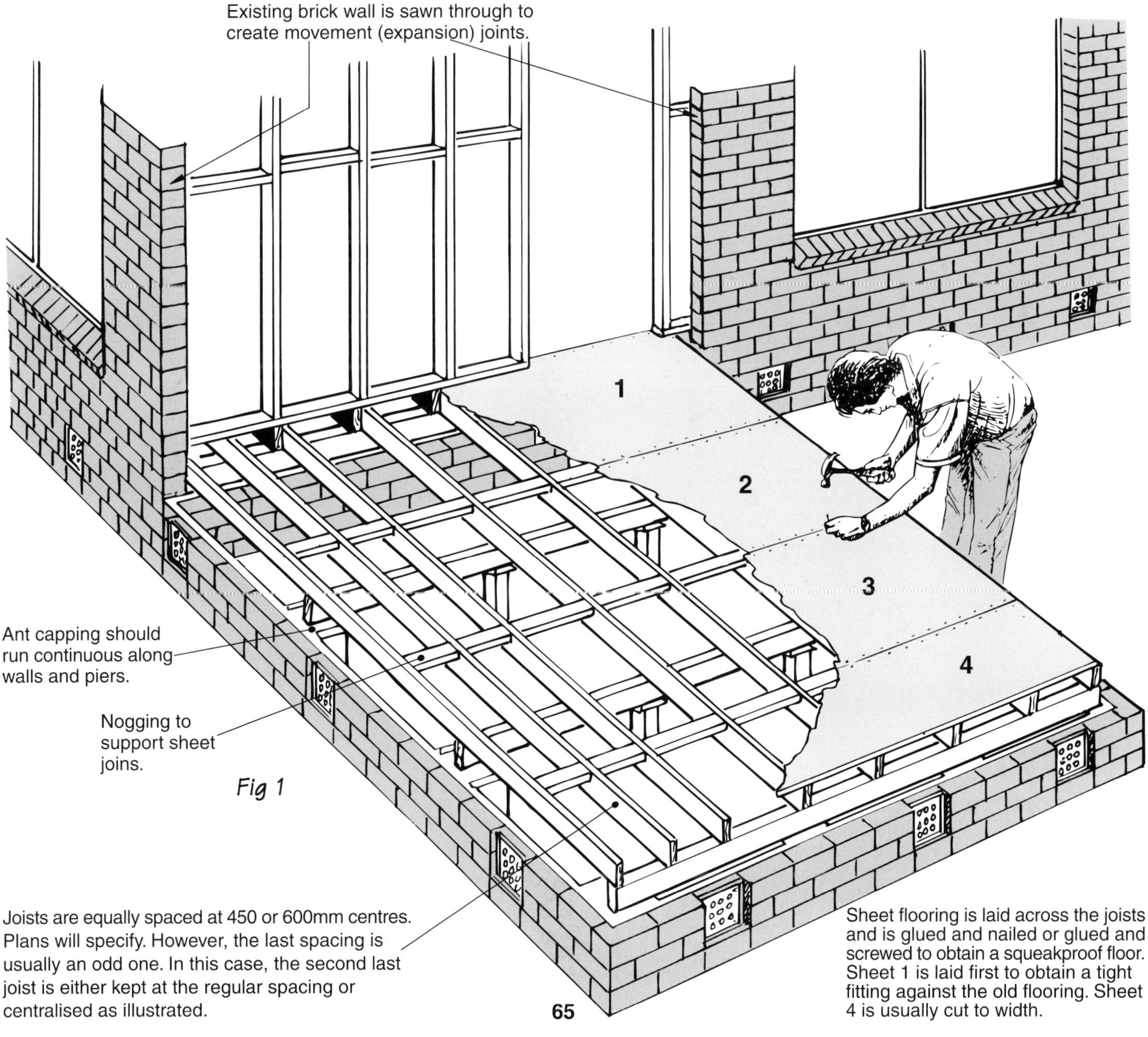

Fig 1

A Quick Easy Extension (for High or Low Set Brick Veneer)

This extension is a simple alternative for extending the brick veneer house without causing too much disturbance to the existing wall or roof lines. Ceiling height will be the first consideration.

If the available ceiling height is inadequate, two options are possible:

a). Lower the extension floor, creating a step down *(by far the simplest option)*; or

b). Raise the roof to the level of the existing top plate. This will entail sawing off the existing eaves.

Reduced ceiling heights are permitted by Local Councils where the room is designated for specific purposes as stipulated in the 'BCA' and building by-laws.

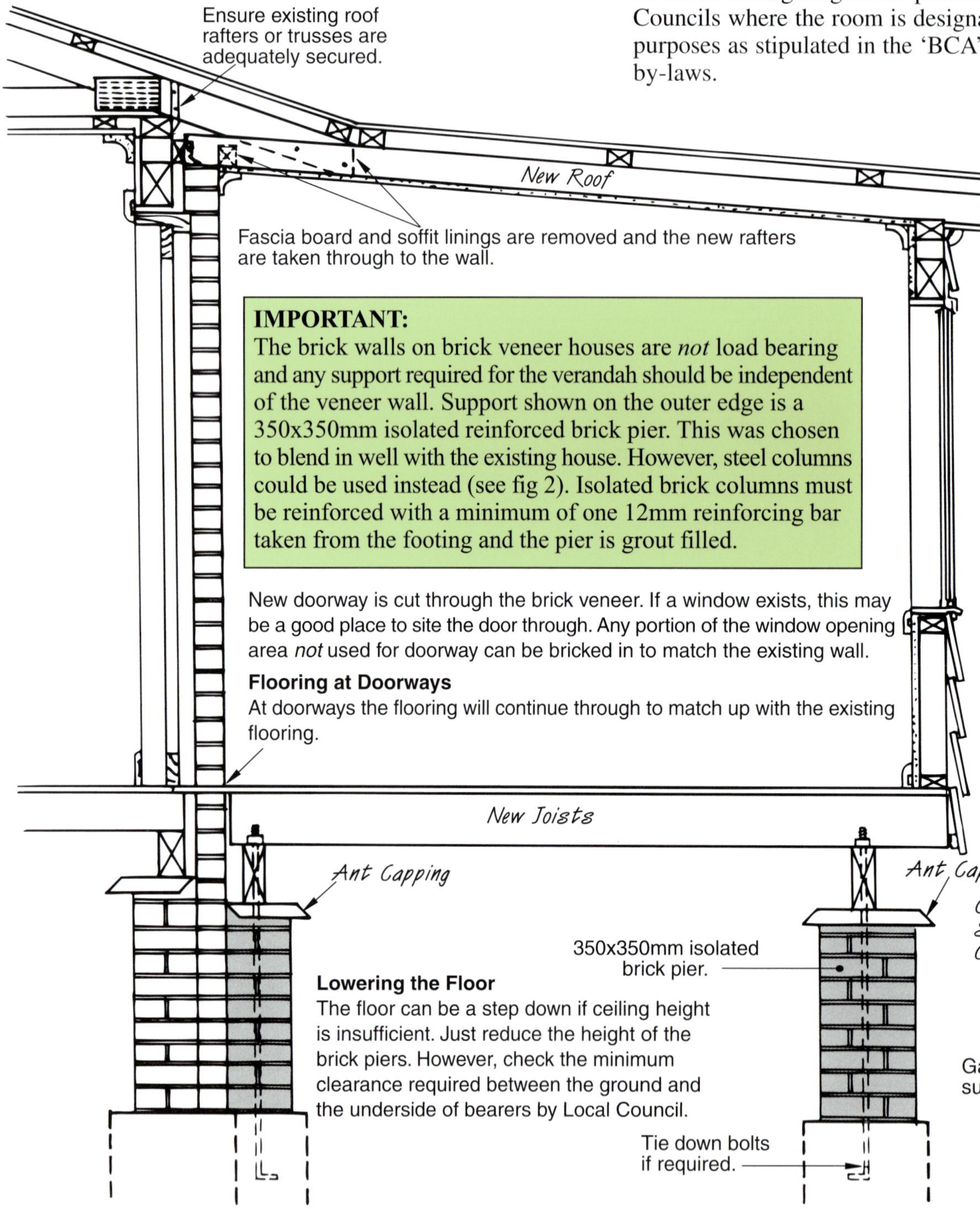

Fig 1

IMPORTANT:
The brick walls on brick veneer houses are *not* load bearing and any support required for the verandah should be independent of the veneer wall. Support shown on the outer edge is a 350x350mm isolated reinforced brick pier. This was chosen to blend in well with the existing house. However, steel columns could be used instead (see fig 2). Isolated brick columns must be reinforced with a minimum of one 12mm reinforcing bar taken from the footing and the pier is grout filled.

New doorway is cut through the brick veneer. If a window exists, this may be a good place to site the door through. Any portion of the window opening area *not* used for doorway can be bricked in to match the existing wall.

Flooring at Doorways
At doorways the flooring will continue through to match up with the existing flooring.

Lowering the Floor
The floor can be a step down if ceiling height is insufficient. Just reduce the height of the brick piers. However, check the minimum clearance required between the ground and the underside of bearers by Local Council.

Hint: when drilling holes through deep timbers, drill through from both sides. This will keep the hole straight. The hole is permitted to be 2mm MAX. larger in diameter than the bolt.

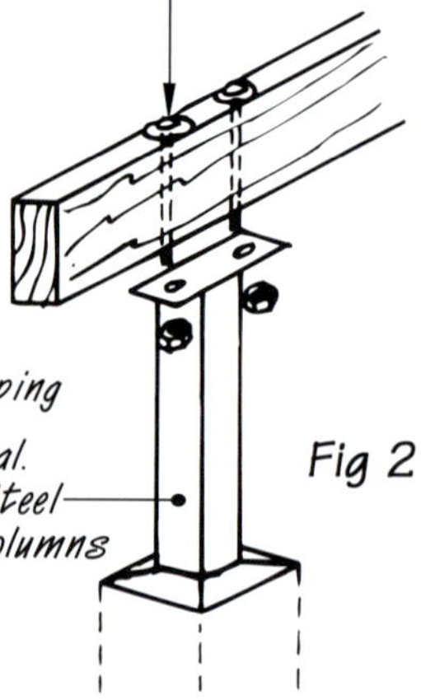

Fig 2

Gal steel columns could be substituted for brick ones.

Constructing Brick Piers

Step 1 Footings of engaged and isolated piers are excavated and concrete is poured with a starter bar embedded in the footing and projecting out of the footing 600mm.

Step 2 The 350x350mm isolated brick piers are constructed with their top finish height marked on the existing wall, making allowance for the bearer, joist and flooring depths.

Step 3 Insert one 12mm threaded gal. reinforcing rod down the pier core to rest on the footing and extend above the pier top sufficiently to anchor timber beams. The brick pier core is then grout filled.

Extending a Weatherboard House

The procedures for constructing a weatherboard extension are almost identical to those already described for brick veneer, with the deletion of brickwork. However, if a brick base is required, that portion including the footings will remain the same.

Constructing a Weatherboard Extension

Step 1 Set out wall alignment on footing profiles as on Page 61, then excavate footing holes for columns or stumps using either concrete, brick or steel. Then concrete the columns in position.

If using steel columns, ensure they are hot dip galvanised and that the concrete is raised up above ground to slope away from columns to prevent water ponding. Arrange for Local Council or other building inspection prior to pouring concrete.

Step 2 Remove cladding from the adjoining wall and protect exposed internal linings from inclement weather.

Step 3 Construct floor framing and lay flooring.

Step 4 Construct and erect wall frames straight, plumb and braced ready for roof construction. *See 'HBM'.*

Step 5 Construct roof framing. *See Pages 69 to 72 and 'HBM'.* Have Plumber fix guttering and valley flashing if any. Roof insulation and cladding can then be carried out.

Step 6 Install windows and external joinery, and, at the same time, have Electrician and Plumber install wiring and pipe rough-in work.

Step 7 Insulation paper then exterior cladding is attached to walls. *See 'HBM'.*

Step 8 Arrange Local Council or other building inspection of framing.

Step 9 Construct eaves and soffit linings and install internal linings and mouldings.

Step 10 Plasterboard joints are finished. Decorate and finish off plumbing. Sand floors and finish off electrical.

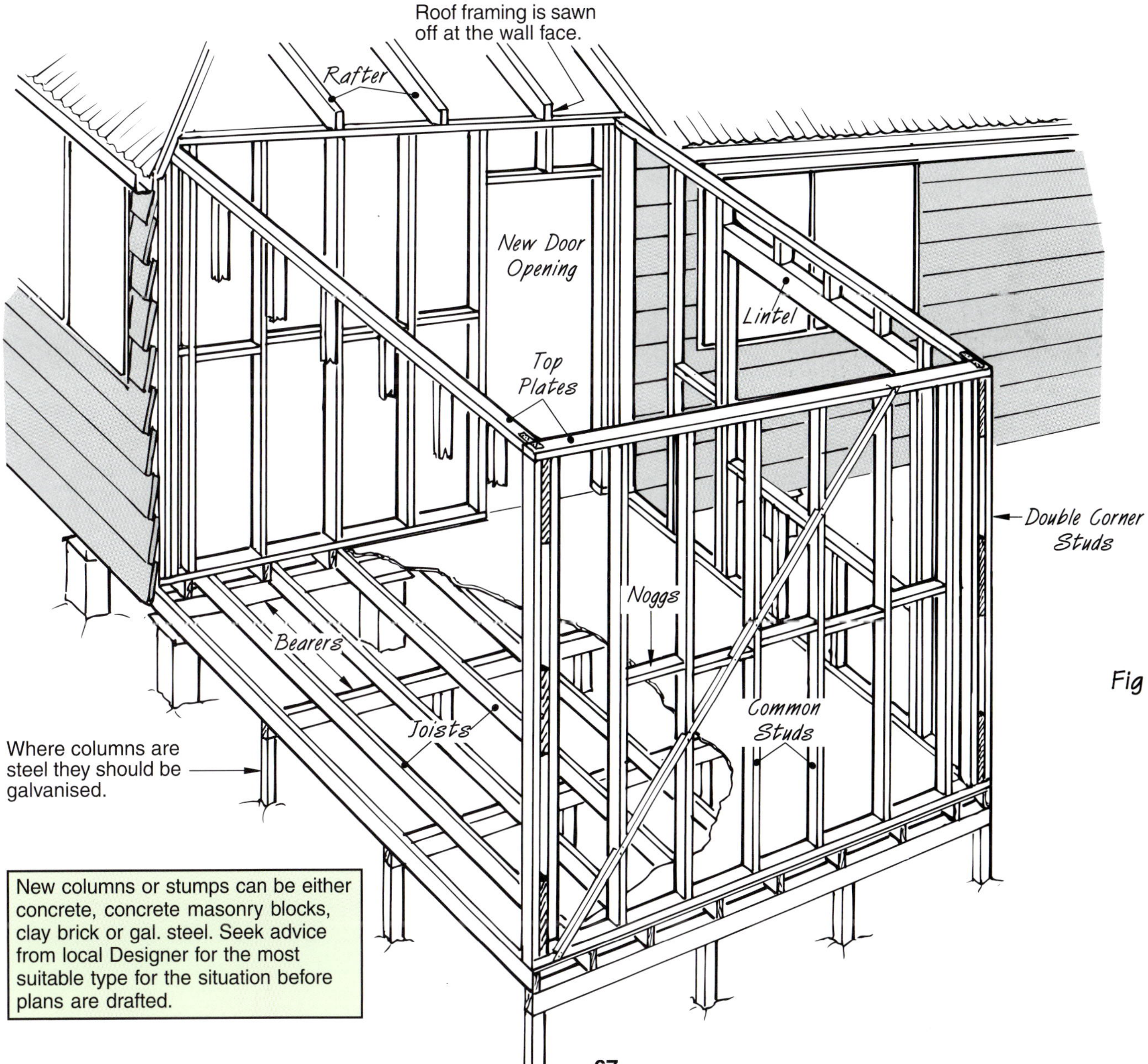

New columns or stumps can be either concrete, concrete masonry blocks, clay brick or gal. steel. Seek advice from local Designer for the most suitable type for the situation before plans are drafted.

Fig 1

Joining Weatherboards

Obtaining Matching Weatherboards

An existing board should be removed, preferably a short length, to use as a sample. A demolition supplier will often be able to supply your total requirement. Timber mills will cut new matching boards. This is often a better option because demolition timber is often extremely hard, requiring every nail hole to be pre-drilled to avoid splitting. Also some lending authorities may *not* approve the use of used materials. Specialist renovation stores may carry stocks of the weatherboard profile you are seeking.

Pre-prime All Weatherboards

All weatherboards should be given a coat of wood primer all round before fitting. All sawn ends should also be well primed.

Joining the New into the Old

The joins between the new weatherboards and those existing should *not* be made in a continuous straight vertical line up the wall if the 'added-on' look is to be avoided. On a wall without openings, it is best to stagger the joins as on the lower portion of the wall in fig 1. This is difficult to perform without removing the existing weatherboards.

If a window or door is not too far away from the join, it is best to remove the existing boards and continue the new ones through to the window or door. Where a vertical join is unavoidable, figs 2, 3, or 4 are often used. If fibre cement weatherboards are used, plastic jointer strips are applied to cover the join. However, joins should still be staggered.

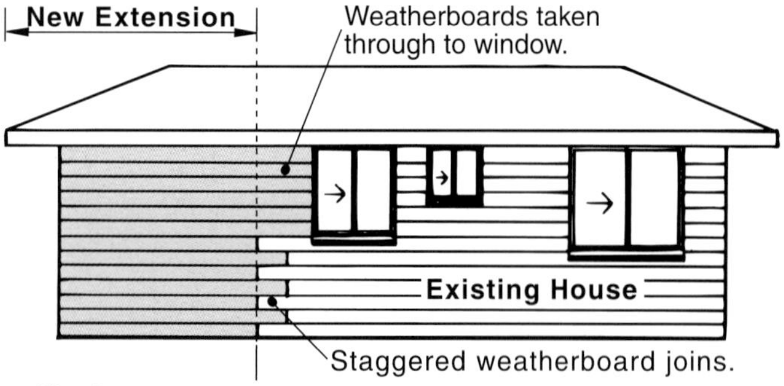

Fig 1

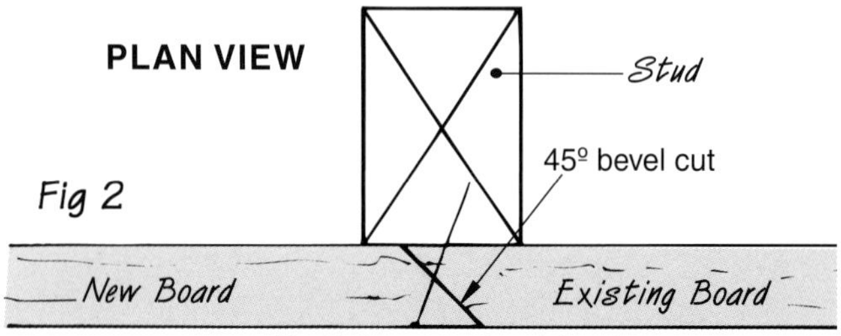

Fig 2

End joins are mitre joined.

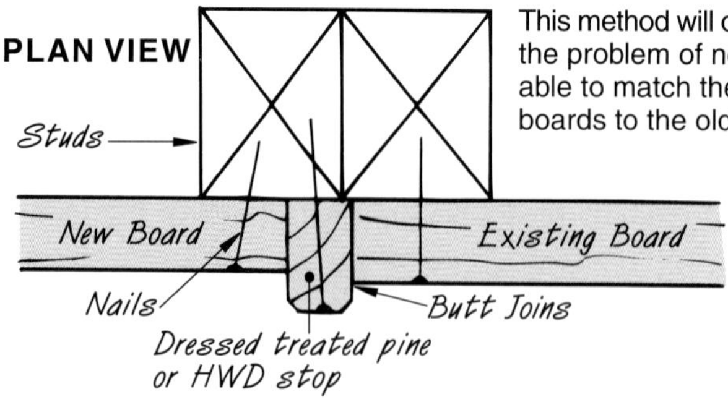

This method will overcome the problem of not being able to match the new boards to the old.

Fig 3

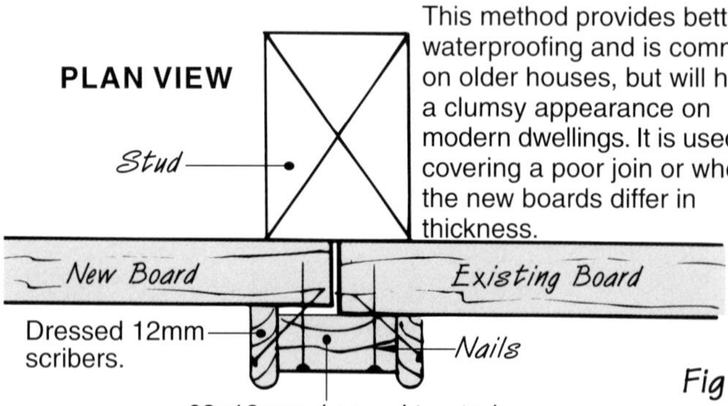

This method provides better waterproofing and is common on older houses, but will have a clumsy appearance on modern dwellings. It is used for covering a poor join or where the new boards differ in thickness.

Fig 4

Fig 5

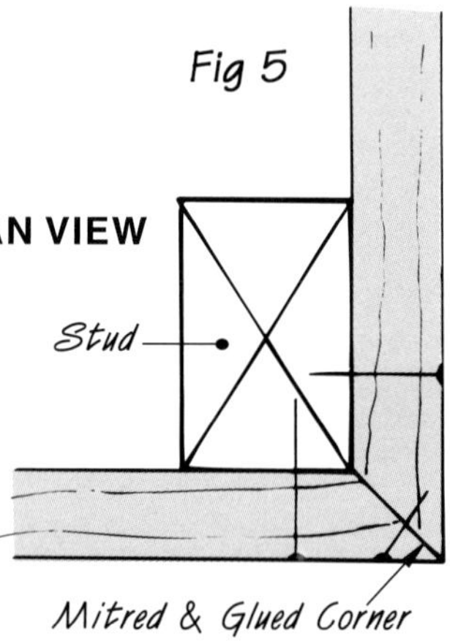

Fig 6

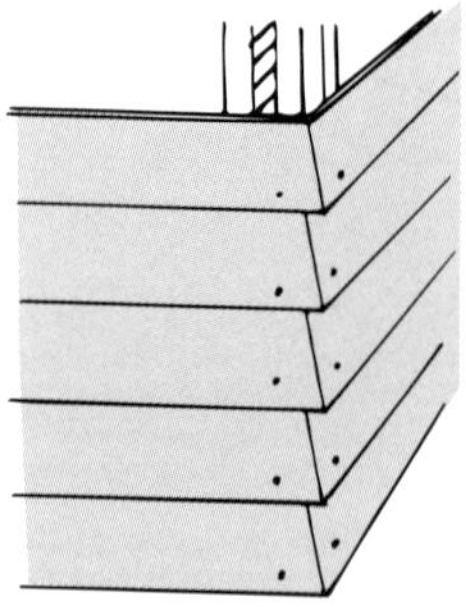

External corners mitred, glued and nailed.

ALTERNATIVE METHODS AT EXTERNAL CORNER

Fig 7

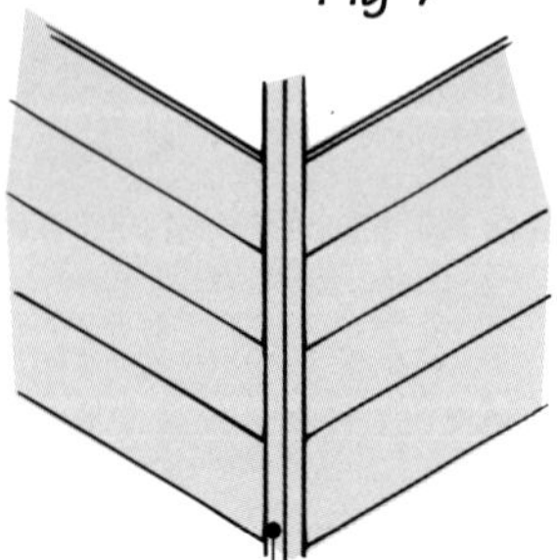

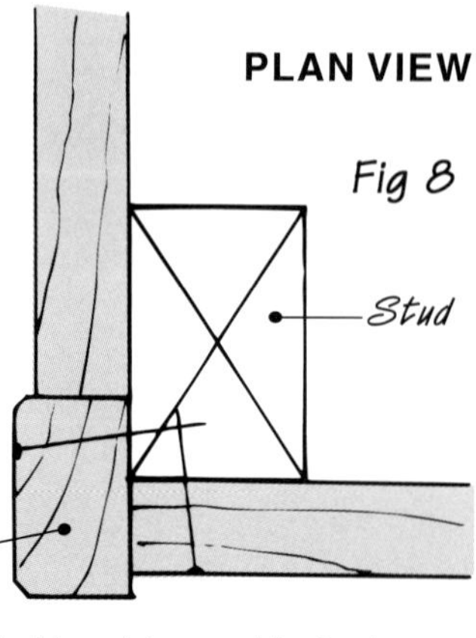

Fig 8

Weatherboards butt-jointed to a 'stop-end-batten' on external corners

Additions to Roofs (using Trusses)

Building the Extension Roof

The basic procedure described here through to Page 72 can be followed for any extension roof which is pitched with hips and valleys. It makes use of manufactured truss components where possible to simplify construction.

Constructing the Roof

Presuming all walls have been straightened, plumbed and braced, proceed as follows:

Step 1 The existing eaves are sawn off through the length of the extension.

Step 2 The station for each roof truss or rafter is marked on the wall top plates (see fig 2). When using trusses, the manufacturer can supply a layout plan.

> *Note:* the use of manufactured roof trusses on an extension roof will simplify and speed up construction time even if the existing roof was pitched using conventional cut-on-site methods. However, on most extensions some conventional roof work will be necessary where the new roof joins into the existing.

Fig 1

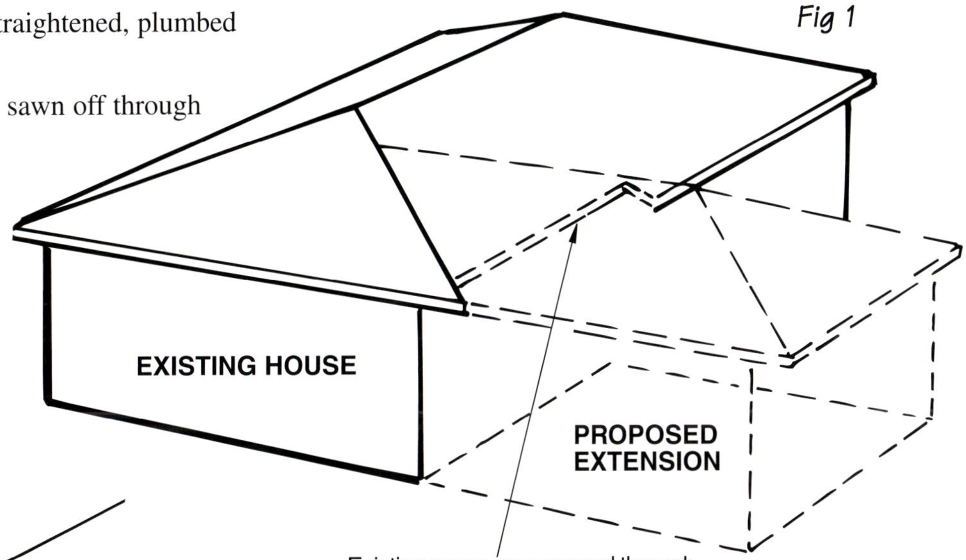

Fig 2

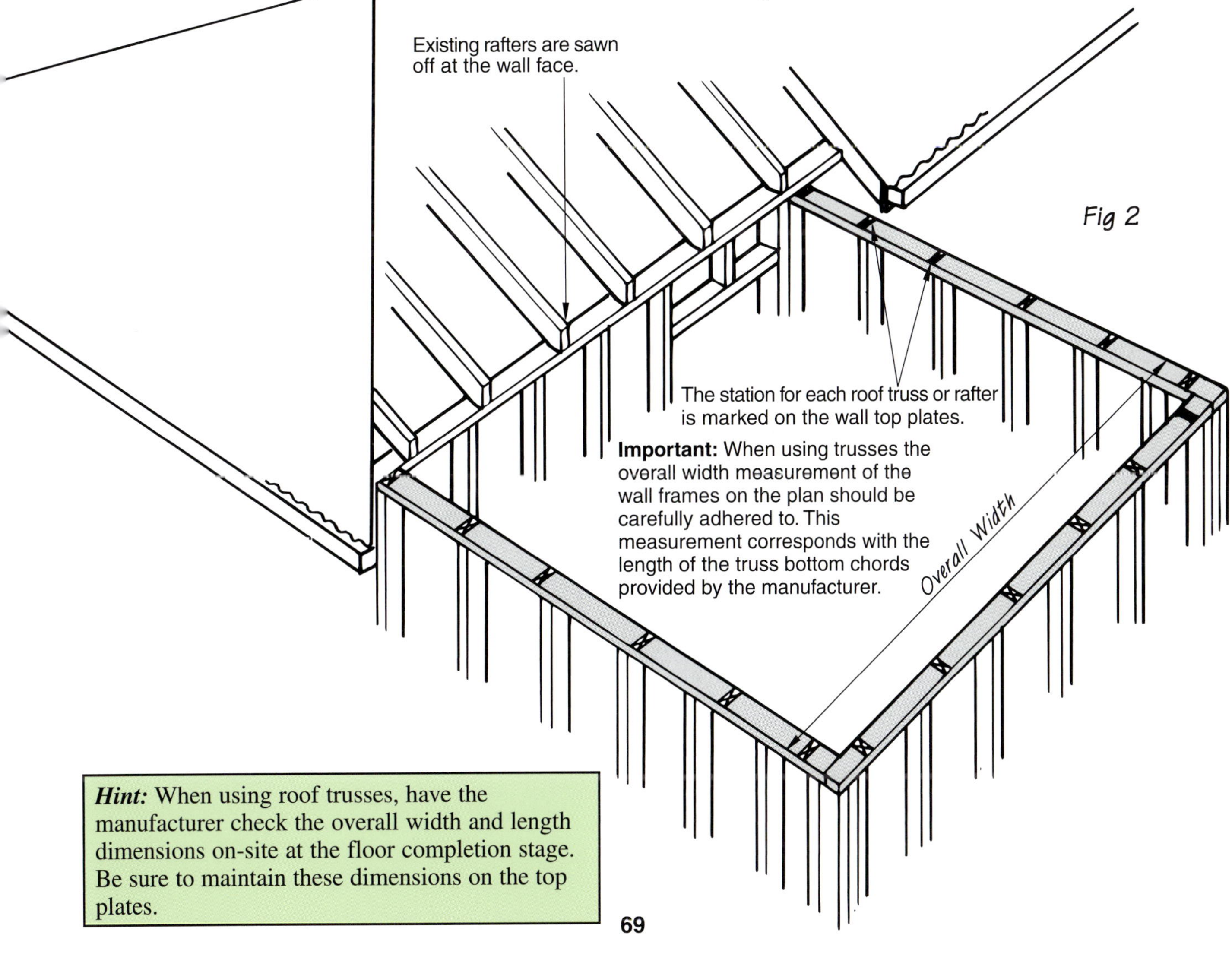

> *Hint:* When using roof trusses, have the manufacturer check the overall width and length dimensions on-site at the floor completion stage. Be sure to maintain these dimensions on the top plates.

Cont.

Each truss should be erected plumb but only tack each end temporarily for ease of correcting any errors later.

Step 3 Position truncated girder trusses first, then the truncated standard truss.

Step 4 Erect hip trusses. Their top ends may require bevelling off on their vertical sides to enable them to fit snugly together. Remaining jack trusses are then installed.

Step 5 The first standard truss next to the truncated standard truss is erected and braced. A string line is then attached to the apex and stretched tight through to the main roof. Ensure the string line is level.

On this type of extension, the string line is attached to the existing hip ensuring the string is square off the main building. This may require a slight adjustment sideways if the apex of standard truss 'A' does *not* line up with the string. On 'T' extensions as in figs 5 & 6. The string is attached to a nogg fixed between existing rafters.

Safety: Laws require the perimeter of roofs to be scaffolded with safety railing during construction.

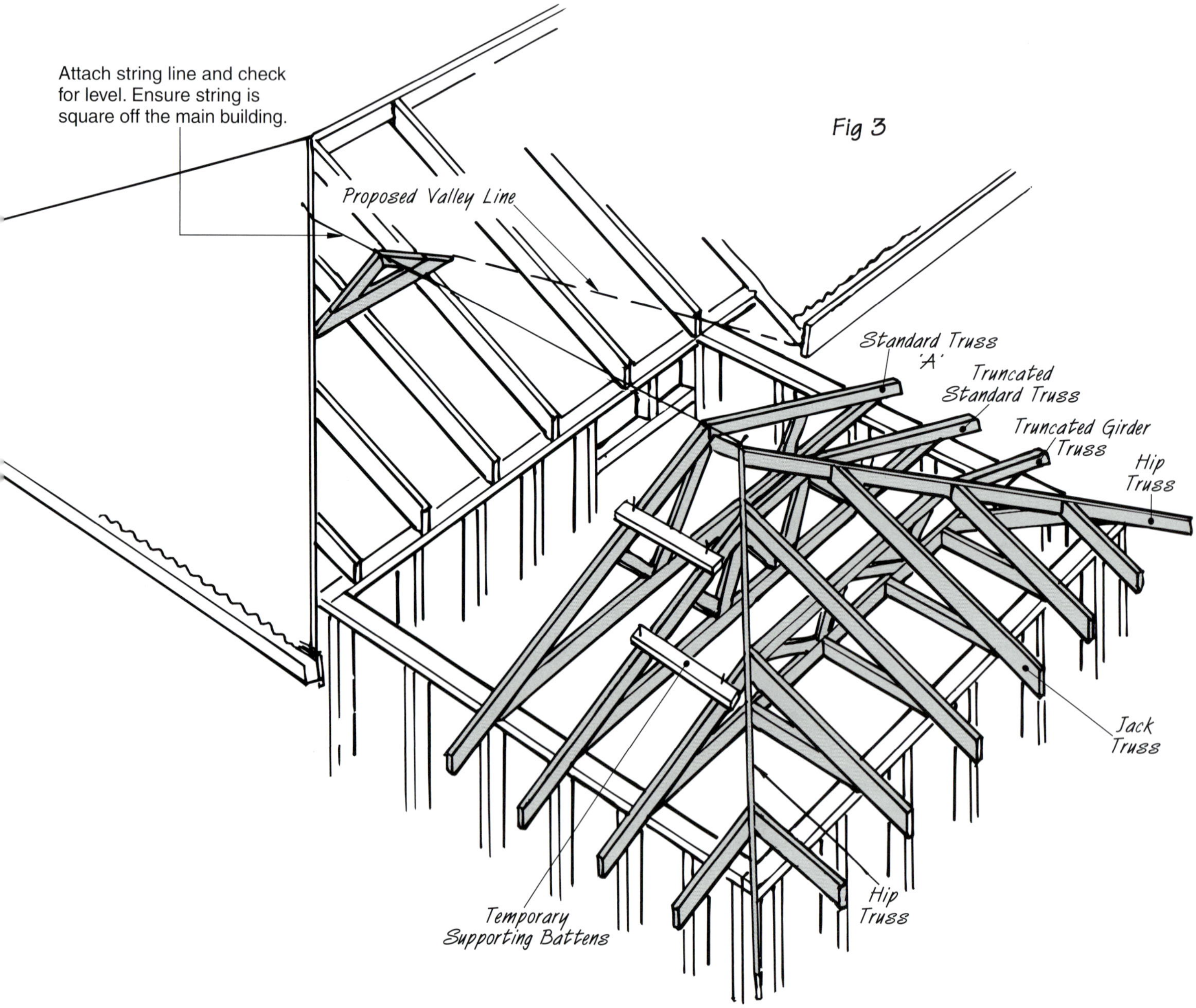

Cont.

Aligning Trusses on 'T' Extensions

Fig 6 illustrates the method of aligning 'T' shape extensions to the main roof. The hip end trusses and first standard truss are erected as on Page 70. Then the string line for aligning the remaining trusses is attached to the main roof, usually to a nogg fixed between existing rafters. Attach the string level and square off the main building as described previously.

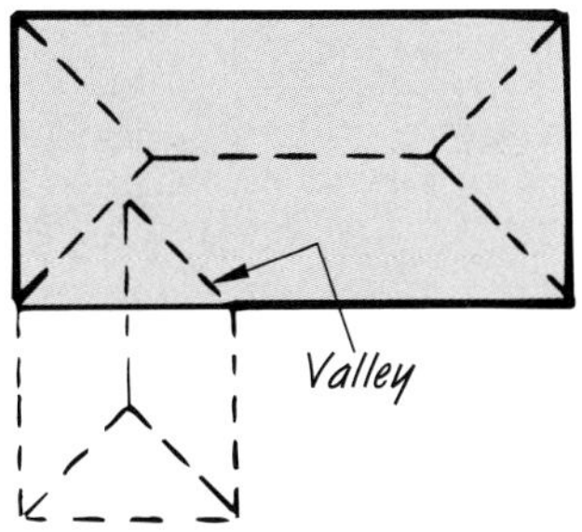

'L' Shape Extension

Fig 4

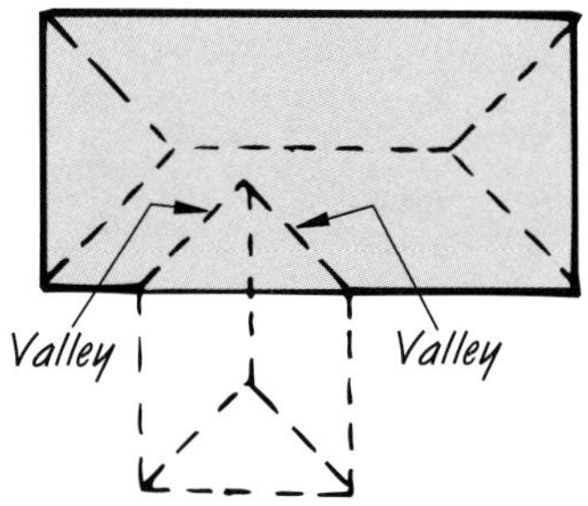

'T' Shape Extension

Fig 5

Fig 6

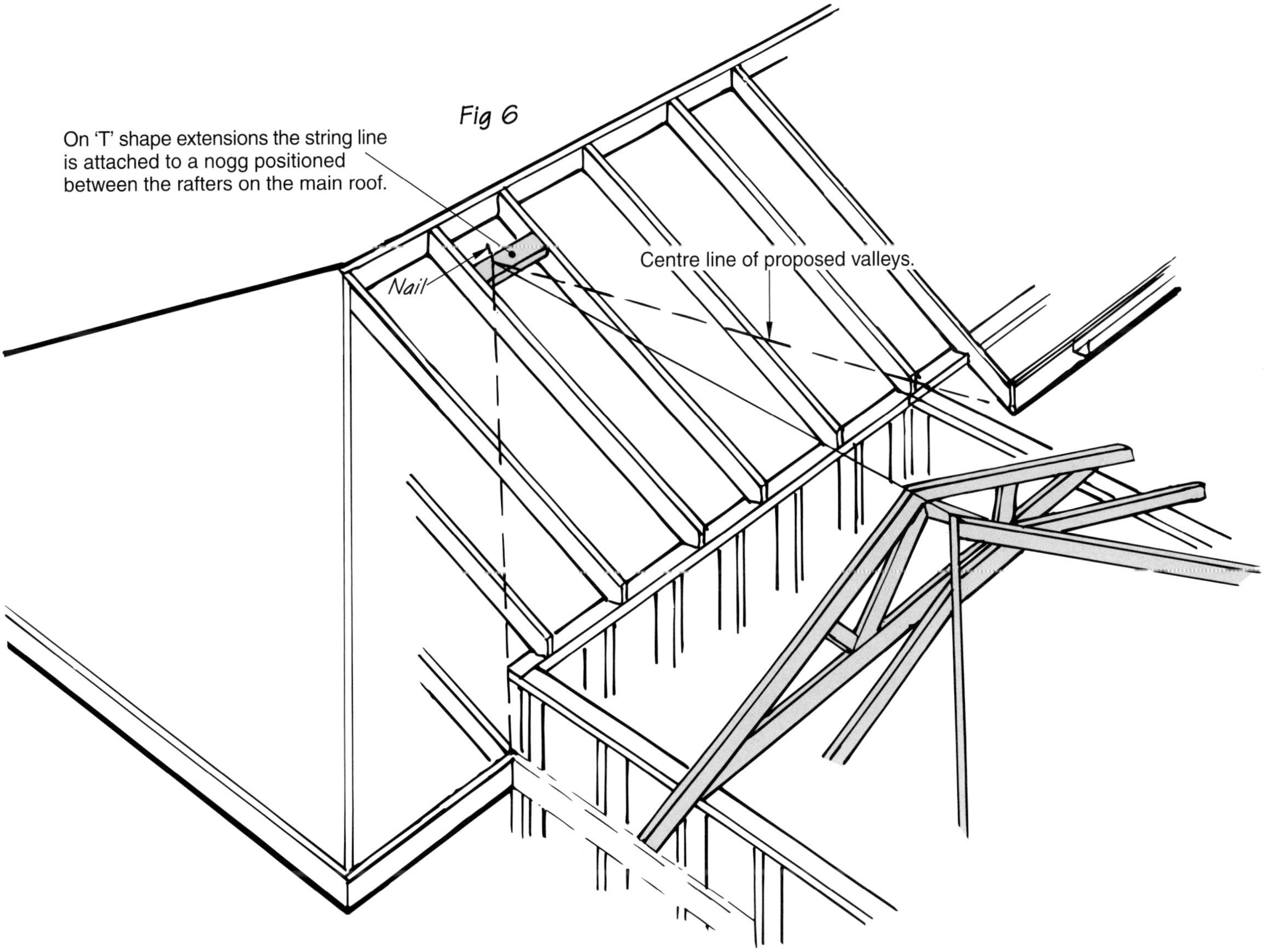

Cont.

Step 6 The remaining trusses are then installed with their apex aligning with the string line. When installing saddle trusses, it is usual to fix a roof batten through the lower side of each truss and attach the trusses to this batten. However, be sure these are square off the wall face to ensure the proposed valley line will be straight. Check the straightness of the valley line before fixing saddle trusses permanently.

Step 7 Attach all triple or multi grips or straps and any specified bracing.

Step 8 Fix fascia boards to a string line. Fix valley boards. The plumber is then required to attach guttering and valley flashing.

Step 9 The roof can then be battened and cladding fixed.

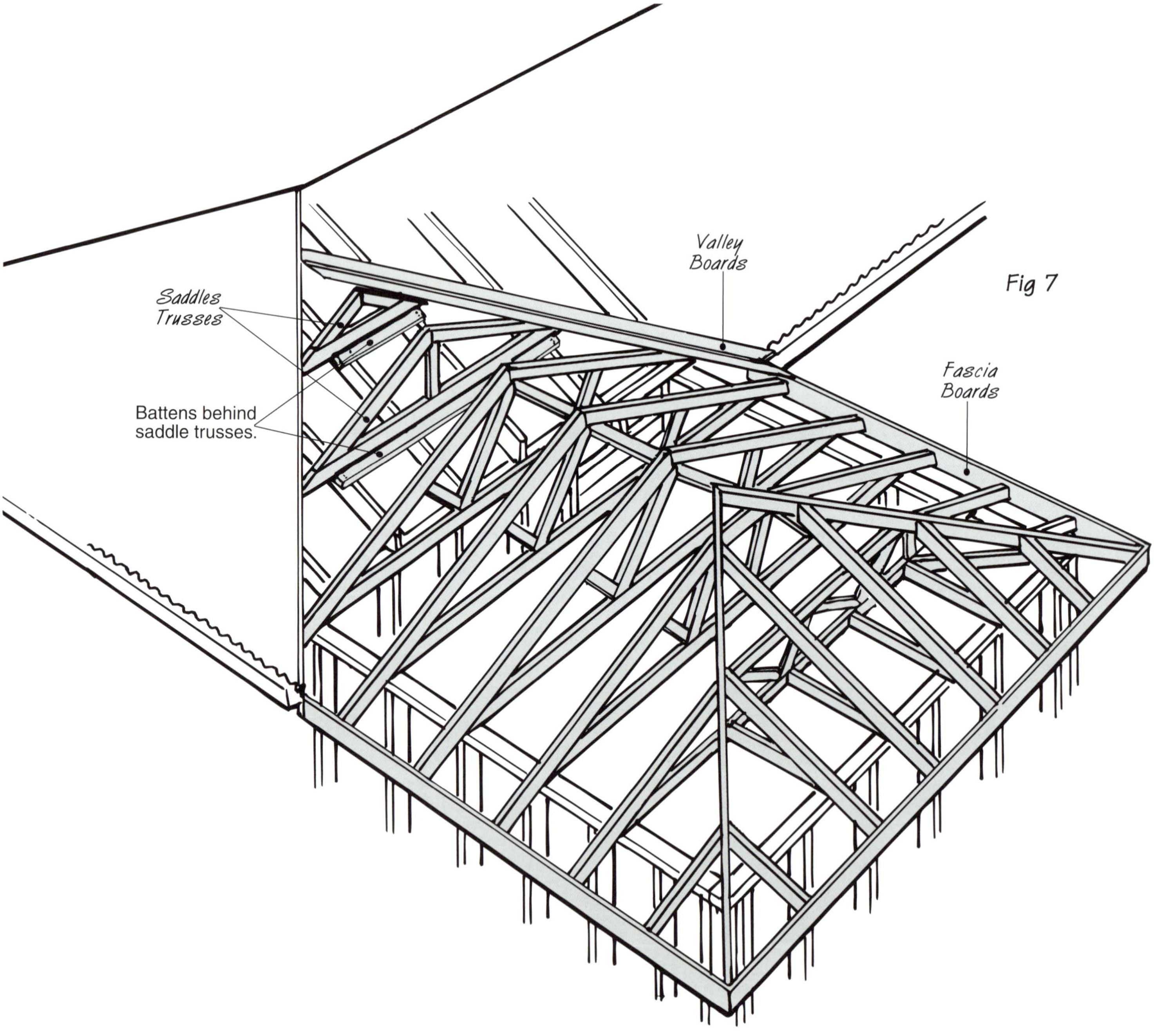

Fig 7

> ***Hint:*** Ensure the correct number of nails is used in each Triple or Multigrip. Short cutting in this tedious nailing job is a major cause for loss of roofs in storms (see the 'HBM').

Adding a Verandah or Carport

Attaching Roofs (for verandahs, patios or carports)

Attaching a cladded roof to existing fascia boards will place stresses on the existing rafter tie downs which may not have been designed to withstand. Ensure existing tie down is adequate or provide additional tie down. *See 'The Australian Decks & Pergolas Construction Manual' for detailed instructions.*

Waterproofing

Waterproofing of verandah roofs at the join to the existing house is often poorly carried out. As most verandah roofs are of a different pitch or a differing roofing material, special consideration is required.

Two methods are described here:

Method A. This simple method provides a waterproof joint, and long run roofing with low pitch capability can be used. The roofing material is folded up at the high end to prevent water penetration (see fig 3). A flashing is fitted also as in fig 2.

Method B. This method is superior to 'A', and will require more effort. If the profile in the new roofing material matches the existing, the guttering is removed and the new roofing is taken well up under the existing sheeting. One or two rows of nailing will have to be released on the existing sheets. If the pitch on the new roofing differs from the old, the new sheets will have to be pre-bent to the desired length (fig 4).

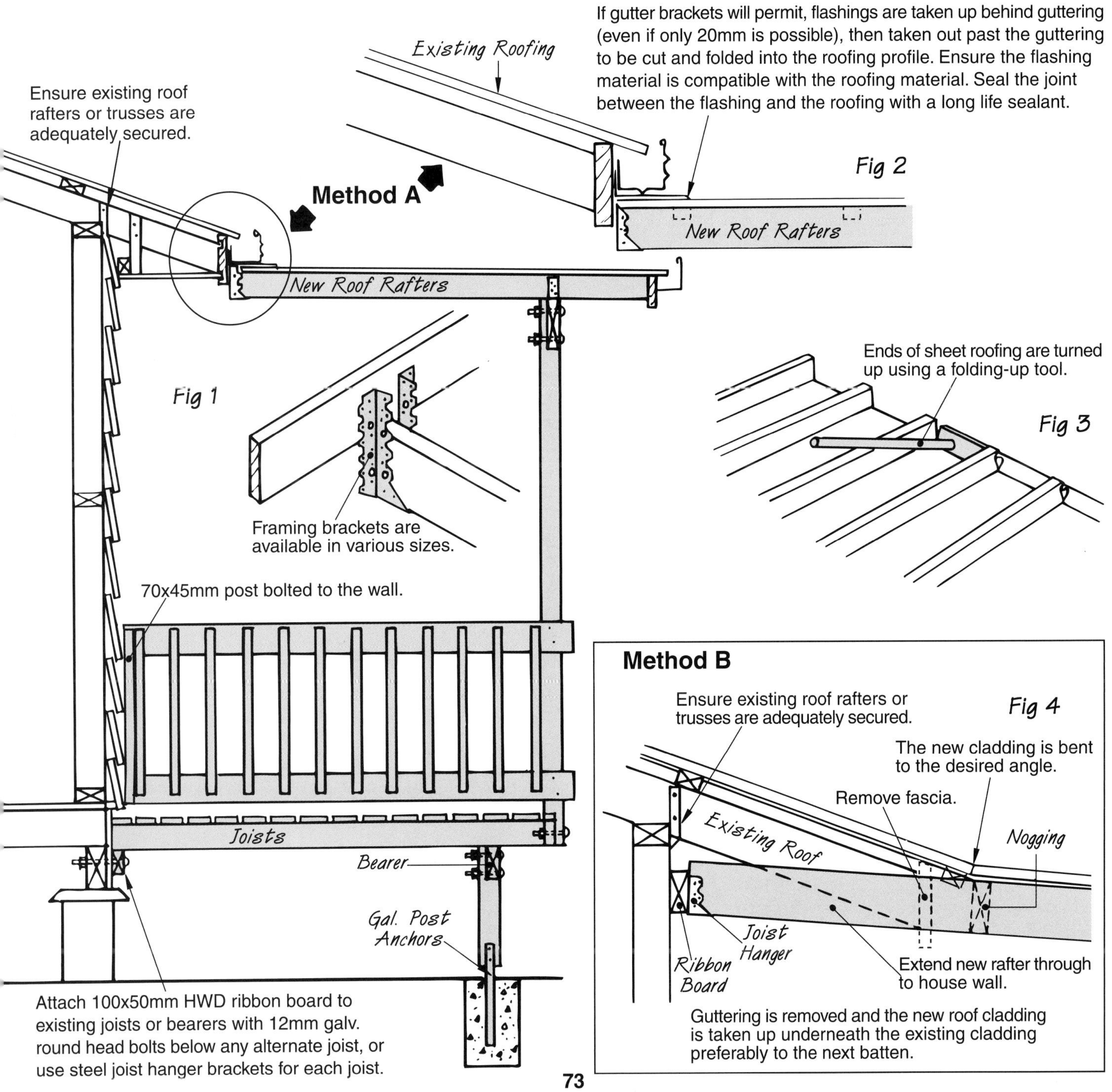

Carport Construction

Council approval must be obtained before constructing.

Constructing a Carport

Step 1 Establish position of carport and erect profile corners as on Pages 114 & 115. Set out all post positions on profiles.

Step 2 Two methods of construction are common for supporting beams.

Method A — erect and brace temporary posts of 100x50mm to support the two side beams. Establish the beams level and complete the roof. Then dig the holes. -Working on sawstools, attach the galvanised MS post stirrups to the permanent posts. Pour concrete then install and plumb posts while concrete is setting.

Method B — dig holes first, pour concrete and insert post stirrups adjusting them into alignment to a string line. Then after a day or so, attach posts plumb and temporarily brace.

Some high wind areas may require the rafters to be strapped to the beams. Wall bracing is applied to one end and one side as indicated by the dotted lines.

Bracing

Although wood compression braces have been illustrated, in the typical plan gal. steel braces could be applied. This should be indicated on the plans. Wood braces should be bolted or strapped each end to the adjoining members.

TYPICAL CARPORT PLAN

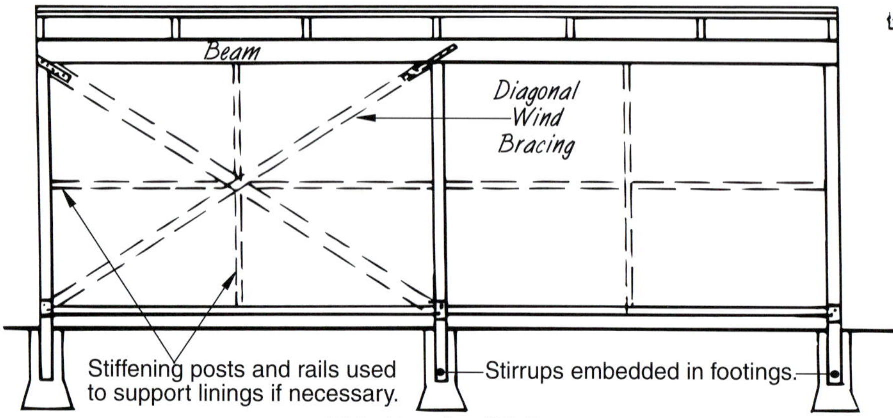

Side Bracing Wall

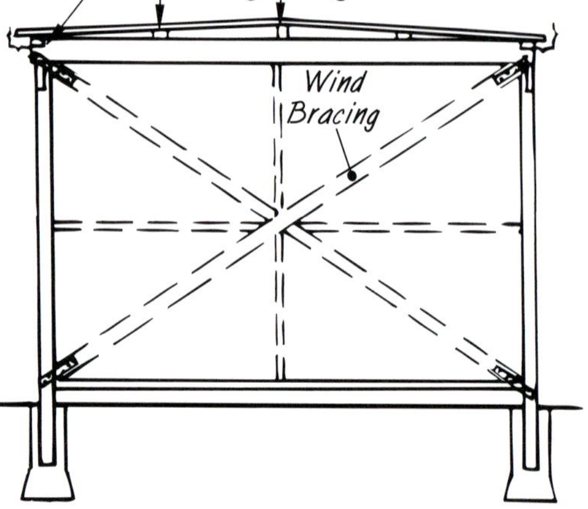

End Bracing Wall

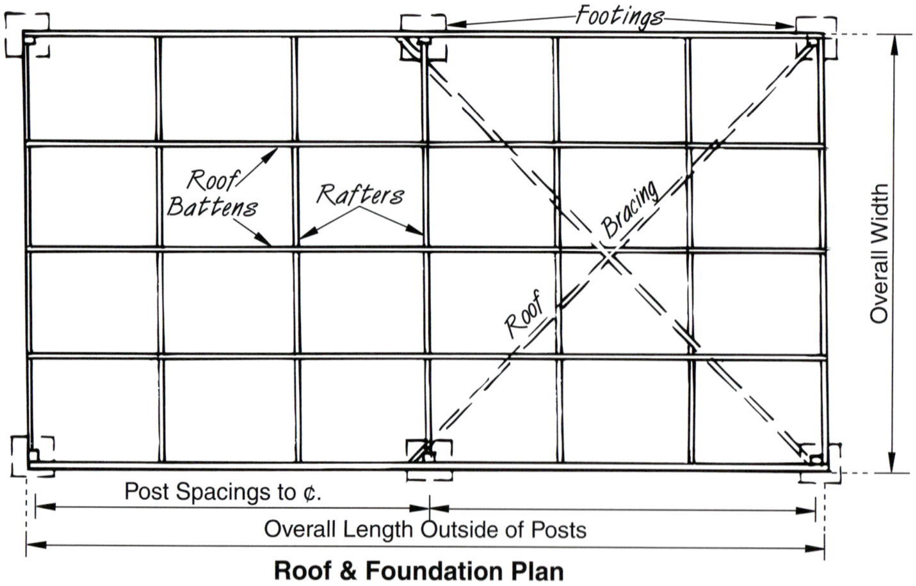

Roof & Foundation Plan

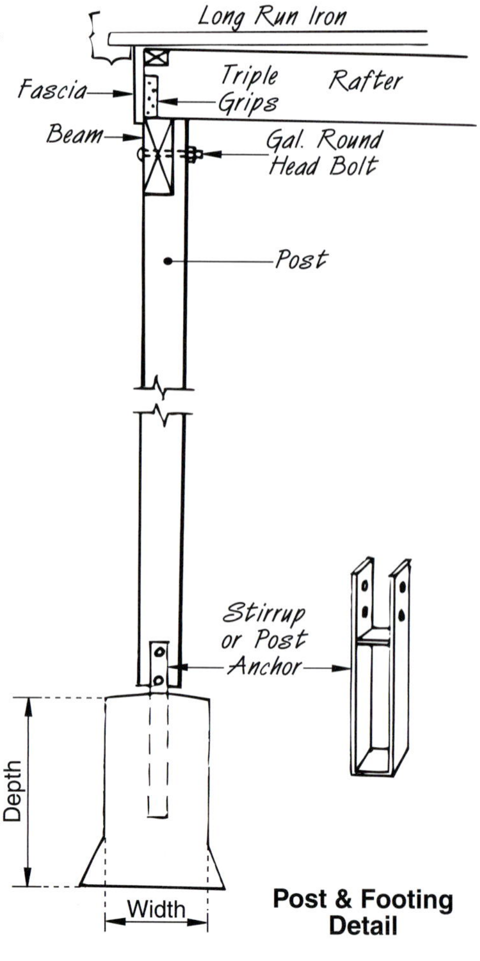

Post & Footing Detail

Carports Attached to the House

It is important to ensure that where the carport is attached to the existing house fascia board that the existing house roof rafters are adequately secured to the walls. This is because those rafters will have to resist additional uplift forces from the new carport rafters. *See 'The Australian Decks & Pergolas Construction Manual' for detailed drawings.*

Buying a House to Renovate

What to Look for:

It is advisable to obtain a building survey and report of the house prior to purchase.

Termites

Where termites are in evidence, the purchase should *not* be considered as it is so difficult to determine the extent of the damage. When buying any house, a Pest Controller should be employed to carry out an inspection and issue a report or clearance certificate.

Structural Soundness

This refers to walls, roof and floor and if acceptably straight, level and plumb. Look for floors that feel like they have slope or doors that are jamming. This may mean a restumping job (which will very often straighten out any roof hollows as well).
See the 'Australian Renovator's Manual' for 'How to Restump'.

Structural soundness should also include that the structure is free of rot. This mainly occurs in material and framing in wet areas behind baths, sinks, basins, shower recesses and laundry tubs. Look for wrinkly paint or if the surface materials and paint have been recently renewed. This may indicate that the renewal was only cosmetic. You may require a skilled professional to inspect for this.

Watertightness from Weather

Repeated water penetration will often cause dry rot in the corners of sills, at joints and in the timber wall, floor or roof framing surrounding these areas.

If the house has been recently repainted, it is possible that signs of water penetration have been concealed. In this case, under floor and ceiling inspections are essential. Check around and under all plumbing fixtures and wastepipes for continually leaking water. These leaks will certainly rot surrounding timber framing. Check timber mouldings around fixtures with your finger nail. It is easy to penetrate rotted timber even if it has been repainted.

Electrical

In many older houses, the wiring insulation has perished or it may *not* be adequate to handle the additional outlets proposed. Rewiring may be necessary.

Plumbing

Check the following:

a). How old is the hot water system? The average system has a life span of seven to ten years.

b). What is the water pressure like?

c). Very old houses have lead waterpipes. These should be replaced.

Drainage

Does the site have adequate surface water drainage to prevent flooding? Ask if there are repeated problems with blocked drains. This could indicate faulty or badly laid drainage or roots from a neighbouring large tree.

Rising Damp

Inadequate or omission of damp proof courses or poor mortar can cause dampness to rise into brickwork. Deterioration is evident if the bricks are discoloured and crumbling. Brick courses nearer the ground should be checked.

To install a new damp proof course requires a portable power saw with a masonry blade to remove the existing mortar joint. Any remaining mortar is chiselled out. The damp proof course is then laid in place and new mortar tooled into the joint. This is done in short sections. The damp proof course must overlap each preceding piece. There are contractors who specialise in this work. Dampness can also rise into the lowest floor members. This will be evident by areas of discolouration and cheesy or soft wood, easily penetrated by a sharp object. If the rot has only affected a limited area or member of timber, the problem can be rectified without too much difficulty. New bearers or joists can be laid beside the old ones.

If dampness is underneath the house, the entire ground may need to be sealed with heavyweight polythene. All joins in the polythene are sealed with pressure sensitive tape. Alternatively, waterproof concrete laid over the area. If the problem is inability of moisture to dry out because of inadequate ventilation, then extra ventilators should be fitted.

IMPORTANT NOTES:

a). When buying a house, check all windows and doors for binding.

If this is evident on a number of doors, this could have been caused by one of the following:

1. The house timber contained a high moisture content when built resulting in more than normal shrinkage. The problem should *not* reoccur. All that is required is to dress the offending windows and doors with a plane.

2. Foundations poorly designed and constructed for the soil type. If plastic clays are present then this is a problem that will re-occur in every drought and every wet season. Check if neighbouring houses have cracked brick base walls or if the fences, gates or posts are crooked. This can also be an indication of plastic soils.

b). If you plan to extend the house, check boundary clearances. In many instances, you may only be able to extend at the rear or on a side which does *not* receive light or breeze, or is unsuitable to your proposed room layout.

Cont.

The Renovation Program

The decision to either 'build new' or 'buy old' and renovate is often the result of such factors as desirable site situation, nearness of transport etc, as well as the availability of money from lending authorities. It is often the case that lending authorities will finance an existing house and then advance a personal loan to carry out renovations.

Points to consider for the buying & renovation option:

1. The House should be basically Sound

Most lending authorities will *not* lend unless their inspector has checked the basic soundness of the dwelling. They often will require a certificate that there is *no* termite infestation. However, it is important for the Owner Builder to establish the extent of renovation required.

It is worth the expense of engaging an advisor to list the defects to ascertain the viability of renovating. Often the cost of alterations, extensions and renovation plus the initial outlay is more than the cost of a new dwelling.

2. Establish an Overall Renovation Plan (and the cost of work before commencing)

A plan should be properly prepared by a Draftsperson in consideration of the following:

a). The most aesthetically desirable position of any extensions as well as aspect and cost efficiency (*see fig 1, Page 57*).

b). Structural considerations such as foundation capacity, positioning or removing of load bearing walls.

c). Local Council regulations such as distance from boundaries, percentage of land permitted to be covered by buildings.

3. Divide the Job into Bite Sized Sections

Each portion of the work is part of the overall plan and should be carried out in a logical sequence to benefit the progression of the entire job.

4. Where to Start

Priorities should be dealt with first:

a). *Waterproofing* — that is, roofing, windows and doors but waterproofing of windows and doors may have to come after 'c'.

b). *Electrical* — rewiring if necessary.

c). *Foundations and damp proofing* — any restumping and placing of damp proof courses should be rectified at this stage.

d). *Other structural work* — such as studs, braces, supports when removing walls and relining.

After these have been completed, then decorating can begin. Decorating is last on the agenda because on-going construction work can fracture finished plaster and paintwork.

Raising a House or Positioning a Removal House

Note: Obtain approval from local building authorities.

Fig 1

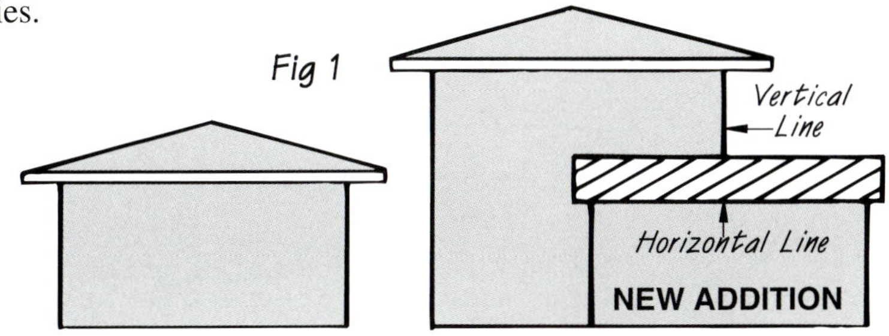

RAISED HOUSE

When the horizontal lines extend across the original vertical one, the top heavy appearance is not only disguised, but the renovation can be greatly enhanced in appearance.

Three benefits of raising a house are:

a). Doubling of existing floor area without a loss in land area. In fact, if the existing house is raised and cantilevered over a new basement, the land area is actually increased.

b). That it can be lived in whilst the work is being carried out underneath.

c). The existing floor area can be doubled in size without requiring additional roofing.

Design is Important

When raising a house, care with the design is important to avoid the top heavy look, especially when the full 2400mm head height is required underneath. This problem can be greatly alleviated by extending balconies, garages or rooms past or over the existing basement area as in fig 1. A Designer should be consulted to obtain a satisfactory proposed front view.

Organisation & Co-operation is the Key

Cracking of wall board lining at corners and joints when raising can be reduced to almost nil if sufficient man power is used to raise all jack points at the same time. Once foundation and fitting connections (that is, bolts, ties or nails), plumbing and drainage pipelines have been released, then the house can be raised in one day. Organisation and co-operation with the Plumber, Drainer and Electrician is the key to a speedy house raising job. The house is temporarily supported by three or four steel joists or RSJ's laid through the length of the house. These joists are resting on sties (criss cross stacks of railway sleepers or 150x150mm timbers). The house is raised using bottle or wallaby jacks. As the house is raised the sty timbers are slid into place. Each steel joist will require three or four pig sties through its length. A house lifting contractor should be used for the actual lift. This will avoid many problems associated with obtaining the necessary equipment.

Raising the House

Step 1 Remove all baseboards and release all bolts or hardware that are holding the house down or are connected to the house. Also disconnect all plumbing and drainage pipelines. This could all be carried out prior to employing the house lifter, to reduce costs.

Step 2 The temporary RSJ's are then positioned and the first sty timbers are bedded nice and firmly into the ground under the RSJ's (see fig 3). The jacks are positioned and if the manpower is available, all jacks raised at the same time. This is the ideal. As sufficient height is gained, extra sty timbers are slid into place. This process is repeated until the required height is obtained.

Step 3 Temporary steps are installed and the Plumber and Drainer are required to connect temporary water pipes and drainage waste pipes if the house is to remain occupied.

Step 4 Footings for new external walls are excavated, reinforced and concreted.

> *Important:*
>
> **a).** Keep all sties away from the line of proposed new supporting walls or columns and their footings.
>
> **b).** The house is raised approx. 100-150mm higher than required to enable easy installation of load bearing walls.

Step 5 *Construction of external load bearing walls are as follows:*

For Weatherboard

A concrete nib is required to seat the walls on (see fig 4). This is formed and concreted at the same time as the footings. Holding down bolts are positioned along the nib at 1200mm centres. Although it is normal to build timber framed walls directly onto the slab floor, this is difficult to carry out on a raised house because the sties are still in place.

For Brick Veneer

The same procedure as for weatherboard. The brick veneer is built after windows, doors etc have been installed (see fig 5).

For Cavity Brick

The two brick cavity walls are constructed. Building codes do *not* permit a single brick leaf to temporarily support the house whilst building the other leaf. Remember to install holding down straps into the brick joints to tie down the top wall plate or bearers. If in high wind areas, use cyclone anchor bolts taken from the footings (see fig 6).

For Concrete Block

Blocks are laid directly onto the footings which contains starter bars. Walls are constructed and reinforcing installed in the stipulated cores and grout poured.

Step 6 After walls are constructed, the house can be lowered and secured to those walls. All sties removed and those centrally located replaced with 100x100mm temporary timber toms (or adjustable steel props). These are firmly braced in position both ways. Alternatively, any permanent beams can be fixed in place with supporting timber or steel posts permanently concreted in place. Where proposed walls occur, the posts may later be concealed within these walls.

Fig 2

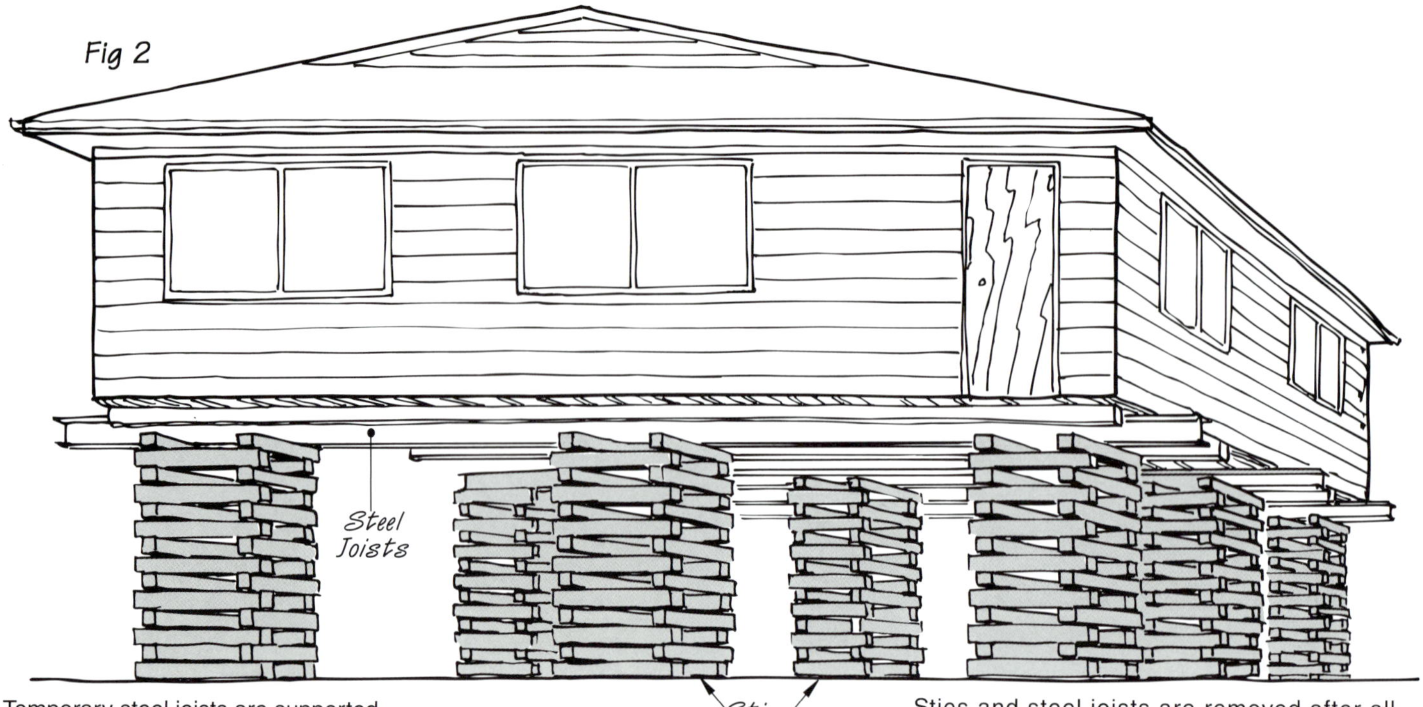

Temporary steel joists are supported along their length by three or four sties. These sties must be kept clear of the line of proposed walls and columns and their footings.

Sties and steel joists are removed after all supporting base walls and/or columns built.

Important: Ensure the top of all walls are level throughout, or at least level at all bearing points, before lowering the house.

Fig 3

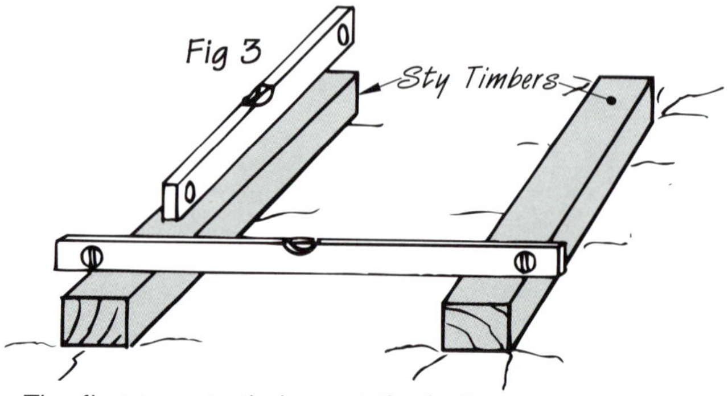

The first two sty timbers at the bottom of each stack should be firmly bedded in the ground level both ways.

Step 7 The concrete slab floor is then laid.

Step 8 All internal partitions are erected and temporary toms removed.

Step 9 All finishing work can now be carried out.

TIMBER FRAME WALL

Fig 4

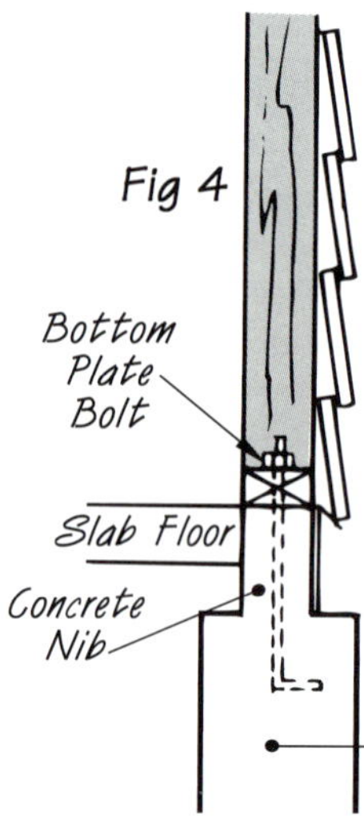

BRICK VENEER WALL

Fig 5

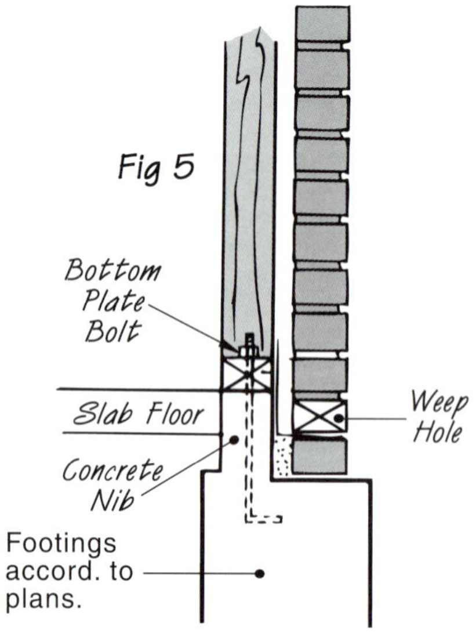

The concrete nib is built to a height of 300mm above finished ground level or according to Local Council requirements. 12mm bolts are positioned along the nib at 1200mm centres maximum also beside doorways and at all internal and external corners.

CAVITY BRICK WALL

Fig 6

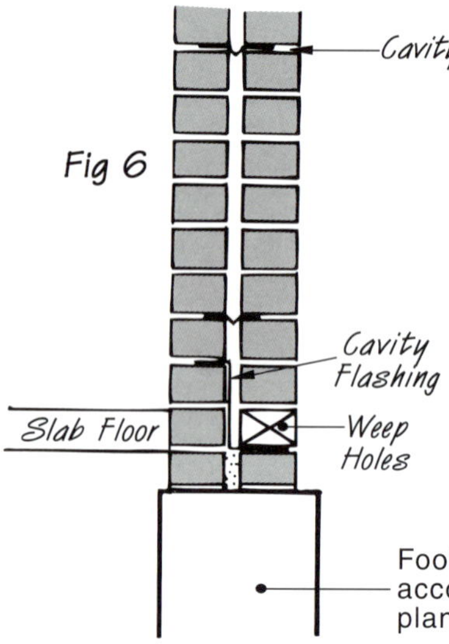

Both brick leaves are built and the concrete floor poured separate from the wall.

CONCRETE BLOCK MASONRY WALL

Fig 7

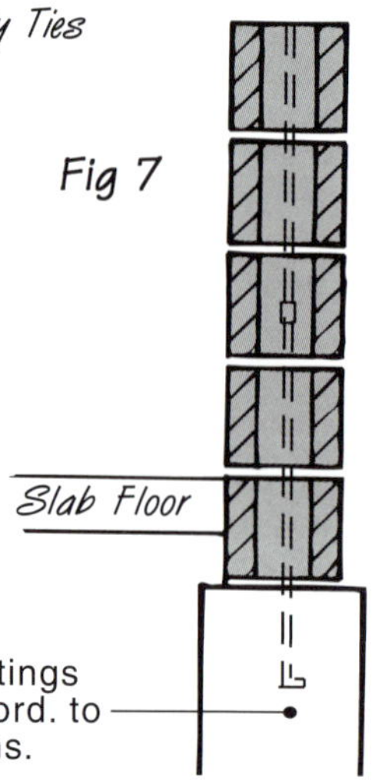

For construction details on 'Concrete Block Masonry Construction' see Pages 47-55.

Planning, Specifications, Sub-contractors & Materials

5

Plan Preparation

A plan is a legal document and should be accompanied by specifications which should contain details of material sizes and methods of construction. Detailed information is particularly important to the owner builder. A scanty plan that will pass minimum council requirements can cause frustration and can result in very costly errors and on-site disputes with subcontractors.

> *Important:* After completion of the house, the plans should be stored in a safe place for future reference.

Establishing the Design

External Appearance

You need to be able to give the designer a developed brief of the style of home design you want.

Room Sizes

These can be established by measuring the rooms you presently live in and simply increasing or decreasing them to suit.

Roof Design

Roof pitch and style, eaves and gable verge widths vitally effect the final appearance of a home. Common pitches today are around 20°. If you are uncertain which pitch to use, designers using computers are easily able to provide a preview of your design with varying pitches.

Windows & Exterior Doors

Size and positioning of windows and exterior doors also impact on the final external appearance. Keep in mind the designer has to locate wall bracing in walls to maintain a structurally sound building. Should you decide to have very large areas of glass you could be limiting bracing placement. The designer can advise.

Remember that elevation appearances of a design will generally appear the same on the completed house taking into consideration the final viewing position as related to ground slope. What this means is that if an elevation view on the house plan appears either out of balance or lacking something, then those faults will *not* go away after construction. So with that in mind, be sure the designer establishes the elevations to your satisfaction before plans are finally printed.

Approaching a Designer

Request addresses of homes previously designed. Obtain at least two quotes.

It is advisable before approaching a Designer to have at least established the floor plan 1:50 (or 1/4") scale. Remember to include the thickness of the walls plus the room sizes.

Also indicate the following in your preliminary drawing:

a). Position and size of the windows and doors.

b). Types of doors and the direction of swing. Cupboards and cabinet layouts.

c). Size and position of all prime cost items, that is, bath, shower, vanity, sink, stove, microwave oven, dishwasher, fridge, tub, clothes dryer etc.

This does require time and effort. It's better to put time into good planning at this stage than to be disappointed later with design faults.

Always try to imagine the consequences of design decisions such as 'If I do this with this element, how will it affect an adjacent element or its effects on sunlight, space, accessibility and comfort, etc'.

> *Notes:* **a).** For comprehensive details on what house plans should contain, see the 'HBM'.
>
> **b).** After plans are completed have the on-site set laminated to withstand rough handling.

How to Obtain Quality Tradeswork

Much of the joy of house building can be spoiled by poor quality tradework. After one has paid thousands of dollars for materials and labour, it is disappointing to find the workmanship is below standard. The only way to maintain quality tradework is to have detailed specifications.

What are Specifications?

The specifications referred to here are a set of documents in booklet form and accompany the plans. Both plans and specifications are legal documents and can be used as a guideline should any dispute arise. Specifications are mainly concerned with the quality of the tradework and materials.

Local building authorities *do not* always require a booklet type specifications accompanying the plans. They do require the plans to contain a full description of the dimensions of all structural timbers and their species, steel reinforcing and their locations, all wall and roof fixing, anchoring and bracing details etc. The plans should also contain notations that the house will be constructed according to the building codes acceptable to the Local building authorities.

How Do Specifications Safeguard the Owner Builder?

Specifications are the Owner Builder's watchdog, protecting him/her from tradespeople who apply underhand and short cut methods. Without specifications, the Owner Builder is really at their mercy with regards to the materials they use and the quality of their work.

For instance, full specifications in booklet form will detail the correct mixture for making concrete and bricklaying mortar, the requirements for the correct placing of reinforcing. Also the minimum quality standards are laid down for proper bricklaying, carpentry, plumbing, drainage, electrical and all other tradeswork. These items are *not* mentioned in the house plans, so without detailed specifications a wide open door exists for faulty or poor quality standard of workmanship to occur. Owner Builders approaching lending authorities will enhance their application for loans if the submitted plan is also accompanied by a complete specification.

Where to Obtain Specifications?

The Builder's Associations is some States have standard specification booklets available for sale to the public. Enquire at your local Master Builders or HIA office.

Some lending authorities have produced their own acceptable standards of construction booklets which are also a specification. When adopting a standard specification, a line is ruled through all clauses *not* applicable to the house being constructed and any additional clauses required in the agenda are inserted.

Policing the Specifications

When a quotation is accepted on the basis of the plans and specification, the subcontractors are asked to sign a copy of the specifications and plans in agreement that they will carry out their tradework in accordance with them. They then become a binding legal document.

During construction, the Owner Builder should read the portion of the specification relating to the particular tradework under construction. If the Owner Builder is sure the work is *not* being carried out according to the plans and specifications, he/she should ask the particular tradesperson to rectify the work. If he is unsure if the work is being carried out as specified, he should seek advice from the Local Building Inspector or Certifier before advising the tradesperson. Policing construction work should be done with a proportion of good sense and fair play.

Employing Sub-contractors or Employees

Obtaining Quotations

a). It is usual to obtain two or three quotations in writing and signed.

b). Make all the conditions clear, any alterations to the plan, method of payment whether weekly or in stages.

c). Ask Subcontractors to provide addresses of previously completed work for you or a Tradesperson to inspect.

d). Beware of Subcontractors who are only temporarily in the district.

e). After accepting a quotation, make an agreement in writing on the quotation stating method of payment, whether in weekly draws or at specific stages. Include the date and signatures of both parties.

Clarify with the Subcontractor the following:

a). Ask to sight the current Contractor's Licence. Does it containlimitations?

b). Current insurance cover for his/her employees plus third party. Is it adequate?

c). Which party is to provide and erect scaffolding.

d). Which party is to perform the cleaning up of the site during construction and on completion.

Keeping Records

It is important to keep all records such as:
Receipts, Inspection Certificates or slips, order numbers, guarantees, payment receipts, concrete dockets (stating the quality, strength and slump figures) and Termite Treatment Certificates etc.

Making Payments

Request an account in writing stating material and labour used to that stage. It should carry the tradesperson's ABN number and Licence number.

Where tradeswork can only be completed in part, it is acceptable practice to retain 5-10% of monies until the remaining work is completed.

5-10% of monies can sometimes be held for thirty days from some manufactured goods where faults could arise within thirty days.

Where inspection of work is to be carried out by any Authorities, withhold payment until such inspections are made. However, be sure to have this as a condition written into the sub-contract agreement.

Local Building Authority or Certifier Inspections are generally carried out for the following stages:

1. ***Footings prior to pouring concrete***
2. ***Slab Floor***
3. ***Frame prior to interior lining***
4. ***Completion of House***

Prescribed Payments' Requirement

The owner builder must register with the tax office as an owner builder under the 'prescribed payments' system. The prescribed rate of tax is deducted by the owner builder from all payments made to contractors or subcontractors. This is sent with the relevant form to your local tax office. A booklet on the 'prescribed payments' system is also available from the tax office.

Do's & Don'ts When Employing Tradespersons

1. *Don't* be aggressive in your requests to workmen on the site. This engenders hard feelings and undoubtedly will lose co-operation and harmony.
2. *Do* leave Tradespersons alone to carry out their work, if and when your assistance is not required. If you must inspect their work while it is in progress, do so unobtrusively if possible.
3. Avoid supplying Subcontractors with second-hand or used materials. It makes all Tradespersons discontented even if you are paying them extra to use them.
4. If paying wages, do so at the same time every week. It is best to have wages drawn the day before or at least eight hours in advance.

Plumbing

All plumbing work must be carried out by a registered Plumber. However, some shires will permit stormwater, guttering and downpipes to be erected by unlicensed persons. Enquire at your Local Council. Owner Builders can assist the Plumber by providing nogging at the positions designated by the Plumber.

Stages to Employ a Plumber

1. Prior to pouring the slab.
2. Metal roof cladding.
3. After fascia boards are fitted for the installation of guttering.
4. After roof installation but prior to lining walls and before Electrician arrives.
5. After lining walls to install fittings, PC items and general completion.

Drainage

Two forms of drainage are to be considered:

1. Stormwater
2. Sewerage or septic

All sewerage and septic work must be carried out by an authorised Drainer. In many shires, the installation of stormwater can be carried out by unlicensed persons, so enquire.

Stages to Employ a Drainer

Laying pipelines should be carried out prior to:

1. Constructing any walls close to boundary fences.
2. Pouring concrete footings, slabs or drives.
3. The Plumber laying waste pipes.

Ensure excavations for drainage *do not* expose the house wall or column foundations. It is good practice to liaise with the Plumber throughout the job.

Electrical

All electrical work must be performed by an authorised Electrician. Meter box position should be planned in consultation with the Electrical Authority prior to erecting any walls. Consider having underground cables installed before deciding on the meter box position.

The wiring procedure entails:
The drilling of holes through framework or brickwork to each room. Fixing of switch boxes followed by the laying of cables terminating at switchboxes, switchboards and meter boards.

Stages to Employ an Electrician

1. To install temporary job power pole.
2. Prior to pouring slabs if they contain any heating systems or wiring.
3. Wiring out — after roof is clad but after Plumber has installed water pipelines.
4. To install fittings and finish off.

Prior to Stage 3, before the Electrician arrives, it is good practice to mark on the frame with chalk the desired positions of lights and power points. Take into consideration proposed furniture, two way switches and outside lighting positions.

Materials

Concrete (Readymix & Homemade)

Ordering Premixed (Readymix) Concrete

These facts are required to place an order for concrete:

1. Quantity *2. Strength* *3. Slump*

1. Quantity

This is ordered in cubic metres and can be calculated by multiplying the length by the breadth and then by the thickness. *See Pages 103-105 also 'HBM' for estimating.*

2. Strength

This is stated in Mega Pascals (MPa) and should be noted on the house plan. *For example,* 20MPa is a common strength used in footings and slabs on ground floors (unless an Engineer specifies otherwise).

3. Slump

This is the plastic quality or state of the concrete. Readymix concrete companies often provide a slump test service for a fee if desired. However, this is *not* a common practice on house sites. The Builder should specify the slump measurement to ensure the mix delivered is *not* too wet or too dry. Concrete manufacturers usually carefully monitor the slump when mixing.

The Slump Recommended for Footings & Slab Floors is 100mm. But when pumping concrete, inform the plant, as the mix has to be designed for that purpose.

When working on steeply sloping ground with stepped footings or similar, the slump could be reduced to 65-70mm to help reduce flow but be prepared to handle stiff concrete.

Adding Water to Readymix Concrete

Do not add water to Readymix either in the truck or on-site without the base plant's approval or you could lose your quality guarantee. Adding water to concrete can reduce its final strength and increase shrinkage and cracking and can cause dusting floor surfaces.

Check & Keep Delivery Dockets

Always check Readymix delivery dockets before the pour to ensure the mix is as you specified and keep your portion in case a resale of the house should require proof of concrete quality.

Pouring Readymix Concrete

To reduce costs, the site should be arranged where possible to enable the truck to discharge its load with only limited use of the wheelbarrow. It takes one hundred wheelbarrow loads to equal five cubic metres of concrete.

The Readymix shute can reach up to approx. 4m from the truck. On limited access sites, it is helpful to know the approx. width and length of a full size concrete truck (see fig 1).

It should be remembered that smaller trucks are available.

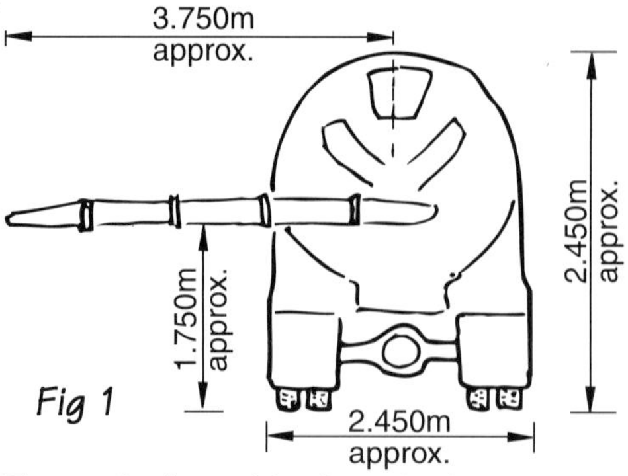

Fig 1

The readymix truck is also 7.3m long approx. and has a turning radius of 8.1m approx. It may carry between 4 and 6m of concrete. Fully loaded, it weighs about 22 tonnes. When hills occur between the readymix base and the site, the payload is reduced to avoid spillage.

Damage by Concrete Trucks

A fully loaded Readymix truck can damage surrounding Local Council footpaths and kerbs. The owner builder is usually held responsible, and the cost of repairs is deducted from his Council road damage bond. Any concrete spilt by the truck on the road, if *not* cleaned up, is also regarded by the Local Council as damage. Ensure that provision is made to ease the truck over any kerbs and *never* permit them to use the concrete driveways or run over waterpipes, drainage or septic areas.

Waiting Time Penalty

A minimum of two people should be on-site when Readymix is being used because a time span is allotted for discharging the load. After this, waiting time penalties can be charged.

Pumping Concrete

Inaccessible or steep sites may require the use of a pump and pipelines from the Readymix truck. A small pump can push concrete 150m horizontally with a 10m rise. The Readymix manufacturer must be informed if a pump is to be used as changes to the normal mix have to be made. Reinforcement for slab floors when using pumped concrete should be a minimum of F72 fabric supported on bar chairs at a maximum spacing of 1m apart and 500mm apart along joins. This is because lighter fabrics and greater spacings of bar chairs are pushed out of position by the force of pumped concrete. Extra manpower is needed to help control and spread the fast flowing concrete.

Curing Concrete Slab Floors

If slab floors are *not* cured, their strength can be reduced by half. In *not* carrying out this simple task, you are paying for potential strength which the concrete is *not* going to achieve.

Cont.

What is Curing?

Curing is slowing down the drying process. Retaining the water in concrete assists the hydration or reaction of cement to develop into a powerful glue. This also reduces shrinkage and surface cracks.

How to Cure Concrete Slab Floors

Cover with polythene right over the edges and weigh down with weights. The polythene should remain on the slab for seven days. New information advises against intermittent wetting down.

Alternatively, a curing compound can be sprayed over the entire surface according to manufacturer's instructions. However, check with the label or the manufacturer that the following tile, carpet or vinyl adhesives will adhere to the surface which has received a coat of curing compound.

Making Your Own Concrete

This method is seldom used today and is *not* recommended because of the near impossibility of achieving the constant quality of Readymix. This is because of the variations in slump control and because of the time span requirement for placement of a large mass.

However, in some situations, such as isolation or strikes etc, the builder may be forced to mix on-site. Sand, gravel, and cement should be mixed by volume using a bucket or box. The mix should continue mixing in a mechanical mixer for a minimum of three minutes. It is a good idea to add the coarse aggregate into the water first, then the cement and sand to ensure the cement does *not* stick to the drum.

RECOMMENDED CONCRETE MIX			
Strength	**Suggested Proportions by Volume**		
15MPa	**Gravel/Metal** 4parts (¾ or 20mm)	**Sharp Sand** 2½ parts	**Cement** 1 part
20MPa	3 parts (¾ or 20mm)	2 parts	1 part

Ordering Timber

It is ideal for timber to be straight. However, this is *not* always possible. It should be requested that certain timbers must be straight such as lintels and beams along their sides, and verandah posts on both edges etc. Sawmills are usually willing for you to select your own timber.

The builder should also consider the use of prefabricated wall frames and truss roofs. This avoids the tedium of having to handle faulty, bowed or very hard timber which may split and may require pre-drilling for nailing. House plans and specifications should contain the specific information for ordering.

There are six requirements to specify:

1. Details of Cross Section
example: 75x35mm S&A (sized & arised)

2. Stress Grading
example: MGP10 or F14

3. Treatment (if required)
example: either treated or untreated. If treated, state what level is required. Example: H2 Specifications should provide this detail (see Page 84).

4. Seasoned or Unseasoned

5. Species
example: Plantation pine, hardwood, Cypress, Oregon. These are the commonly used building species.

6. Quantity
example: timber can be ordered in lineal or cut lengths. e.g. '100 lineal metres or 40 @ 2.4m'.

An order would read similar to this example:
75x35mm SAR MGP10 treated H2 and seasoned plantation pine 40 @ 2.4m .

1. Details of Cross Section

Framing timber can be bought rough sawn or sized. Rough sawn leaves a variation in cross sectional dimensions from one piece of timber to the next, whilst sizing will convert the whole order to the same dimensions. Sizing can be performed on one or more sides.

Following are the correct abbreviations to use when ordering:

RS	Rough Sawn
SAR	Sized All Round
S4/S	Sized 4 Sides
S&A	Sized and Arised (all sides are sized and corners rounded). Commonly ordered for hardwoods to avoid splinters.
S1S	Sized 1 Side
S2S	Sized 2 Sides
S1E	Sized 1 Edge
S2E	Sized 2 Edges
S1/E1/F	Sized 1 Edge & 1 Face
S2/E1/F	Sized 2 Edges & 1 Face

Floor joists can be sized on one edge only. This is sufficient to reduce all the joists down to the same depth. Ceiling battens need to be sized on two faces. Most professional builders today prefer sized timber in order to avoid a multitude of carpentry problems which delay progress.

Dressed Timber

Timber used for finishing etc may be 'dressed'. That is, one or more faces and edges are given a smooth planed surface.

Below are the abbreviations to use when ordering:

DAR	Dressed All Round
D1S	Dressed 1 Side
D2S	Dressed 2 Sides
D1E	Dressed 1 Edge
D2E	Dressed 2 Edges
D1/S1/E	Dressed 1 Side & 1 Edge
D2/S1/E	Dressed 2 Sides & 1 Edge

2. Stress Grading

The higher the stress rating the greater the strength. In many situations the higher stress rating may enable the use of smaller sectional sizes. Pine is graded with 'MGP' (Machine Graded Pine) followed by the MPa stress rating which also utilises a different value system from hardwood. The stress grading is stamped on the timber. If it is not, then pine is automatically graded as MGP10 and hardwood as F8. The house plans or specifications should indicate which stress grading is required for specific members.

3. Treatment

Timber treatments to prevent rot and termite infestation can be specified. Various levels of treatment are available depending on the application the timber will be put to. Treated timber is noticeably green or olive in colour. The treatment strength is designated by an 'H' (Hazard) followed by the level, e.g. 'H3' is suitable for timber exposed to weather above ground and 'H4' and 'H5' for in-ground. Ask for treated timbers which carry a guarantee.

USING TREATED SOFTWOOD

END USE	'H' TREATMENT LEVEL
ABOVE GROUND for Posts in stirrups, bearers, joists, ledgers, handrails, step stringers, step treads, bracing timber, deck flooring, pergola beams, joists & battens.	H3 Common species Radiata, Slash Pine & Hoop
Should only be used for non-structural landscaping.	H4
IN GROUND or EMBEDDED IN CONCRETE Posts or stumps	H5
IN MARINE CONDITIONS Posts for decks or jetties	H6

Dry-after-Treatment or Seasoned after Treatment

Dry-after-Treatment or Seasoned after Treatment for softwoods is preferred as they will be more stable. The timber is firstly kiln dried to 10-15% moisture content then put through the vacuum pressure to receive the preservative treatment then kiln dried again to 10-15% moisture content. Request 'treated and seasoned' (this may or may *not* be available in hardwoods).

User Safety Precautions

The following safety precautions apply when using all preservative treated timbers.

a). Wear gloves

b). Wash hands and face before eating, drinking, or smoking.

c). When sanding timber, provide good ventilation and wear protective clothing plus dust mask.

d). NEVER USE IN FIRES FOR HEATING, COOKING OR B.B.Q.'s.

Termite Treatment for Pine House Framing

Even in brick veneer construction, termites could gain access to the frame through weep holes or cracks in the mortar or slab. Termites are capable of extensively damaging a house frame. It would be worth the minimal extra expense when ordering the framing timber to request 'H2' treatment. Cypress pine is a good alternative as it is naturally resistant to termites.

4. Seasoned or Unseasoned

Seasoning is the term used for timber which has had its moisture content reduced by either kiln or air drying. Moisture control quantity is expressed in percentages e.g. 12% moisture content. Unseasoned and green timber is likely to shrink or suffer distortion (warping, bowing etc) after installation. *Decking (flooring)* will perform better if seasoned.

5. Species

Sometimes a certain species will be specified in the plans or specifications to fulfil a particular function, and should *not* be ignored and a substitute used without careful consideration. *For example:* if pine is substituted for hardwood for framing members, the cross sectional size will most likely have to be increased.

6. Quantity

When ordering lineal metres, the total quantity will be supplied in running metres of varying lengths including short pieces which could be of no use. In that case, request that short lengths be no less than a specified length. If some lengths are required to be extra long, you will need to stipulate the lengths. When ordering cut lengths, allow sufficient for trimming on-site. Timber is ordered in lengths commencing at 900mm and increased in multiples of 300mm.

Important Notes:

a). Deliveries of badly 'twisted, cupped, split or collapsed' timber *do not* have to be accepted. However, make sure that complaints are made within 24 hours of delivery.

b). Timber should be neatly stacked and protected out of the sun and wind immediately after delivery.

Storing Materials

When selecting storage sites, ensure main work areas *do not* become clogged with materials ordered too soon. This hampers the tradesperson whose time you are paying for, and also engenders accidents.

Theft

Theft can be a real problem on building sites.

How to minimise:

1. Keep materials on-site to a minimum.
2. Avoid making obvious the presence of materials. *For example,* a hot water system left in the middle of a floor or too close to the road could become 'easy pickings'.
3. Lock up as soon as possible. Even if the external cladding is *not* fixed, it is a lesser temptation for thieves if there is *no* door or window access, even if the walls are only screened off with insulation paper.

Putting materials together and watching the house grow can be very rewarding. It is not so pleasurable when the weatherboards won't 'sit' properly and the doors are warped because of weather damage due to incorrect storage.

Here are some tips on storing materials:

Windows

Protect from wind breakage by securing upright to a partition with ropes. Cover to protect woodwork from warping and twisting by sun, dew or rain. Factory primed reveals, or site primed on arrival, will alleviate this.

Doors

Must be protected by stacking flat. Always lay three or four equal thickness chocks underneath and the full width of the doors. Leaving a door in the sun for even thirty minutes can result in warping.

Prime Cost Items

Stoves, benchtops, baths etc are better purchased just prior to installation. Ensure when fixed into position they are well protected from damage. Quite often subcontractors will stand or rest tools on stoves, kitchen cupboards and vanities whilst working and the end result is often a scratch or dint on the finished surface. Cover these items properly with thick, soft material before tradespeople arrive on-site.

Timber

Ensure when timber loads arrive that a flat and accessible space has been cleared. Chocks should be placed to keep timber from contact with the earth. Strapping of timber bundles not only keeps the stack even, but prevents petty thieving from the site. Cover the load with a tarpaulin or polythene and allow ventilation.

Bricks & Concrete Blocks

These generally arrive on pallets. Locate them in a convenient space close to where they will be laid. This will save undue and costly double handling by the bricklayer. Cover concrete blocks to prevent moisture penetration as they should be laid in a dry state.

Cement

The slightest dampness will commence deterioration of cement. Store on chocks and cover with polythene.

Particle Board Flooring

Take care *not* to damage the tongue and edges of grooves when unloading also the edges and tongue and groove in this material will swell with moisture. Install as soon as possible. Cover stacks with polythene sheeting overnight.

Estimating Total Costs

Approaching Lending Authorities

The Owner Builder who presents details to the lending authority in a well presented manner will receive more favourable consideration for finance. The proposed plan should be submitted accompanied by a typed list such as the one set out below and supported by subcontractor's written quotations. *Lending authorities will give higher priority to the Owner Builder who can submit estimated dates of:* **a).** Commencement, **b).** Roof Completion & **c).** Finishing

The following items will cover most types of construction. Rule a line through items that are not applicable. Most hardware merchants and tradespersons will give a 'take-off' quote on the plan but it still remains your responsibility to check that all items are included in the quotation.

Labour & Materials	**QUOTE $**
EXCAVATIONS	
Allow per hour + travelling	
Bulldozer & Backhoe	
Chaindigger for footings	
Bobcat to level slab	
Truck Hire to Remove Fill	
Fill if required	
Labour	
FOOTINGS & SLAB	
Steel Trench Mesh	
Stirrups & Starter Bars	
Lengths of Steel Bars	
Slab Mesh, Tie Wires & Bar Chairs	
Concrete Stumps	
Termite Protection	
Labour	
Concrete required for:	
Footings	
Slab or Suspended Floor	
Cement Grout	
Drives & Paths	
Column Bases	
Labour	
STEELWORK	
'U' Beams	
Steel and Open Web Joists	
MS Angles & Flats	
Steel Step Stringers	
Plates & Saddles	
Welder's Labour	
TIMBER	
Profiles, Formwork (boxing) & Pegs	
Subfloor Framing:	
Bottom, Top Plates, Sills & Noggs	
Studs, Lintels	
Bracing	
Floor Framing:	
Wall Plates	
Bearers & Beams	
Laminated Beams	
Floor Joists & Bridging	
Strutting	
Nogging for Flooring	
Verandah Plates & Joists	
Verandah Flooring	

Labour & Materials	**QUOTE $**
Wall Framing:	
Bottom, Top Plates & Noggs	
Studs	
Window Sills	
Lintels & Door Heads	
Wall Plates for Brick Walls	
Bracing	
Roof Framing:	
Roof Trusses & Anchoring	
Ceiling Joists & Noggs	
Ceiling Binders	
Hanging Beams	
Strutting Beams	
Exposed Beams	
Laminated Beams	
Roof, Hip, Ridge & Valley Rafters	
Valley Boards	
Collar Ties	
Under Purlins	
Struts	
King Posts	
Bracing	
Dragon Ties	
Fascia Boards	
Barge Boards	
Gable Framing	
Sundry Timber	
EXTERNAL WALL CLADDINGS	
Chamferboards or Weatherboards	
Vertical Cedar	
FC planking	
Any other Claddings	
Carpenter's Labour required to:	
Set Out Profiles	
Cut Out & Erect Subfloor Framing	
Bearers, Joists & Flooring	
Cut & Erect Wall & Roof Framing	
Fix Gable Ends & Soffits	
Exterior Wall Linings	
Interior Wall Linings	
Install Battenings or Claddings to Basement	
Erecting Scaffolds	
Install Bath, Shower	
Cabinets, Pantry, Wardrobes & Linen Cupboards	

Labour & Materials	**QUOTE $**
BRICKWORK	
Brick Base & Veneer Walls	
Brick Piers	
Steps	
Arches	
Veneer & Cavity Ties	
Cement, Sand, Lime & additives	
Labour	
BLOCKWORK	
Concrete Blocks	
Steel Reinforcing Rods	
Cement, Sand & Lime	
Plasticiser	
Labour	
ROOFING	
Battens & Tiles	
Cladding & Moulds	
Sarking	
Skylights & Ventilators	
Labour	
PLUMBER	
Labour & Materials	
DRAINER	
Sewerage or Septic	
Stormwater & Surface Drainage	
Labour	
ELECTRICIAN	
Light & other Fittings	
Labour & Materials	
INTERNAL LININGS	
Plasterboard	
Plasterer's Labour	
Materials	
FC Sheeting or other claddings required for:	
Soffit Linings	
Garage Linings	
Sheeting behind Tiling	
Ceilings	
Walls	
Gables	
Insulation	
Tiles & Materials	
Tiler's Labour	
Laminate Linings required for:	
Kitchen Cupboards	
Shower Recesses	
Around Bath	
Benchtops and Laundry	
FLOOR SANDING	
Labour & Materials	
PAINTING	
Labour & Materials	

Labour & Materials	**QUOTE $**
HARDWARE	
Nails, Screws & Hinges	
Anchor Bolts & other Bolts	
Metal Angle Bracing	
Framing Anchors	
Door Handles, Locks & Stops	
Glue & Sealants	
Primers & Sandpaper	
Waterproofing Agents	
Soffit Ventilators	
PRIME COST ITEMS	
Stove & Hot Plates	
Hot Water System/ Solar Hot Water	
Kitchen Sink	
Laundry Tub, Handbasin, Bath & Shower Tray	
Water Closet	
Vanity Unit & Laundry Cabinets	
Clothes Hoist	
DOORS	
Exterior Solid or Hollow Core	
Interior Hollow Core or Special	
Garage plus jambs & fittings	
WINDOWS	
Materials & Labour	
OTHER MATERIALS	
HIRING GEAR	
Jackhammer or Kanga Hammer	
Power Pole & Extension Cables	
Power Saws & Sawbench	
Power Drills	
Concreting Equipment	
Pneumatic Nailing Equipment	
Ramset Nailing Gun	
Temporary Water Closet	
Scaffolding	
Tile Cutting Machine	
Miscellaneous	
FEES & COSTS	
Plans	
Insurances required for:	
Contractors' All Risk Public Liability	
Workers' Compensation	
Council Fees & Bonds	
Power Pole Fee	
Underground Power Fee	
Water Connection Fee	
Rates While Under Construction	
Other fees	
SAFETY MARGIN	

Ready to Start Building

Tools Required

It is unnecessary for the Owner Builder to be as tool equipped as the professional Builder. Many tools are readily available from hire equipment establishments. Your tool needs will depend on whether you are building in masonry or timber. Buy only tools that will be required frequently. As far as electrical tools go, a 175mm portable circular saw and a 10mm two-speed reversible impact drill are a must. The 175mm saw is light enough to use with one hand, yet big enough to cut all timbers in a house frame. Also purchase sufficient extension cables to reach all job extremities.

If you are to perform extensive masonry work, it will be necessary to purchase an electrical concrete mixer, a wheelbarrow and other appropriate hand tools. If it is intended to carry out carpentry, work in conjunction with a Tradesperson. Some basic carpentry tools will be required as Tradespeople do *not* appreciate their tools being continuously borrowed.

Insurances

Three insurances are essential and considered as normal building contracting expenses.

1. Contractors All Risks

This is a policy covering all eventualities on the building site such as damage or loss while under construction, through storm, wind, fire, theft, collapse, explosion, malicious damage and glass breakage. Minimum cover should be for the completed value of the house including labour and should be taken out prior to building commencement.

2. Public Liability

Usually this policy can be included as a single package with the Contractors All Risk. It provides financial protection for actions brought against you as a result of your legal responsibility for accidents causing injury, loss or damage to persons or the property of others. The minimum cover should be discussed with your insurance company.

3. Workers Compensation

This insurance is compulsory if one is employing workers on wages even if they are on the site temporarily. If one is engaging subcontractors, ensure they have current worker's compensation policies. Do *not* neglect to cover yourself.

Tee up Your Subbies

Prior to commencing construction, the following subcontractors should be organised regarding approximate commencement dates and material needs.

You will need to organise:

a). Excavator & trencher or post hole digger

b). Electrician (for temporary power)

c). Plumber *d). Concretor*

e). Carpenter *f). Bricklayer*

Other subbies to be organised as job progresses:

a). Electrician (for permanent power)

b). Gyprock fixer and Plasterer

c). Roofer *d). Tiler*

e). Floor Sander *f). Painter*

Suppliers to arrange materials & approximate delivery dates for the following:

a). Sand, gravel and filling

b). Bricks and/or blocks

c). Hardware supplies

d). Concrete

e). Timber

f). Roofing

g). Windows & doors & other joinery

h). Tilta or rolla or overhead doors

i). Wallboard or plasterboard

j). Kitchen supplies

k). Paint and/or wallpaper

l). Light fittings

Ready-to-Go Check List

a). Ensure title on property is cleared.

b). Ensure finance is approved in writing and ready to use.

c). Obtain your 'Owner Builder Licence' from the Authority concerned.

d). Have plans and specifications approved by your Local Council.

e). Erect job sign with 'Lot No., name and Owner Builder's registration number' displayed if this is required.

f). Erect temporary power pole in conjunction with the Electrician.

g). Erect temporary W.C. or E.C.

h). Have water connected to the site.

Write it Down

Post a note pad somewhere to jot down materials for each day. It's *not* so much going to the store for materials that is the bug-bear, but getting in the queue and waiting that will fritter your time away.

Before driving back to the site, examine that what the sales assistant gave you is what you asked for. It is more important to find out that in the little packet just handled to you is really the *100mm* ***galvanised*** *coach screws* rather than the *100mm* **non-galvanised** ones the sales assistant gave you.

Cont.

The Building Schedule

Speedy Completion

Contrary to the thinking of most Owner Builders substantial cost savings can be achieved through speedy completion.

The three major areas where loss occurs through delay are:

1. Loss of time from permanent place of employment.

2. Additional rents expended on accommodation whilst building.

3. Inflation on materials during construction.

Obviously 'No. 1' will *not* affect those who are on long service leave etc, but for most people who have a short span of free time available, such as four weeks annual leave, by using one of the methods for part-time builders on Pages 6-8 they will avoid the problem of taking extended leave. Of all the part time methods, the best for money saved and speed is 'A Quick Building Program' on Page 8.

Overall Time Schedule

It is important that time is not lost through disorganisation. For this reason, prepare an 'Overall Time Schedule'. The graphic example (illustrated opposite) could be used as a guide and a long term bird's eye view of progress.

It will also inform on which materials should be ordered for the long term. This schedule should be readjusted when times have been reduced or increased.

A Weekly Diary

To prevent delays, a weekly diary should be kept to inform which materials and tradespersons should be ordered for that particular week. It should be checked each night for the following day's ordering.

How to Speed up Construction

Construction times can be improved with the use of prefabricated wall frames and roof trusses, pre-hung doors and windows with pre-fitted reveals. Subcontractors can be used to attach Gyprock linings and a carpenter for door hanging and fitting mouldings.

SUBCONTRACT LABOUR ALLOWED FOR IN THE OPPOSITE SCHEDULE INCLUDE:

Concrete floor layer, Bricklayer, Drainer, Plumber, Electrician, Roof Plumber or Tiler.

CONSTRUCTION TIME PROPOSED:

(for an Average House)

90 Days Approx.

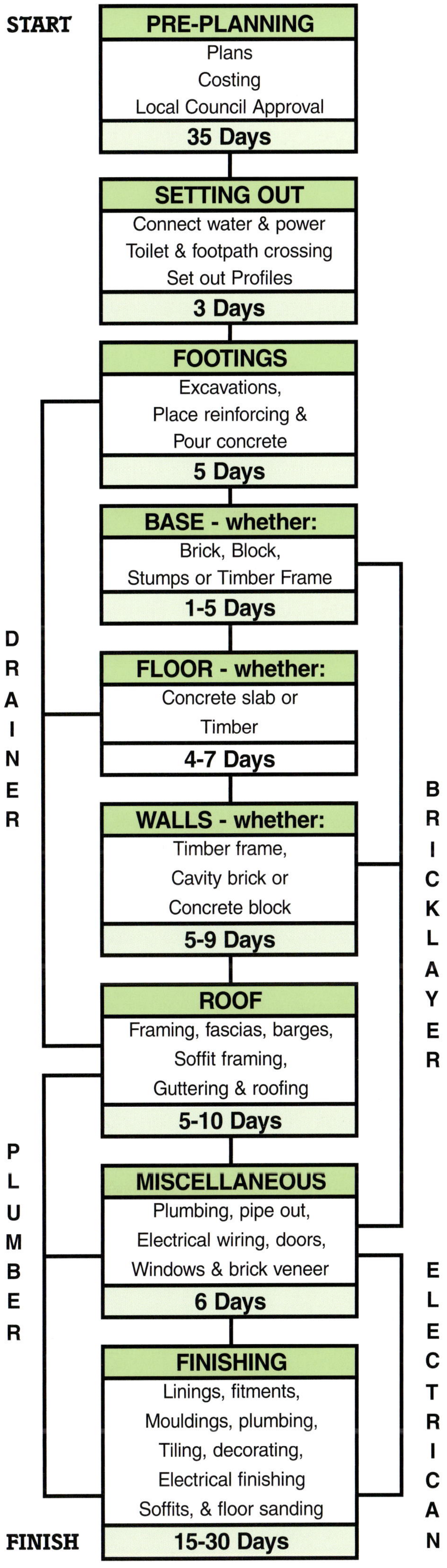

6 Identifying Improper Building Practice & Common Problems

This chapter is designed to draw attention to common problems and faulty or unacceptable building practices. When the house is under construction, each day refer to this chapter and the page dealing with that particular stage. Check that correct building practice is being adopted. If a subcontractor has performed unacceptable work, point this out and have it rectified before the work advances further. If uncertain if the work is unacceptable, seek the advice of the Designer or a Local Building Inspector.

IMPORTANT NOTE:
All tradeswork involves the use of essential accessories such as flashings, DPC materials and many other hardware items *not* visible after the work is complete. These items should be on site prior to commencement of the work. If not, some tradespeople will either substitute or ignore their use. The completed work *will not* betray this substitution or failure, but the strength or quality of the work may be (and in some cases is) seriously impaired.

Setting out Foundations & Footings

Building on the Wrong Site

Correct Procedure: Inspect Local Council allotment plans for other lots in the same street with the same lot number. Check the numbers carved into each peg to ascertain correct identity. If in doubt, consult a Surveyor.

Subsoils Unstable

Correct Procedure: Enquire with Local Council Engineer if the land developer has placed fill on the site. Also, before purchasing land, have an Engineer carry out a pre-purchase soil test. Obtain permission first.

Boundary Infringement

At some stage during the life of the building a neighbouring house could employ a Surveyor to check their alignment pegs. This investigation could prove your house or theirs is infringing on the adjoining boundary. This can result in litigation.

Correct Procedure: Ensure boundary pegs are in their correct position before setting out profiles. These can sometimes be in the wrong position. If so, physical boundary measurements will differ from the measurements on the Local Council plans. To double check, take measurements of adjoining boundaries. This will give a good indication whether pegs are correctly sited. The only certain method is to employ a Surveyor to carry out a check.

Wall Lengths & Proposed Positioning Incorrectly Measured onto Profiles

Correct Procedure: Always carry out a double check after the subcontractor has left for the day. Ultimately, the responsibility will be yours as Owner Builder *(see fig 1, Page 91)*.

Walls Positioned on Profiles Out-of-Square

Correct Procedure: Wall positions should be checked first, then two diagonal measurements taken from opposite corners. The two rear nails represent the two side walls and are adjusted together until both diagonals are of identical length (see figs 1 & 2). *See also Pages 114 & 115.*

Cont.

Fig 1

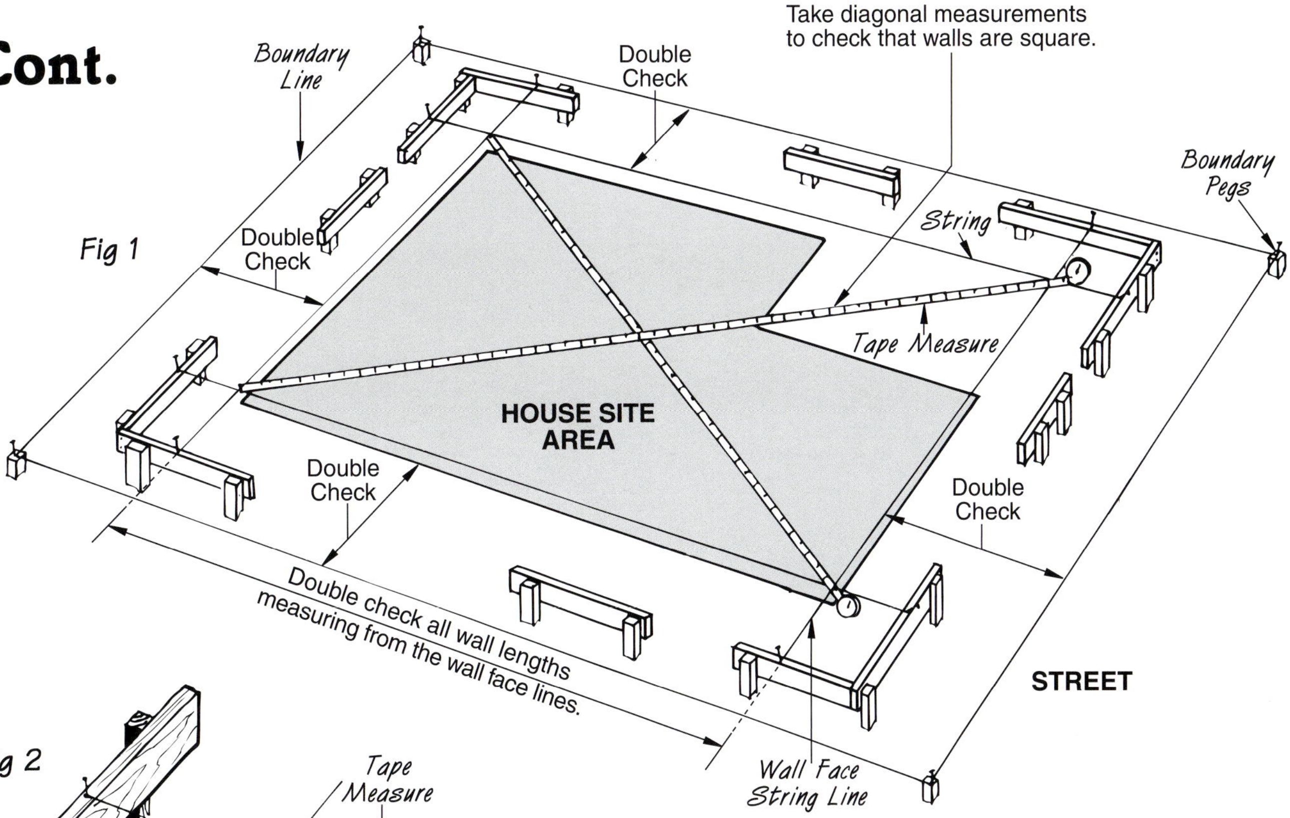

Fig 2

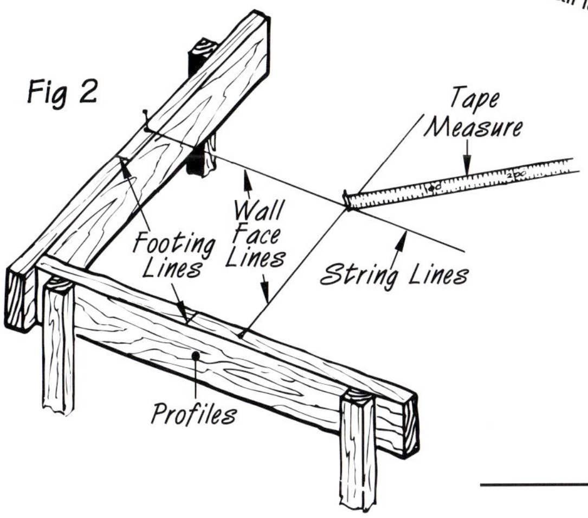

Wall positions are marked on profiles with a nail or a saw cut. The wall lengths and their positions should be checked; then the whole building checked for square. This is carried out by stretching string lines to represent the four external wall faces onto the profiles as above. An assistant is required to hold the tape accurately on the crossing of the strings (as in fig 2) while the diagonal measurement is taken. Both diagonal measurements should be the same. To correct, move both rear positions sideways until the diagonals correspond.

Footing Excavations

Damage to Service Lines

Correct Procedure: Ensure machine operator is advised of position of sewerage and water pipes etc prior to excavating.

Footing Trenches dug Narrower or Wider than required

Correct Procedure: Advise machine operator the size of trenches so the correct sized spade or bucket is brought to the site.

Trenches too Shallow. Crooked or Cave-ins

Correct Procedure: *Do not* leave the trenching operator without on-ground assistance. The trench depth should be measured constantly to ensure correct depth is being maintained and also to advise where best to cut footing steps. Shore up any cave-ins prior to pouring concrete. All trenches must be straight whether machine dug or straightened later with a spade.

Footing Reinforcement

Reinforcement has Insufficient Laps

Correct Procedure:

All longitudinal joins in reinforcing must be well tied together and have specified laps as follows:

Round Bars — Forty-five times the diameter of the bar.

Deformed Bars — Twenty-three times the diameter of the bar.

Trench Mesh — (at end-to-end laps): 500mm overlap
(at 'T' junctions & corners): Fully overlapped.

Reinforcement Improperly Supported

Correct Procedure: Reinforcement should not be supported on bricks or lumps of clay or rocks. Dampness will soak through these materials and rust the steel. This is turn will cause blowouts to the concrete. Reinforcement can be supported on trench mesh chairs or by battens and wire hangers (see fig 3 where both methods are illustrated).

Cont.

Fig 3

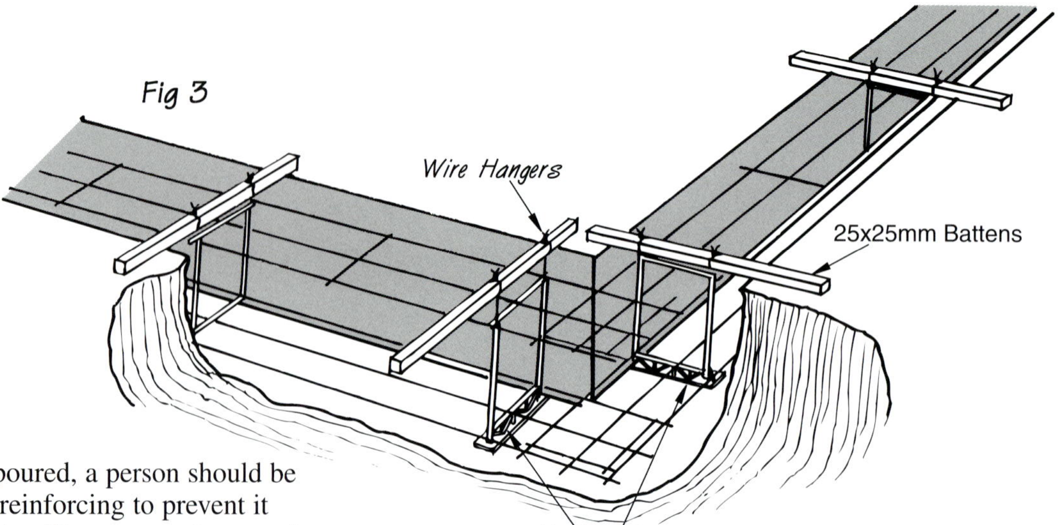

Reinforcing is supported on bar chairs or suspended by wire ties from battens. Both methods are illustrated in fig 3. However, only one method is necessary.

While concrete is being poured, a person should be manually supporting the reinforcing to prevent it shifting and to ensure that a 40mm concrete cover is maintained at sides and ends.

Concrete Slab Floor Preparation

Fig 4

Check plans for depth of slab and basecourse. Then check these depths measuring down from a string line stretched from one side of the slab formwork to the opposite side at regular intervals.

Height of Slab Floor Surface Incorrect

Correct Procedure: Slab surface height above finished ground level or paving should be designated on the house plans or if not, according to local requirements. Slab height should be established at time of setting out profiles.

Thickness of Slab/Basecourse Incorrect

Correct Procedure: Check plans for depth of slab and basecourse. Double check measurements with a string line stretched from one side of slab formwork to opposite at regular intervals (see fig 4).

Failure to Correctly Apply Termite Proofing

Correct Procedure: Apply termite proofing as required by the 'BCA' and the 'Australian Standards Code' or according to Local Authority requirements *(see 'HBM' for further details).*

Incorrect Concrete Mix. Poor Quality or Too Wet

Correct Procedure: Readymix is preferable. Strength will be indicated on the plan. *Refer to Pages 82 & 83 for details on how to order and mix concrete correctly.*

Polythene DPC Incorrect Grade

Correct Procedure: The plans will specify the polythene thickness. All laps around pipes and all punctures should be sealed with pressure sensitive tape. Allow 200mm laps at joins and seal with pressure sensitive tape.

Reinforcing Mesh or its Positioning Incorrect

Correct Procedure: This should be stated on plans. When overlapping, the two outer transverse bars on one panel should overlap the two outer

Cont.

transverse bars on the other and tied with tie wire. Bar chairs should be spaced at *not* more than 800mm apart or approx. 3 per sq. metre.

When using one layer of mesh throughout, chairs should support the mesh 25mm below the slab surface or according to specifications.

Rebate Step in Slab Edge

This step is *not* required on weatherboard houses.

Correct Procedure: The step or rebate in the edge of slab floors is essential for brick veneer and double brick walls. It provides a means for moisture on the back of the outer brick leaf to escape from the cavity. *See 'HBM' for construction details.*

Curing Concrete Inadequate

Correct Procedure: Concrete is strengthened by slowing its drying time (known as curing). This can be performed by different methods *(see Page 83)*.

Brickwork

Incorrect Mortar Mix

If too strong, cracking will occur which permits water penetration, too weak (lack of cement or too much chemical additive) crumbling results and breakdown of joints.

Correct Procedure: *See the 'HBM' for the table of correct mortar mixtures for above and below DPC at the specific distances from the ocean or polluted environments.*

Important Notes when mixing mortar:

a). All mixtures are by volume.

b). Sand should be sharp, clean, washed pit sand.

c). Measure all ingredients by bucket or box, *not by shovel.*

d). Mix for a minimum of three minutes in a mechanical mixer to ensure adequate blending.

e). Additives should be used strictly in accordance with directions.

Joints in Brickwork too Thick or too Thin & Brick Joints Poorly Finished

Correct Procedure: Brick joints are normally 10mm thick as an average thickness and 13mm as a maximum.

Raked Joints
All joints should be raked clean and any holes in the mortar joints should be filled.

Ironed Joints
Preferable for prolonging the life of bricks in salty or polluted atmospheres. Joints should be smooth with all holes and gaps filled.

Soiling of Brick Face with Mortar

Correct Procedure: Ensure all mortar is removed with a brush prior to setting, and bricks washed well if required, using a sponge.

Brick Patterns or Textures Laid Upside Down or are in an Unacceptable Pattern

Correct Procedure: Check bricklaying prior to whole walls being completed to ensure pattern and style *has not* been laid the wrong way around or large patches of colour appearing in an unpleasing pattern. To avoid this, the bricklayer should be forewarned that you want the brick colours evenly distributed or the odd colours laid below ground level or on an inconspicuous wall. Textured bricks should have the texture lying downwards to prevent dirt accumulating in the texture. When deciding on a mixture or pattern, commence on a rear or inconspicuous wall.

Brick Veneer Construction

Damp Proof Courses Incorrectly Applied

Damp proof courses should prevent moisture rising and gaining access the timber wall framing and also protect the brickwork from deterioration.

Correct Procedure: *Damp Proof Courses on:*

Slab Floors — Ensure damp proof course is on-site before bricklayer commences. It should be laid throughout the slab edge step as in fig 1. Corners are fully overlapped end-to-end joins lapped 150mm *(see also fig 1 on Page 94)*.

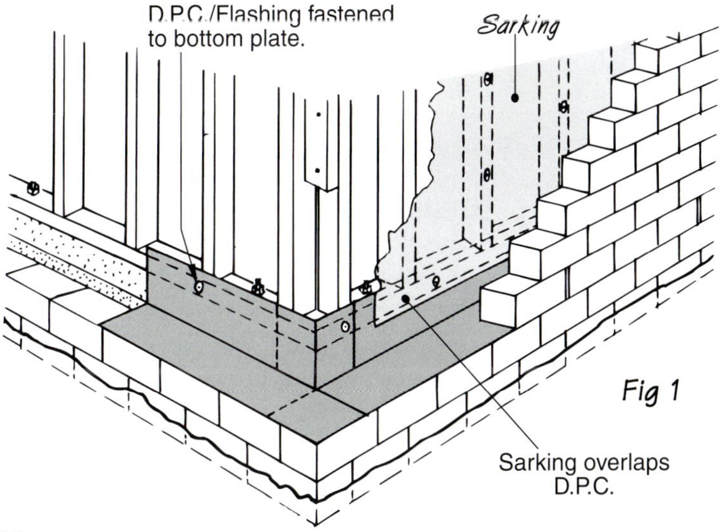

Fig 1

Cont.

Timber Floors — One layer at two courses or 150mm above ground surface and in high set houses, an extra layer should be placed directly below the lowest timber floor members.

Incorrectly Positioned Brick Veneer Ties

Correct Procedure: Brick veneer walls *must* be anchored to the timber frame at regular intervals with brick veneer ties horizontally and vertically.

Variations in the spacing requirements exist between the different wind category locations. Check with plans or local building authority. Additional ties are positioned at floor level on timber joisted floors at 300mm centres.

Veneer spacings vary between the various wind categories. *See the 'HBM' for the table and further specific details on selection and installation.*

Mortar Allowed to Collect on Veneer Ties

This can cause moisture to cross to the timber frame.

Correct Procedure: Brick veneer ties should be kept free of mortar droppings as work progresses.

Mortar Droppings Left on Cavity Bottoms

This can prevent moisture escaping in wet weather.

Correct Procedure: Mortar catching battens should be used and raised as brickwork progresses. Also where sarking is not required, it is desirable to delay internal wall lining to enable easy access to clean out cavity bottoms.

Sill Flashing & Shrinkage Allowance

Correct Procedure: Sill flashings must be fitted to prevent moisture damage to the timber frame *(see fig 2, Page 34)*. A shrinkage gap must be provided between brick sills and window frames to allow for timber frame shrinkage (see same figure).

Cavity Brick Construction

Damp Proof Courses Incorrectly Applied

Correct Procedure: *Damp Proof Courses on:*

Slab Floors — Ensure damp proof course is on-site ready for use. It should be applied throughout the brick courses of both leaves as in fig 1. Ensure weep holes are provided along this course.

Timber Floors — Ensure a damp proof course is laid across both brick leaves two courses or 150mm above finished ground level as in fig 2. Fill the cavity below the damp proof course with grout.

Ensure a damp proof course is also laid beneath any bottom plates or bearers resting on brickwork.

Fig 1

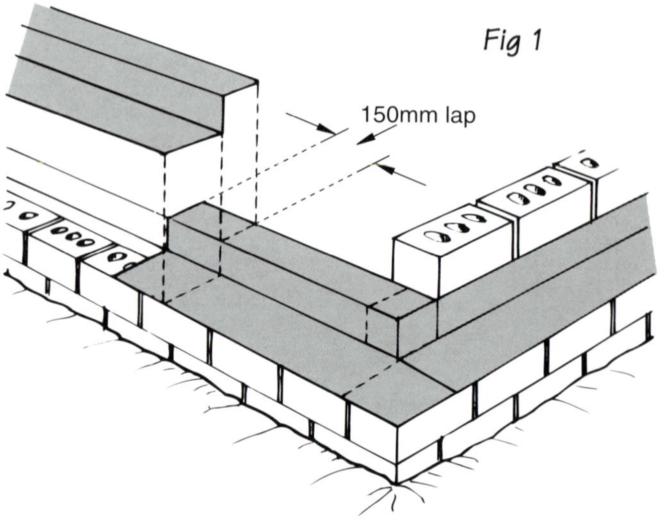

Damp Proof Course and Ant Capping on Cavity Brick

Damp Proof Course and Ant Capping on Cavity Brick.

Fig 2

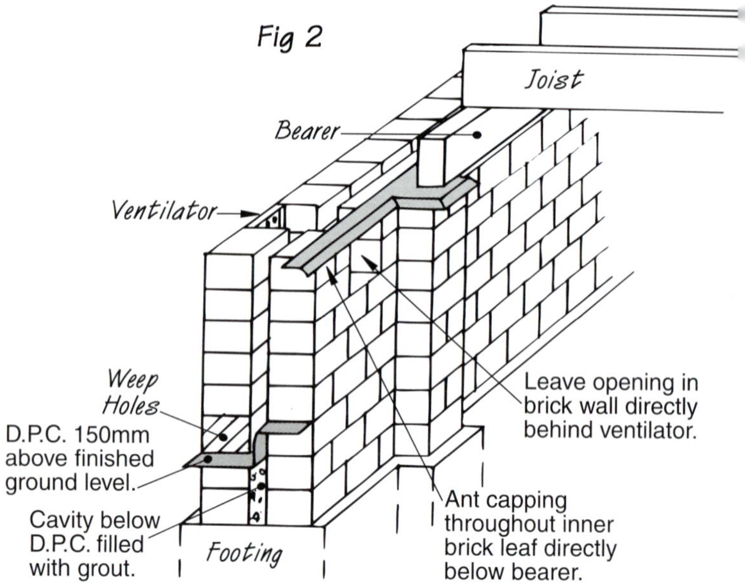

Construction of Brick Walls before Installation of Joinery

Correct Procedure: Joinery should be on-site prior to brickwork commencing and should be fitted while brickwork is being constructed to ensure tight fitting work around frames. This method also ensures that horizontal brick joints at window head heights arrive at the correct height. The builder can erect, plumb and brace joinery into position for the bricklayer.

Mortar Droppings Left on Cavity Bottoms

This will result in moisture being prevented from escaping in wet weather.

Correct Procedure: Mortar catching battens should be used and raised as brickwork progresses. Also at cavity bottom level a brick can be left out temporarily at suitable spacings to enable the cavity bottom to be cleaned out.

Mortar Droppings Left on Cavity Ties

This could result in permitting moisture to cross to the inner brick leaf.

Correct Procedure: Cavity ties should be kept clean as work progresses.

Sill Flashings Incorrectly Fitted

Correct Procedure:
Moisture can easily reach the inner brick leaf if a sill flashing is *not* fitted *(see fig 8, Page 45). See also HBM.*

Incorrectly Positioned Anchor Bolts & Straps

Correct Procedure:

Anchor Bolts & Straps
House plans should indicate if and at what spacings anchor bolts and straps should be positioned.

For detailed diagrams of tie down and attachments, see 'HBM'.

Concrete Block Masonry Construction

In concrete block masonry careful attention should be paid to correct reinforcement and grouting of the vertical and horizontal cores, lintels and bond beams. Blocks on the first bed joints should be fully bedded, that is, shell edges and cross webs embedded in compo.

Also load-bearing columns should be fully bedded. Remaining block work above *should not* have cross webs bedded.
All cores should be kept free of mortar droppings.

Starter Bars Incorrectly Positioned

Correct Procedure:
If starter bars previously set into footings were found later to be outside of the stipulated core, the bar is *not* permitted to be cranked over (see fig 1).
For correct positioning of starter bars see 'HBM'.

If blocklayers discover bars set out of alignment they will very likely either crank them over, leave them out of position, or cut them off. Correct procedure would be to engage the blocklayers on another wall whilst the builder replaces the starter bars.

How to Replace Misaligned Starter Bars
Use a proprietary fixing such as a chemset bolt or 150x12mm dyna bolt and anchor into footings 75-100mm and attach a female anchor bolt coupling with a 500mm length of threaded rod attached, alternatively, weld a length of starter bar to the side of the dyna bolt.

Fig 1

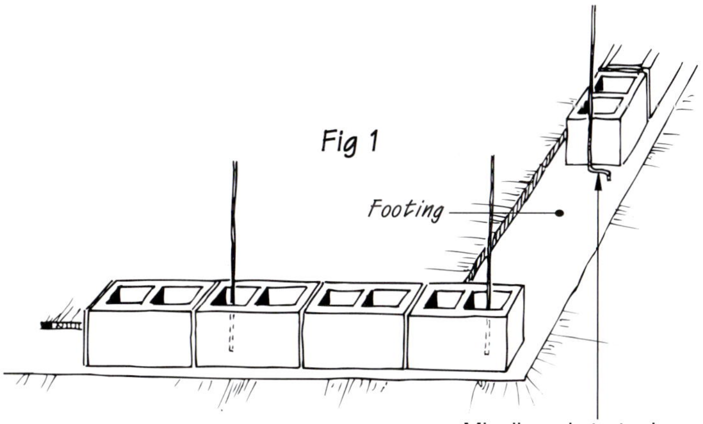

Misaligned starter bars should *not* be cranked as illustrated.

Incorrect Blocklaying Mortar Mixture

If too strong, cracking will occur. Too weak and joints will break down and crumble.

Correct Procedure:
See the 'HBM' for the table of correct mortar mixtures for above and below DPC at the required distances from the ocean or polluted environments.

Cont.

Important Notes when mixing mortar:

a). All mixtures are by volume. Measure all ingredients by bucket or box, *not* by a shovel.

b). Sand should be sharp, clean, washed pit sand.

c). Mix for a minimum of three minutes in a mechanical mixer to ensure adequate blending.

d). Additives should be used strictly in accordance with directions.

Laying Blocks Upside Down

Correct Procedure: The thicker edges of the shells and webs should be laid uppermost.

Incorrect Reinforcement & Grouting of Vertical Cores & Bond Beams

Correct Procedure: Vertical cores should have all waste mortar removed. Clean-out blocks are laid at the base of the cores for this purpose. A vertical rod is used to knock mortar dags off.

Vertical Cores: Vertical reinforcing bars should lap starter bars a minimum of 450mm. Top ends are bent and tied into top course bond beam reinforcing.

Lintels & Beams: Lintels should be reinforced according to plans and specifications. Horizontal joins should be lapped 45 times the diameter of the bar for round bars and 23 times the diameter of the bar for deformed bars then tied together.

Concrete Core Fill for Cores & Bond Beams: Readymix concrete to cores, lintels and bond beams should be a minimum strength of 20MPa. You **must** inform the plant that the concrete is to be pumped so the mix can be designed for that purpose. Cores should be tamped down to remove any honeycombing.

Walls Inadequately Waterproofed

Correct Procedure: (see Pages 47&54) and block manufacturers recommendations.

Window & Door Installation Incorrect

Correct Procedure: Window and door installation should take place after waterproofing block jambs and reveals. Flush jamb and reveal blocks should be used, *not* slotted or grooved ones.

Carpentry

Using Secondhand Building Materials

Correct Procedure: Often the time taken to intergrate these into new materials can be more expensive than using new materials.

Timber Deliveries Incorrect

Correct Procedure: All timber delivered to the site should be checked before the truck leaves the site. *Check for:*

a). Correct quantity and sizes

b). Correct species and treatment if any

c). Correct stress grade

If the plan stipulates the grade, it should correspond with grades stamped on the timber or on the sales docket.

d). Faulty timbers

Incorrect Measurements of Room Sizes & Timber Lengths

Correct Procedure: Measure all dimensions twice to establish room sizes and timber lengths when cutting framing.
Remember 'measure twice and cut once'.

Flooring, Weather Damaged after Laying

Correct Procedure: Tongue & Groove (T&G) flooring is best laid after enclosing the roof and walls. Particle board flooring which has been temporarily waterproofed is okay to install prior to constructing walls.

Sarking to Walls & Roof Incorrect

Correct Procedure: The correct sarkings should be stipulated on the plan or in specifications.

Wall or Roof Bracing Incorrectly Applied

Correct Procedure: The correct wall or roof bracing type will be stated on the plans.

These points should be checked:

a). All metal bracing to be fixed in a straight line.

b). Speed bracing should have its ends bent over the top and bottom plates and secured, as required in manufacturer's literature.

d). All bracing should be secured strictly according to manufacturer's specifications.

Failure to Apply Damp Proof Course

Correct Procedure: Damp proof course should be supplied on-site well in advance of requiring it and used wherever there is a risk of dampness penetrating the timber work. On slab floors, DPC should be used under all untreated pine bottom plates.

Cont.

Failure to Apply Flashings

Correct Procedure: Flashings should be installed around the perimeter of all openings (see fig 1). Flashings should be used wherever there is a risk of water penetration for specific situations.
See 'HBM' for further information.

Metal flashing should be of a longlife material such as Colorbond, copper or zincalume coated or anodized aluminium.

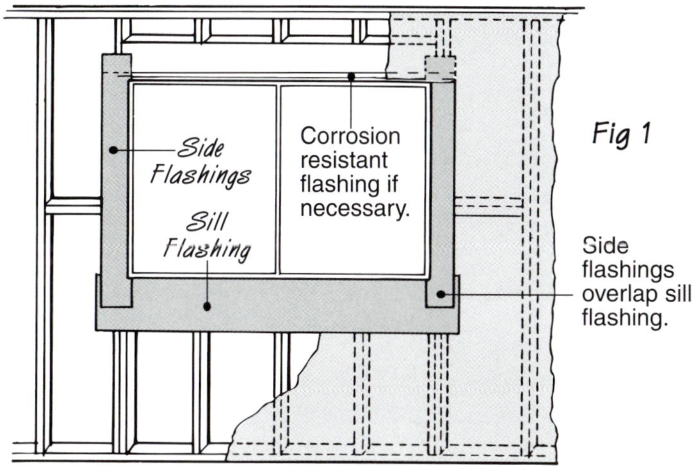

Fig 1

Failure to Correctly Apply Anchor Bolts & Straps

Correct Procedure: Anchor bolt positions and spacings are determined at subfloor stage and should be stipulated on the plan. Prior to fixing the roof covering, all anchor bolt nuts should be checked for tightness. In cyclone areas ensure that cyclone washers have been used. Check that all holding down straps are correctly secured prior to lining walls.
See plans and specifications or manufacturer's leaflets for more information.

Inadequate Fixing of Trusses to Top Plates

Inadequate nailing of triple or multigrips is common. Ten nails are required, four into the truss, four into the side of the top plate and two into the top of the top plate. Use 30x2.8mm gal. connector nails MIN.
Not clout heads.

Correct Procedure: The truss manufacturer or the plans should specify the anchoring method. A common error when using multi or triple grips is that the fixing holes arrive against the steel gang-nail-plate on the truss preventing the proper fixing of the triple grip. In this case, the triple grips should be moved to the opposite edge of the top plate or straps used in lieu of triple grips. *See 'HBM' for details.*

Roofing

Concrete or Terra Cotta Tiles

Tiles Insufficiently Tied or Fastened Down

Correct Procedure: This can lead to lifting or flapping in strong winds, permitting rain penetration. Manufacturers specify which tiles should be tied down. This varies according to the wind category of the area.

Cracked Tiles

Result of walking on roof.

Correct Procedure: If *no* roof sarking exists - which shouldn't be the case except in older dwellings, check for cracks from inside the roof. Otherwise check externally. Because of the possibility of cracked tiles through walking on, it is advisable to sark the underside of all tile roofs whatever the pitch. If possible, use long life non-tearable sarking.

Sheet Metal Roofing

Application of Lead Materials When Run-off is Used for Drinking Water

Correct Procedure: Lead flashings must *not* be used when run-off water will be used for drinking. Plumber should be advised.

Incorrect & Insufficient Nailings & Fastenings

Request Draftsperson to stipulate these requirements on the plans.

Correct Procedure:
In high winds, sheet metal roofing can be stripped from a house if *not* adequately fastened to purlins. Nails should be preferably ring nails. The spacing and type of fastenings will be according to the wind category of the area. High wind areas will require screw fixings — refer to manufacturers requirements.

Joining Incompatible Metals

Correct Procedure: Joining incompatible metals will cause corrosion.

Follow the table on the following page:

Cont.

COMPATIBLE METALS & FLASHINGS

Roof or Wall Cladding	Compatible Flashing Material
Zincalume	Zincalume or Aluminium
Galvanised Iron	Galvanised Iron (never Zincalume)
Colorbond Steel	Colorbond Steel or Aluminium
Zincalume Metal Tiles	Colorbond Steel or Aluminium
Aluminium	Aluminium
Decrabond Tiles	Decrabond or Aluminium
Concrete or Clay Tiles	Aluminium, Colorbond or Zincalume
Fibrolite Sheet	Aluminium, Colorbond or Zincalume
PVC Acrylic	Aluminium, Colorbond or Zincalume

Plumber & Drainer

Use of Galvanised Shower Trays

Correct Procedure: These *should not* be permitted. Stainless steel is preferred and should have 150mm MIN. high sides *(see HBM)* and all joints sealed including the joint around the waste. Avoid copper trays as they tend to corrode at the joints.

Metal Angle Flashing in Contact with Copper Shower Tray *(see above clause)*

Correct Procedure: These metals may not be compatible and *should not* come into contact. Use a bitumen coated aluminium DPC or PVC.

Liquid Membrane Shower Floor Failure

Correct Procedure: Liquid membranes are notorious for failing when *not* installed strictly according to manufacturers instructions. These are best applied by a certified applicator. A major cause of failure is *not* allowing the stipulated curing times prior to working over.

Drainage Trenches Too Close to House Foundations

Correct Procedure: These *should not* be closer than 600mm away from house foundations when running parallel to them except in exceptional circumstances. Seek a Local Council Drainage Inspector's advice.

Drainage Trap Tops Built over Weep Holes in Brick Walls

Correct Procedure: Drainage trap tops *should not* be built over weep holes. If unavoidable, make another weep hole on either side of the trap.

Electrician

No Provision for Future Power Requirements

Correct Procedure:
Ensure the meter board is of sufficient size to contain future electrical requirements should the house be extended or a flat added on.

Incorrectly Positioned Meter Box

Correct Procedure:
Should be located within 2000mm from front of house down either side of building. It should be recessed into the wall with its top no higher than permitted by local power authority. Seek an Electrician's advise.

Thin Section Render (Polymer modified cement and sand render and heavy bodied acrylics).

Various faults can manifest in the use of thin section rendered coatings. Use a solid plasterer tradesperson if possible (few applicators are). Faults can emerge soon after the coatings have cured or in the future. These can be caused by incorrect installation of the substrate (base materials upon which coatings are applied), the trim or the actual coatings. *The following will provide guidelines.*

Substrates

Must be fixed according to manufacturers recommendations.

Brick or Concrete Block *Substrate*

These are the most stable substrates and will provide the most reliable surface for applying the coatings. Joints are flush finished and the wall wetted down to create neutral suction for the first coat. Fibreglass, while *not* generally applied, will provide additional protection against future cracking due to movement especially if applied across the entire surface.

Hebel Panels or Blocks *Substrate*

Fairly reliable. *Refer to the CSR Hebel Render System booklet.*

Polystyrene Panels (EPS) *Substrate*

Whilst these are in widespread use, many problems can surface. Coatings must *not* be applied too thinly as hail can then damage the wall.

Installation: An impervious vapour barrier must be applied first across the frame as in some situations the polystyrene causes condensation on the rear side especially in air conditioned spaces.

Cont.

This condensation can damage the frame. However, impervious barriers also restrict the frame from breathing which in turn is not healthy for the frame. Request guarantees that the impervious barriers will *not* cause damage to the frame through restriction of airflow.

After installation and where exposure to the elements has caused yellowing or surface deterioration, the panels must be broomed off before applying coatings.

Flashings and fastenings: Details are too numerous to include here. *See manuf. specifications.*

QT Eco Series Wall Panels *Substrate*

This is a reconstituted polystyrene panel which also contains cement and sand. It is vermin and fireproof. It requires the frame to be battened, permeable sarking attached and weepholes inserted. The system is superior to the above 'EPS' one if manufacturer recommendations are followed.

FC Base Sheets such as Harditex (Blueboard) or Cemintel *Substrate*

Used as part of the manufacturer's dedicated coating system. Or applied as a base sheet for acrylic renders only. *Do not use cement/sand based polymer modified renders over this substrate.* Check Manufacturer's recommendations regarding coatings.

See also 'HBM' for 'Installing Harditex Base Sheet'.

Areas in which to take particular care:

Vapour permeable barrier This must be provided behind the sheets as recommended.

Fastenings, Control joints and Flashings must be provided as specified. 6mm wide sealant filled gaps must be provided at internal corners. It is advisable to avoid dark colours in finished coatings as heating up of the substrate could result in movement in the base sheet.

Fibreglass Mesh for All Substrates

This should be 15oz and have a hole size of 10x10. This mesh is applied across the entire surface of polystyrenes and is a good practice for all substrates. Apply accord. to manuf. specifications.

Trim and Corner Mouldings

A skilled plasterer could dispense with corner mouldings especially for such thin coatings. Corners would be formed wet and with little difference in labour time but minus the problems associated with plastic trim as well as their expense. Stainless steel trim, while expensive, is preferred as plastic has a limited life-span. After renders have been applied, exposed corners or portions of trim must be painted with a full paint system to protect from the elements.

Fastening as specified by the manufacturer.

Coatings

Polymer modified cement/sand or lime

Usually manufacturers make their own formula. There is no specific Australian Standard for them or the consumer to rely upon. Mix according to manuf. requirements. Substrates are generally wetted to prevent undue suction on the first coat. It is usually applied 4-6mm thick. Fibreglass mesh (when applied) is then trowelled into the wet render in vertical runs working from the centre out. A 2-4mm thick top coat is then applied encasing the mesh then screeded or floated to the specified finish.

Curing the Render 3-4 days is required. If hot, dry or windy conditions prevail, the render is wetted down continually for the first 2 days.
The surface then receives its acrylic texture or a quality acrylic paint system.

Acrylic Render Systems (with heavy bodied acrylics)

These should be applied by the manufacturer's trained applicators. The coatings are generally applied over Harditex or Cemintel base sheets with fibreglass mesh over joints. However a superior system, though not common, would sheath the entire wall in fibreglass. *This would be performed as follows:* A first coat of acrylic is applied; the mesh then bedded in and a final coat of acrylic applied over the top encasing the mesh. Acrylic coatings are generally *not* thicker than 2mm. They are *not* applied over polystyrene (EPS). They can be applied over previously painted brick or block accord. to manufacturers recommendations.

Cement Rendering (Traditional)

Only a coverage of pertinent areas is possible here. With decriptions limited to brick and concrete block substrates in general purpose M3 locations. These include elements on marine and non-marine environments not subject to saline wetting and drying or elements in fresh water or non aggressive soils. On brick substrates leave joints raked to provide a better key.

Suction in Substrates

It is vitally important that suction in substrates be assessed before applying coatings to ensure that moisture is not sucked out of the coatings too quickly. Otherwise, the coatings will suffer damage. Suction is controlled by wetting and/or the application of splash coats or scratch coats.

Hot, Dry & Windy Conditions

The tradesperson must be prepared to take extra precautions in these conditions to ensure coatings are *not* drying out abnormally fast. Additional pre-wetting of the background may be necessary or the erection

Cont.

of shade covers or a reduction in the area to be worked to enable easy application and finishing without fighting suction.

Splash Coat and Mixture

This is applied to very hard impervious surfaces to create a key and to reduce and equalise suction across the surface, scabbling may be necessary or a bonding agent or both. ***Mixture is:*** 1 cement to 2 coarse river sand blended into a thick slurry with a bonding agent and applied with a splatter trowel or scoop. Apply to a moist substrate. *Do not* allow splash coats to dry out quickly, they should cure slowly over three days. Bonding agents i.e. Bondcrete must be applied according to the label.

Scratch Coats *(referred to as the first coat or undercoat in the tables on this page).* These are applied to create a key to reduce and equalize suction and to fill undulations. Applied directly to the substrate or over a splash coat. The surface is scratched with horizontal scratches to one third of the depth of the coat using a scratching comb with points spaced at 10-12mm to 20mm MAX apart. *Do not* allow to dry out too quickly. Allow three days to dry before applying top coat.

Existing Expansion Joints should continue through the surface of the render to avoid irregular cracking.

Ventilators should not be blocked off and the render should be neatly finished around them.

Weep Holes Where these occur, the render should be cut out neatly to expose them. Should these be blocked off, internal flooding can occur.

Bagging A bagging finish is a single coat of thin slurry rubbed over the substrate with a bunched up piece of hessian, sponge float or similar, working in a circular motion. The same consideration for background suction and adhesion applies. ***Mix proportions:*** 1 cement: ½ lime: 4½ sand for moderately strong backgrounds plus a bonding agent if necessary.

Table 1. Substrate Identification & Recommended Process

SUBSTRATE	PROCESS
Dense Strong and Smooth Substrates	***Off-form concrete and impervious bricks*** provide poor suction or adherence for render. These require scabbling then a splash coat using bonding agents.
Moderately Strong Substrates	***Most porous clay masonry.*** A splash coat is recommended as also are raked joints. If necessary, a scratch coat may be applied over the splash coat. Otherwise the final coat may be laid directly over the splash coat.
Moderately Weak to Weak Substrates	***Concrete block and porous concrete.*** Dampen surface lightly and apply a normal scratch coat. Allow to cure for three days then apply the final render coat.

Table 2. **Typical Render Mixes -** ***for General Purpose (GP)*** **M3 environments - these mixtures will cover M2 environments as well.**

Parts by Volume: Cement: Lime: Sand			
Material Ratio	**Location**	**Application**	**Render Thickness (mm)**
1:½:4½	External	First and second undercoat on dense, strong substrates.	8-12
1:1:6	External	Final coat on dense, strong substrate. Undercoat or final coat on mod-strong substrate. Undercoat on no-fines concrete.	8-12

Much of the above material on traditional cement rendering kindly supplied by 'Cement, Concrete & Aggregates Australia'.

Using Building Tools & Materials

7

Measuring & Marking Out

The Retractable Tape Measure

The retractable tape measure has enlongated rivet holes in its hook as in figs 1 & 2 enabling it to take outside measurements as in fig 3 or inside measurements as in fig 5.

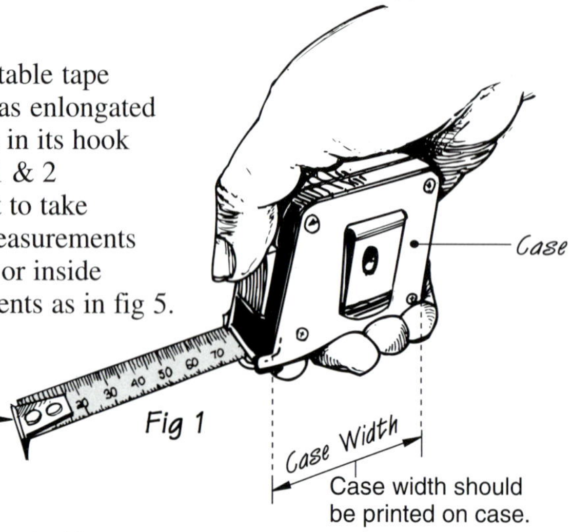

Fig 1

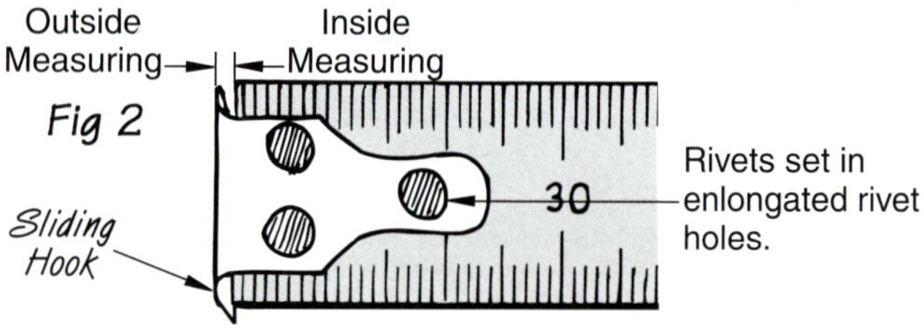

Fig 2

Taking Measurements

When measuring external lengths of material, place the hook over the end of the material as in fig 3 and lay the tape in a straight line parallel to its edge to ensure accuracy.

Fig 3

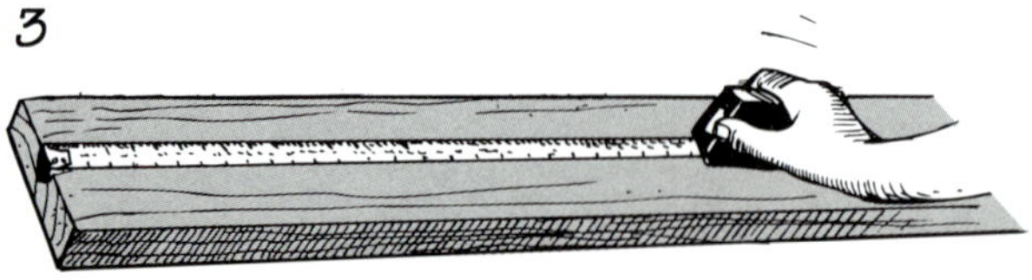

Fig 4

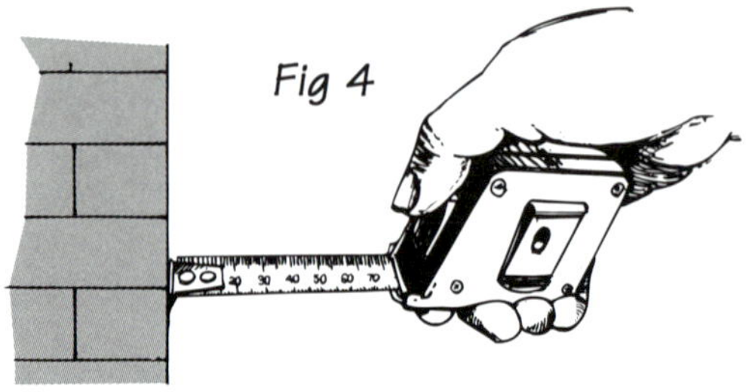

Measuring when abutting to surfaces.

For internal measurements include the inside of case.

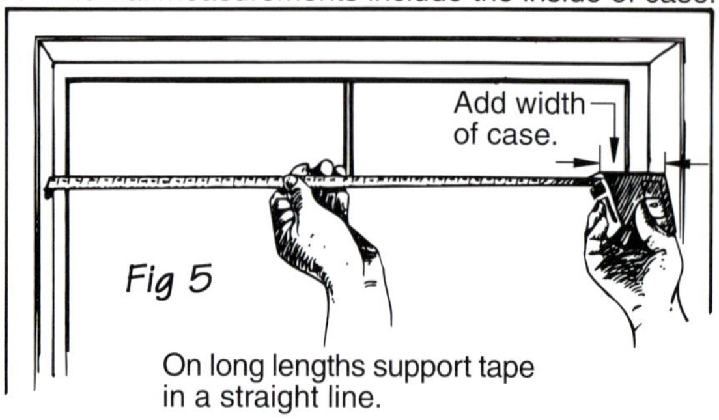

Fig 5

On long lengths support tape in a straight line.

Marking out

Again hold the tape in a straight line and parallel with the material then roll its curved bottom until the edge is in touch with the material. Then make the mark sighting from directly above.

Fig 6

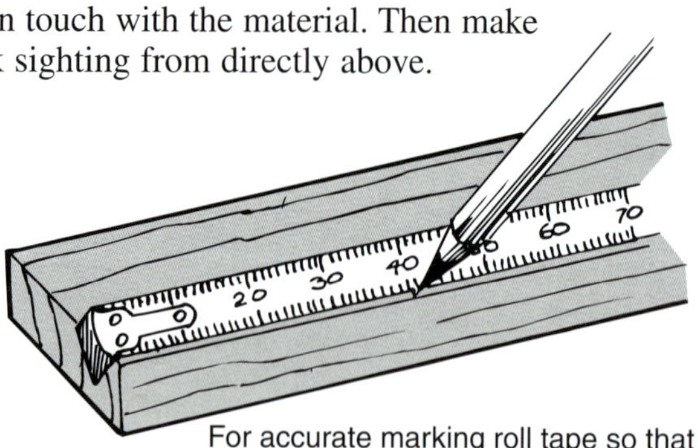

For accurate marking roll tape so that one edge touches the material.

Metric Rules or Tapes

In metric rules used in building construction each increment represents one millimetre. Longer dimensions are marked every five, ten and 100 millimetres. The exception is rafter squares where increments are marked every two millimetres.

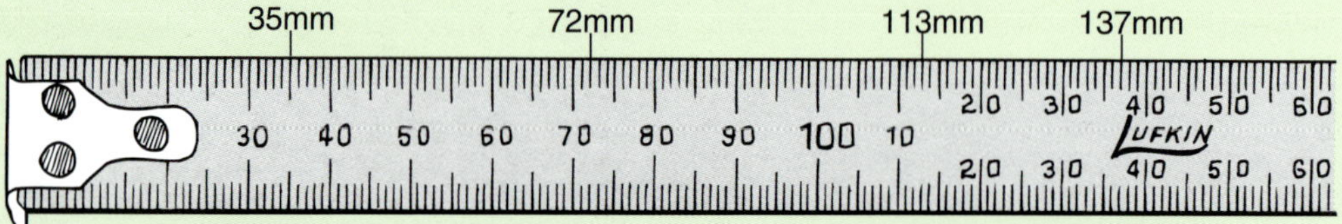

TAKING MEASUREMENTS FROM A METRIC RULE OR TAPE

Hints:

a). When retracting, be sure to restrain the adjustable hook from slamming into the case as this will enlarge the rivet holes and render measurements inaccurate.

b). Double check measurements especially when cutting expensive beams or sheet material etc.

Using the Scientific Calculator in Building

The type and brands of calculators available are many and varied and therefore difficult to generalise. However, most calculators with the features described in this chapter will be similar to the one shown in Fig. 1.

Fig 1

It is important that the operating manual be read in conjunction with these notes. Many keys feature an alternative or 'second' function in addition to that printed on the top of the key. This is printed on the body of thc calculator abovc thc kcy.

To activate this second function, depress the [2nd F] or [SHIFT] or [INV] before the main key. Depending which your calculator has.

All unit measurements must be the same in each calculation. For example, all in metres or all in millimetres, all in dollars or all in cents. For ease of working, most linear measurements are best calculated in metres. Always cancel previous entries before attempting a new calculation.

For all the following examples and all other basic arithmetic calculations, the calculator must be set to **COMP** or **DEG** mode. Refer to the instrument's manual to enter this.

Addition and Subtraction

Keys: [+] [−] [=]

Example: Add the following three figures 4 965mm, 17 470mm & 11 135mm then subtract 475mm

Procedure:

4.965 [+] 17.47 [+] 11.135 [−] .475 [=]

Answer displayed: 33.095 metres

Practical Example: Find the length of the privacy screen as in fig 2. It is taken to the rear fence less 915mm for gate opening and has a 968mm return to the deck at the opposite end.

Fig 2

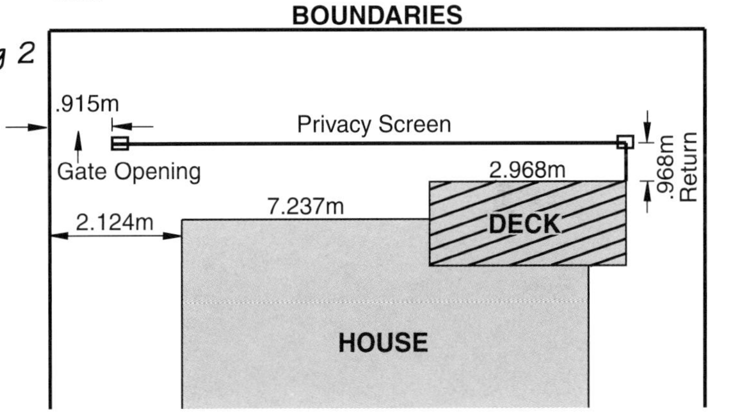

Procedure:

2.124 [+] 7.237 [+] 2.968 [+] .968

[−] .915 [=]

Answer displayed: 12.382 metres

Multiplication and Division

Keys: [×] [÷] [=]

Example: A floor area 13 750 long and 9 100 wide is to be laid with T&G flooring with a cover width of 65mm. Calculate the linear quantity of boarding.

Fig 3

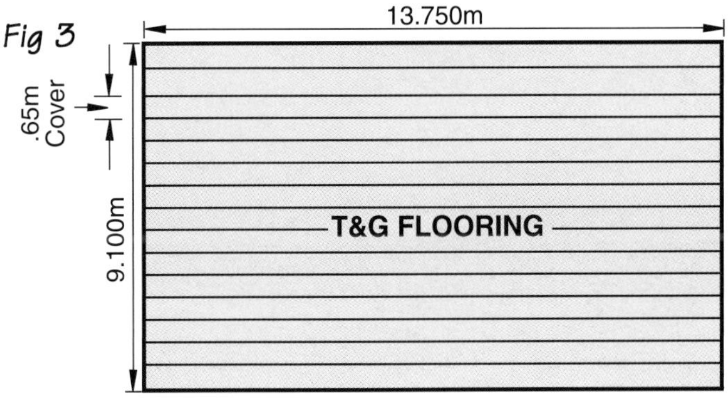

Procedure:

13.75 [×] 9.1 [÷] .065 [=]

Answer displayed: 1925 metres

Squaring and Square Root

Keys: [√] [x^2]

(A second function may be required).

Usage: Triangulation

Example: For squaring purposes, determine the length of the diagonals of the rectangular building set-out as in fig 4.

It measures: 9 480mm long by 6 720mm wide.

i.e. $\sqrt{9.48^2 + 6.72^2}$

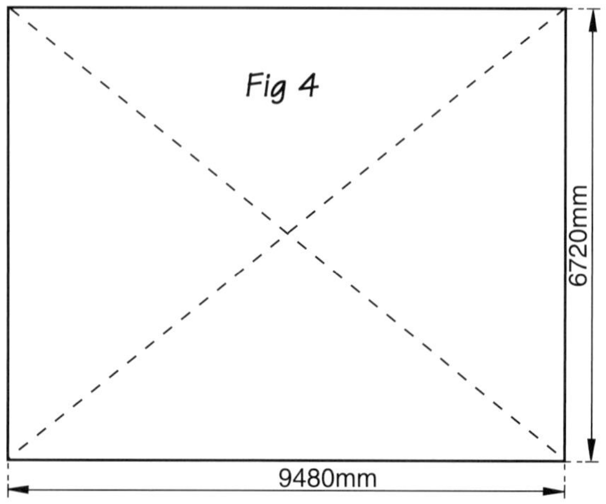

Procedure:

9.48 [x^2] [+] 6.72 [x^2] [=] [√] [=]

Answer displayed: 11.620 metres

Percentage

Percentage Symbol

Keys: [%] or [=]

(This may be a second function as above).

Usage: Calculation of discounts or percentage reduction and percentage increase such as wastage allowances, tax, profit, and overhead expenses.

The previous example of T&G flooring quantity for multiplication and division fig 3 gives the flooring requirement for a given area but allowance for wastage was not provided. This is usually added as a percentage of the total.

Example (a): Determine the allowance for wastage of flooring for fig 3 Page 104. Allow 5%. The present flooring total is 1925m without waste allowance.

Procedure:

1925 [×] 5 SHIFT [=]

Percentage of waste is displayed 96.25

To add to total: [+]

Answer displayed: 2021.25 metres

Example (b): Allow and add 15% for wastage on an estimated 17.5 m³ or cubic metres of concrete.

Procedure:

17.5 [×] 15 SHIFT [=] [+]

Answer displayed: 20.125m³ or cubic metres.

Example (c): An order for 840 metres of flooring was 21 metres short. What percentage should have been added for cutting and waste?

Procedure:

21 [÷] 840 SHIFT [=] [−]

Answer displayed: 2·5%

Example (d): Take 7½% discount from $179.20

Procedure:

179.2 [×] 7.5 SHIFT [=] [−]

Answer displayed: $165·76

Example (e): The amount of tax included in $21 340. Taxable rate is 10%.

Procedure:

21340 [÷] 110 SHIFT [=]

Displays the net amount of $19 400

Tax: 21340 [−] 19400 [=]

Answer displayed: $1,940

Example (f): The amount of discount included in an item purchased for $1296.25. Discount rate is 15%.

Procedure:

1296·25 [÷] 85 SHIFT [=]

Displays the marked price of $1,525.

Discount: 1525 [−] 1296.25 [=]

Answer displayed: $228.75

Independent Memory

Keys: [M+] (M– M) [RCL] (STO)

(Some may be activated by second function).

[M+] (M– M) adds/subtracts displayed figures to/from an accumulated memory. [RCL] recalls and displays accumulated memory. This figure is held in memory even when the instrument is turned off. It must be manually cleared.

Always clear memory before commencing a new calculation.

Usage: Where a number of separately calculated quantities are required as part of a final result.

Example: Determine the total linear quantity of timber from the list.

145 / 2.4, 22 / 2.7, 5 / 3.3, 14 / 4·2

Procedure:

145 [×] 2.4 [=] [M+]

22 [×] 2.7 [=] [M+]

5 [×] 3.3 [=] [M+]

14 [×] 4.2 [=] [M+]

To recall the total accumulated memory:

[RCL] [M+]

Answer displayed: 482·7 metres.

To clear this stored memory for further calculation:

[0] [SHIFT] [RCL] (STO) [M+]

Parentheses

Keys: [(] [)]

Usage: This procedure is mainly useful to a builder who has frequent use for it.

Multi-function calculations. Mathematical rules dictate an order of process. Any part of a problem contained within brackets must be calculated first, followed by multiplication and division, then finally, addition and subtraction. (BOMDAS)

Example: Determine the number of floor tiles required for the bathroom as shown in Fig 5. Tiles are *not* required under the bath or vanity unit.

Fig 5

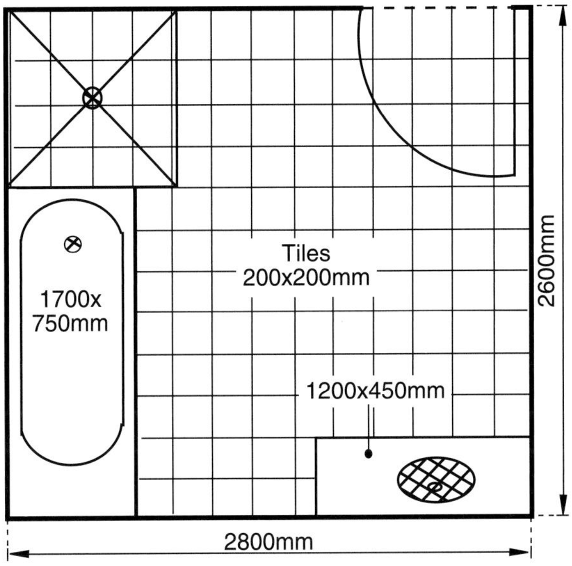

Procedure:

((2.8x2.6) - ((1.2x.45) + (1.7x.75))) / (.2x.2)=

[(] [(] 2.8 [×] 2.6 [)] [−]

[(] [(] 1.2 [×] .45 [)] [+]

[(] 1.7 [×] .75 [)] [)] [)] [÷]

[(] .2 [×] .2 [)] [=]

Answer displayed: 136.625 rounded to 137 tiles.

Explanation: To explain the above process, the 2.8 x 2.6 is the total room area.

The vanity 1.2 x 4.5 has two brackets '((' in front which tells the calculator to carry out this multiplication before applying the '-' then the bath area 1.7x.75 is added to the vanity area.

The ')))' brackets are telling the calculator to add the two areas together before deducting them from the 2.8x2.6 area.

The resulting total is then divided by .2x.2 which is the individual tile size, in order to obtain the total tile quantity of 137.

How to Mark Parallel Lines

(a). Where precision is *not* necessary lines can be marked using the end of finger tips as a gauge against the material see fig 1.

(b). For gauging a measurement quickly of a greater width for medium accuracy use a rule or the retractable tape as in fig 2.

(c). Where even greater precision is necessary a combination square is adjusted to required depth and a sharp pencil as well is the end of the finger are held firmly against the end of the blade for the whole to act as a single tool. The gauge handle trails behind to prevent binding and the tool is pulled toward the body as in fig 3.

(d). Where further accuracy is required the marking gauge is applied (see figs 4 & 5).

Fig 3

For accuracy pull tool towards your body and keep middle pencil finger just touching the end of the blade and maintain continuous movement.

Fig 1

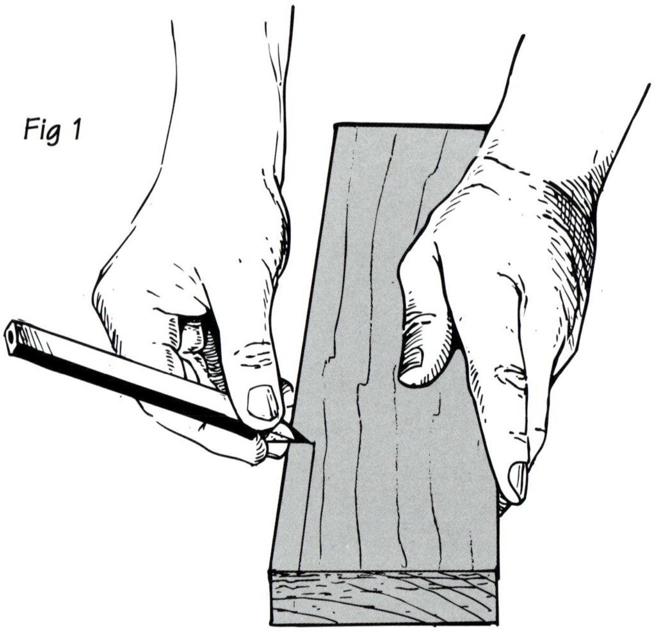

Sliding middle finger firmly along edge to gauge a line.

Fig 2

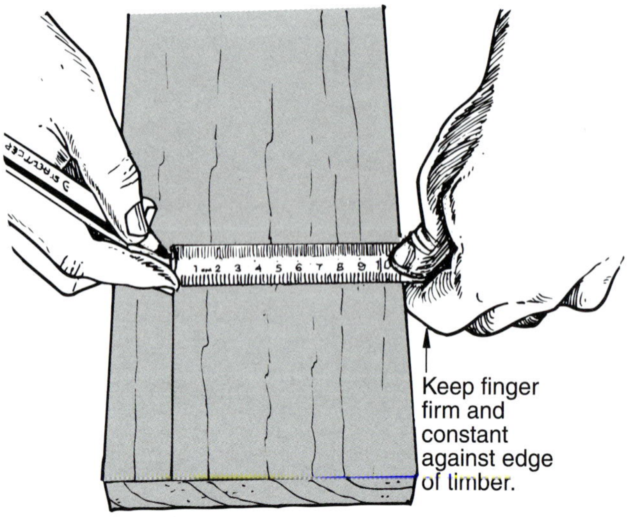

Using a tape or rule as a depth gauge. Keep the pencil and fingers against the end of the tape and make a continuous movement through the length.

Gauging Parallel Lines with the Marking Gauge

This tool should have the pin set to very short around 1-2mm. The tool is rolled to its forward edge and pushed away from the user. Keep the stock firm against the material. Carry out a few practice runs on scrap until you can produce a clean even line of the same depth.

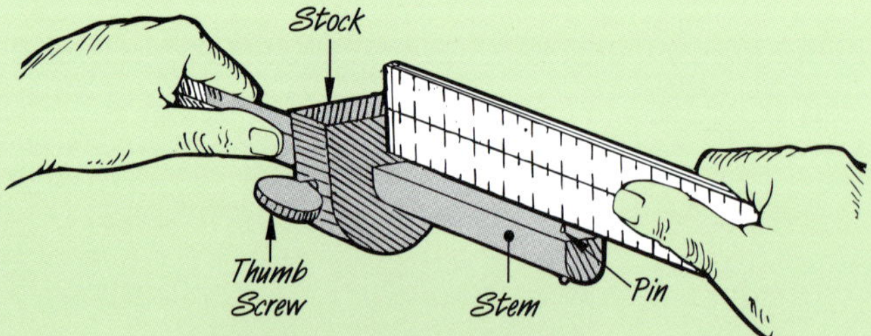

Release thumb screw and adjust stem to the required depth and retighten screw.

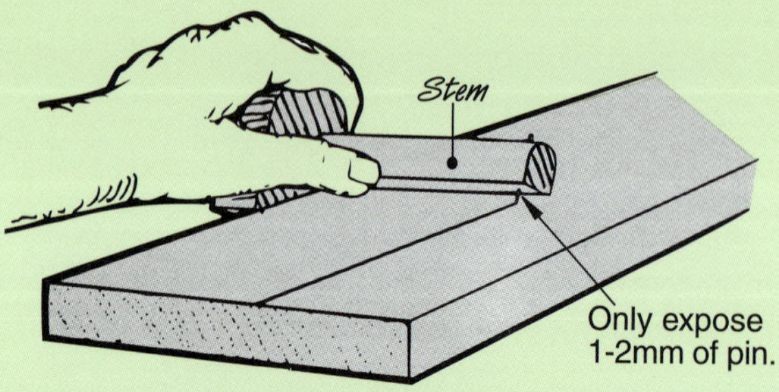

Roll gauge onto the forward edge of the stem and push away from your body with even pressure.

Scribing

Scribing is simply transferring one surface contour or profile onto another. This can be performed with a pair of dividers, a pencil and small block or just a pencil. On new construction, joins at internal corners of mouldings such as skirtings can be achieved by simply mitre cutting the corner in a mitre box then cutting away the outlined shape using a coping saw as described in the 'Australia House Building Manual'. Without the need for scribing but when fitting new mouldings to large or old existing ones it is often necessary to transfer the shape with dividers.

Using Dividers

Step 1 Square cut the first moulding then butt-fit it between the walls. Then lay the loose adjoining mould with its end against the fixed one as in fig 1.

Step 2 Open the dividers to slightly wider than the widest gap.

Step 3 Commence to scribe the shape of the fixed mould onto the loose one by following the contour with one point. Maintain the dividers parallel with the contours (see fig 2).

Step 4 Cut away the scribed waste with the coping saw.

Fig 1

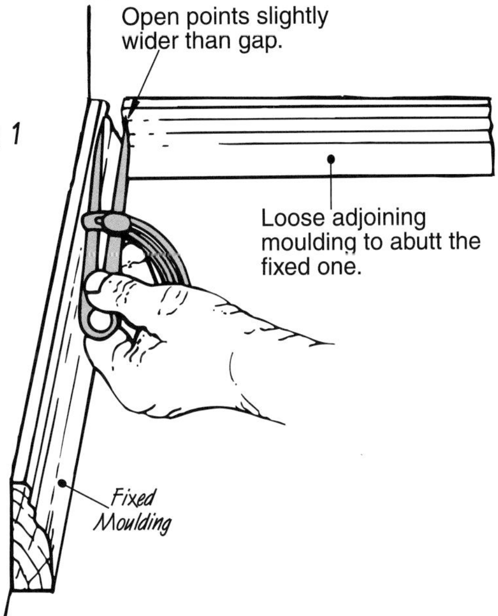

Fig 2

Ensure points and arms of the dividers remain parallel with the contours.

Fig 3

A moulding may be scribed to fit against weatherboards at the sides of windows and door frames instead of using sealant alone. *See the 'HBM' for complete details.*

Using the Pencil & Block Method

One example is when fitting the end of a weatherboard into another on internal corners.

Step 1 Move the loose board to abutt the fixed ones.

Step 2 Slide the block down the fixed board and scribe a line onto the loose board following the board as in fig 4.

Fig 4

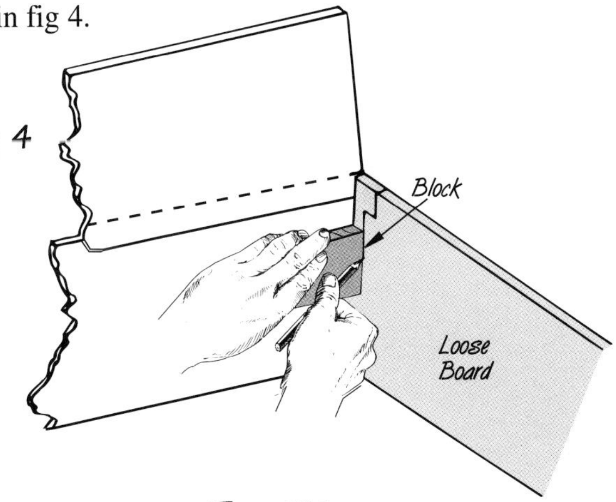

Fig 5

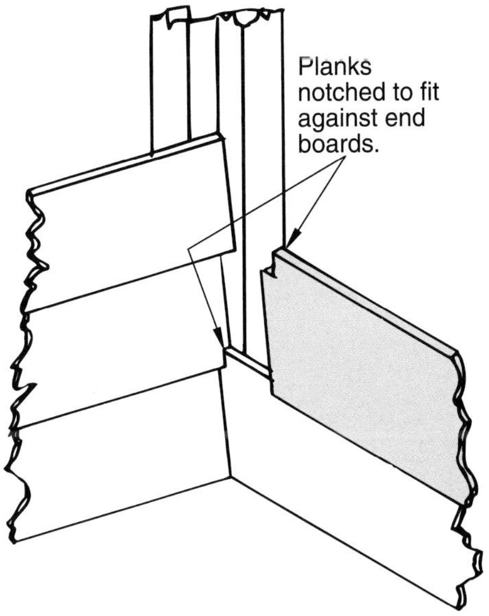

Cont.

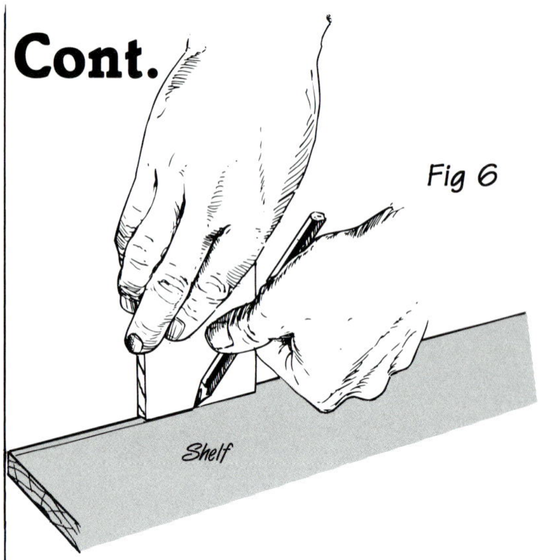

Fig 6

Another common use for this method is when fitting a shelf or similar against a wall that has an uneven surface. The same result can often be achieved with the pencil alone as in fig 7.

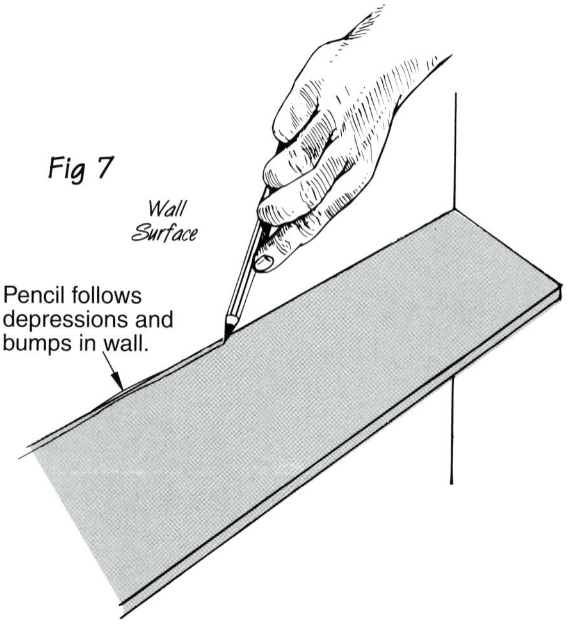

Fig 7

Marking Equal Distances using Dividers

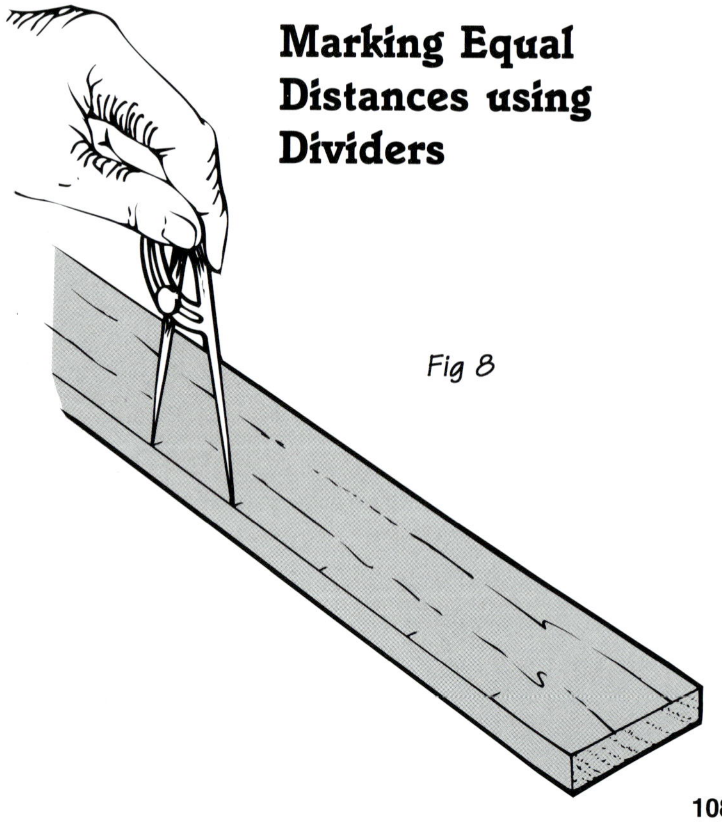

Fig 8

Dividing Material into Equal Parts

Material can be divided any number of equal parts. You don't need to know the width of the board e.g. to divide the board by say, four. Select a measurement that can be divided equally by four and which is also larger than the width of the board. Below we chose 100mm i.e. 4x25mm=100. We could have chosen 120mm which would have given 4x30mm. Then angle the rule till the 100 touches the corner of the timber and space out 4x25mm.

Fig 9

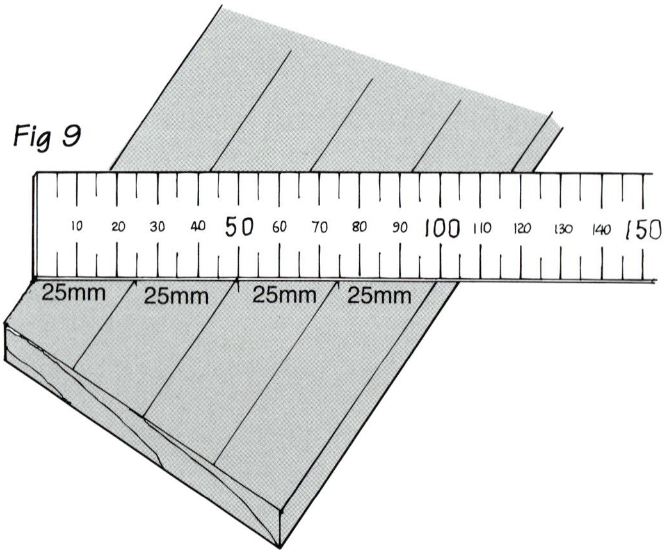

How to Divide a Line or Element by Ratio

This is useful when setting out a pattern or several elements by differing proportions. Say we want to divide a line into three parts, five parts and seven parts. Firstly add these dimensions together 3+5+7=15. Draw the right angle A,B,C. Then draw line A D. It's length will divide into 15 equal parts. Firstly adjust the rule up or down until its 15th part intersects B C.

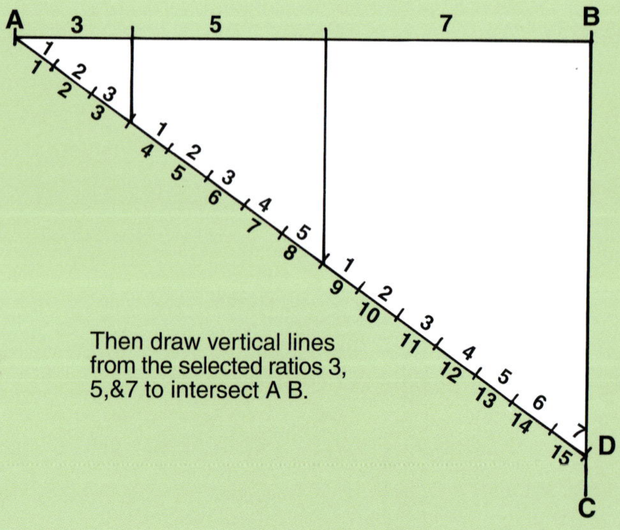

Squaring Bevelling & Gauging Tools

Combination Square

This tool if, accurately square can replace the trisquare and it does have many applications. It has a level and a steel scriber in the handle. It pays to keep this elsewhere to avoid loss. The scriber can be used instead of a pencil on metal or to create an etched mark for a sharp chisel to follow.

Before use, the tightening screw should be tightened otherwise the blade could be out of square in its loose position.

Use this tool for:

(a). Squaring lines at 90º (see fig 1).
(b). Marking 45º lines (see fig 2).
(c). Gauging depths (see fig 3).
(d). Gauging parallel lines (see fig 4).
(e). Squaring objects (see fig 5).
(f). Checking faces for flatness (see fig 6).
(g). Checking edges for square and true (see fig 7).

Fig 4

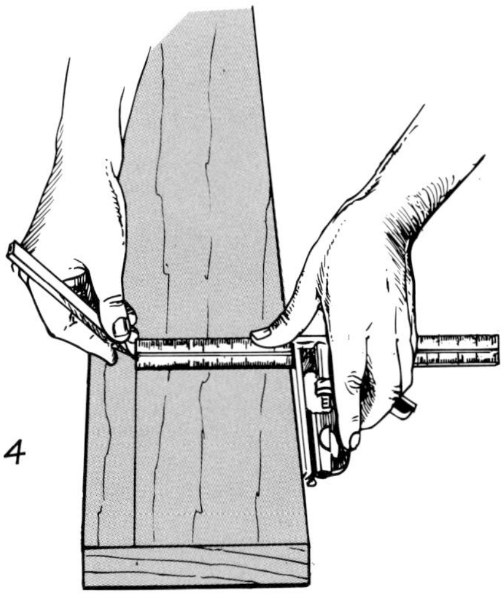

Using the square as a marking gauge.

Fig 1

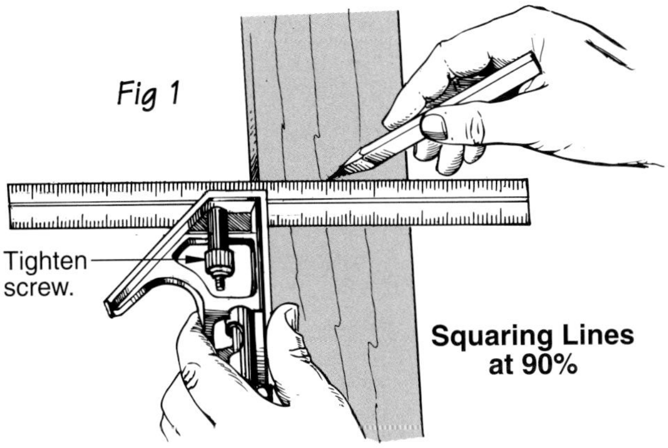

Squaring Lines at 90%

Fig 5

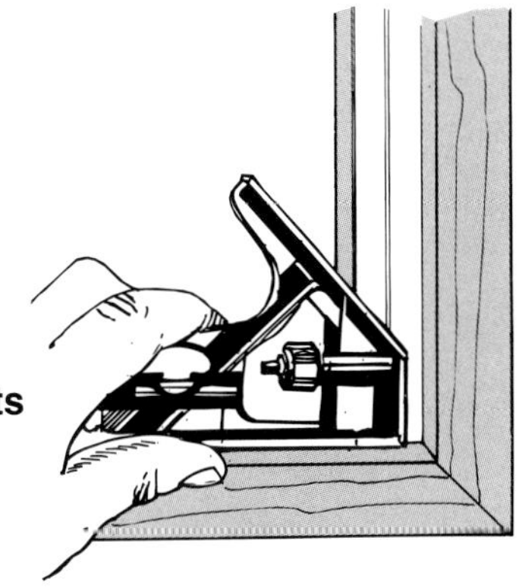

Checking objects for square.

Fig 2

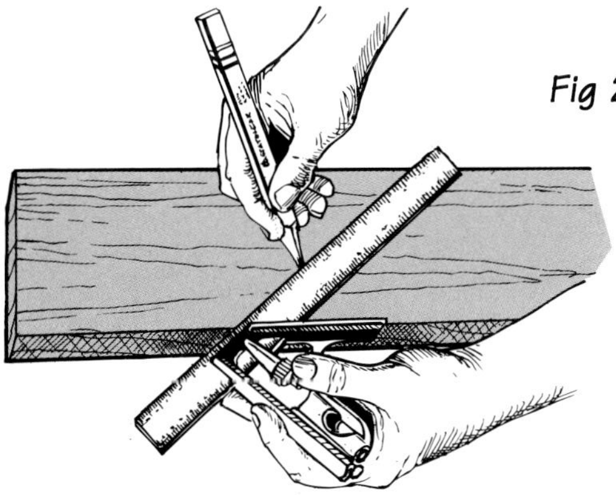

Marking 45° Bevels

Fig 6

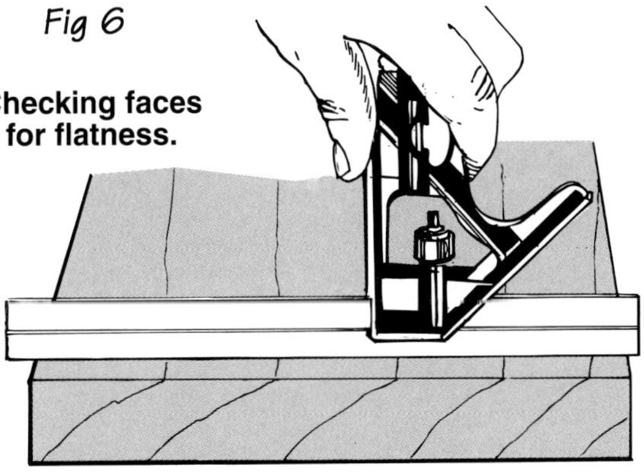

Checking faces for flatness.

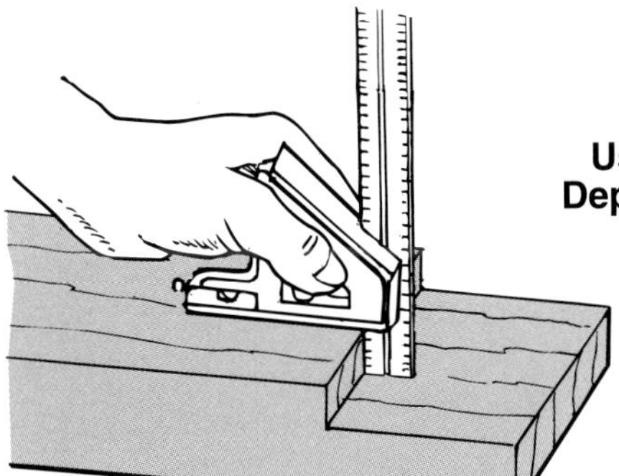

Used as a Depth Gauge

Fig 3

Fig 7

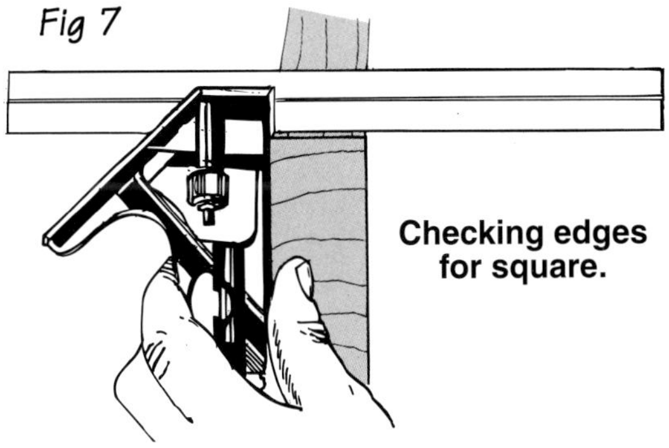

Checking edges for square.

The Adjustable Bevel

The adjustable bevel is invaluable for obtaining or transferring angles. For greater accuracy purchase the steel model of a well known brand rather than wood or plastic.

Use this tool for:
(a). Obtaining existing angles.
(b). Transferring angles to material.

Fig 1

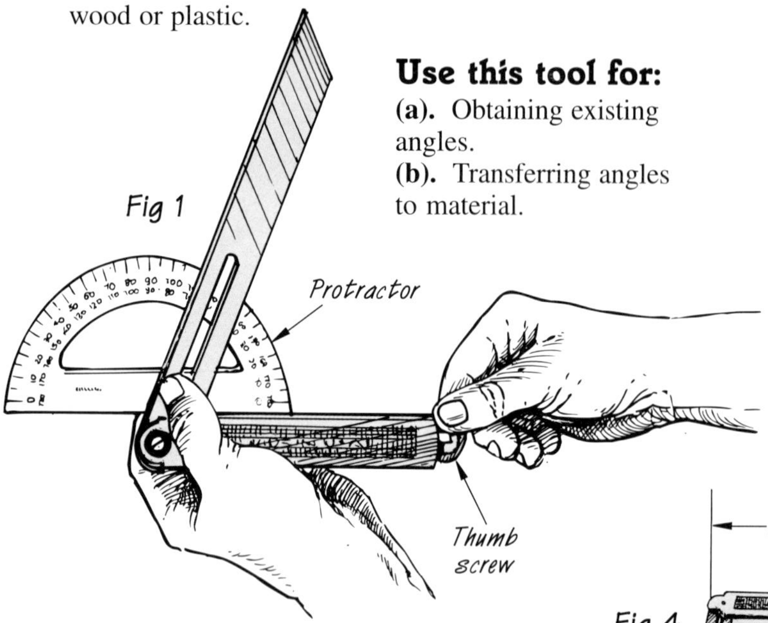

Obtain bevels from the protractor, rafter square or from existing angles on site. Larger protractors will enable more accurate bevel adjustment.

Fig 2

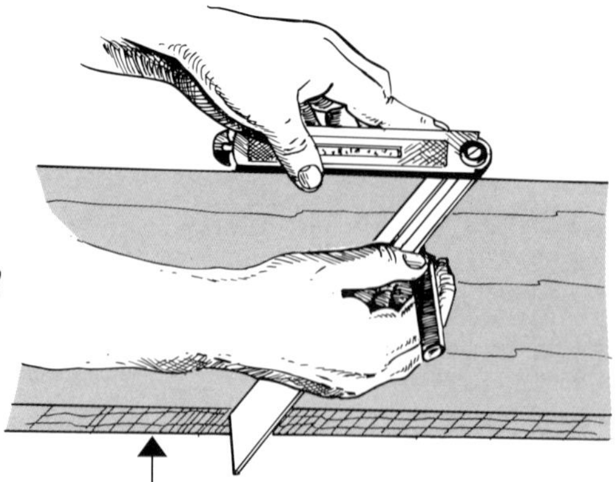

Once the tool is adjusted to a specific bevel, it can be transferred to the material.

Fig 3

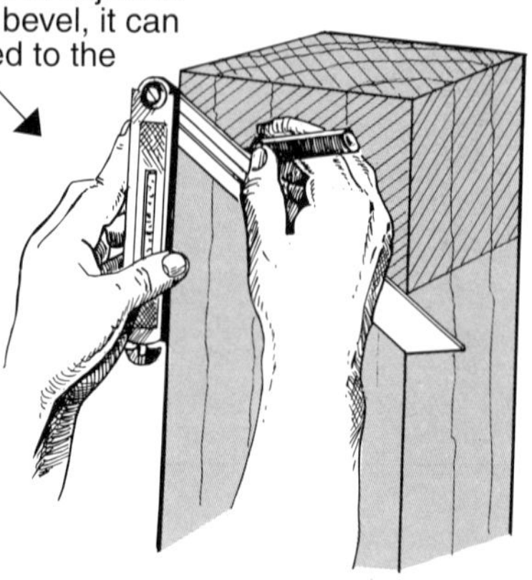

Fig 4

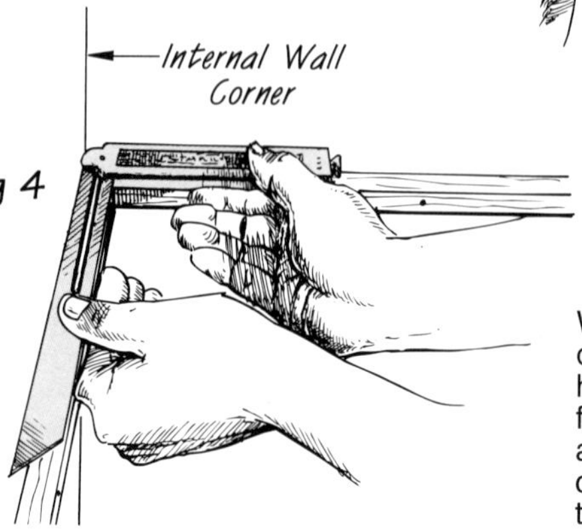

Walls are *not* always square to one another especially on older houses. Obtain the corner angle for cutting shelving etc by adjusting the bevel in the actual corner then transfer this angle to the material.

Adjustable Tool for Cutting Struts, Braces etc

This tool is most useful to have in the kit for roof struts or sub-floor bracing requiring two sets of angles founded on an angle as in fig 2.

The end squares could be made from plywood and the central arm from 42x12mm dressed timber.

Fig 1

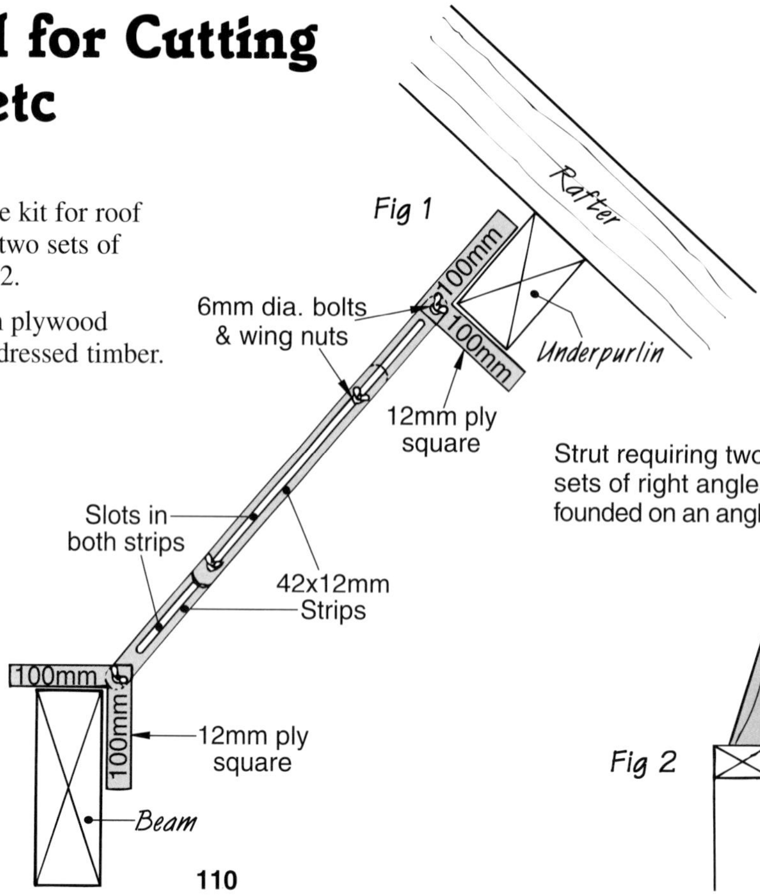

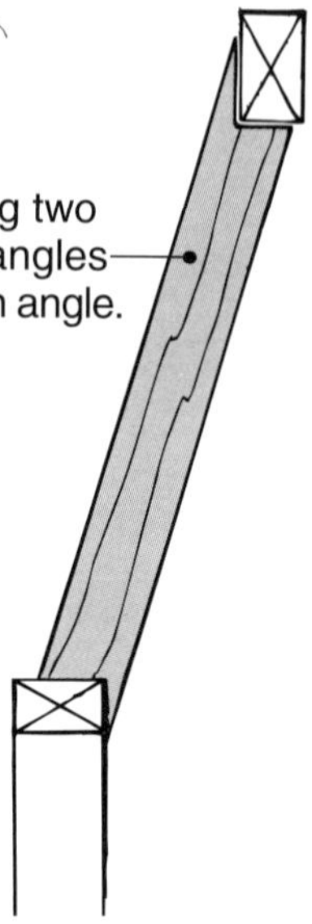

Fig 2

The Rafter Square

The rafter square is indispensable. A fence or steel guides can be attached as in figs 1 & 2 for setting out rafters or stair stringers. It is used for ensuring cabinets and frames are square as in fig 3. Use it for marking square lines on sheet material or multiple members such as studs as in fig 4.

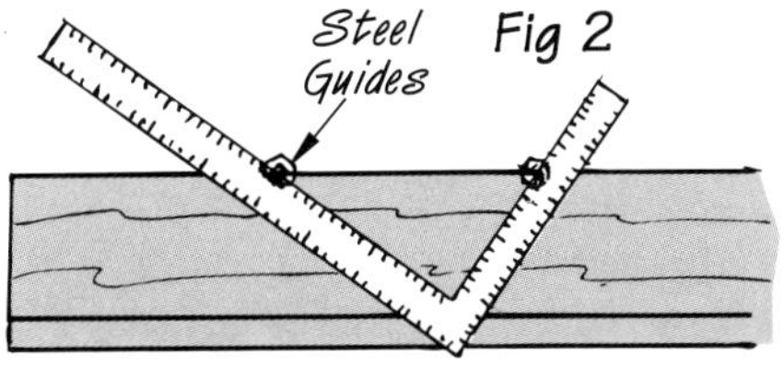

Steel guides are available from hardwares. Use for setting out rafters or stair stringers.

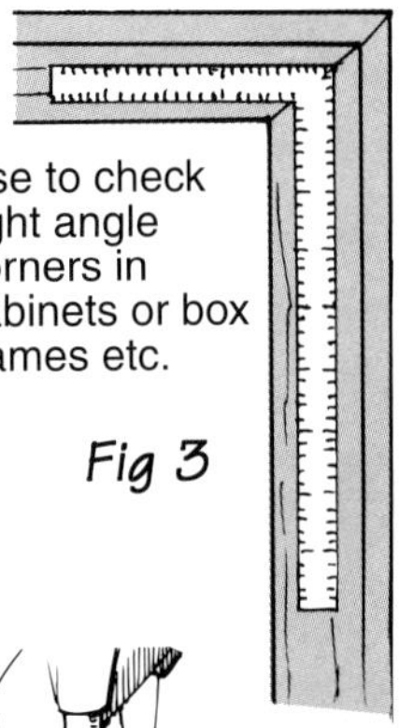

Use to check right angle corners in cabinets or box frames etc.

Fig 3

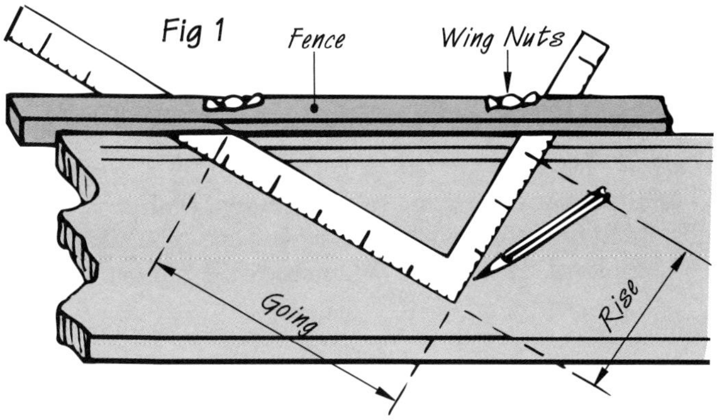

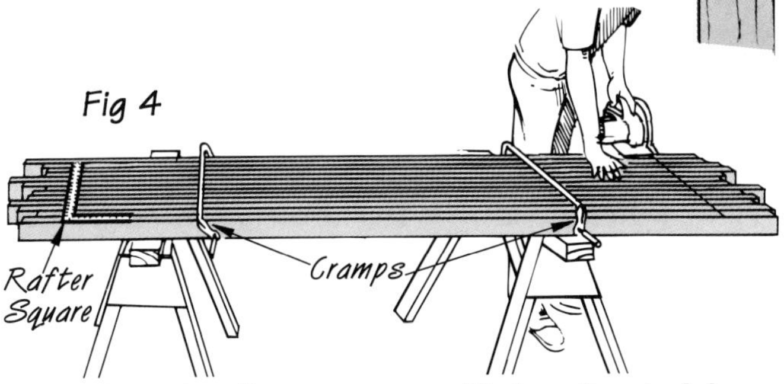

Squaring lines across multiples of material

The Spirit Level

It is essential to have a 1200mm long model and if possible a 450mm for short work. Take care *not* to drop as the impact can misalign the bubble.

How to Check for Accuracy

When purchasing, apply the level to a flat surface and mark its position. Note the position of the bubble then rotate it, holding it in exactly the same position. The bubble should align in the same position both times. The same test should be carried out on the plumbing bubbles rotating the level and end for ending it.

Using a Spirit Level for Levelling

Hold one end on a fixed point as in fig 1 and raise the other end until the bubble is located centrally in the vial. Then mark a level line or apply packers beneath the object or lower one end until level. If the bubble is not central in the vial, it's *not* level. Always rotate the level to check that the bubble rests in the same position. If it doesn't, the object will require adjusting until the bubble maintains centrality on rotation.

Plumbing Objects

Always check the level is touching the surface throughout and it's not being deflected by a lump etc. This is the same as for horizontal levellings. The surface or edge must be adjusted until the bubble is located centrally.

Fence, verandah and framing posts, whether embedded in concrete or soil or installed in saddle anchors will have to be plumbed on both sides of the posts. When the posts are in saddle anchors, they will require braces both ways until the concrete hardens. Where stiff concrete is used, braces can often be omitted.

Plumb both sides of posts.

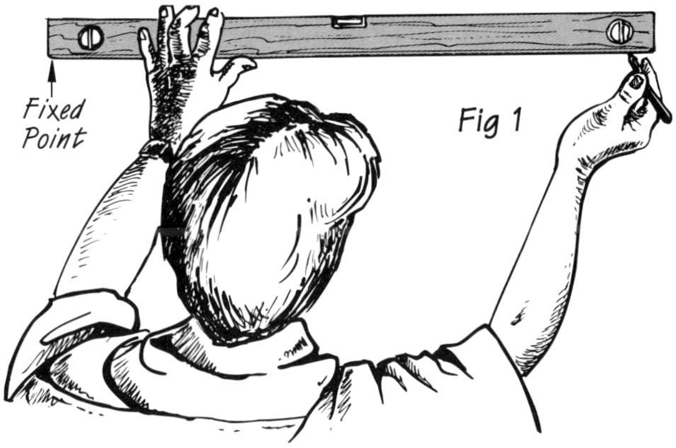

Plumbing & Levelling a Patio Door Frame

Fig 3

How to Set-out a House or Extension Profiles

Establish the Boundaries

Buildings are *not* uncommonly erected on the wrong site or encroach onto adjoining boundary space. This often involves litigation. Have a Surveyor confirm boundary pegs to be accurate. Ground movement and people do move them.

Preliminary to Setting up Profiles

Profile hurdles are required to enable the proposed foundation and sub-floor to be erected in square and true alignment and for walls to be accurately sited and aligned. But first their location is pegged as follows.

Step 1 Drive a nail in the centre of the boundary pegs and stretch string lines through.

Step 2 Roughly peg the proposed corners of the house or extension (see fig 1). Roughly square the area using 'Pythagoras Theorem' or the '3,4'5' method *(see the 'Australian House Building Manual' Chapter 2 for more information).*

This can also be carried out using diagonal measurements as applied in 'Squaring the Area' Step 7 and fig 1. Alternatively, after pegging two sides. They can be squared using the scientific calculator and the square and square root function.
See below:

Squaring using the Calculator

Example on 'How to Square two sides of known length': To bring the two sides into square, the length of the third side is required. The calculator will provide this - using the x^2 & √ buttons.

This example measures: 9 480mm long by 6 720mm wide. i.e. $\sqrt{9.48^2 + 6.72^2}$

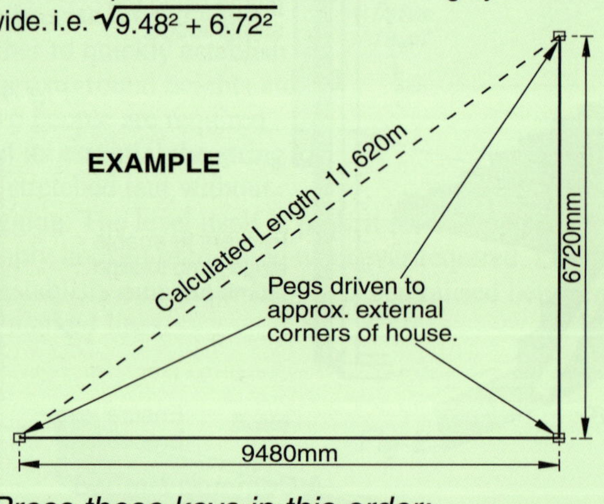

Press these keys in this order:

9.48 x^2 + 6.72 x^2 = √ =

Answer displayed: **11.620 metres**

Step 3 After establishing the four external corners of the house with pegs and into roughly square alignment, erect profile hurdles outside these pegs as in fig 2. Allow space for excavating machinery to manoeuvre. Profiles need to have all their top surfaces on the same level plane. Use an automatic level or laser level. Be sure to peg and brace hurdles over 1200mm high to maintain rigidity.

Setting out on the Profiles

Step 4 Mark the front external wall face on the profiles. Establish it's distance from the front boundary by measuring back from the front boundary string line.

Step 5 Mark the rear external wall face measuring from the front external wall face.

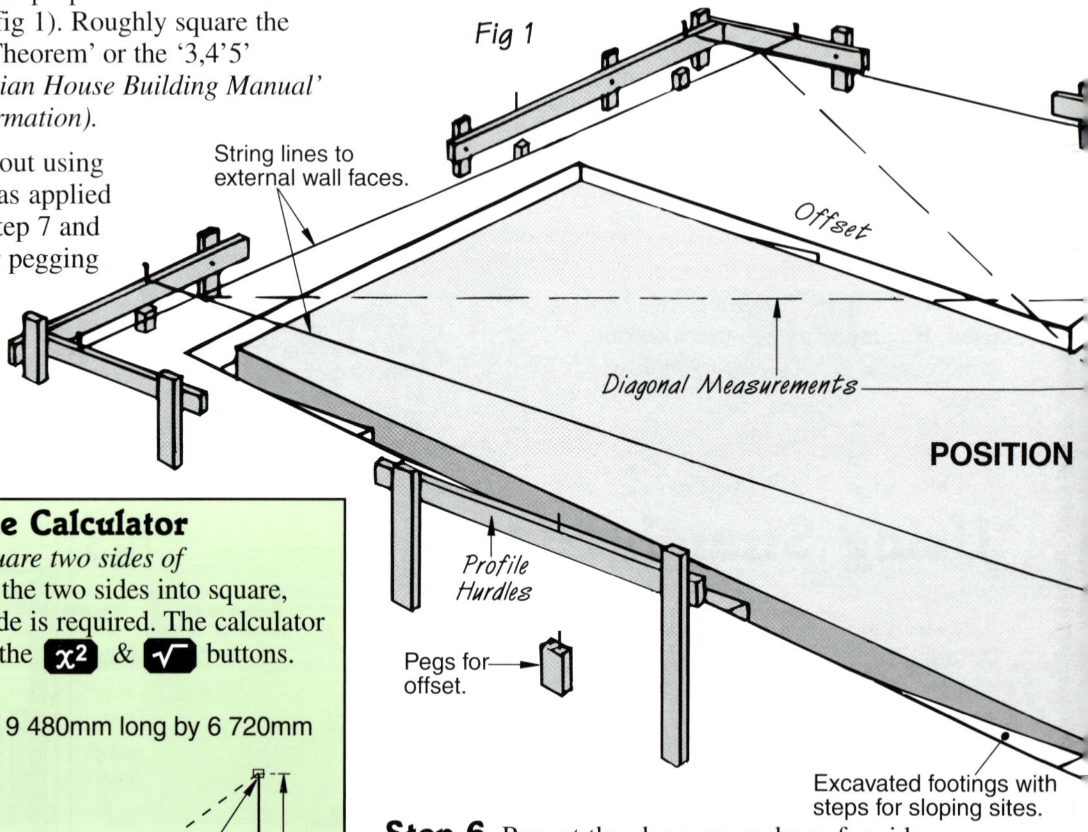

Step 6 Repeat the above procedures for side walls. Don't be concerned about offsets at this stage. Drive nails to these points and stretch string lines through.

Square the Area

The points where the string line intersect will be the proposed corners of the building. This area is now brought into square alignment.

Step 7 Take diagonal measurements from the string line intersections as indicated by the dashed line as in fig 1. These lengths should correspond.

Step 8 If these measurements don't correspond, and they probably won't, adjust the two rear nails supporting the side wall string lines. Adjust both the same amount until the diagonal measurements correspond.

The Rafter Square

The rafter square is indispensable. A fence or steel guides can be attached as in figs 1 & 2 for setting out rafters or stair stringers. It is used for ensuring cabinets and frames are square as in fig 3. Use it for marking square lines on sheet material or multiple members such as studs as in fig 4.

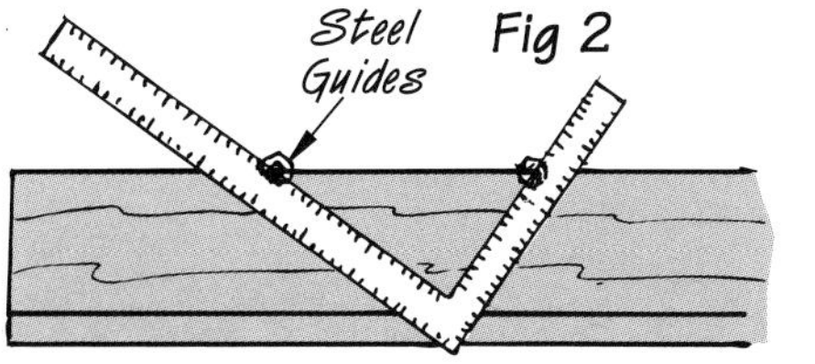

Steel guides are available from hardwares. Use for setting out rafters or stair stringers.

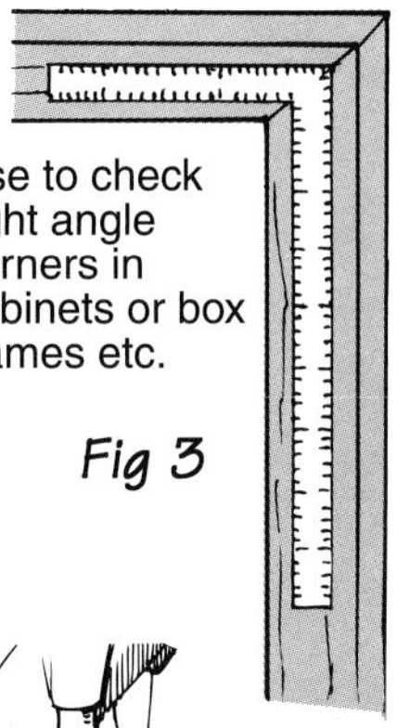

Use to check right angle corners in cabinets or box frames etc.

Fig 3

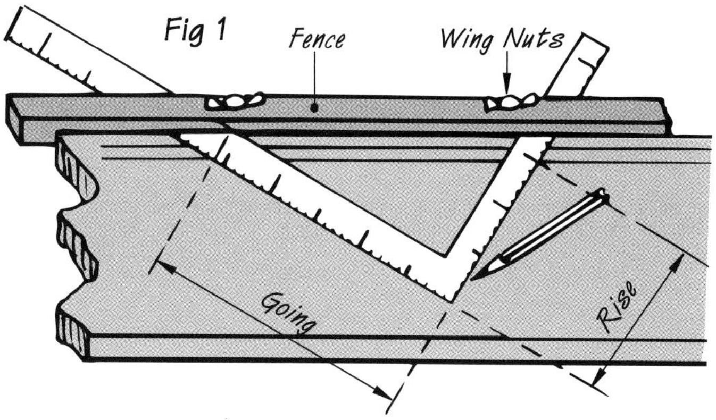

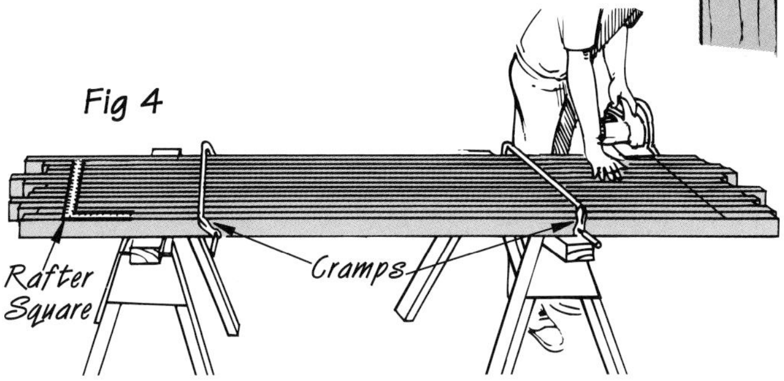

Squaring lines across multiples of material

The Spirit Level

It is essential to have a 1200mm long model and if possible a 450mm for short work. Take care *not* to drop as the impact can misalign the bubble.

How to Check for Accuracy

When purchasing, apply the level to a flat surface and mark its position. Note the position of the bubble then rotate it, holding it in exactly the same position. The bubble should align in the same position both times. The same test should be carried out on the plumbing bubbles rotating the level and end for ending it.

Using a Spirit Level for Levelling

Hold one end on a fixed point as in fig 1 and raise the other end until the bubble is located centrally in the vial. Then mark a level line or apply packers beneath the object or lower one end until level. If the bubble is not central in the vial, it's *not* level. Always rotate the level to check that the bubble rests in the same position. If it doesn't, the object will require adjusting until the bubble maintains centrality on rotation.

Plumbing Objects

Always check the level is touching the surface throughout and it's not being deflected by a lump etc. This is the same as for horizontal levellings. The surface or edge must be adjusted until the bubble is located centrally.

Fence, verandah and framing posts, whether embedded in concrete or soil or installed in saddle anchors will have to be plumbed on both sides of the posts. When the posts are in saddle anchors, they will require braces both ways until the concrete hardens. Where stiff concrete is used, braces can often be omitted.

Plumb both sides of posts.

Plumbing & Levelling a Patio Door Frame

Fig 3

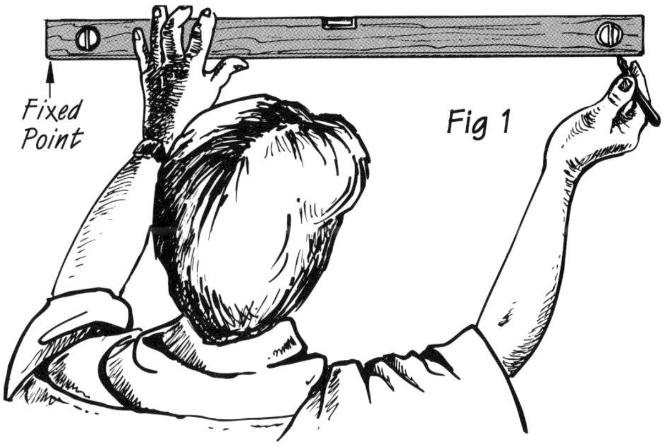

The Water Level

> *Hint:*
> Remember to always check the water level for evaporation and bubbling before commencing.

The water level is accurate and ideal for use in awkward situations or where walls or obstructions prevent the use of other methods. It should be kept out of the sun to reduce evaporation.

How to use a Water Level

Step 1 Have an assistant hold one end on a Datum line as in fig 1. (A Datum is the reference point from which to establish other levels).
The Datum point is not altered. All other points are made to align with the Datum. In the situation below the Datum is Point 'A' and is most likely the highest point as it is easier to raise bearers with packers than it is to lower them.

Step 2 Hold end 'B' of the level on the object to be adjusted and level the object or simply mark a level line.

How to Make a Water Level

Obtain a suitable length of 10 or 12mm clear plastic tubing available at hardware stores.

Step 1 One end is plugged or folded over and tied.

Step 2 The tube is then filled with water and checked for any air bubbles, these must be flushed through then the other end blocked off. Leave about 300mm of each end empty of water.

Step 3 The ends are held together as in fig 2. When the water has settled in a line across both ends, a felt tip pen line is drawn across one tube at the water level. This end is held at the datum point.

Datum (reference height) 'A' is the fixed point from which to establish all the other levels.

Fig 1

Point 'B' is the point which is to be altered to align with the Datum 'A'.

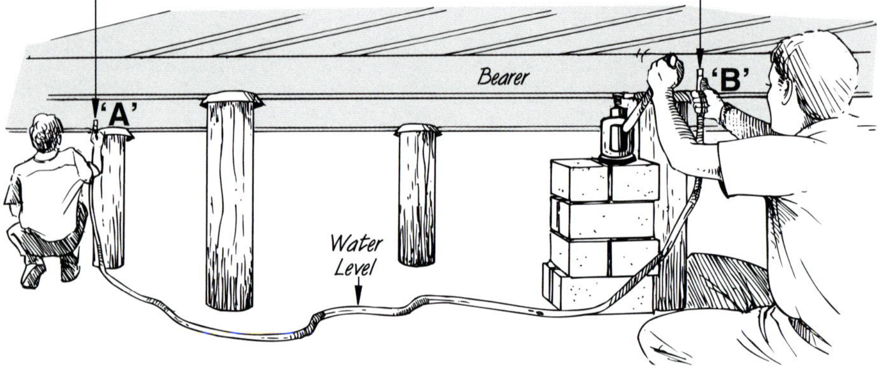

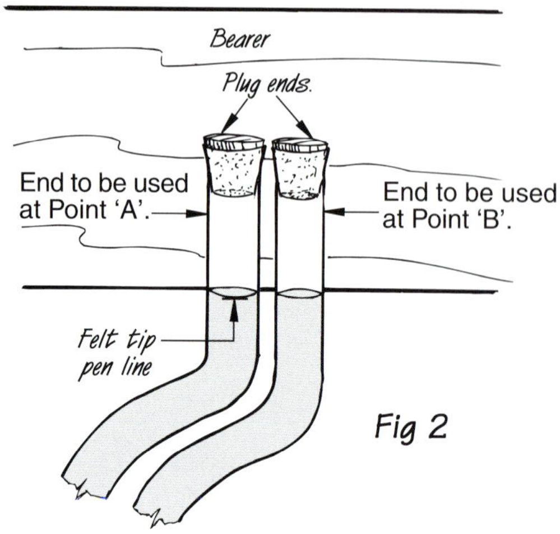

Fig 2

The String Line Level

String line levels are *not* used for precise levelling but rather to quickly establish approx. ground heights etc. Two people are required and its essential the string be stretched taut without sagging. The level itself is a spirit level which is simply hooked onto a line whenever required. Level is established once the bubble is centralised between its marked lines.

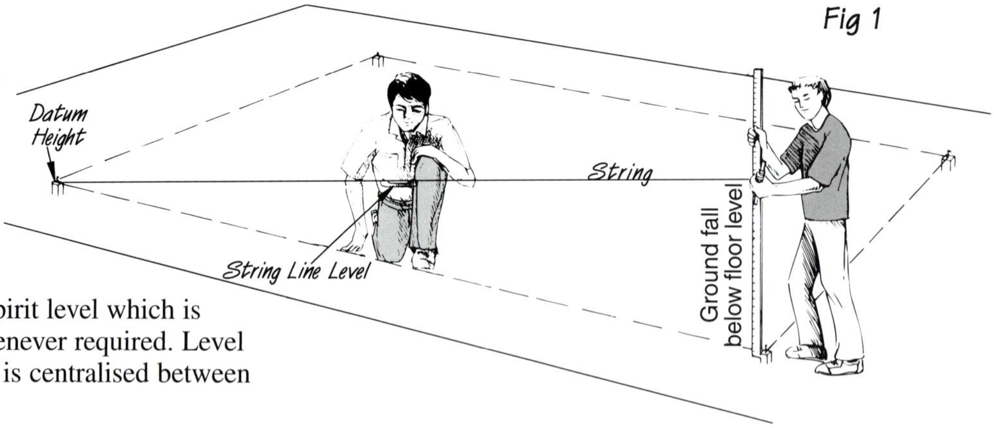

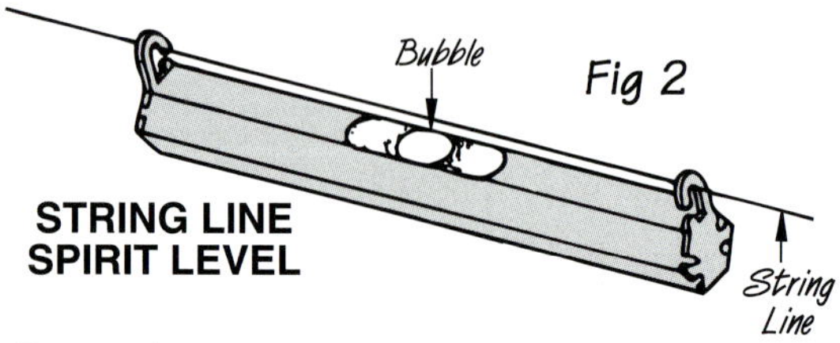

Step 1 Attach the line at the Datum height.

Step 2 Stretch the line taut without sagging.

Step 3 The level is positioned centrally along the line.

Step 4 Raise or lower the line at the opposite end until the level bubble is centralised. Then mark the level height on the height stick or other.

Step 5 Rotate the level on the line and mark another level line.

Step 6 Accept the centre between the two level lines as nearest to true.

String Lines & Gauge Blocks

Another useful method for straightening members is with string line and gauge blocks. This is commonly used for top and bottom plates of stud walls. Fasten the ends of the plates first then attach gauge blocks of equal thickness to all external corners on the edges of the bottom plates. Stretch a string line onto the face of these gauge blocks. Then using a spare gauge block, at regular intervals, slide it between the plate and string until it slides neatly between barely touching the string. Nail the bottom plate at these points. Continue this procedure, straightening the centres and larger bows first and working towards the ends.

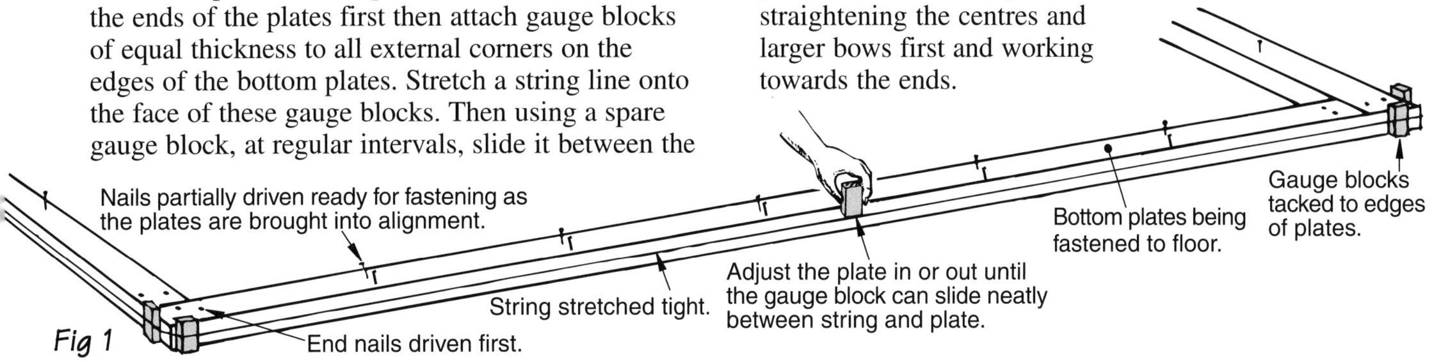

Fig 1

Using the Chalk or String Line

The chalk line is used for aligning horizontal and vertical fixtures such as house frames on a floor surface or for aligning vertical timber plates or pre-fabricated partitions. Also for providing a guide for trimming members or marking out a pattern for attaching decorative elements. Different colours can be used. Be careful *not* to use a colour which could be difficult to remove later.

Fig 1

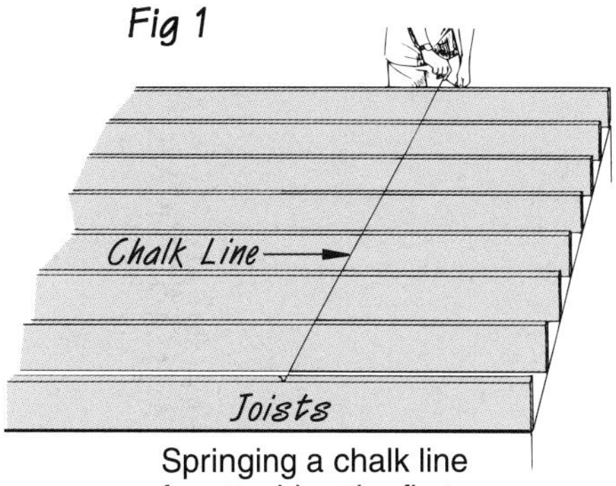

Springing a chalk line for attaching the first flooring panel.

Fig 2

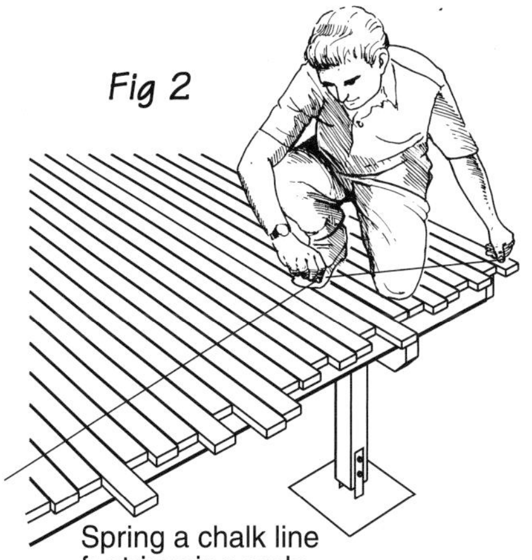
Spring a chalk line for trimming ends.

Using Straightedges

The straightedge is constantly used on the building site. Aluminium box section is ideal. If wood, select dried timber of Oregon or Cedar 75-90x19mm. It's used for checking the alignment of floor joist tops as in fig 1. The sides and tops of brickwork corners as in fig 2.

For aligning stud walls, two small packers are tacked to its ends as in fig 4. These will rest on the top and bottom wall plates. Their purpose is to enable the straightedge to stand clear of any bows in the studs. The level is then applied. Sometimes these have a level built-in.

Fig 2

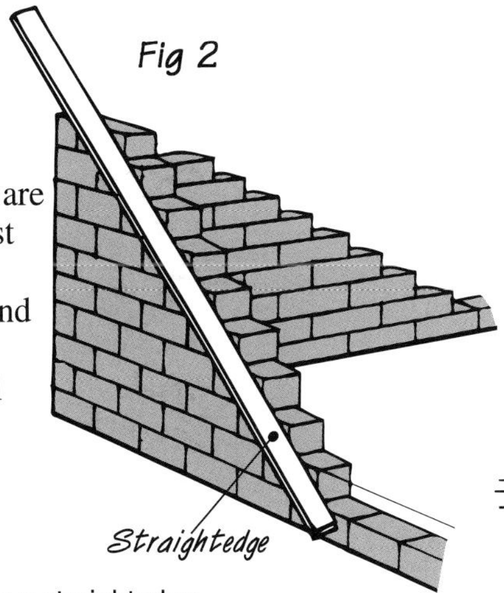

Fig 1

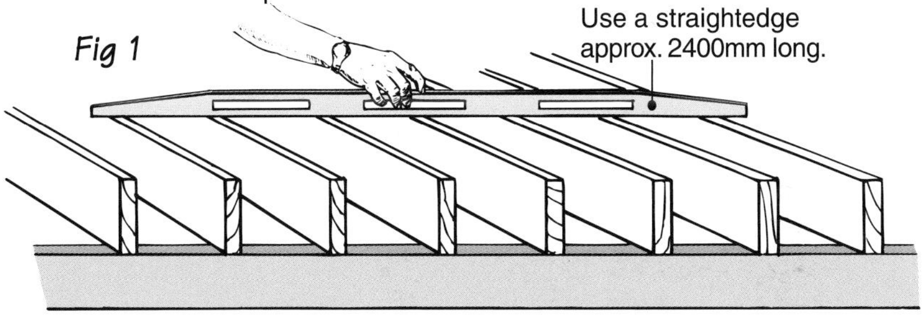

Fig 3

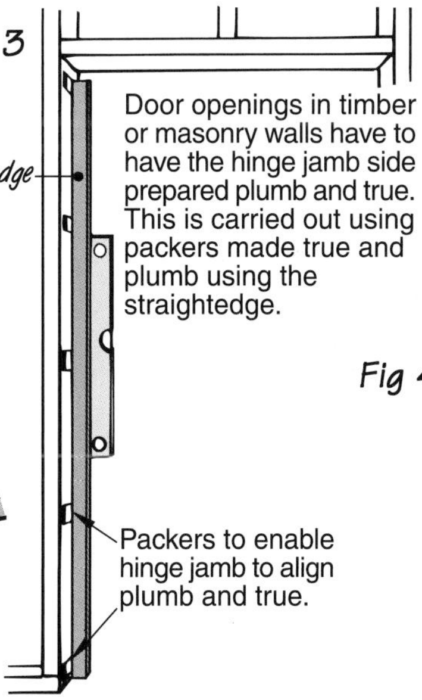

Fig 4

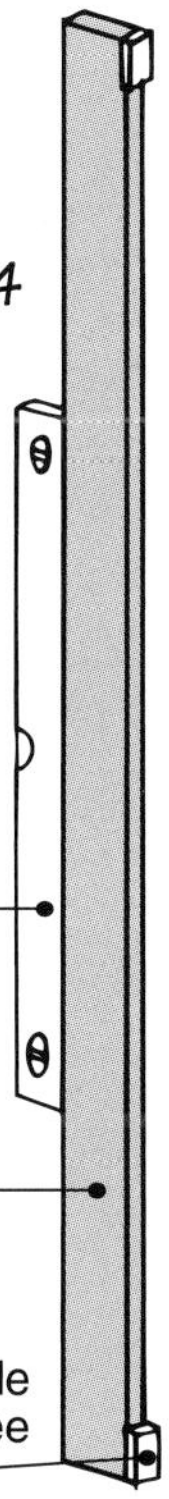

A Common Method of Plumbing Wall Studs

How to Set-out a House or Extension Profiles

Establish the Boundaries

Buildings are *not* uncommonly erected on the wrong site or encroach onto adjoining boundary space. This often involves litigation. Have a Surveyor confirm boundary pegs to be accurate. Ground movement and people do move them.

Preliminary to Setting up Profiles

Profile hurdles are required to enable the proposed foundation and sub-floor to be erected in square and true alignment and for walls to be accurately sited and aligned. But first their location is pegged as follows.

Step 1 Drive a nail in the centre of the boundary pegs and stretch string lines through.

Step 2 Roughly peg the proposed corners of the house or extension (see fig 1). Roughly square the area using 'Pythagoras Theorem' or the '3,4'5' method *(see the 'Australian House Building Manual' Chapter 2 for more information).*

This can also be carried out using diagonal measurements as applied in 'Squaring the Area' Step 7 and fig 1. Alternatively, after pegging two sides. They can be squared using the scientific calculator and the square and square root function. *See below:*

Squaring using the Calculator

Example on 'How to Square two sides of known length': To bring the two sides into square, the length of the third side is required. The calculator will provide this - using the x^2 & √ buttons.

This example measures: 9 480mm long by 6 720mm wide. i.e. $\sqrt{9.48^2 + 6.72^2}$

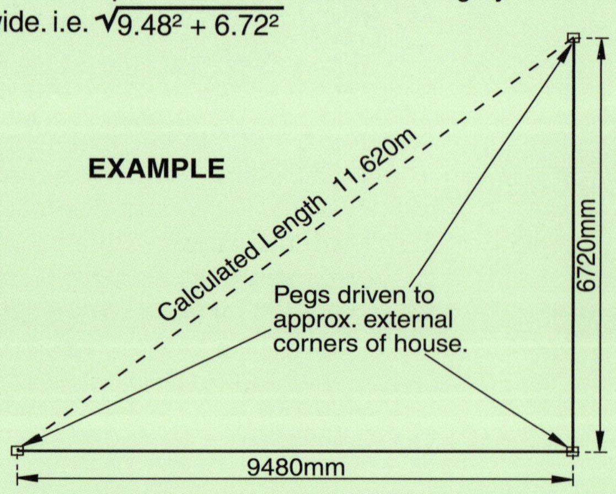

Press these keys in this order:

9.48 [x^2] [+] 6.72 [x^2] [=] [√] [=]

Answer displayed: **11.620 metres**

Step 3 After establishing the four external corners of the house with pegs and into roughly square alignment, erect profile hurdles outside these pegs as in fig 2. Allow space for excavating machinery to manoeuvre. Profiles need to have all their top surfaces on the same level plane. Use an automatic level or laser level. Be sure to peg and brace hurdles over 1200mm high to maintain rigidity.

Setting out on the Profiles

Step 4 Mark the front external wall face on the profiles. Establish it's distance from the front boundary by measuring back from the front boundary string line.

Step 5 Mark the rear external wall face measuring from the front external wall face.

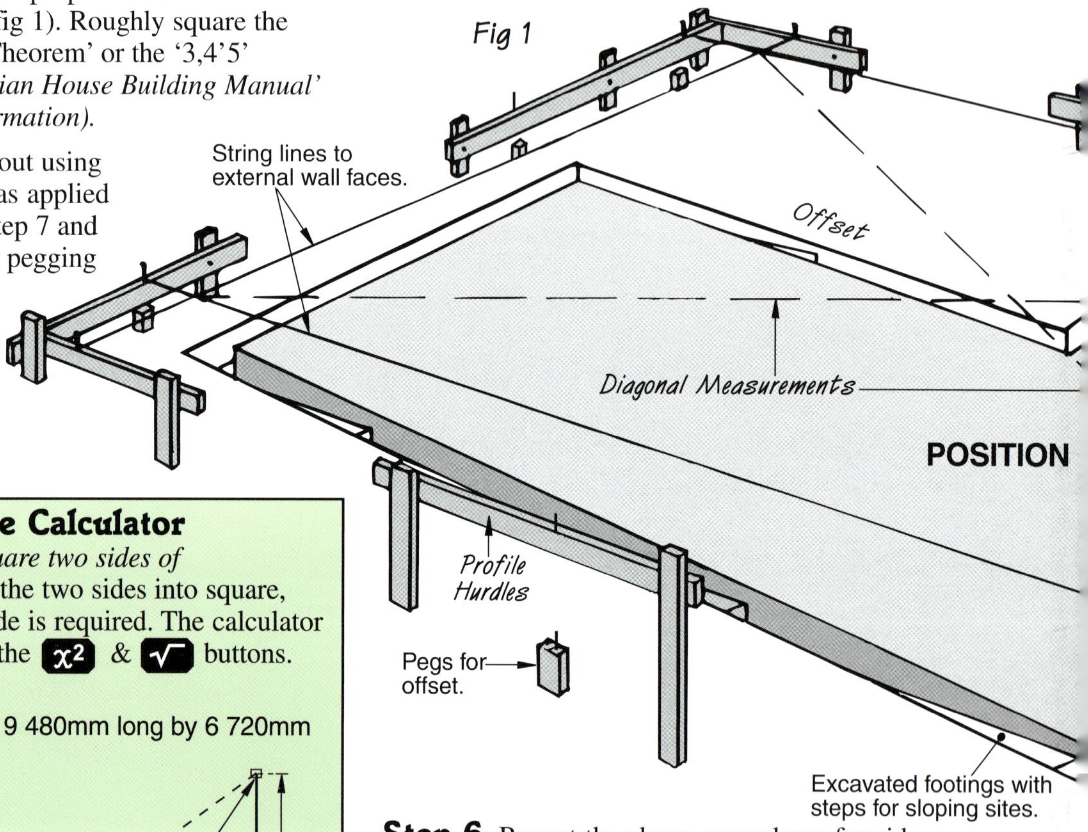

Step 6 Repeat the above procedures for side walls. Don't be concerned about offsets at this stage. Drive nails to these points and stretch string lines through.

Square the Area

The points where the string line intersect will be the proposed corners of the building. This area is now brought into square alignment.

Step 7 Take diagonal measurements from the string line intersections as indicated by the dashed line as in fig 1. These lengths should correspond.

Step 8 If these measurements don't correspond, and they probably won't, adjust the two rear nails supporting the side wall string lines. Adjust both the same amount until the diagonal measurements correspond.

Setting out Offsets

Step 9 Now that the area is in square alignment, offsets can be marked. An offset is anywhere the building steps in or out as in 'L' or 'H' shape designs (see fig 1).

Taking the offset distances from the house plan, measure and mark them from the outside walls, working along the profile hurdles. Drive nails and set strings also to these. After establishing the alignment points, write beside each one on the hurdles what it represents.

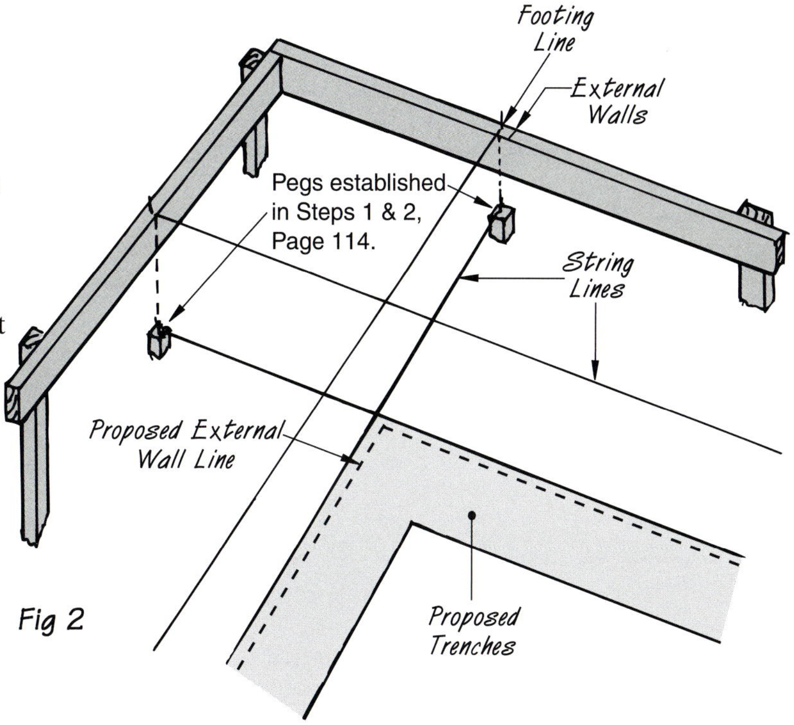

Fig 2

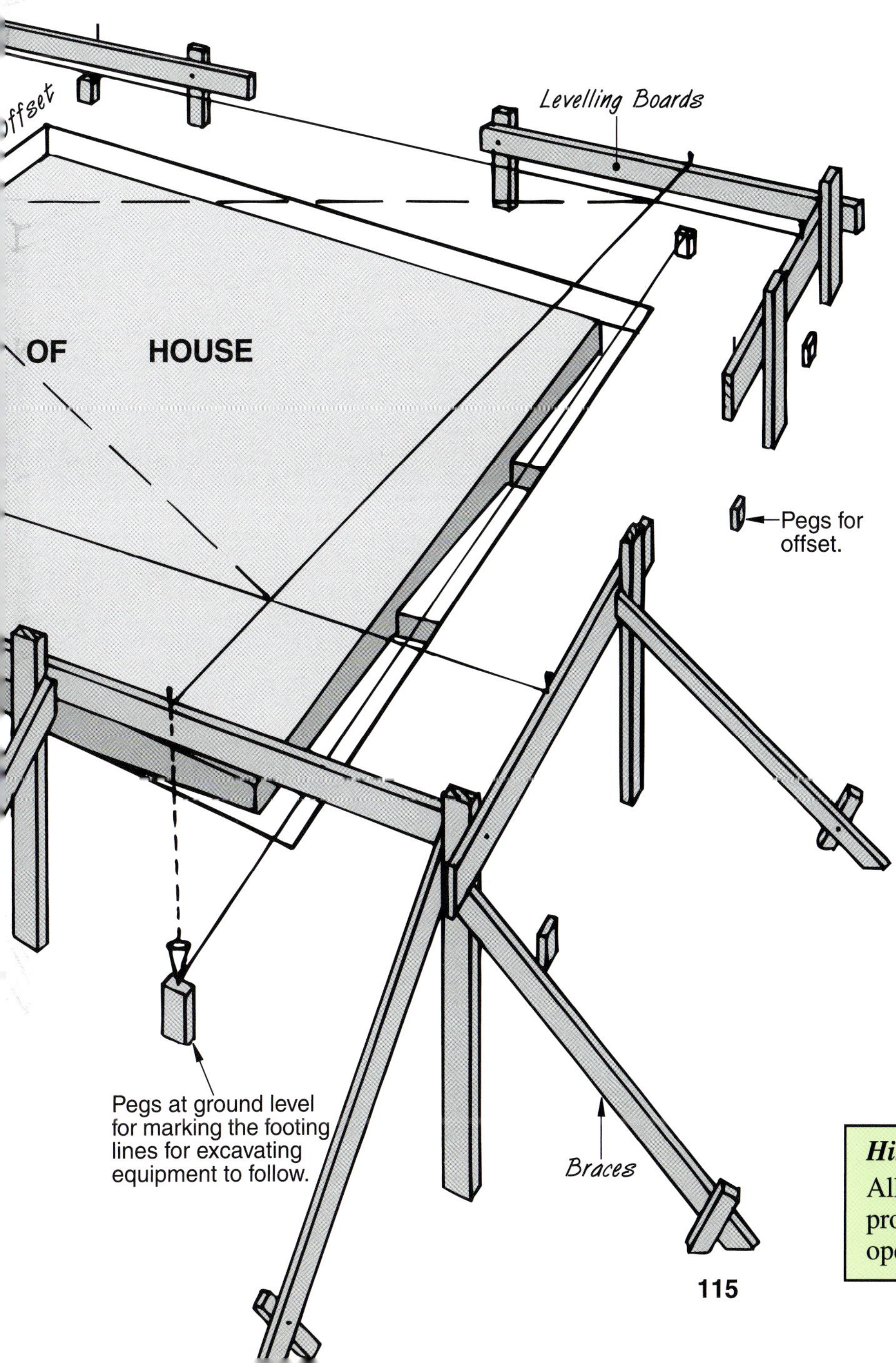

Siting Footings

The footings may be centralised beneath the upper walls or they may have their outer edge in alignment with them. This will be the case should the footings be raised above ground to act as a termite barrier.

Marking out Footing Lines

Step 10 Mark the outside line of the footings on the profiles then drive nails to these points and stretch string lines to these.

Step 11 Using a plumb bob or level, transfer the intersection points of the string lines to pegs driven directly below and drive nails to these points and stretch string lines to the nails.

Step 12 Using a funnel in a narrow necked bottle or similar, fill with lime or plaster dust and spread a white line directly below these lines. The trench digger will use an excavating bucket of the same width as the footing. One side of the bucket will follow the white lines. Footing depth can be established using a laser level as the excavation is in progress.

> ***Hint:***
> Allow at least 1200mm between profiles and proposed footings for trenching machinery to operate.

8 Fastening

Using the Claw Hammer

> *Hint:* A crown which is dirty will also bend nails. Sandpaper the crown until it shows bare steel.

Most useful size is 20oz for both carpentry and woodworking. 24oz is good for house framing but only for a person with a large hand.
The 16oz and 7oz are really useful for cabinet work. Choose a hammer that is balanced and comfortable in the hand, has a forged steel head and a fine claw for withdrawing small nails. A cheap hammer with a flat crown will always bend nails. When purchasing, check that the head has a rounded crown (see fig 1).

Fig 1 Fig 2

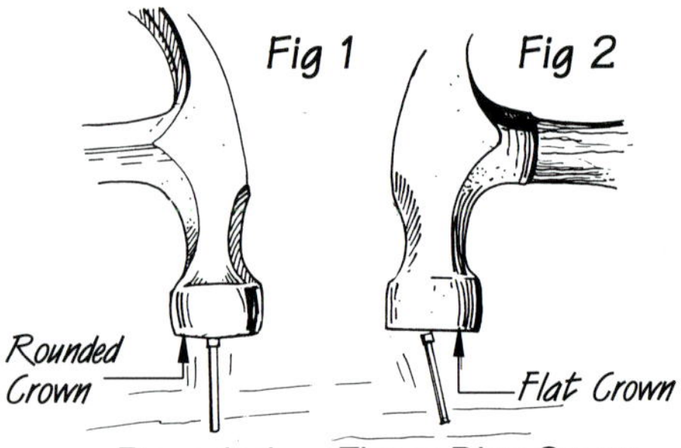

Rounded Crown   Flat or Dirty Crown will bend nails.

Fig 3

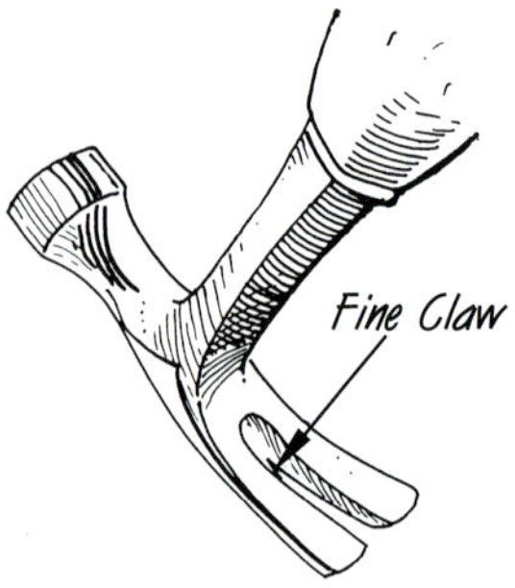

When purchasing, check that the claw has a fine 'V' for pulling small nails and for slipping under objects as in fig 4.

Fig 4

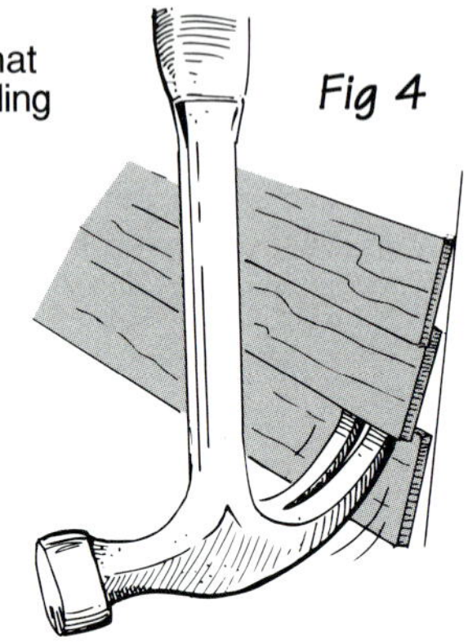

How to Drive Nails

Step 1 Lay a length of pine (say 100x50mm) on a flat surface and take a few 50mm long bullet head nails.

Step 2 Hold the hammer at the grip with around 35-40mm of its end exposed at the lower end of the handle as in fig 5. *Don't* allow your hand to creep up the handle.

Step 3 Hold the nail in position with the free hand and lightly tap into the surface as in fig 5. Remove the free hand. Begin to drive the nail harder ensuring that the hammer head strikes the nail at about the moment when the handle is level otherwise it will bend the nail. Keep your eye on the nail head. When you gain confidence try some 75mm nails. *Don't* give up if you have a few failures, everyone has them.

Fig 5

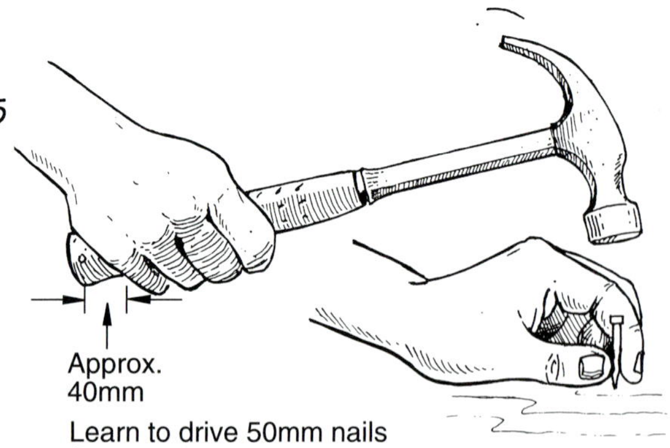

Learn to drive 50mm nails first then larger.

Fig 6

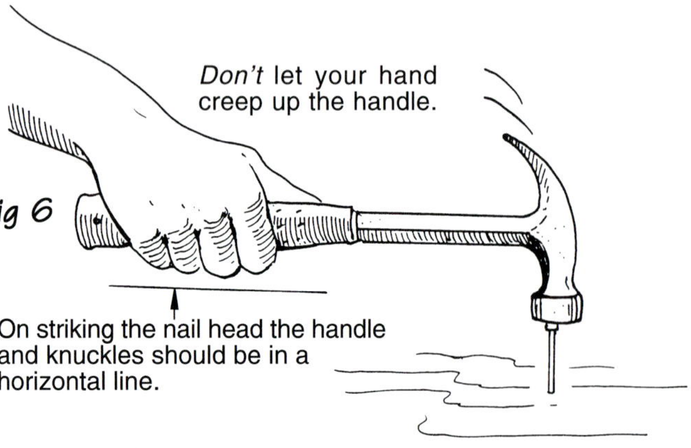

On striking the nail head the handle and knuckles should be in a horizontal line.

Driving Small Nails

For ease of driving very small nails or tacks push them through a strip of cardboard first as in fig 7.

Fig 6

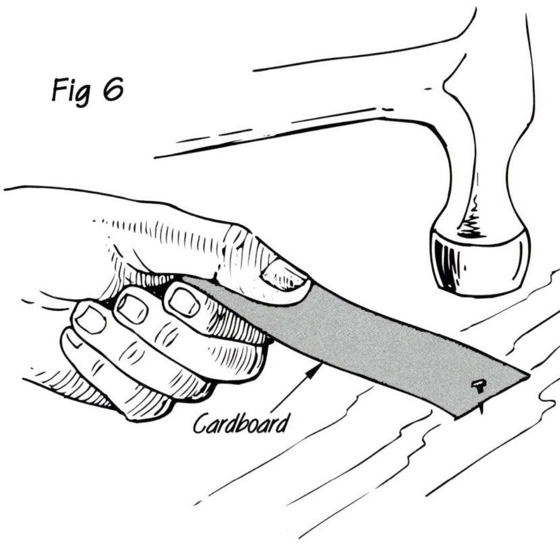

Fig 9

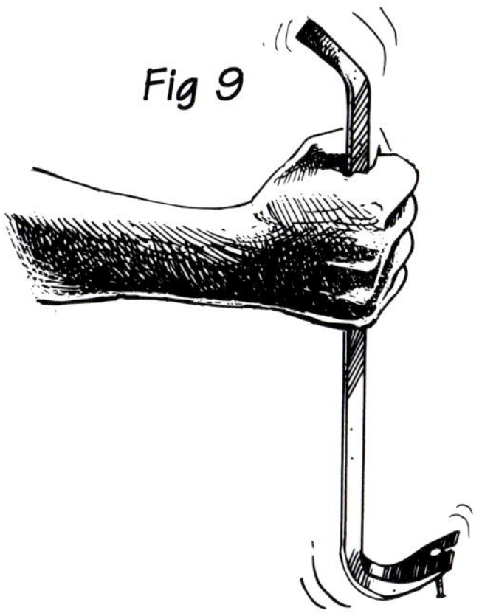

The larger the nail the larger the pinch bar required.

Fig 10

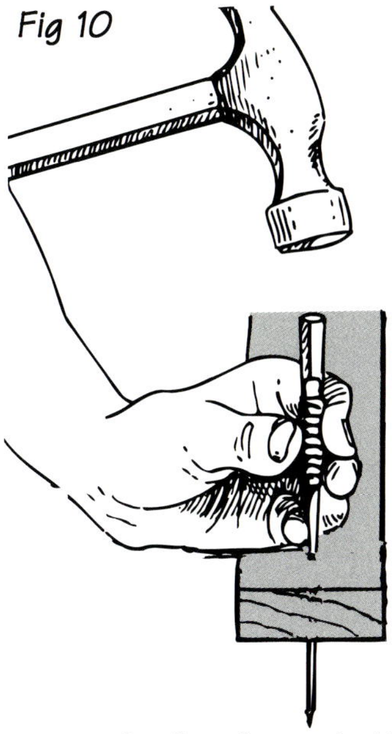

A nail can be punched back then extracted from the back with the fine claw of a hammer or pinch bar.

Withdrawing Nails

Use a block of scrap wood under the hammer or pinch bar to prevent damage to dressed timber (see fig 7). Use pincers to remove small nails (see fig 8). Use a pinch bar on nails over 60mm long to prevent damage to the claw on hammers (see fig 9).

The larger the nail the larger the pinch bar should be. Where an embedded nail must be removed, it can be punched back through with a punch and extracted from thc back sidc with a hammcr or pinch bar which has a fine claw.

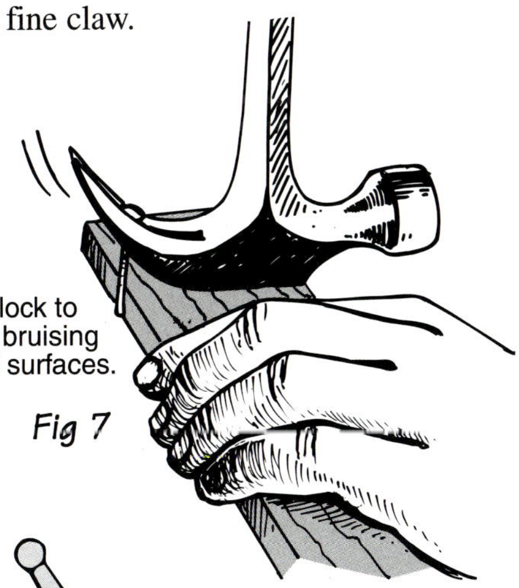

Use a block to prevent bruising finished surfaces.

Fig 7

Fig 8

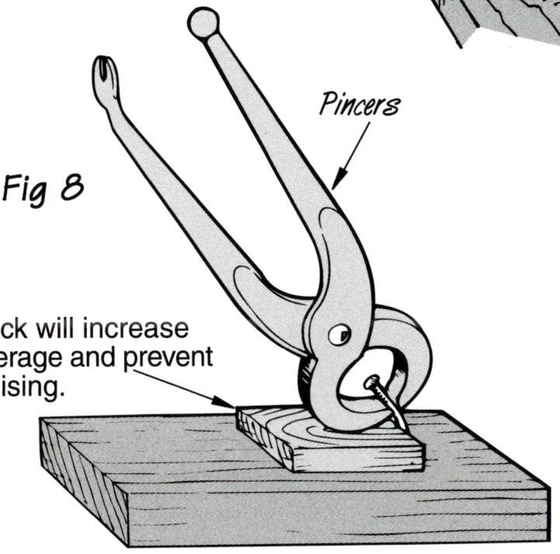

Block will increase leverage and prevent bruising.

Using the Nail Punch

The nail punch is used to punch nails below the surface. To prevent the hammer head leaving an impression on finished surfaces, the nail head is first left exposed then driven below the surface using a nail punch with a driving point just slightly smaller in diameter than the nail's head diameter.

Punched Depth

Don't punch the head so deep that the punch begins to increase the hole diameter but deep enough so that filler will not easily pop out later about 1-2mm.

Fig 11

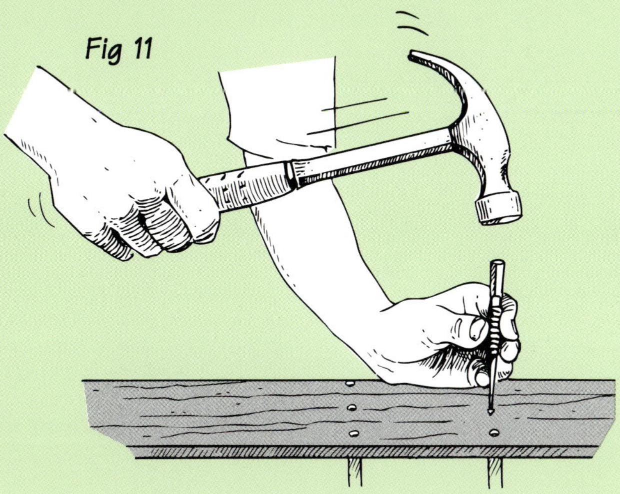

Cont.

Nailing Requirements

The length and type of nails when used in a structural situation should be as specified in approved plans and specifications or according to the building code.

When fastening a member into the **side grain** of a receiving member the nail should penetrate ten times the diameter of the nail. But when into the **end grain** of the receiving member it should penetrate 15 times the nail diameter (see figs 1 & 2).

Fig 1

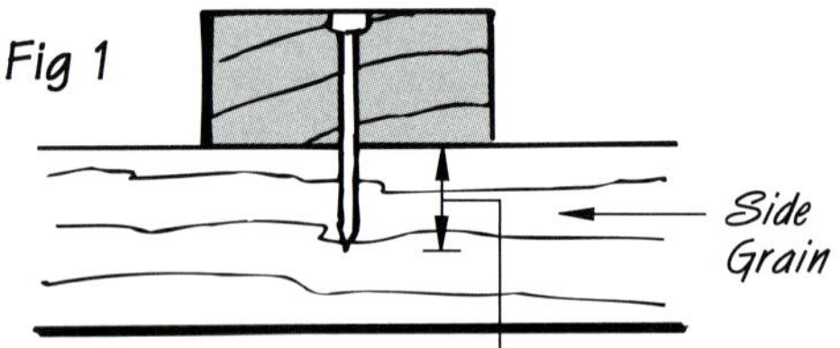

Penetrate the receiving member ten times the dia. of the nail into side grain.

Fig 2

Penetrate the receiving member fifteen times the dia. of the nail into end grain.

Skew Nailing

This type of nailing is often necessary for attaching insitu members such as studs-to-plates, noggings-to-studs etc and for attaching members to existing structures. Pre-drilling is often necessary when fastening joists and rafters etc to prevent splitting. Apply two nails to each joint.

Correct Skew Nailing

Fig 3

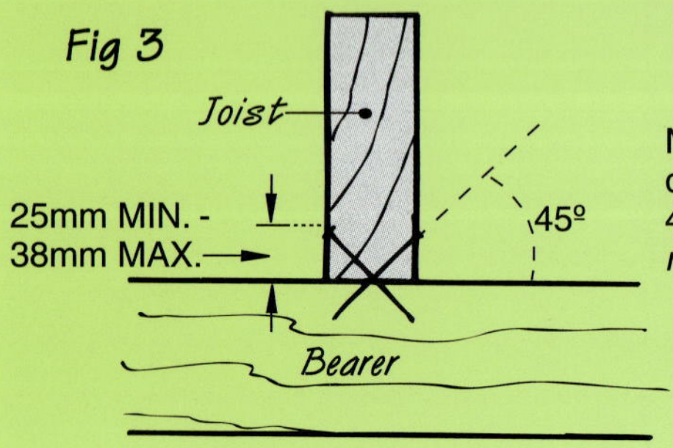

Nails should be driven at or close to 45º to the joist but *not* less than 30º.

Angled Nailing

Nails driven at an angle (see fig 4) provide a stronger joint.

Fig 4

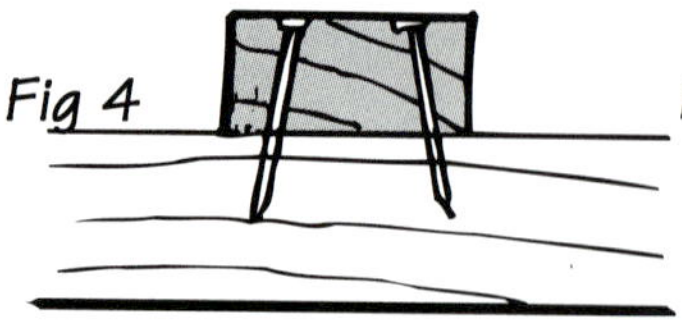

ANGLED NAILING

Fig 5

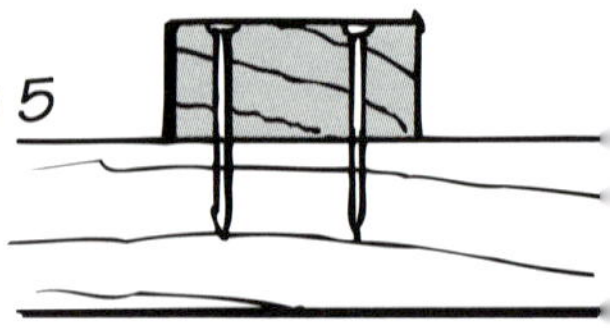

STRAIGHT NAILING

How to Avoid Splitting Wood

To blunt the point of a nail with the hammer will often be sufficient to prevent splitting (see fig 6).

To dip the nail into some lubricant such as grease will also help especially in hardwood.

Avoid driving nails in a line into receiving members as in fig 7. Rather, apply a staggered pattern as in fig 8 unless nails are sufficiently spaced. Pre-drill nail holes where there is any risk of splitting. Use a drill bit slightly smaller than the nail diameter.

Fig 6

Blunt the nail point to prevent splitting.

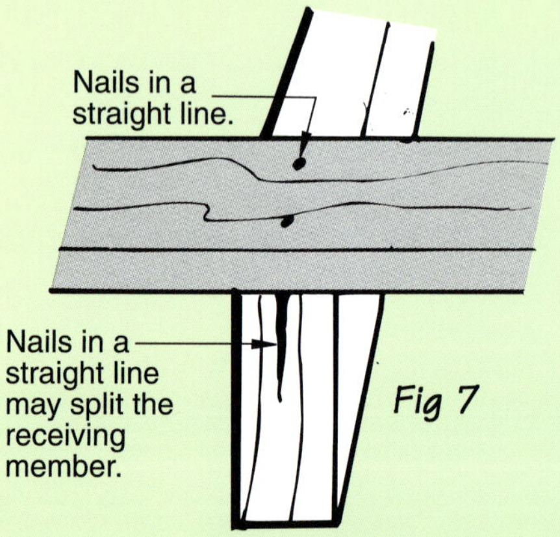

Fig 7

WRONG

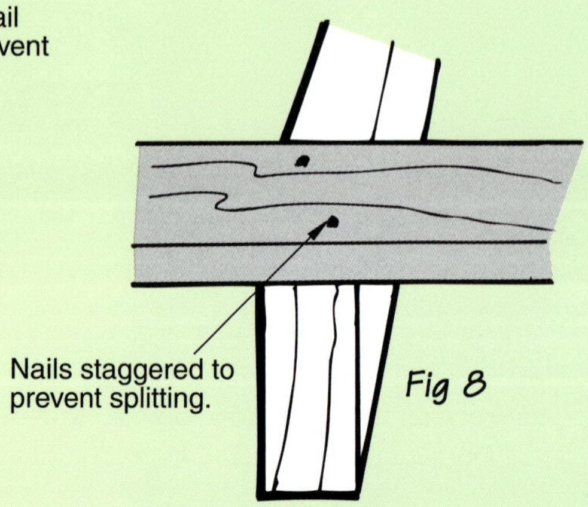

Fig 8

RIGHT

Screw Fastenings

Powered screw drivers and new materials have altered the shape and diversity of screw design.
Each design has a specific purpose and incorrect substitution can often be detrimental to the associated material or to the screw or its holding power and longevity.

While most screws are power driven sometimes manual driving or power driving into pre-drilled holes is necessary.

How to Drive Screws either Manually or into Pre-drilled Holes

For driving countersunk wood screws through an attaching member into a receiving member.

Step 1 Clamp or fasten the two members together. Mark the centre of the screw point.

Step 2 Drill a hole the same diameter as the core of the thread (see fig 1). Depth can be marked by wrapping a strip of masking tape around the bit or by using a screw-on depth gauge. Tape is usually OK.
In very hard wood you may need to ream out the hole a little to prevent binding or overheating the screw; a common cause for the screw head separating from the screw.

Step 3 Drill a larger hole through the attaching member. This is usually the same diameter as the overall thread diameter to enable easy passage through the attaching member, see fig 2. On tapered screws make the hole the same diameter as the shank.

If you are using press-in screw caps later, *don't* countersink too deep or the caps will fail to snap in.

Step 5 Drive the screw. Select the correct driver. If it's Phillips head, select the matching Phillips cross recess bit otherwise you can damage the head. If it's the rarely used 'slotted head'.

Fig 5

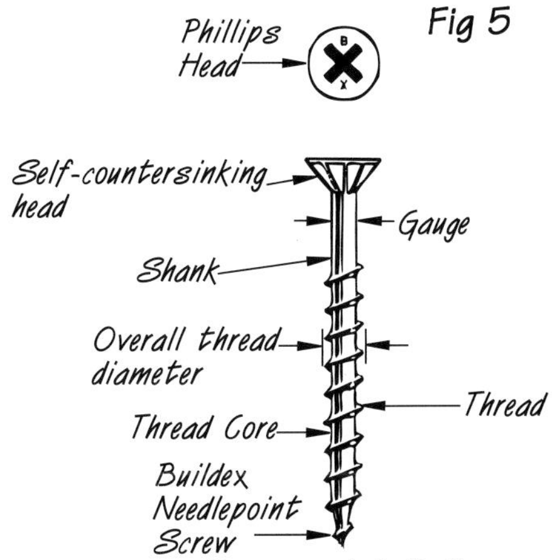

Countersink Self-driving Wood Screw

Fig 1

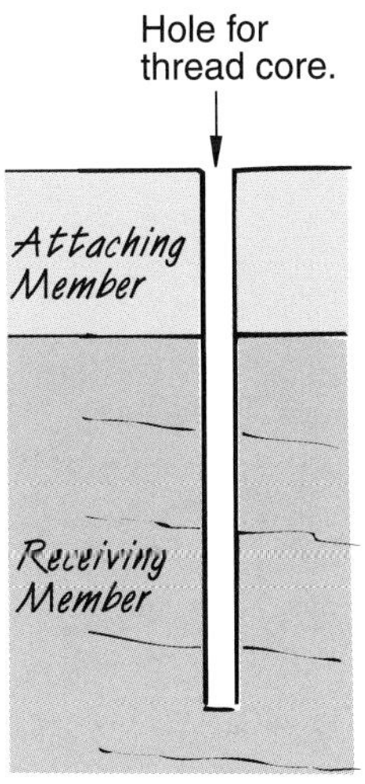

Fig 2

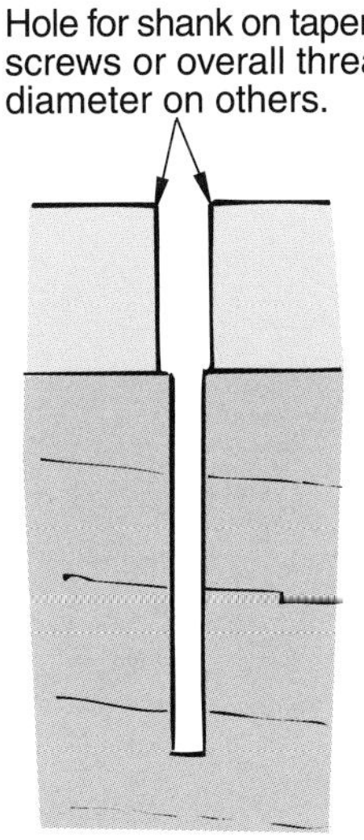

Fig 3

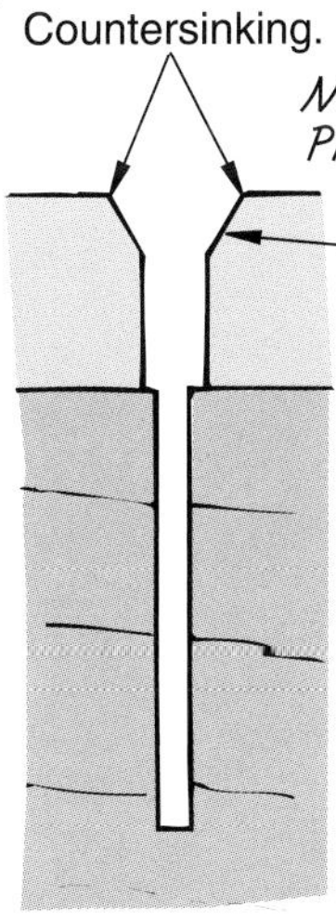

Fig 4

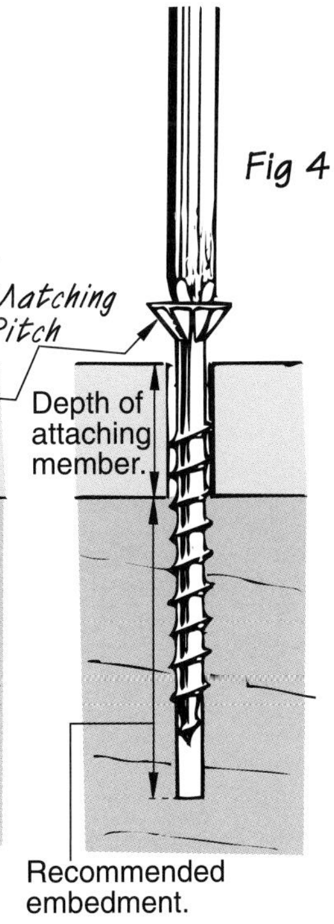

Step 4 The countersink hole is formed (see fig 3). Be sure to obtain a countersink bit with a pitch which matches the screw's pitch. Some have a steeper slope than others. Have the screw on hand when purchasing the bit.

Test the countersink by inserting the screw head first to see if it is flush or recessed and by how much.

The slotted driver must fit the slot nearly. *Not* loose, especially in soft metals such as brass otherwise the slot will easily damage. If the screw is too tight for the driver to install, remove it and ream the hole out a little or re-drill with a larger bit. When the screw is properly installed the attaching member should tighten firmly onto the receiving member.

Screw Heads Points & Threads (based on Buildex Self-drilling Screws)

Countersink Head

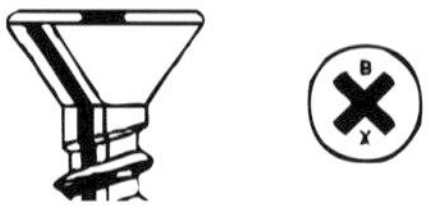

Originally designed for countersinking into timber for a flush or recessed finish. It can also be used for industrial hinges and similar applications. Driven with a Phillips #2 Cross Recess Bit.

Countersink Rib Head

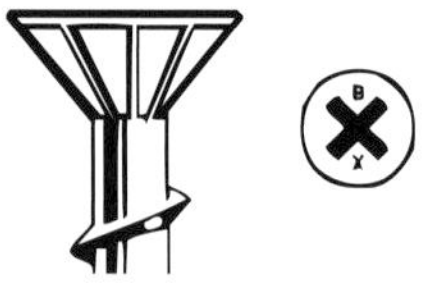

Used for countersinking into composite material such as chipboard and timber. The ribbed head enables easy self-countersinking. Driven with a Phillips #2 Cross Recess Bit.

Bugle Head

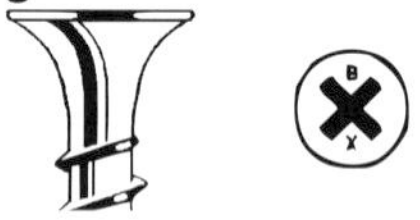

Has a smooth curved surface on the underside of the head designed to spin on the face of the plasterboard without tearing the surface. When set, this head is slightly below the surface for neat finishing. Driven with a Phillips #2 Cross Recess Bit.

Bugle Head Batten

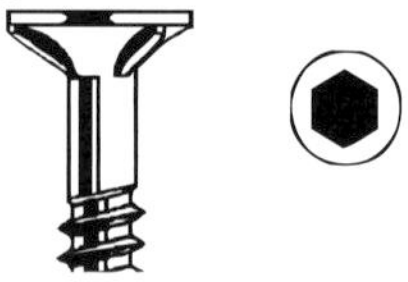

A bugle head with ribs designed to be embedded into timber for a flush head finish. Batten fastening to timber rafters in cyclonic areas is a major application. Driven with a 5mm internal hexagon drive Bit.

Self Embedding Head

Has a special flattened head with cutters and flutes, designed to ream into sheeting and hardwoods. The head type will achieve a flush or recessed finish. Driven with a Phillips #2 Cross Recess Bit.

Button Head

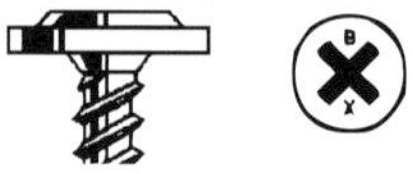

A low profile head with a flat underside. This design enables the fastener to sit level on the surface behind the plasterboard being fastened. To drive use a Phillips #2 Cross Recess Bit.

Wafer Head

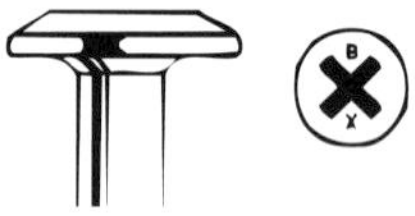

A versatile head style used for many fastening applications. When used with fixing clips, the low head design eliminates the risks of dimpling the roof when tradespeople walk on it. Driven with a #2 Phillips Cross Recess Bit.

Tamper Resistant Head

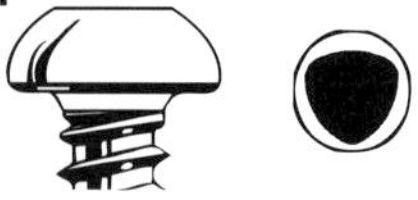

Has a descending diameter from the base to the top to prevent tools such as pliers and spanners being used to undo it. The driver is trilobular and available only through the Buildex Customer Service Centre.

Note: The above information kindly supplied by Buildex.

Pan Head

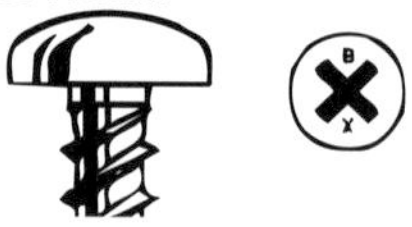

A round head with a flat underside fully threaded for accurate clamping. Designed for applications fixing against metal surfaces. Driven with a Phillips #2 Cross Recess Bit.

Hexagon Head

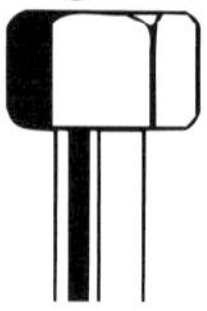

with washer

Gives greater strength and ease of torque input. Available in 1/4", 5/16" and 3/8" socket sizes. For water tight sealing use a bonded washer.

Special Pan Head

A low profile head found on Buildex Ripple Tek screws. Used for fixing mini-corrugated sheeting, it seals without a washer and *does not* deform the sheeting. To drive use a Phillips #2 Cross Recess Bit.

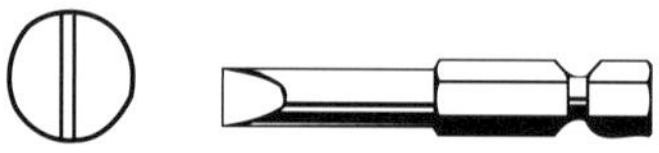

Slotted Bit

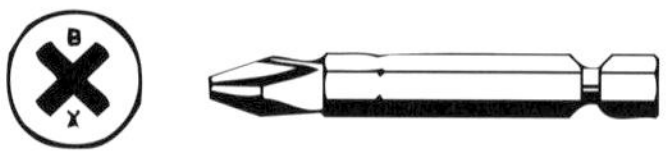

Phillips Bit

Hexagon Socket Bit

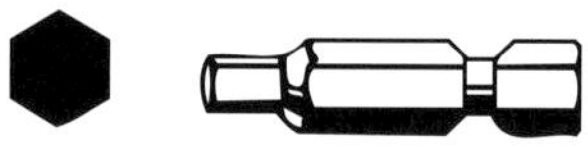

Internal Hexagon Drive Bit

Tamper resistant Pentagon Bit

Tamper resistant Trilobular Bit

POINTS

Needle point for easier starting.

Self-drilling point for wood.

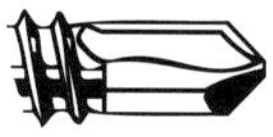

Tek point for fastening to steel.

THREADS

Course threads. For timber and for roof cladding.

Fine threads. For metal threads for steel only.

Buttress threads. For best holding power in thin metal.

Twin Start Thread. For low grade fixing such as plasterboard which is glued as well.

Tap Tight Thread. For steel and plastics. These form their own thread.

High-Low Thread. For soft timber, plastics and thin metal. These screws have superior holding power in these materials compared to conventional threads.

Selecting the Cordless Driver

Where a professional requires a driver to consistently drive screws to a set depth at great speed and efficiency **a dedicated screw gun** with 380-650watts and operating between 2000-2500RPM is used for e.g. Buildex TEK® screws and 500-2000RPM for Type 17 self-drilling screws.

However, for other operations and DIY usage a drill driver is adequate.

The following options should be considered:

a). Voltage 9-24volt. 12-14volts being most commonly used on building sites. Remember the higher the voltage the heavier the tool. 9-12volt is quite adequate if the battery is a fast charging one. The general purpose tool is 14volt for consistent light work. 9volt is OK and is commonly used by cabinet makers and in factories where two are used, one for boring and one for driving screws. This saves constantly changing bits.

b). Always purchase *two batteries*. Time taken to recharge will reflect in the purchase price of the tool. Usually the faster the charge the dearer the tool. Some poorer quality batteries and chargers left on charge overnight will damage the battery making it unable to hold a decent charge.

c). Look for *2-gears* or speeds plus. Most drivers have 2-speeds. The first will take the RPM from e.g. 0-500 while the second will be 0-1200. These vary from drill to drill and is often printed on the drill also *variable speed* and *reverse* are essential.

d). *Multi-stage torque control* is also necessary. This enables driving to a pre determinated depth.

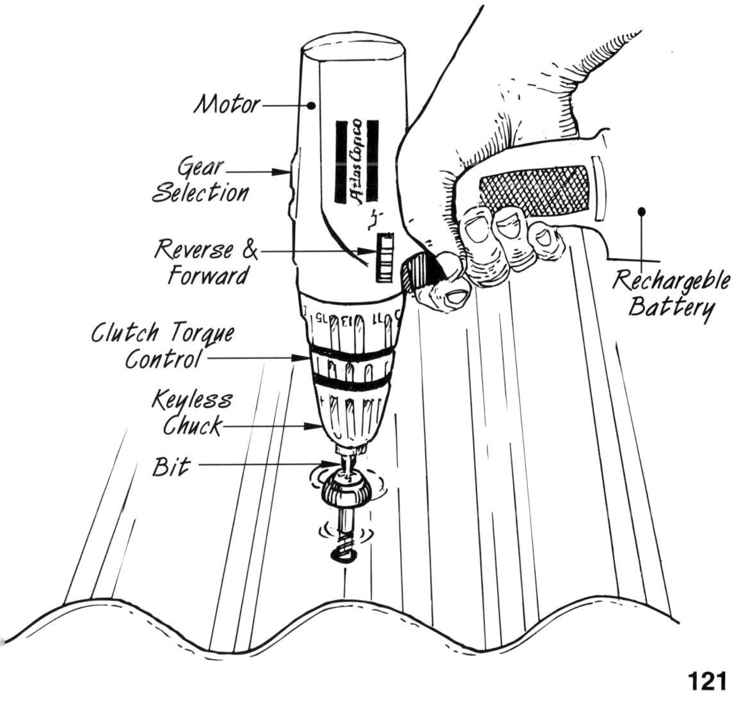

Selecting Screws

Check the following:

a). The gauge — This is the diameter of the shank as in fig 5, Page 119.

b). Head type — e.g. *countersink rib head*

c). The length and recommended embedment into the receiving member plus the depth or thickness of the attaching member (see figs 1-5, Page 119).

d). The type of metal and its protective coating — e.g. ***a.** steel; **b.** zinc plated; **c.** gold plated; **d.** Climaseal; **e.** stainless steel.*

Wood Screw Plain C/S head for hinges, brackets, general use thread, with cutting tip.

C/s Particleboard Screw. Ribbed head and needle point both for powered driving.

Pan head for general fixings.

Wafer head for where a low profile head is required.

Self embedding head for general use.

Roof Cladding Screw.

Roof Cladding Screw. The plain shank portion is where the edge of the sheet touches. This safe guards against corrosion of the threads which would normally rub on the sheet at this point.

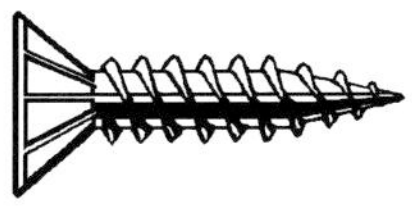

Villaboard Fibre Cement Screw

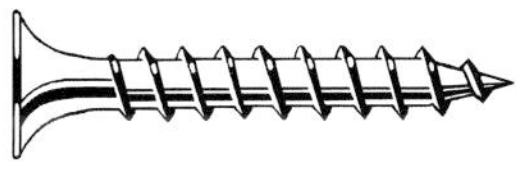

Bugle head plasterboard screw. Countersinks without damaging the paper surface.

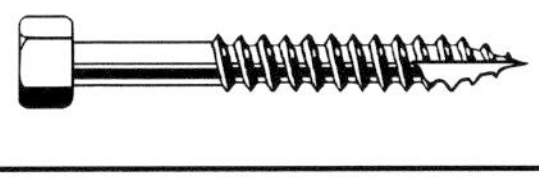

Hex. head screw where greater leverage is required. Available with bonded and sealing washers attached.

Driving Self-drilling Screws with Powered Drivers

How to Drive Chipboard & Timber Screws

Step 1 Select a screw that will give the required and recommended thread embedment into the receiving member.

Step 2 Set the torque on the driver to the setting that will drive the screw to the desired depth. This may require a practice run to establish required torque. Better to begin with too little than too much. You can always increase the torque.

Step 3 Hold screw into bit and press into the material then drive bit until the head sits flush with the surface or slightly below if that is desired. For hardwood it may be necessary to pre-drill pilot holes. For Bugle Batten screws use a 5mm hex. drive bit.

How to Drive Type 17 Screws into Timber

Select Head to Suit

Step 1 Choose the screw with the correct head type and length as required and recommended.

Step 2 Adjust the torque setting to ensure the attaching member is pulled tight.

Step 3 Insert the screw into bit and drive it with a firm consistent pressure. Be sure at the start of the drive that it will travel straight.

How to Drive Plasterboard Screws

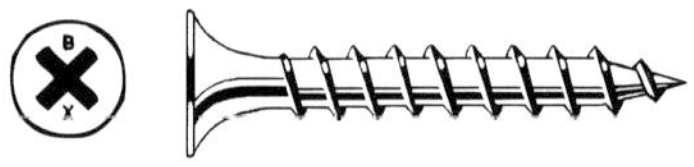

Step 1 Measure the total thickness of the materials being fastened and choose a screw long enough to provide 20mm MIN. of thread embedment into the timber receiving member.

Step 2 Adjust the torque setting to drive the screw until it pulls the plasterboard tight to the base with its head just countersunk. Be careful *not* to over drive. When fixing into steel be sure the screw is long enough to have at least three threads protrude past the steel thickness.

How to Drive Stitch Screws

Step 1 Measure the combined thickness of the materials to be stitched and select the screw of the correct length and head type.

Step 2 Insert screw into bit and press sharply on driver to make a start point in material then drive screw. Do *not* overtighten otherwise strip-out could occur.

How to Drive Polyteks & Type 17s into Polycarbonate & Fibreglass Cladding

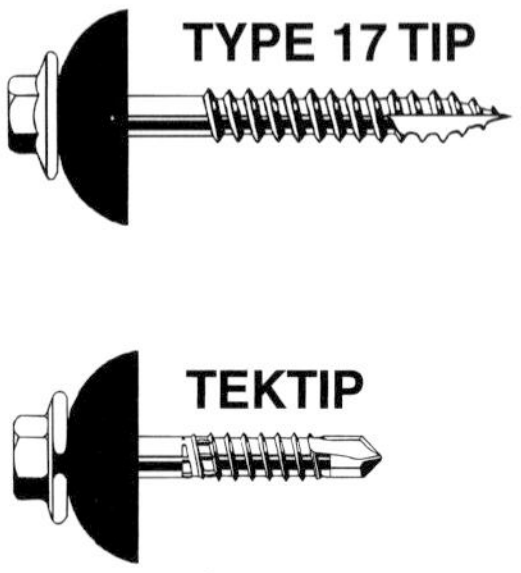

Step 1 Drill a 10mm hole and fix according to roof manufacturing instructions.

Step 2 Insert the screw. Ensure the washer is covering the hole. Drive screw with a $^{5}/_{16}$" hex head socket. Take care *not* to overtighten.

TEK® is a registered trademark of ITW Buildex.

How to Drive Fibre Tek Screws through Fibre Cement to Metal Battens

For 6-12mm cladding use c/s rib head. For 4.5mm cladding use bugle heads.

Drive screw for a flush fit. Set torque after a trial run.

How to Install Masonry Anchors

(applications below are based on Ramset Fasteners)

Masonry anchors vary in type. Some more suitable than others for a specific situation. Some being capable of greater holding power. Check with the manufacturer's representative or literature to make the correct choice. Also anchor performance can be optimised by the use of a correctly tensioned torque wrench.

Check the edge distance required for the specific bolt also recommended location of bolts in hollow masonry blocks or bricks which contain holes.

Chemical Anchors

A variety of types are available for selection and installation see the manufacturer's representative or literature.

Sleeve Anchor (Dyna Bolt)

Step 1 Mark the centre of the hole using the hole in the fixture as a guide. Select a drill bit the same diameter as the Dyna Bolt. Drill the hole to the required depth.

Step 2 Clean the hole with the correctly sized brush and remove the dust with the hole cleaning blower or compressed air.

Step 3 Insert the bolt through the fixture with sleeve, washer and nut attached as below. If you have to hammer the bolt into the hole, the hole is too small. It should slide in.

Step 4 Tighten with a spanner. The nut will tighten down the fixture firmly onto the base material. For optimum anchor performance use a torque wrench.

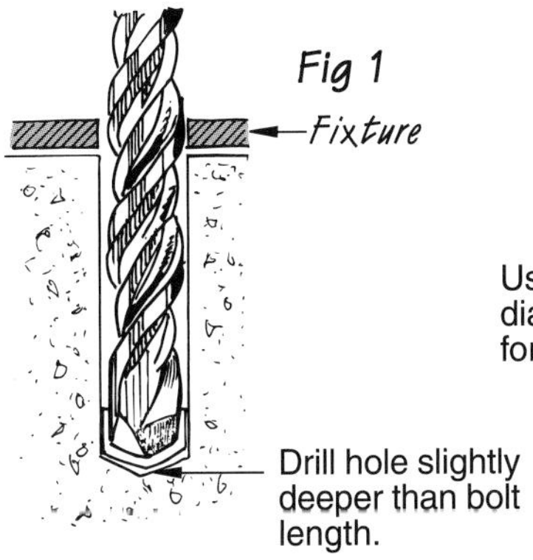

Fig 1

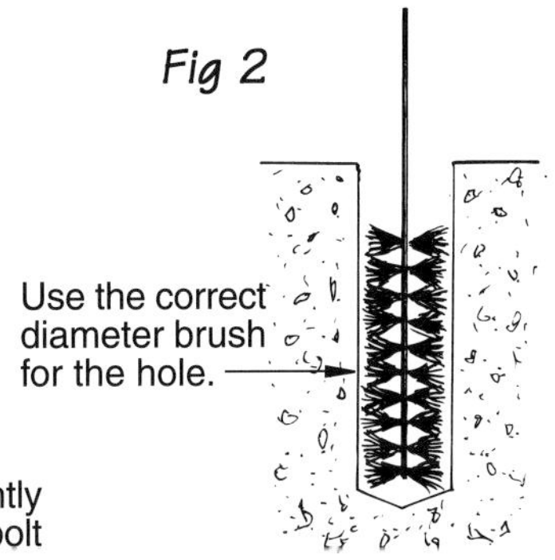

Fig 2

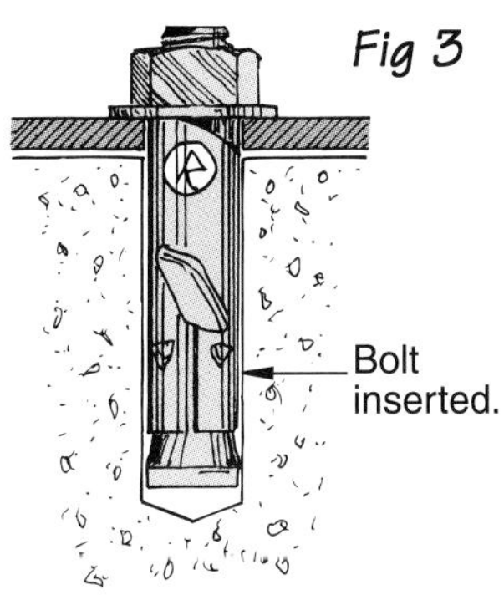

Fig 3

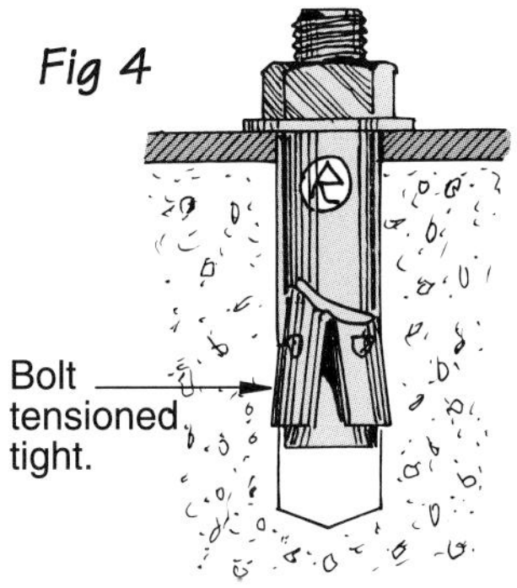

Fig 4

Screw-in Anchor (AnkaScrew)

Step 1 Drill the hole the same diameter as the screw. Use the centre of the hole in the fixture as a guide and drill to recommended depth.

Step 2 Remove debris using a hand pump or compressed air.

Step 3 Install anchor through fixture and tighten. If resistance is experienced, unscrew one turn and retighten. Be sure *not* to overtighten. Use a torque wrench to obtain optimum performance.

Fig 5

Wallboard Anchors

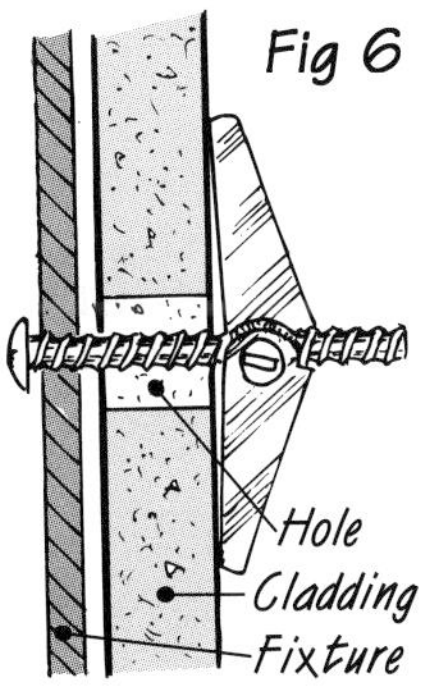

Fig 6

Spring Toggles

Step 1 Mark the hole centre.

Step 2 Drill the hole using a bit dia. to receive the toggle with its wings in closed position.

Step 3 Insert the screw through the fixture then with the screw just threaded into the wing, insert through the hole. Allow the wings to unfold then tighten screw.

Wall Mates

These are plasterboard screws with a threaded hole in the head to insert a fixture screw.
Simply cuts its own thread using a screwdriver.

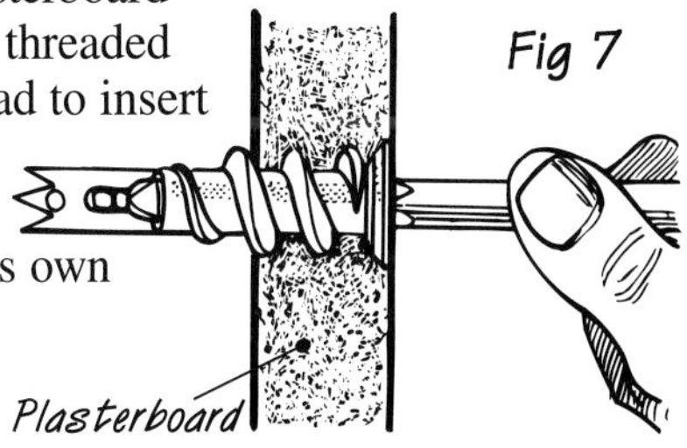

Fig 7

Installing Plastic Masonry Anchor Plugs

(based on Ramset Plastic or Ram)

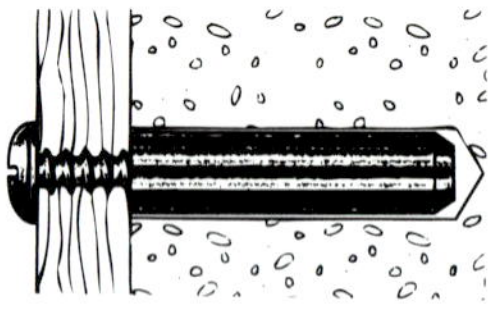

STAR PLUG OR PLASTIC PLUG

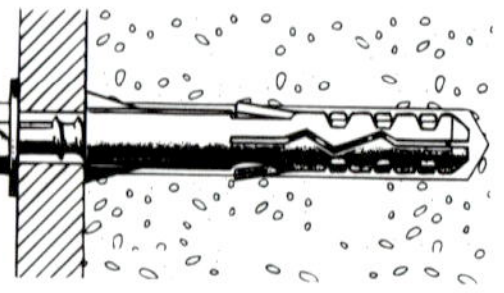

RAM PLUG

Step 1 Use the table to establish screw and plastic plug size. For Ram Plug check the specifications on the packaging or request the Ram Plug specifications. The principles of installations are the same as provided here except for screw diameter latitudes.

COLOUR	PLUG DIA. (mm)	SCREW GAUGE	DRILL BIT DIA. (mm)
White	5	4.5-6	5
Red	6	8-9	6
Green	6	10-12	7
Blue	12	14-16 or ¼" coach screw	8

Step 2 Hold the fitting on the surface and mark the centre of the screw holes.

Step 3 Using a masonry bit the same diameter as the plug. Drill the hole using an impact drill. Take care to frequently withdraw the bit to remove waste. To establish the depth, wrap a small strip of masking tape around the bit as a depth guide.

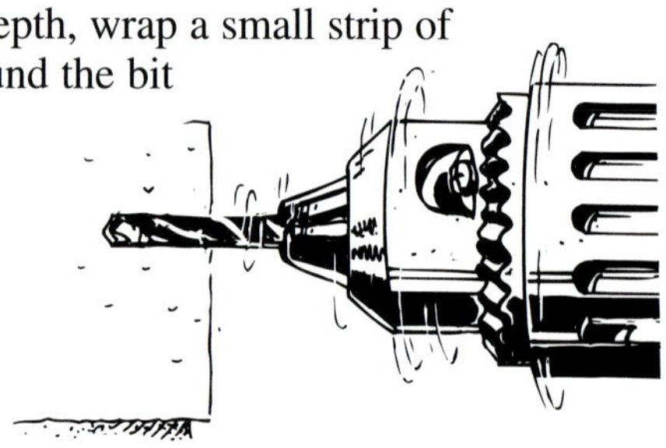

Step 4 Blow the dust out of the hole with a drinking straw and test the depth using a nail, inserting it head first.

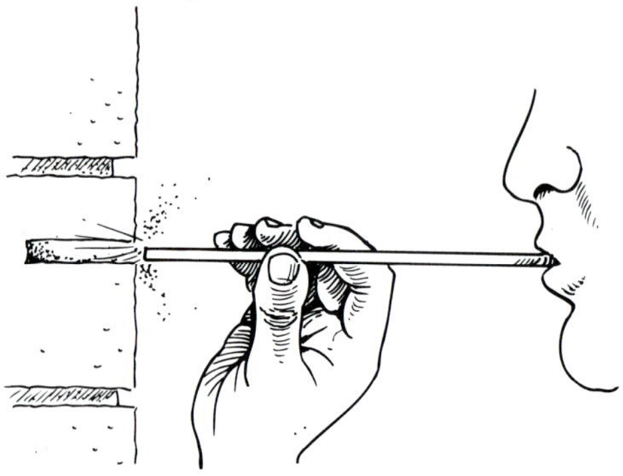

Step 5 Cut the plastic plugs to length or use purpose made plugs or Ram Plug. Be sure when installed they finish just below the surface.

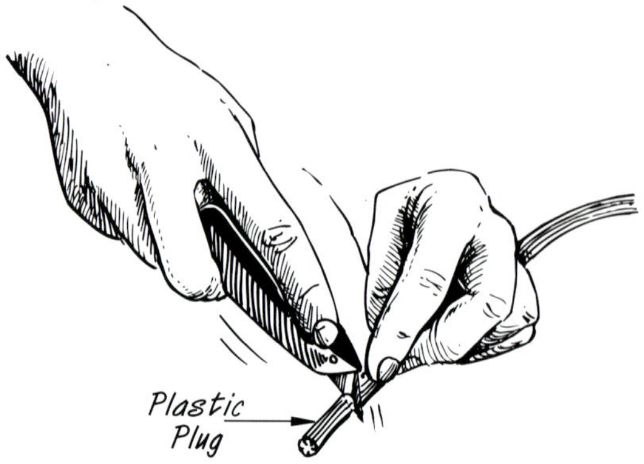

Step 6 Insert the plug.

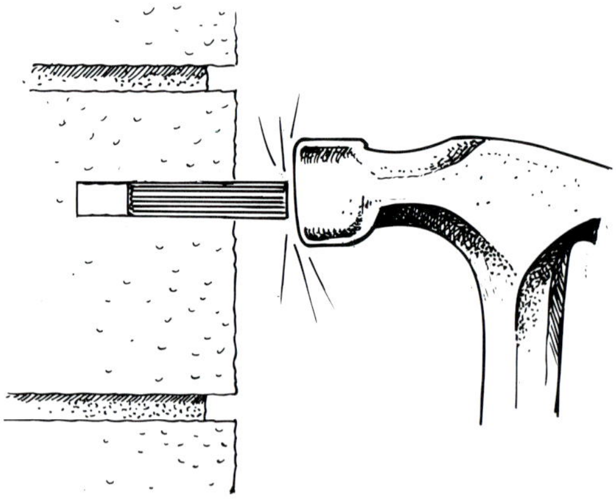

Step 7 Install the screws through the fitting into the plugs.

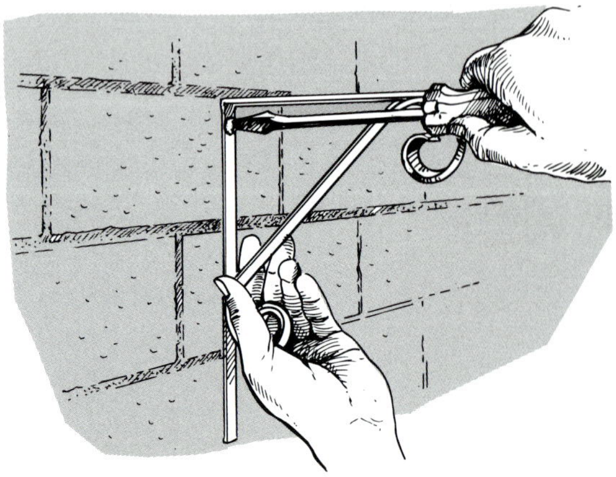

Cutting, Planing & Jointing

9

Hand Saws

There are basically three types of hand saws:
Panel, Cross cut and Rip.

A saw's length is indicated by the length of the blade as in fig 3, for example a 600mm blade represents a 600mm saw.

Panel Saws 450-500mm, 10-12 points per 25mm for making finer cross and rip cuts.

Cross Cut Saws 550-700mm, 5-9 points per 25mm. The most suitable for general work has 6 points.

Rip Saws 600-700mm, 3-6 points per 25mm. Their chisel-edged teeth are at right angles to the blade making it much easier to rip heavy timber with the grain as in fig 2. This process is only used today on specific work as it is mainly performed by the power saw.

Fig 3 **Parts of a Saw**

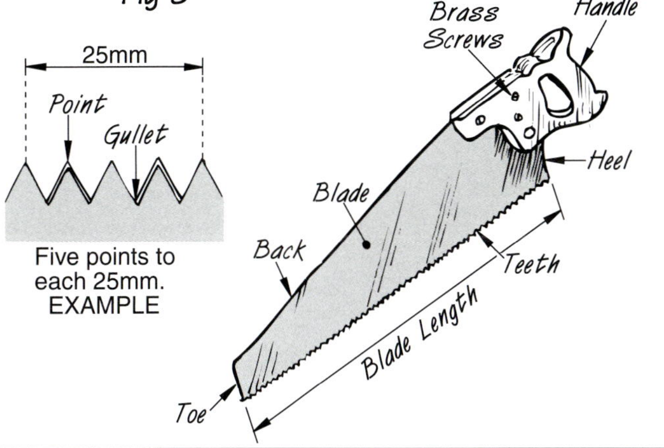

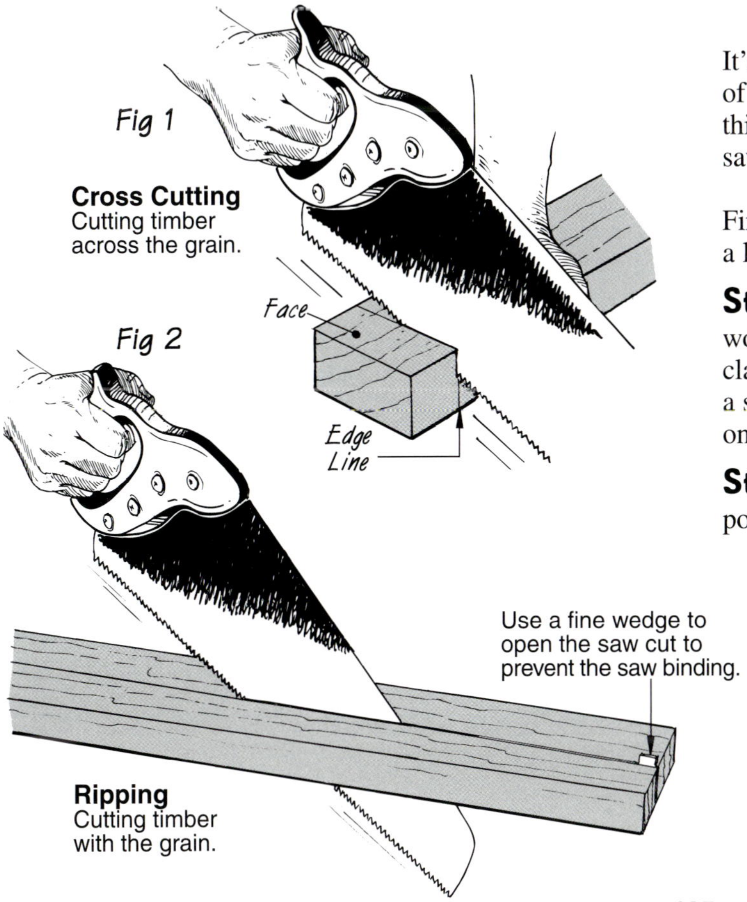

Fig 1

Cross Cutting
Cutting timber across the grain.

Fig 2

Ripping
Cutting timber with the grain.

How to use a Hand Saw

It's best to learn to saw using a panel saw on a piece of scrap pine or soft wood approx. 90x20mm. Once this is mastered it won't be difficult to use a larger saw on harder or thicker wood.

Firstly, the saw must be sharp and be nicely polished, a little oil or CRC on both sides will help.

Step 1 Draw several lines square across the scrap wood about 20mm apart and place in either a vice or clamped to a saw stool, see fig 6. It's good to learn on a sawstool as a vice is *not* a normal luxury when out on site. Use clamps to hold firm.

Step 2 Hold the handle with the index finger pointing along the handle as in fig 4.

Fig 4

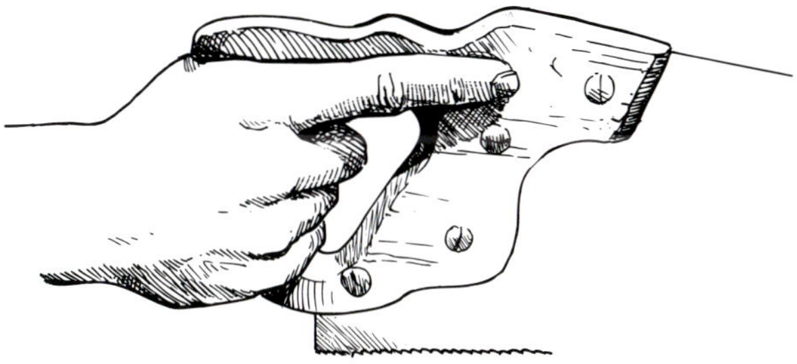

Step 3 Commence to cut just outside the edge of the line on the corner so the line will remain visible after cutting. Start by pulling the saw backwards at a low angle as in fig 5 & 6 and at the same time keeping the blade steady with the thumb of the free hand. Just touching the side of the blade above the teeth. Drawing the blade first will make a groove for the teeth to follow on the downward slope.

Don't rush the first cuts. As the saw cut deepens, the blade angle can be raised as in fig 7. Keep your eye on the line and learn to maintain a steady even backwards and forwards motion, as you approach the end slow down and lower the angle of cut to prevent the last splinter from breaking out inside the line.

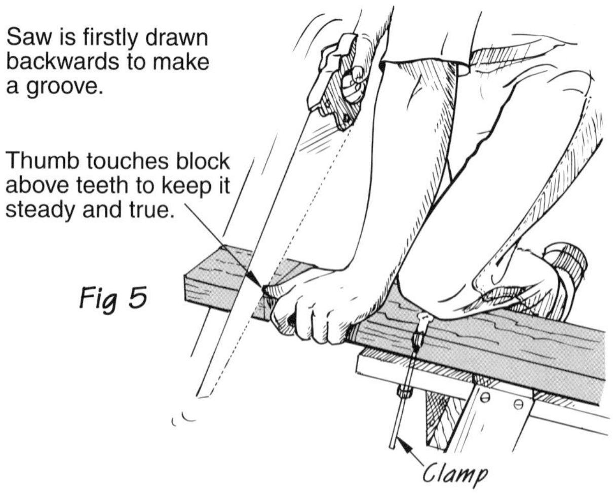

Fig 5

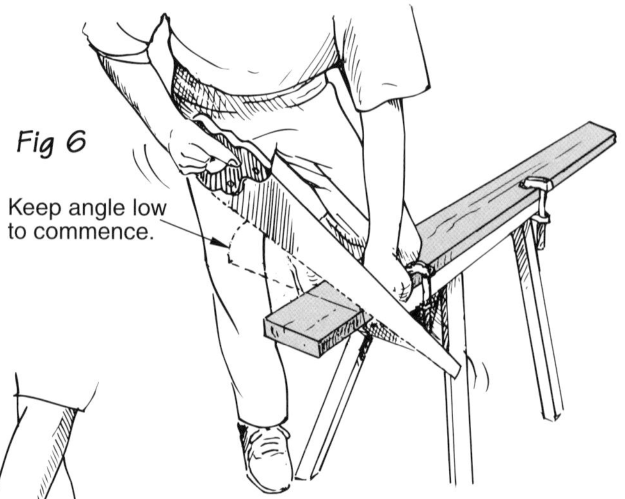

Fig 6

Making a Square End

After mastering a straight cut, you will need to learn how to cut a square end on thicker wood.

Step 1 Take a 90x45mm length of softwood and mark a line about 150mm back from the end and square lines on the edges as well, as in fig 8.

Step 2 Commence to cut in the same manner but this time after three or four strokes along the corner and face, raise the blade to cut three or four strokes down one edge line as in fig 8. Then return to follow the top line. Continue this process until the blade has cut to the bottom of the edge line.

As you near the final two or three strokes reach over with the free hand and support the off-cut, as in fig 7 to prevent break-out and ensure a nice clean full square end.

On thicker timber such as beams, it is necessary after taking the blade part way down on one edge of the beam to cut to about 10mm depth on the opposite edge to ensure the cut will be maintained square. Then continue to cut both edges, through the blade will still be at an angle cutting the front edge through first.

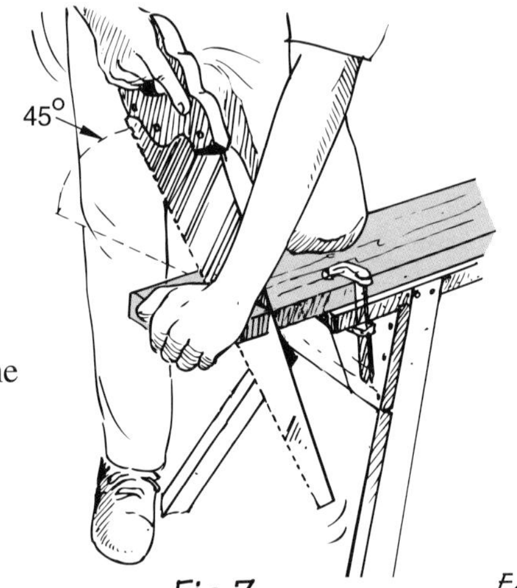

Fig 7

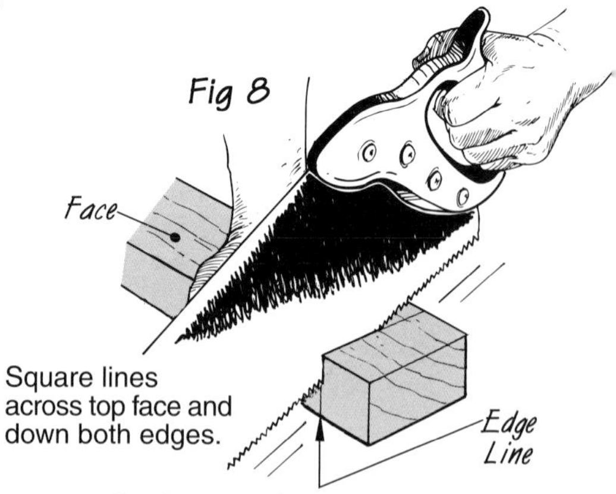

Fig 8

Cut 3 or 4 strokes on the top face and corner then 3 or 4 down the edge.

Cutting Sheet Material

Step 1 Lay the sheet material on two timber runners, say 70x45mm on two sawstools. Mark each end of proposed cuts using a tape measure and join the marks using a straight edge, steel rule, long level or square.

Should it be important to prevent all splintering on the back side you can transfer the lines there as well and run adhesive tape such as sticky masking tape or clear tape over the lines. This is removed after the cuts are complete.

Check any return lines are square with the adjoining one, use a rafter square to check.

Step 2 Ensure the runners are placed either side of the line to support the cut and prevent bulging and sagging of the material while cutting.

Commence to cut with the saw in a lowered angle, to prevent splintering on the back side, it's best to make the cut at a low angle.

As the cut gets longer the side of the cut will tend to bend the blade and this will cause splintering on both sides. Avoid this by supporting one cut side a little above the other. Use your free hand or work with an assistant.

Portable Circular Saw

A first time user should have a demonstration on its use. Begin with a 185mm tool and fit a combination or cross cutting blade for cutting wood. Ensure it is sharp.

Step 1 Adjust the blade into square with the base plate as in fig 1 using a try or adjustable square.

Step 2 Adjust the depth of the blade so that only approx. 6mm of the teeth pass through the material as in fig 2.

Fig 1

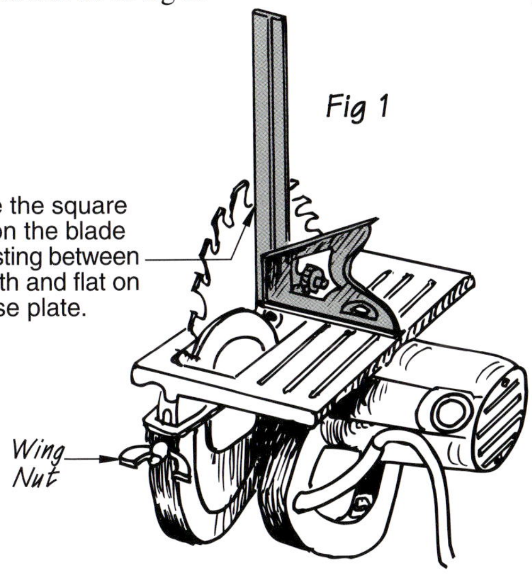

Fig 2

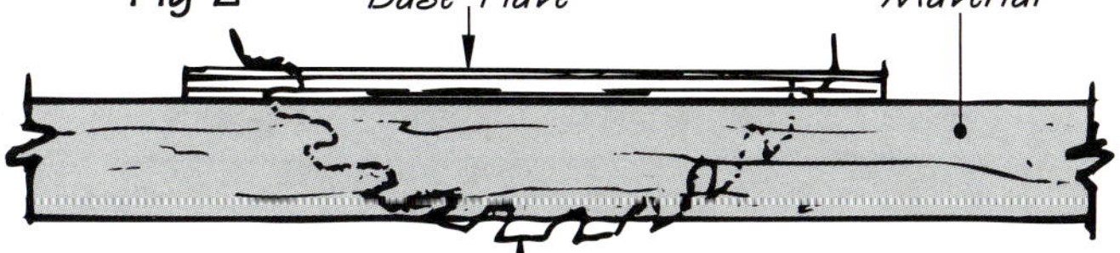

The teeth should only extend through the material approx. 6mm.

> **IMPORTANT:** Always check the blade guard is rotating and returning freely. Wear a pair of safety spectacles and shoes or boots.

Step 3 Commence with a length of 100x50mm clamped to a pair of sawstools. Have the timber extended over one stool.

Step 4 Plan to make several off-cuts. Using a pencil, square several lines across the face about 25mm apart at one end.

Step 5 Check that the power cable is well behind the tool. Commence to line up the cutting guide mark, slot or V on the front plate of the saw with the line.

Plan to cut along the outside edge of the line. Hold the saw as illustrated in fig 3 with one hand on the handle and trigger and the other also supporting the saw with the handle and the thumb used to raise the guard just to commence as in fig 4. Once the blade is cutting, the guard can look after itself. Do *not* use the locking button. Ensure the saw teeth are clear of the wood when the motor is switched on.

Fig 4

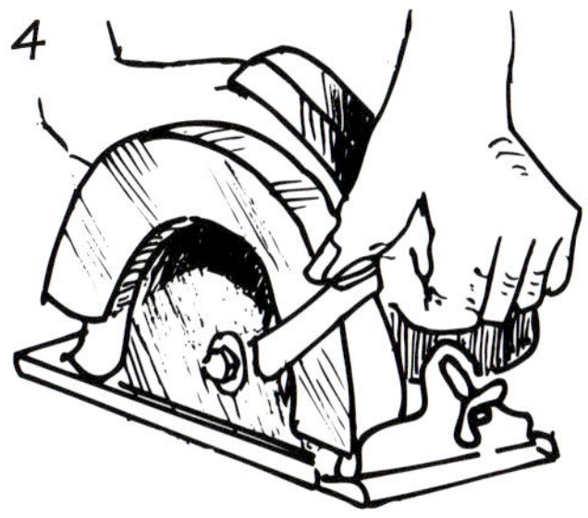

Raise the guard only on commencement of the cut.

Fig 3

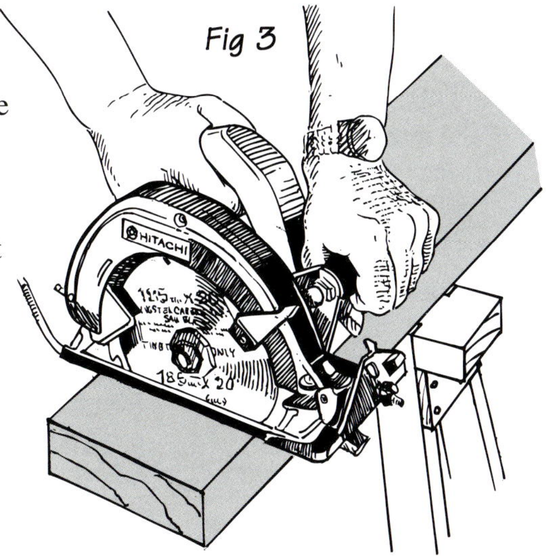

Fig 5

Plan to cut right through without stopping, keeping your eye on the line. Learn to push the saw through in one even continuous movement *not* stopping until the offcut drops on the floor.
Don't try to save it with one hand!
Don't slow the tool down just before the last 10mm of the cut otherwise, when cutting a larger offcut, it can break off taking a corner of the adjoining material with it.

Only a skilled operator should operate the saw with one hand.

> **Important**
> As soon as the offcut drops away the saw blade will be exposed until the guard returns. After cutting away keep the tool in the air clear of the cable and your body until the guard returns.
> A common scenario is that the user rests the tool on the floor not noticing that the guard hasn't retracted and the saw instantly races across the floor over the cable or the user's foot. The cause is often that sawdust (possibly wet) has clogged the guard return mechanism.

Continue to practice cutting the remaining offcuts aiming to achieve a straight clean cut. You'll soon find it is not difficult at all.

When cutting long lengths of material on pairs of stools *never* cut between the stools as in fig 6. Always mark the cut overhanging the stools and allow the waste to fall.

Fig 6

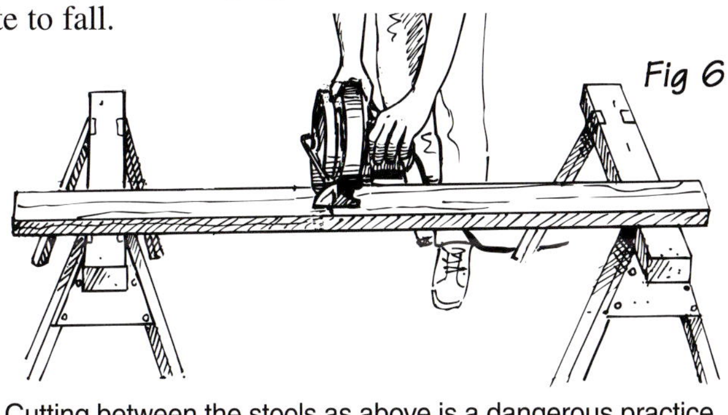

Cutting between the stools as above is a dangerous practice. Kickback can occur and thrust the blade back into your body.

Hand Planing & Chiselling

Hand Planing

The No. 4 (60x250mm) plane is the one of choice for the building site and for DIY use. The No. 5 & 7 are for cabinet/hand jointing work. If you own a bench jointer (planer) you can do without these.

The No. 5 (63x370mm) is 14 inches long and the No. 7 (73x557mm) 22 inches long. Oil after every day's use and you should get your investment back even after a lifetime of use.

How to Dismantle & Reassemble the Plane

To use a plane successfully, you must learn how to dismantle and reassemble the plane. In particular the blade assembly which will require regular setting, waste removal and resharpening.

It's really very simple, just follow the steps:

Always check the frog is in correct alignment. *Follow 'Checking the Frog Alignment' Page 131.*

SIDE VIEW

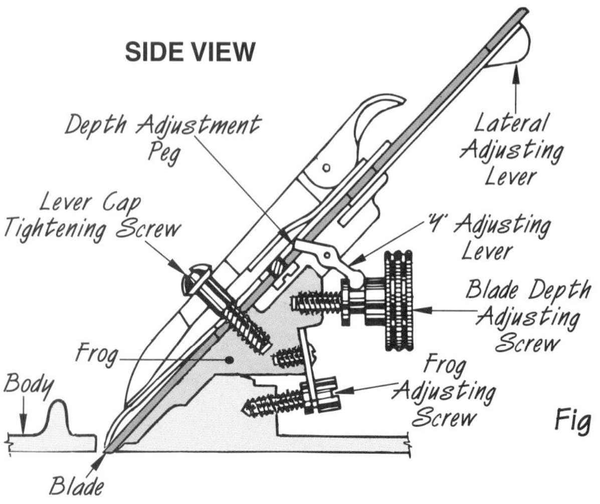

Fig 2

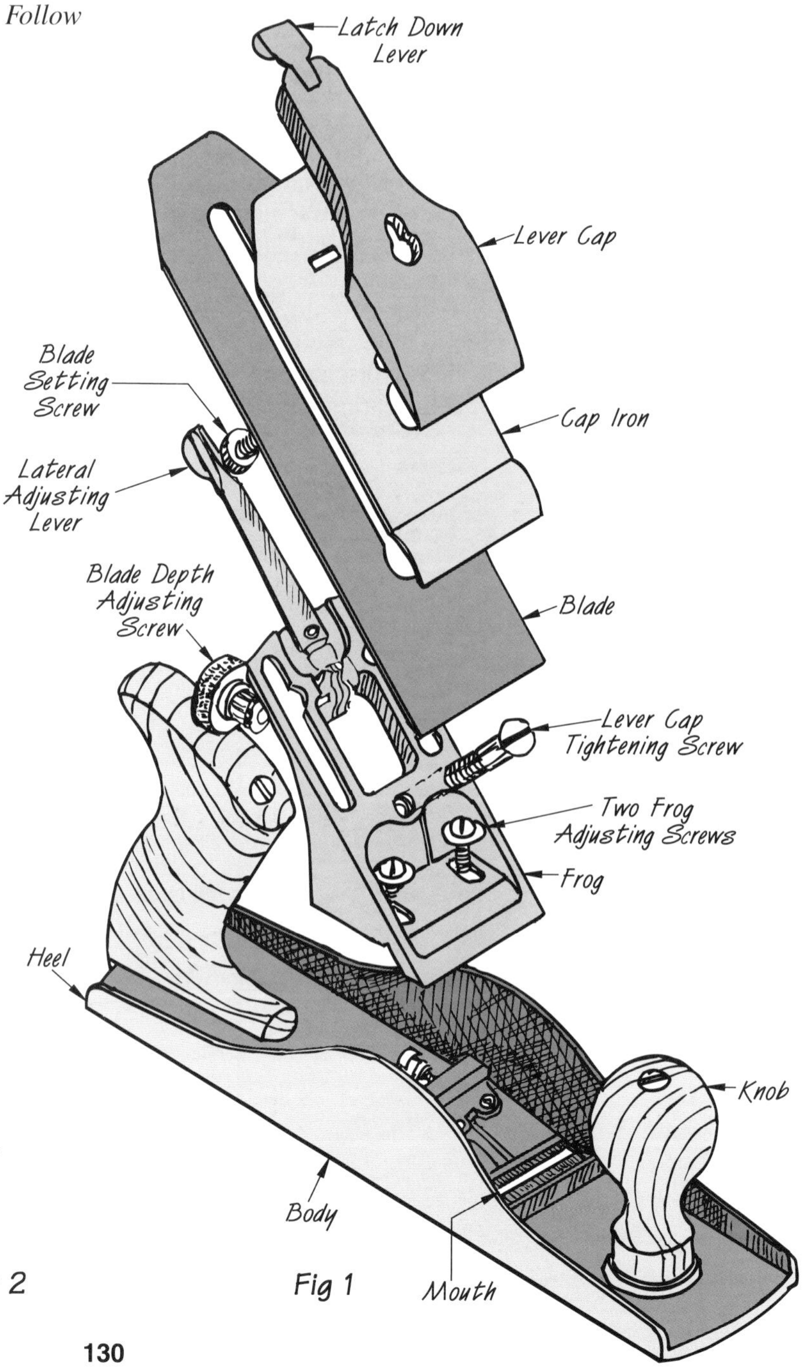

Fig 1

Portable Circular Saw

A first time user should have a demonstration on its use. Begin with a 185mm tool and fit a combination or cross cutting blade for cutting wood. Ensure it is sharp.

Step 1 Adjust the blade into square with the base plate as in fig 1 using a try or adjustable square.

Step 2 Adjust the depth of the blade so that only approx. 6mm of the teeth pass through the material as in fig 2.

Ensure the square is flat on the blade and resting between the teeth and flat on the base plate.

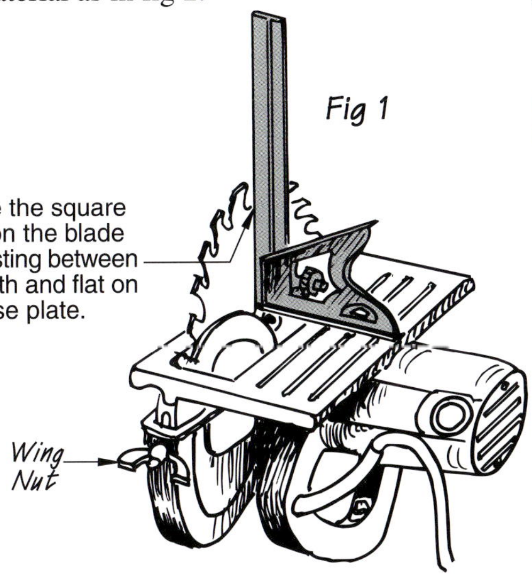

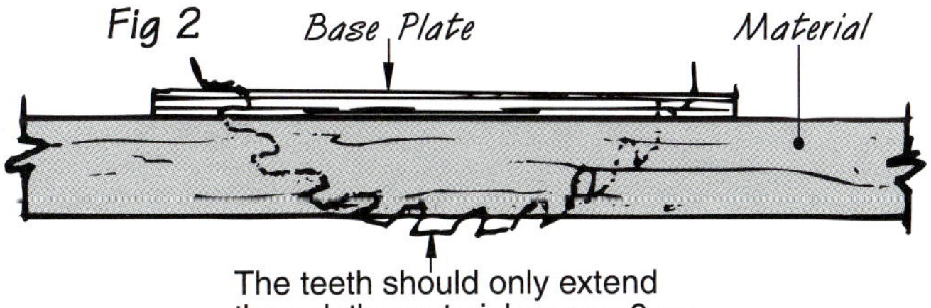

The teeth should only extend through the material approx. 6mm.

IMPORTANT: Always check the blade guard is rotating and returning freely. Wear a pair of safety spectacles and shoes or boots.

Step 3 Commence with a length of 100x50mm clamped to a pair of sawstools. Have the timber extended over one stool.

Step 4 Plan to make several off-cuts. Using a pencil, square several lines across the face about 25mm apart at one end.

Step 5 Check that the power cable is well behind the tool. Commence to line up the cutting guide mark, slot or V on the front plate of the saw with the line.

Plan to cut along the outside edge of the line. Hold the saw as illustrated in fig 3 with one hand on the handle and trigger and the other also supporting the saw with the handle and the thumb used to raise the guard just to commence as in fig 4. Once the blade is cutting, the guard can look after itself. Do *not* use the locking button. Ensure the saw teeth are clear of the wood when the motor is switched on.

Fig 4

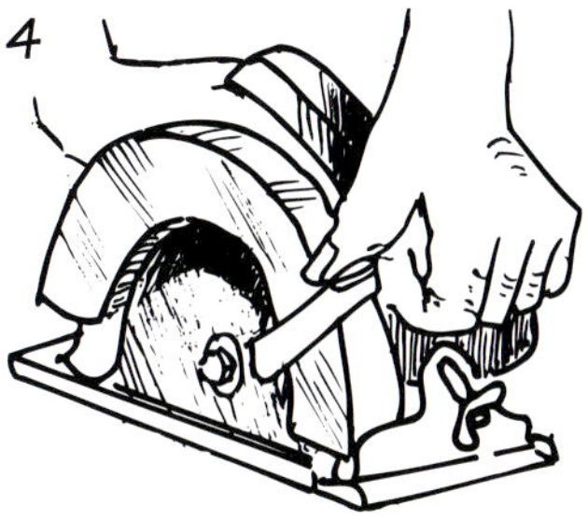

Raise the guard only on commencement of the cut.

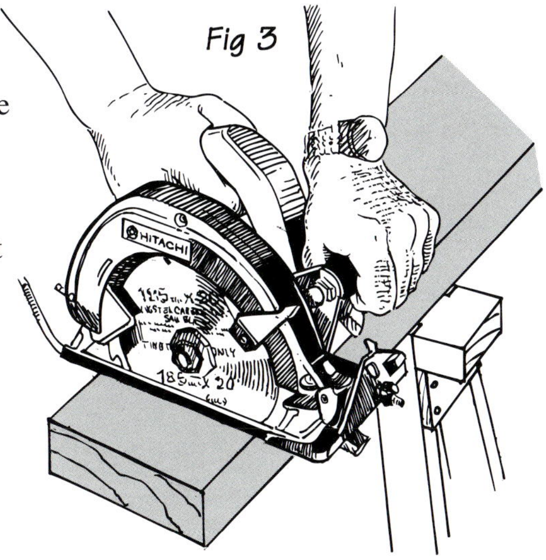

Only a skilled operator should operate the saw with one hand.

Plan to cut right through without stopping, keeping your eye on the line. Learn to push the saw through in one even continuous movement *not* stopping until the offcut drops on the floor.
Don't try to save it with one hand!
Don't slow the tool down just before the last 10mm of the cut otherwise, when cutting a larger offcut, it can break off taking a corner of the adjoining material with it.

Important
As soon as the offcut drops away the saw blade will be exposed until the guard returns. After cutting away keep the tool in the air clear of the cable and your body until the guard returns.
A common scenario is that the user rests the tool on the floor not noticing that the guard hasn't retracted and the saw instantly races across the floor over the cable or the user's foot. The cause is often that sawdust (possibly wet) has clogged the guard return mechanism.

Continue to practice cutting the remaining offcuts aiming to achieve a straight clean cut. You'll soon find it is not difficult at all.

When cutting long lengths of material on pairs of stools *never* cut between the stools as in fig 6. Always mark the cut overhanging the stools and allow the waste to fall.

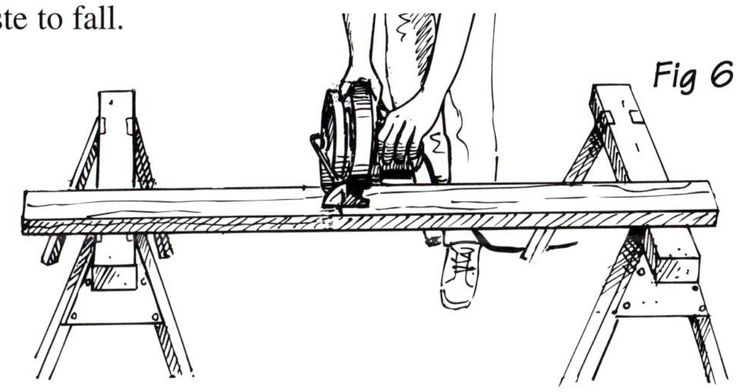

Cutting between the stools as above is a dangerous practice. Kickback can occur and thrust the blade back into your body.

How to Rip Cut

Mark the cutting line and set the blade to correct depth. Then install and adjust the width gauge to the desired width and carry out a test cut on scrap material and either clamp the material or have an assistant support one end.

Commence the cut ensuring the width gauge is running firm along the edge of the material.
If cutting between stools, as you approach the stools, switch off, release the clamps and adjust the material to avoid cutting the stool.

How to Cut Sheet Material

Step 1 Lay two lengths of timber (runners) on the stools to support the material and to keep the blade above the top of the stools.

Step 2 Mark the cutting lines and position the runners to support the material one on each side of the cutting line.

Step 3 Adjust the blade depth and make the cut. An assistant may be necessary to support the sheet and hold the cut apart to prevent the blade binding and also to prevent damaging the corners as the blade passes through the final millimetres of the cut.

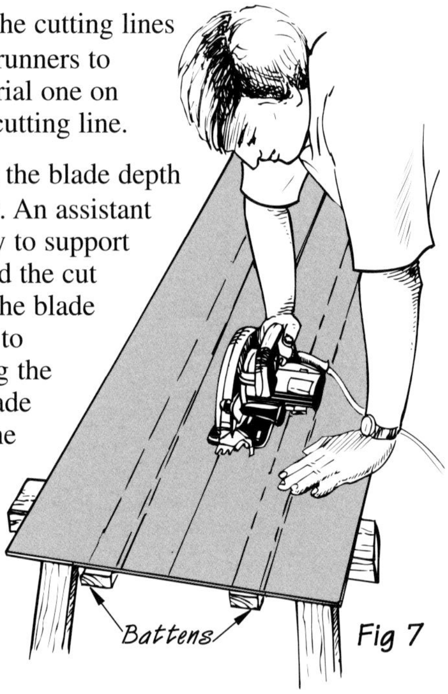

Fig 7

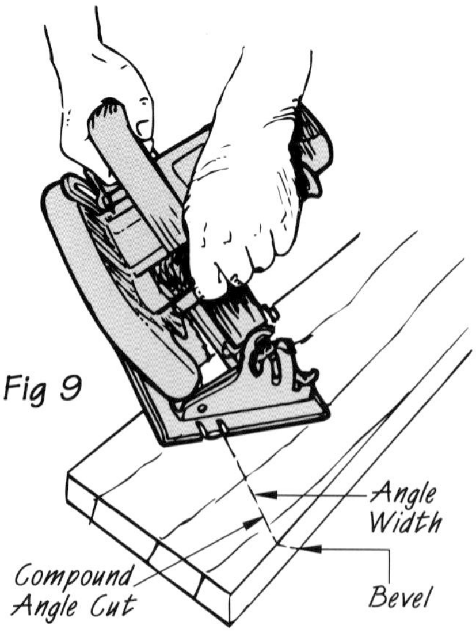

Fig 9

Pocket Cutting

Pocket cutting is safer performed with a jig saw but can be done with a circular saw. Set the blade to depth and lower the saw into the material as in fig 10. The saw must *not* be allowed to move backwards or kickback may occur. Also after making the cut, wait for the blade to stop before retracting.

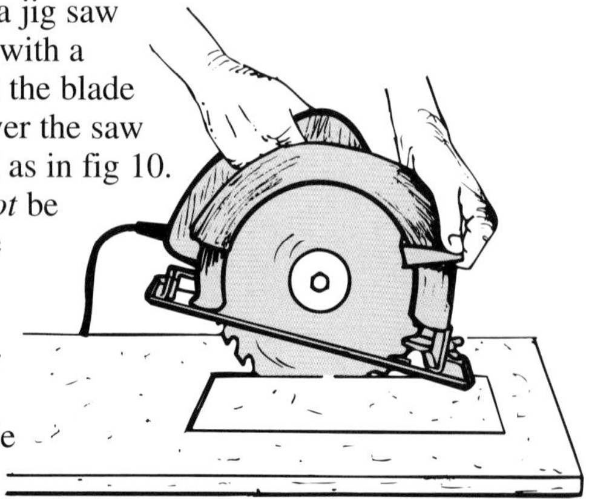

Fig 10

How to Make Compound Angle Cuts

This is the same as for making 90º cuts except that the base plate position is adjusted to the required angle.

Step 1 Obtain the bevel angle required and set this on an adjustable bevel.

Step 2 Unplug the tool and release the base plate screw just enough for the plate to be moved (see fig 8). With the tool upsidedown, hold the blade guard back and adjust the plate until you have the desired bevel. The bevel should rest firmly on the blade between the teeth and on the plate.

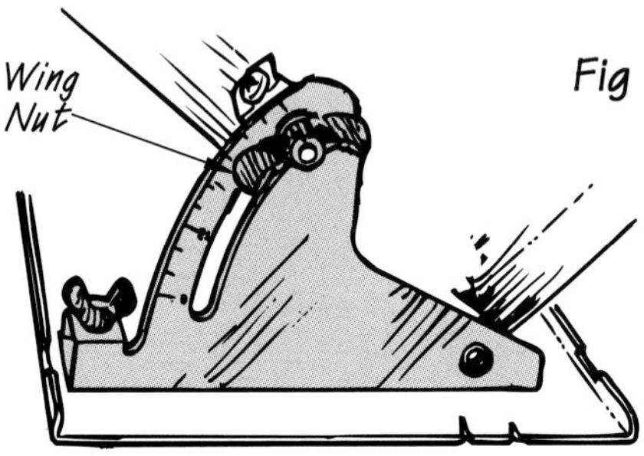

Fig 8

Hold the bevel tool between base plate and blade the same as the square is held in fig 1. Adjust and tighten the wing nut.

Blade Types

Fig 11

COMBINATION BLADE
Used for cross and rip cuts.

CROSS CUTTING BLADE

RIP CUTTING BLADE

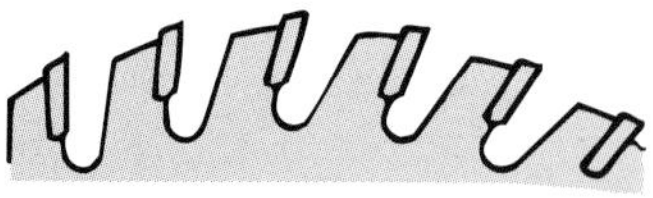

TUNGSTEN CARBIDE TIPPED

Using a Portable Power Plane

How to use the Planer

Read the safety instructions for the tool.

Step 1 Mark the line to dress down to then unplug the planer and turn it upside-down. Sighting the cutter blades are in parallel alignment with the base; the same as for hand planes as in fig 6, Page 131 and adjust them if necessary. Then adjust the Cutting Depth Plate with the Depth Adjustment Knob (see fig 1). For deep removal of material, make several passes. For fine dressing adjust the Depth Cutting Plate and carry out a test on scrap material. Make sure you first practice passes on a length of 40-50mm wide material in a vice or clamped to a stool. Before switching the planer on, hold the tool with its nose on the material but with the blades not yet in contact with the wood. Check the cable is well clear.

Step 2 Switch on and commence the cut with one hand in the handle trigger and the other on the adjustment knob as in fig 1. *Don't use the locking button.* That is only for experienced users. Hold the planer on the same level plane as the material not cocked up or down. Ensure the front plate is flat on the material. Plan to pass the plane over the material in one continuous movement *not* stopping and starting. It's better to undercut the line than remove it. You can always make another pass. When coming to the end of the material, take care not to lower the nose of the plane. ***Note:*** If shavings are not discharging freely a blockage will probably need clearing. Unplug the tool before attempting this.

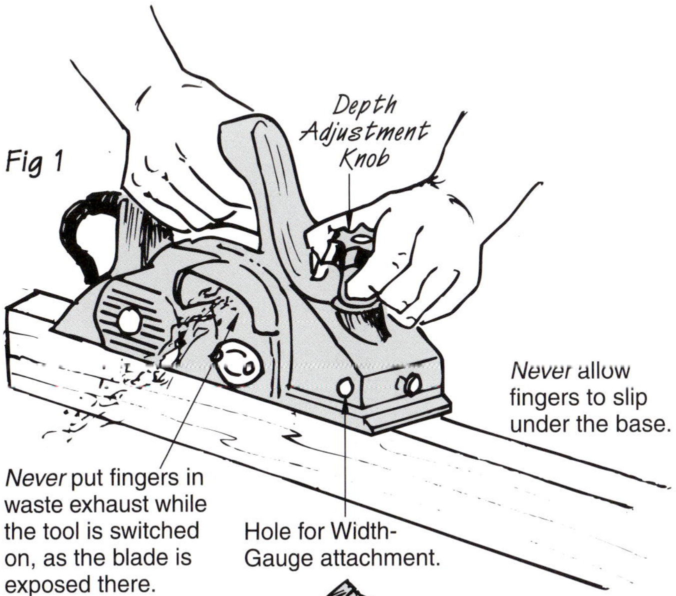

Fig 1

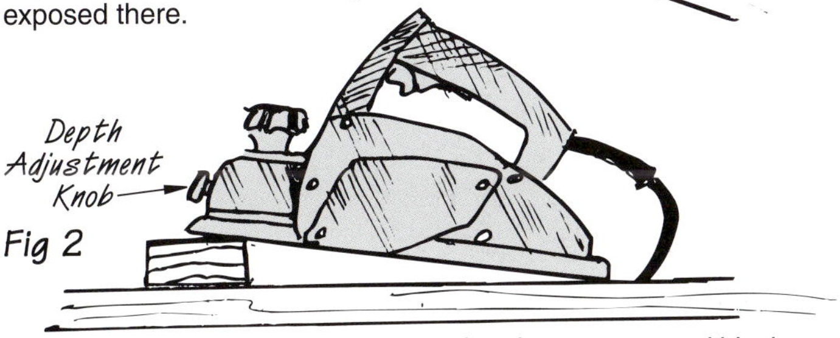

Fig 2

After completion of the task rest the planer on a wood block to protect the blades and the bench surface.

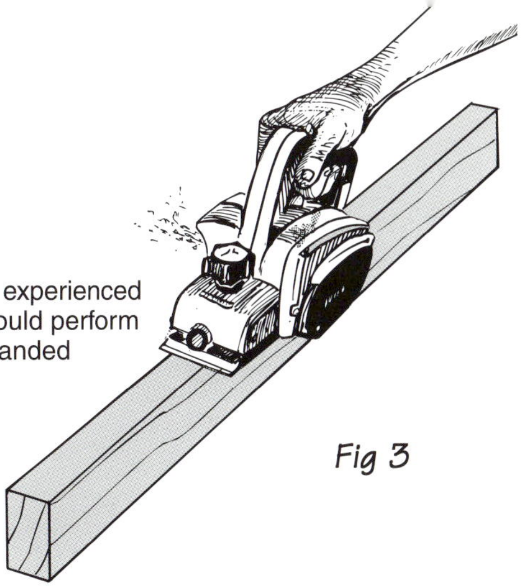

Fig 3

Making Rebates with the Power Planer

Step 1 Mark the lines of rebate.

Step 2 Adjust the cutting depth plate.

Step 3 Attach the Width-Gauge Attachment.

Step 4 Carry out a test, if the rebate is deep, perform it in two or three passes.

Step 5 To perform the cut precisely ensure the material is secure and keep your eye on the Width Gauge that it remains following firmly against the material and that the nose of the tool remains flat and square with the material. Again plan to make the cuts in single, even, continuous passes.

How to Make Bevelled or Chamfered Corners

The planer has a V-groove formed in the underside of the Depth Plate to help start a chamfer. To ensure the chamfer is equally cut at 45° to the corner, you need to hold the tool at a consistent 45° to either side. This is *not* difficult to perform and you will soon master the technique. However, an accessory tool is available for this. Carry out a few practice runs on scrap. Where you are uncertain as to the bevel size required, dress down in stages a little at a time.

Fig 4

SAFETY: With power planers always be mindful of where your fingers are in relation to the blades. Wear a dust mask as some wood dust can cause permanent lung damage and after completing a task, check that the blades have stopped rotating before resting the tool.

Hand Planing & Chiselling

Hand Planing

The No. 4 (60x250mm) plane is the one of choice for the building site and for DIY use. The No. 5 & 7 are for cabinet/hand jointing work. If you own a bench jointer (planer) you can do without these.

The No. 5 (63x370mm) is 14 inches long and the No. 7 (73x557mm) 22 inches long. Oil after every day's use and you should get your investment back even after a lifetime of use.

How to Dismantle & Reassemble the Plane

To use a plane successfully, you must learn how to dismantle and reassemble the plane. In particular the blade assembly which will require regular setting, waste removal and resharpening.

It's really very simple, just follow the steps:

Always check the frog is in correct alignment. *Follow 'Checking the Frog Alignment' Page 131.*

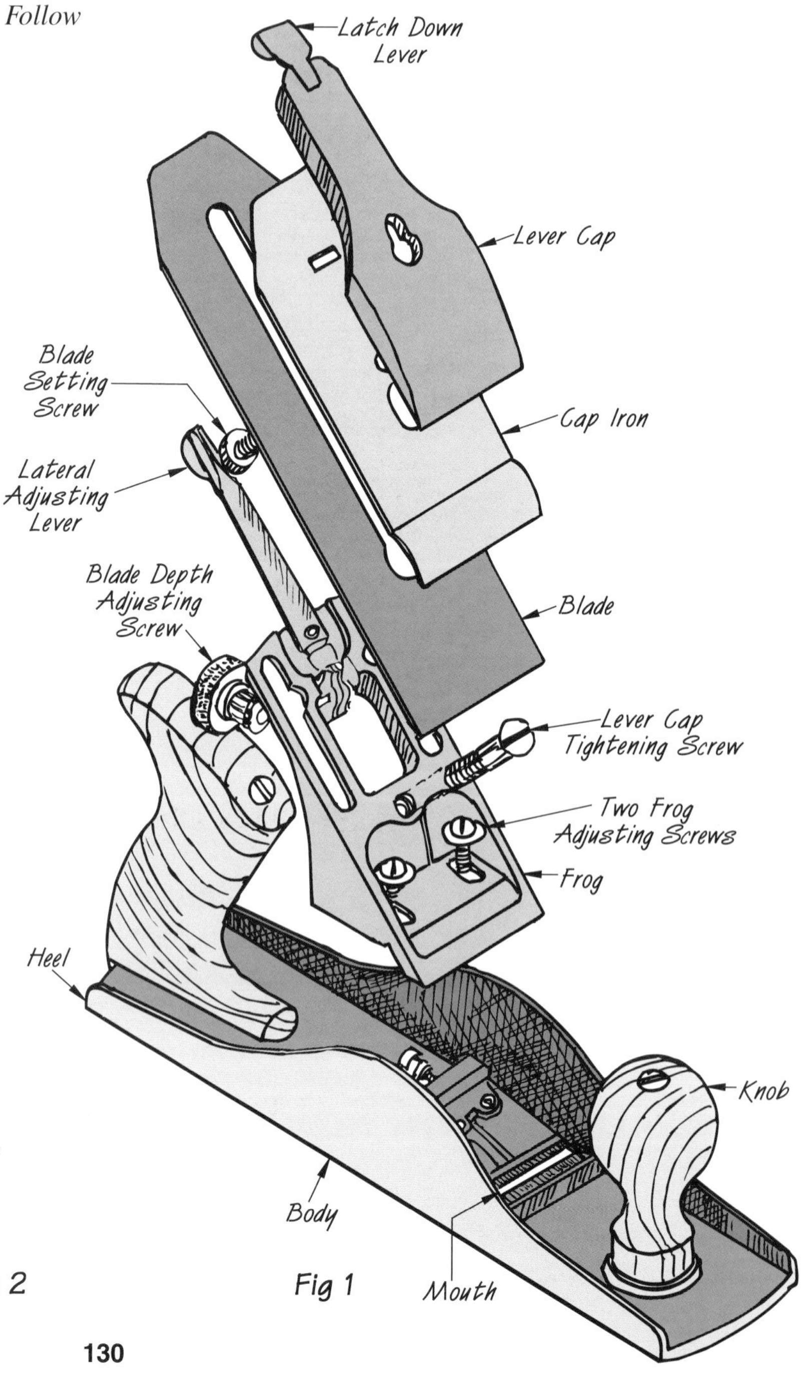

Fig 1

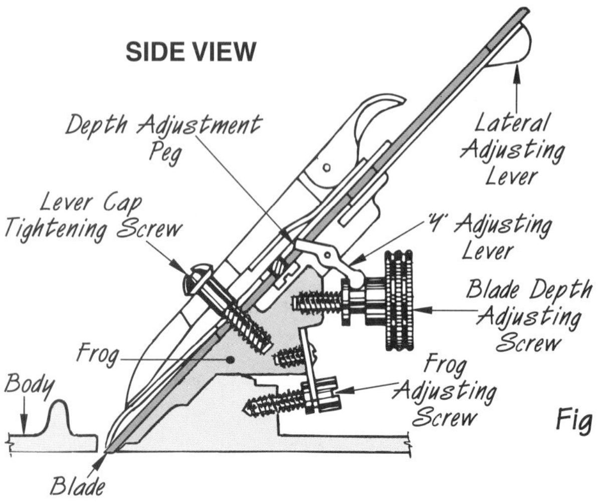

Fig 2

Checking the Frog Alignment

Check that the frog is resting in line with the mouth bevel as in fig 3. It should *not* be behind the mouth bevel.

Adjusting the Frog

To begin, if the frog is resting flush in line with the mouth bevel then leave it alone. If it's not, release the top pair of frog adjusting screws just a little then adjust the frog in or out with the single Rear Frog-Adjustment-Screw. When in alignment, simply tighten the upper pair of screws. A fine shaving will give a smooth finish. This will require the frog to be adjusted forward slightly to narrow the mouth opening.

Fig 3

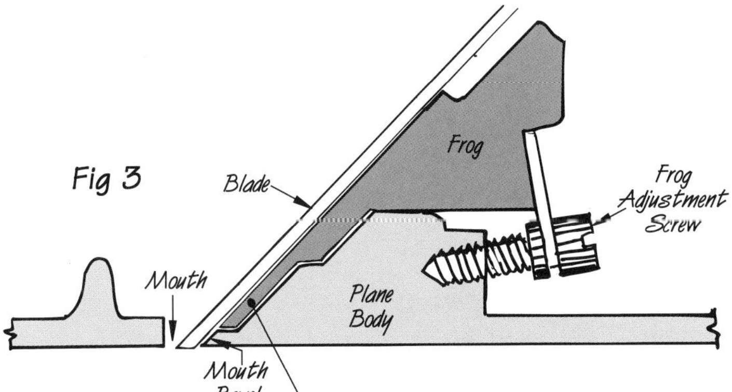

Frog in line with mouth bevel. It should *not* be any further back.

Fig 4

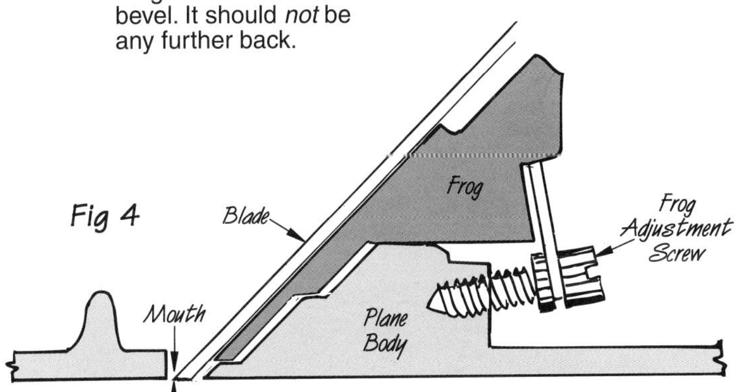

Frog adjusted forward leaves narrow mouth for fine shavings.

When shavings get forced between the cap iron and blade, remove the Cap Iron to clean to ensure it rests tight on the blade.

When repositioning the Cap Iron, take care not to touch the sharpened blade edge with the iron. Be sure to fix the cap iron parallel with the blade edge (see fig 5).

Fig 5

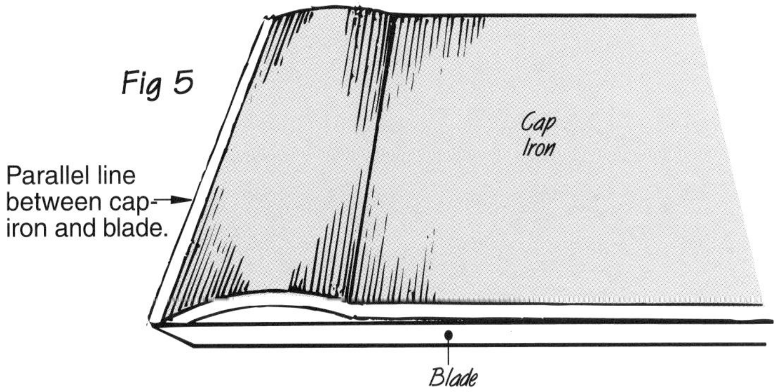

Reset the Blade to Depth

Once the blade is reinstalled onto the frog, it has to be adjusted for depth and parallel. Sight along the plane base from its toe as in fig 6 and at the same time adjust the Lateral Adjusting Lever until the line of the protruding blade is parallel with the base. Then set the depth with the Depth Adjusting Screw. Once the blade is parallel its depth can be adjusted as you work. To ensure the setting you've chosen doesn't move, check the Lever Cap Screw is tight.

Dismantling and Re-setting the Blade Assembly

Step 1 Release the lever on the Lever Cap (see fig 1) and remove.

Step 2 Remove and separate the blade and cap iron but before doing so, take note of the following as in fig 2.

a). How the rectangular hole in the cap iron rests over the Depth-Adjustment-Peg;

b). How the cap iron is attached on the back of the blade and set close to the blade edge;

c). How close the cap is set to the blade edge.
The closer it is the finer the shaving.
For general work usually between .5-.7 of a millimetre.

Fig 6

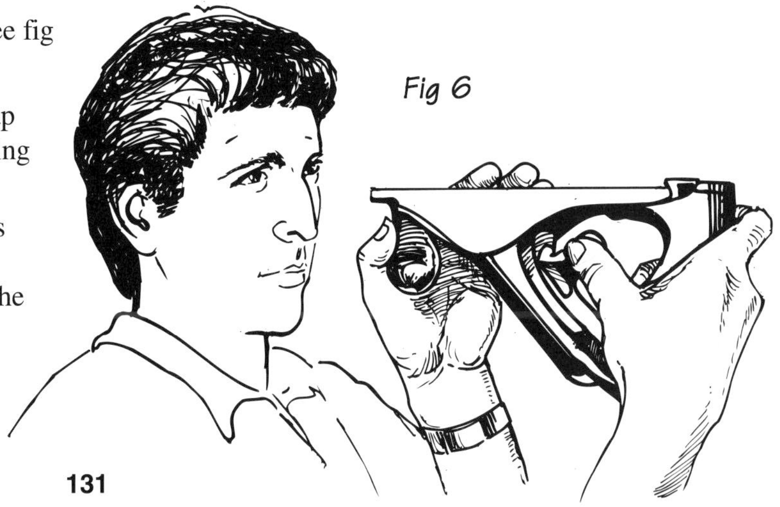

Using Hand Planes

The following is intended for those unfamiliar with using hand planes. It is best to start with edges before attempting flat surfaces.

Jointing Edges

Step 1 The blade should be razor sharp and should extend beyond the base showing just a fine parallel line when sighted as in fig 6, Page 131. Adjust the blade parallel using the Angle Adjustment Lever. To extend or withdraw it, turn the Depth Adjusting Screw (wheel).

Step 2 Start by dressing the edge of a length of pine or softwood say around 75or100x20x500mm long, place in a vice on edge. But first check the grain direction see figs 1 and 2. The plane should follow the direction of the grain *not* oppose it.

Step 3 Hold the plane as below and commence to plane. If it's biting in and sticking, the blade may require withdrawing a little or the plane is opposing the grain direction.

The position of your feet and legs is important to help carry the forward motion and bear some of the pressure. Continue to plane until you can remove an unbroken peel of shaving from the whole length of wood.

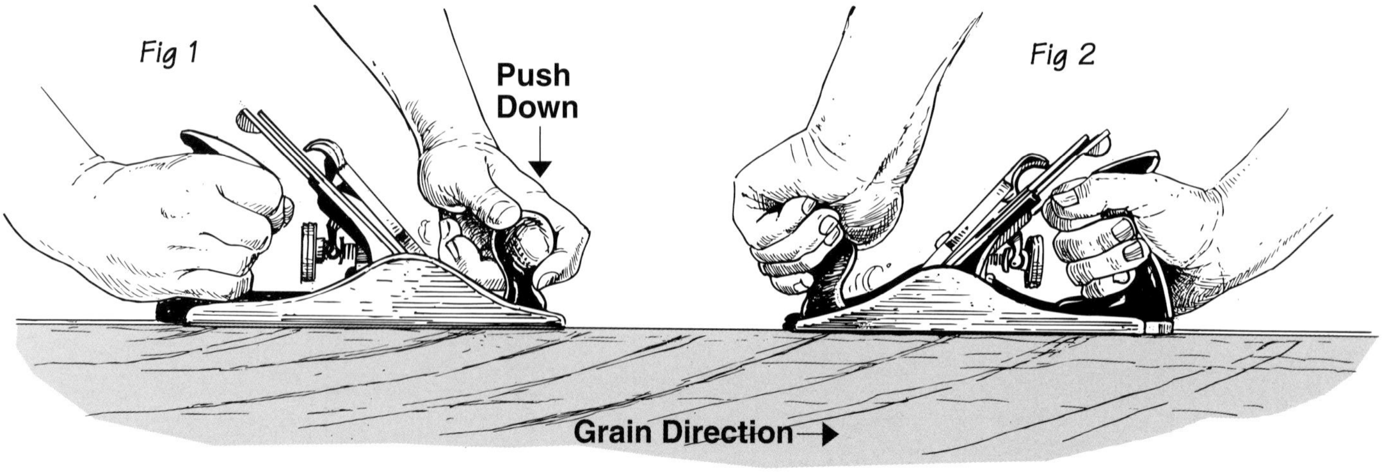

RIGHT

Once the blade is correctly adjusted, push the plane through in one continuous movement using the legs and body. An unbroken shaving will prove you have mastered the technique.

WRONG

Planing against the grain will cause the plane to dig in and chatter the surface and also block up the mouth.

Planing End Grain

Step 1 Secure the timber in a vice and clamp a length of scrap timber on the leading edge end as in fig 3 to prevent break-out as has occurred in fig 4.

Step 2 Adjust the blade to extend only a small amount also it must be sharp.

Step 3 Push the plane across the end at an angle slicing using a slightly sideways movement.

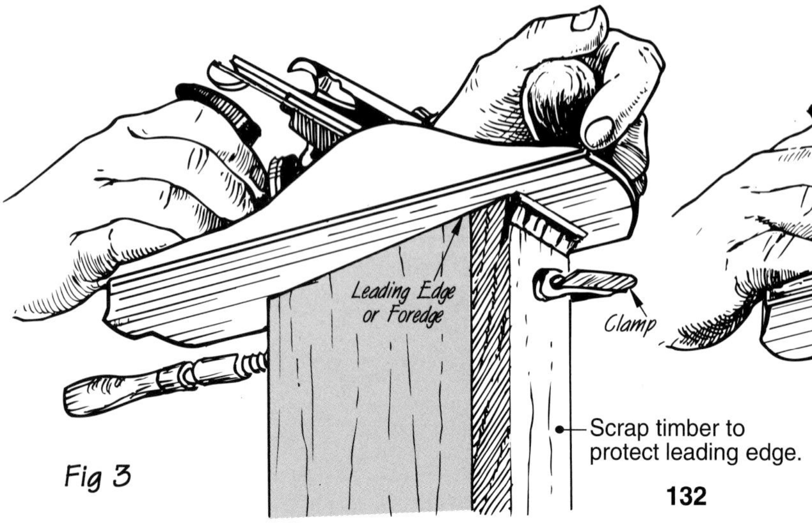

Fig 3

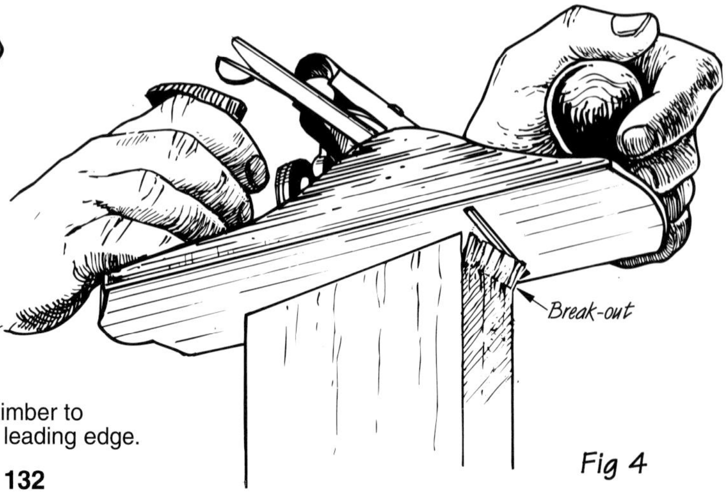

Fig 4

Cont.

Jointing Edges

This is often necessary to create a tight edge fit or when edge joining timber in order to create a wider panel, see fig 1.

Step 1 Presuming the timber has been thickened that is, dressed on both faces and only the edge requires dressing. This operation is usually performed on a stationary powered jointer (planner) but when using hand planes a No 5. or 7. Remember the longer the timber joint the longer the plane required to make it straight.

Step 2 Rest the plane on the timber and support the base flat and square to the edge using one hand with fingers extended underneath to rest on the timber to act as a supporting gauge as in fig 2.

Never attempt to remove too thick a shaving. Your aim is to attempt to follow through in one continuous movement ending up with a single shaving. If the blade is set correct and is razor sharp, you will soon discover one of the greatest pleasures of hand woodworking.

Fig 1

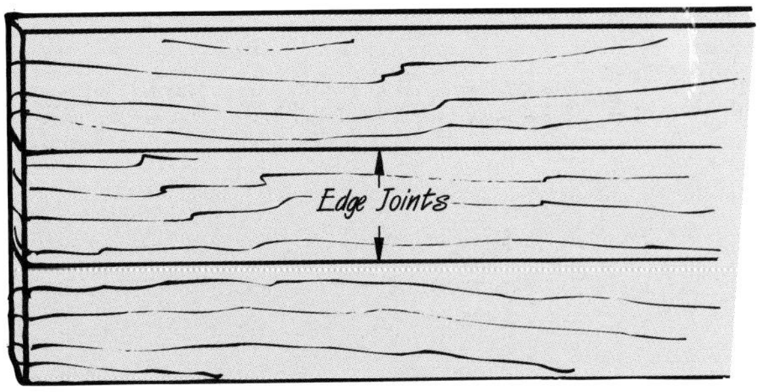

A wider board is created by edge jointing two or more pieces together.

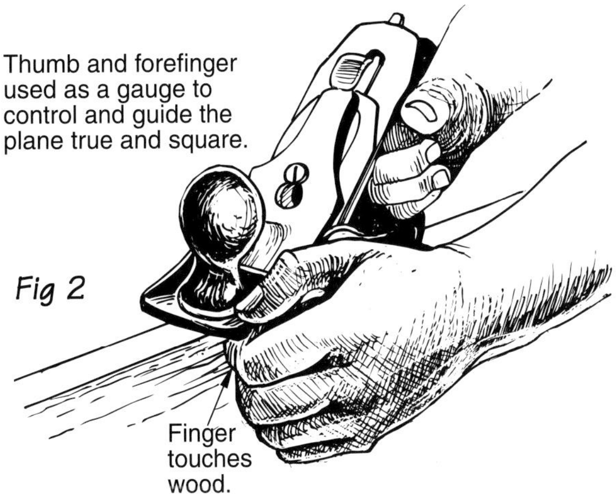

Fig 2

Joints & How to Make Them

The instructions for making the following joints are basically the same for all the joists on Pages 133-135.

Making Halves in Corners & T's (Cross) Joints

Step 1 Check that the ends of both pieces are of identical width and thickness. Clamp the timber to a stool or in the vice for marking. Set the marking gauge or combination square to half the width of the timber to be halved. Mark the edges as in fig 3.

Step 2 Use a tenon saw for a fine joint or fine panel saw for a not so perfect joint. Cut the cross cuts first on the waste sides of the lines. For corner joints use the saw to make the end grain saw cut. To assist waste removal make several saw cuts as in fig 4.

Step 3 For 'T' and cross joints you will then remove the waste using a chisel. Commence with the bevel of the chisel on the underside as in fig 6 and commence to remove half the waste from one side. Then repeat the process from the opposite side as in fig 6. Continue the process down to just clear of the line from both sides. A wood mallet can be used. Finally remove the last millimetre or two of wood using the chisel on its flat with the bevel side uppermost as in fig 7.

Fig 1

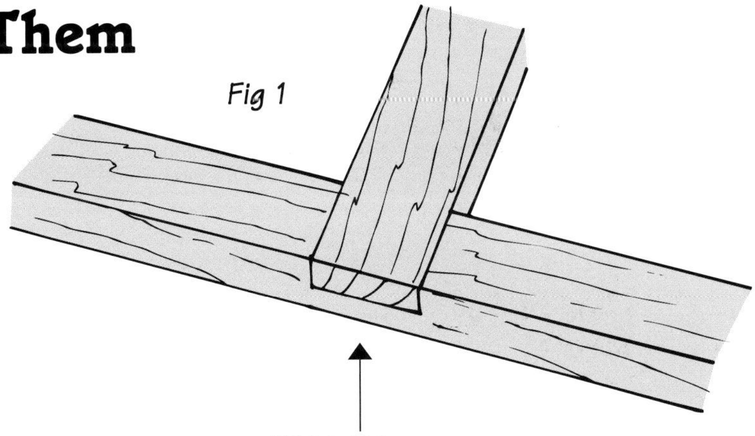

'T' Half Lap or 'T' Halving

Fig 2

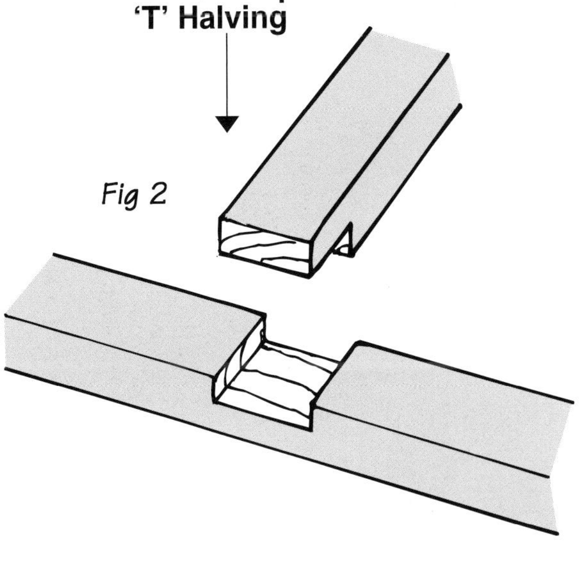

Cont.

Step 1 Ensure both lengths of timber are exactly the same width and thickness. Set the adjustable square or marking gauge to half the thickness of the material.

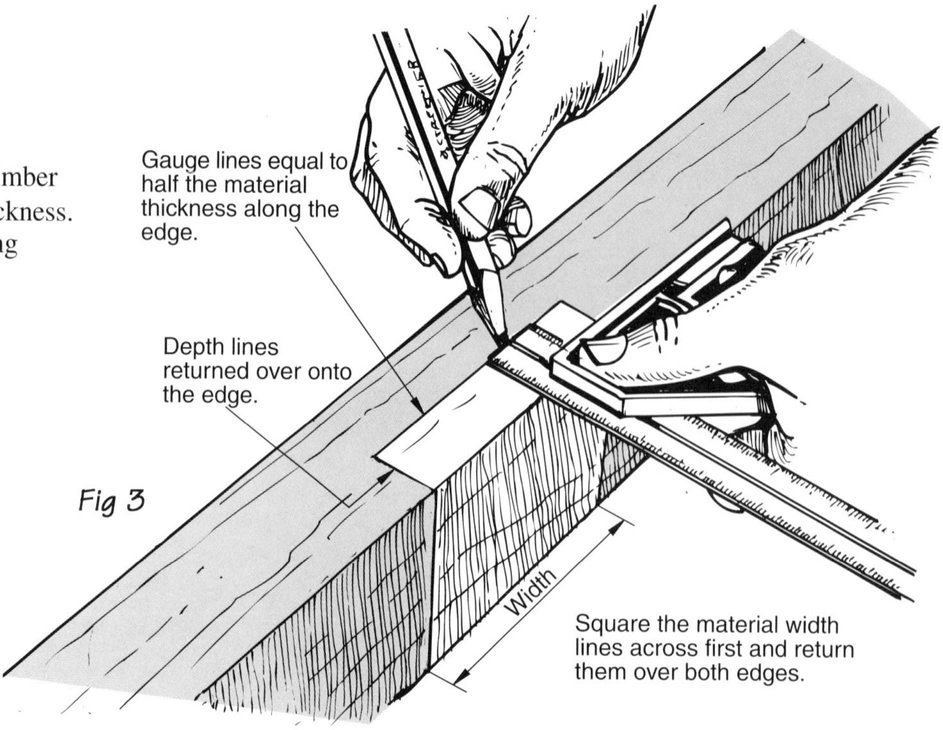

Fig 3

Fig 4

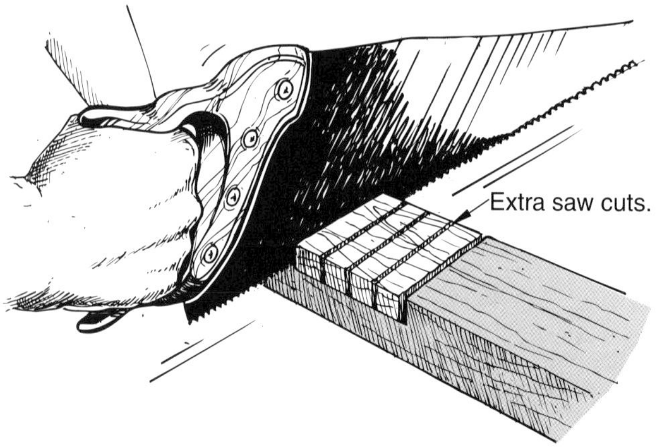

Step 3 Remove waste from both sides down to a millimetre or two from the bottom using the chisel with its bevelled side underneath to prevent digging in.

Fig 6

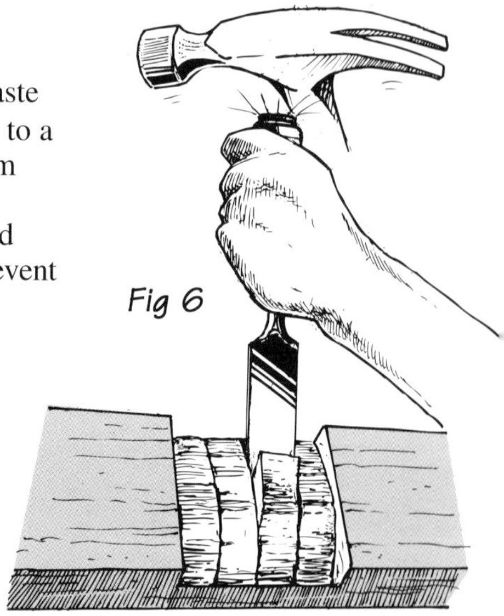

Step 2 Saw cut carefully up to the width lines and down to the thickness line. Then several saw cuts can be made to make work easier for the chisel (see fig 4).

On Stopped 'T' housings use the saw to make the side cuts before chiselling out the waste.

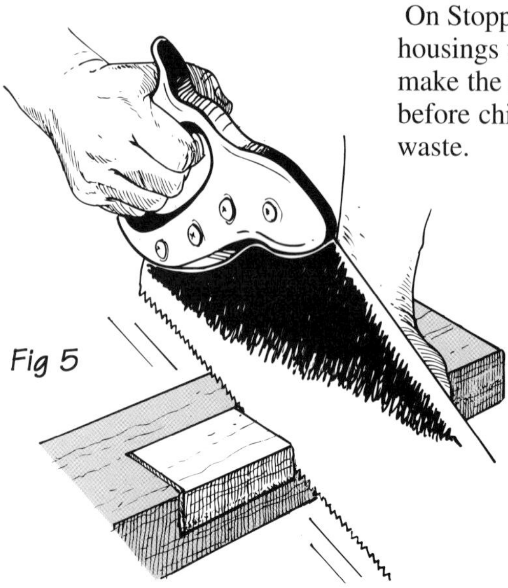

Fig 5

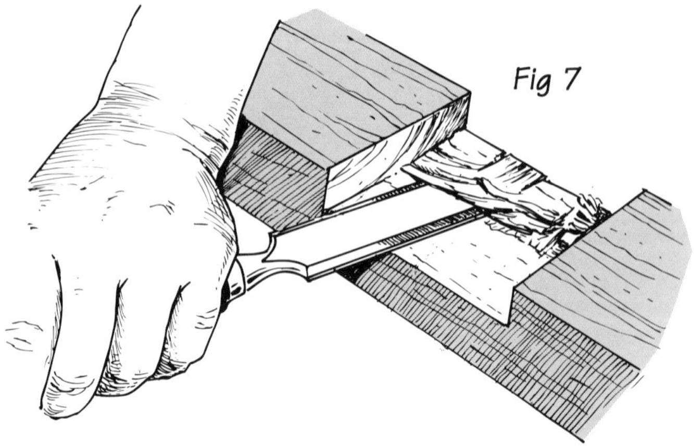

Fig 7

Step 4 For removing the last millimetre or two turn the chisel over onto its flat. You may *not* require the hammer just a firm hand paring action if the chisel is very sharp.

Cont.

Common Building Construction Joints

The following illustrations cover most joints encountered in the building construction industry and the principles of making them are in the main illustrated on Pages 133 & 134.

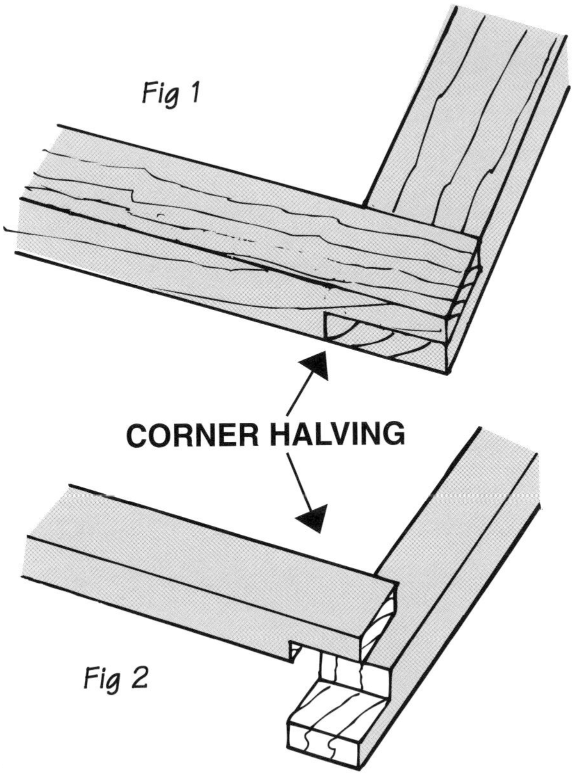

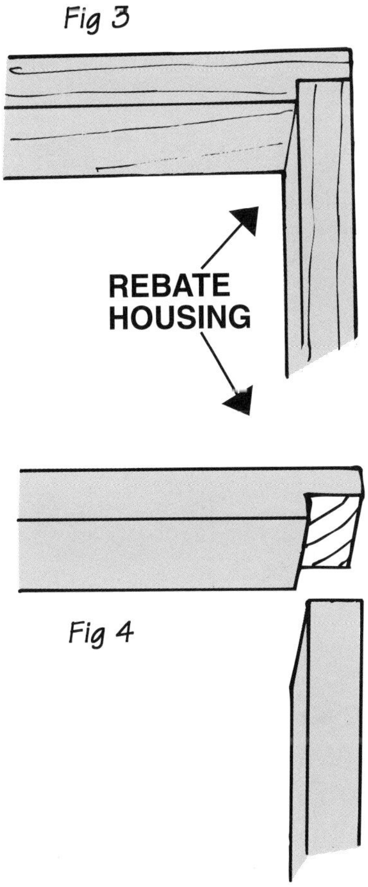

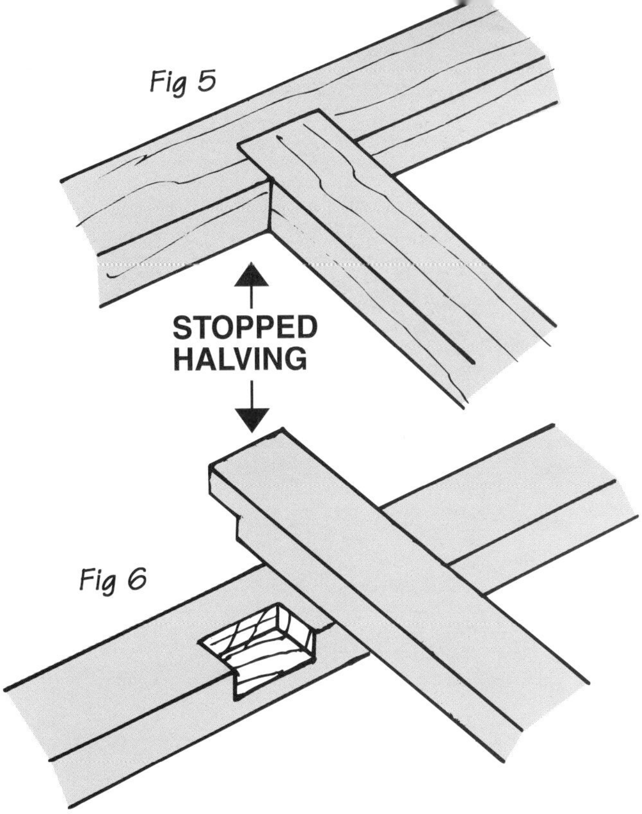

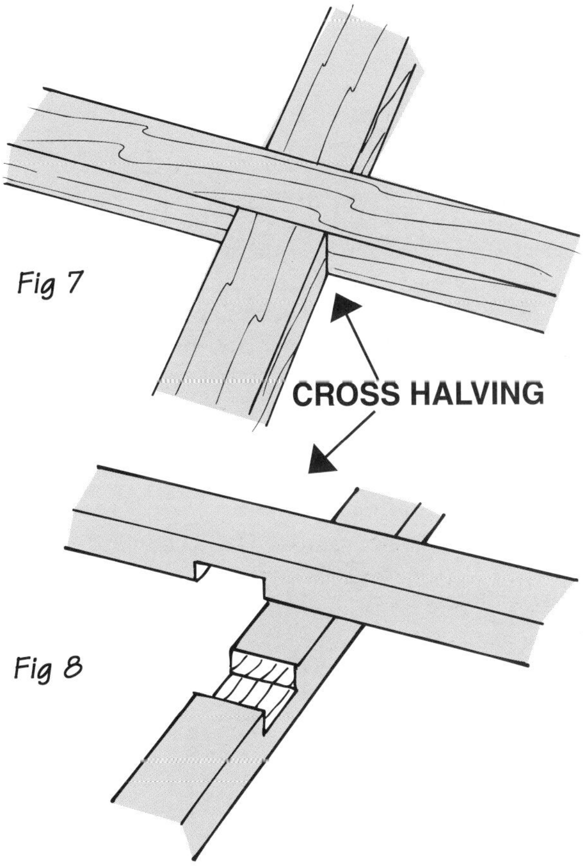

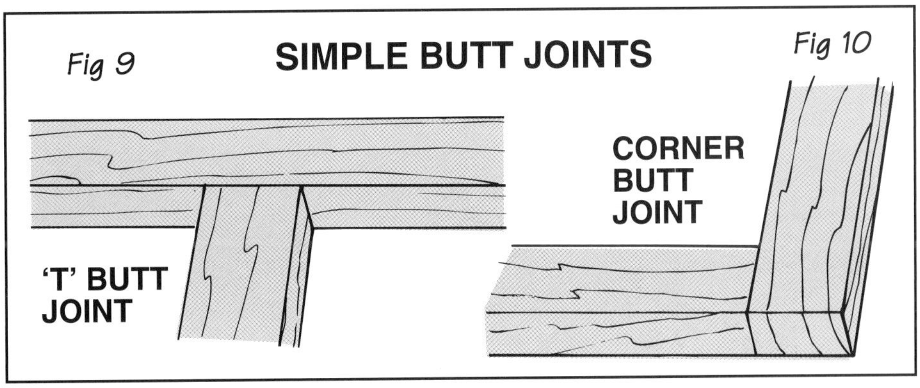

10 Extra Building Know How

Bricklaying

Bricklaying Mortar

(Refer to the 'HBM' for the various mixtures for various situations)

An improved mixture is obtained by using a mechanical mixer. The mortar consistency or its pliability and stickiness is a very important factor to successful bricklaying. A small to medium quantity of mortar on the trowel should be capable of being held upside down without falling off *(see Step 1, Page 137)*. Too wet or too dry a mixture will impair progress considerably.

Laying Bricks

Mortar joints are usually 10mm thick but the wet mortar is laid to about 20mm thick to allow for mortar to be squeezed out when a brick is positioned. String lines are attached and pulled taut. The horizontal bed is laid first then the unlaid brick is buttered on one end and laid up against the preceding brick, then tapped down to the string line. Any squeezed out mortar is then removed. Corners are built up to a maximum of 1200mm high and intermediate sections filled in (see fig 1 & 2). This enables mortar joints to set evenly throughout. Jointing is carried out as mortar firms a little. Brush or damp sponge the completed brickwork down or use a piece of bagging when sufficiently dry.

Jointing

Although the raked joint is popularly in use, the ironed joint offers superior protection for the clay brick from the elements. Where joints are exposed to salt air, it is preferable to apply ironed joints.

Constructing Brick Walls

One of two methods can be used for levelling and gauging the height of each course. The first one (see fig 1) more desirable for application by the inexperienced requires the erection of corner profile posts with nails driven at each course for attaching string lines, The second consists of building up raked or stepped corners using a level and straightedge as in fig 2 and filling in between.

Preparing Profile Posts (as in fig 1)

90x45mm straight edged posts or hired metal posts are erected at each corner (see fig 1). Bracing them accurately plumb, indicate the first course on all profile posts using a Builders automatic level or water level. Alternatively, simply level off the floor if you are sure it is level. A gauge rod is then made using 42x19mm dry and dressed stock or similar and all brick joint positions indicated on one edge. This rod is held on the profile posts aligning with the first course previously marked and all joint positions transferred across. Nails are driven in these marks to support the string line. This method relieves the Bricklayer of all levelling and height measuring while laying bricks.

Fig 1

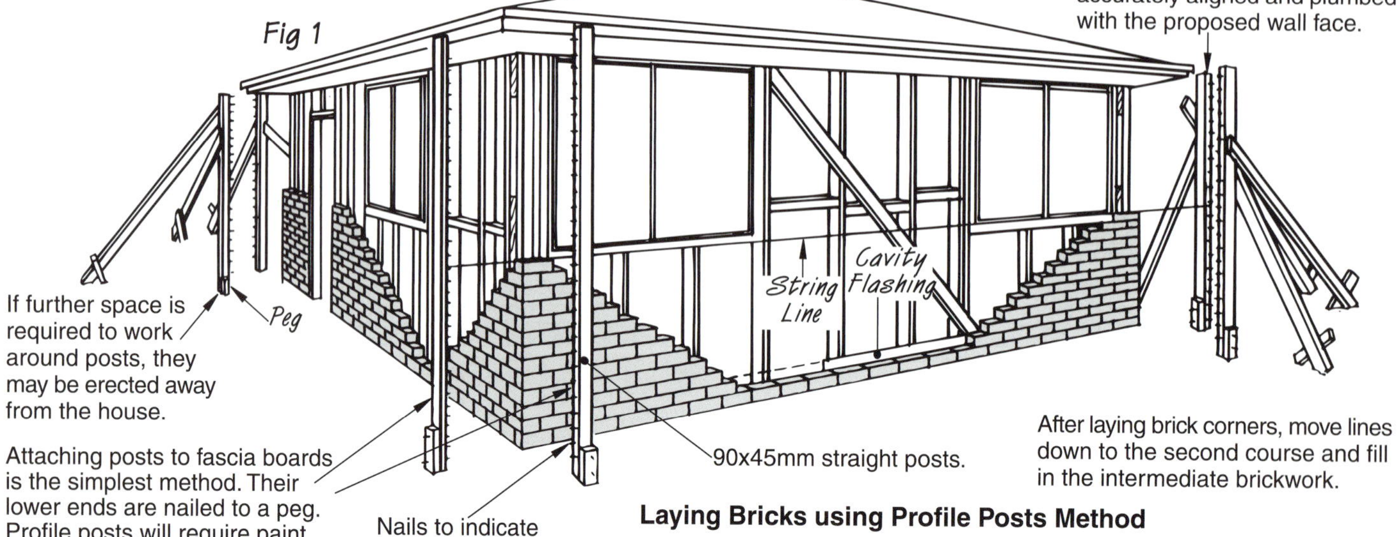

Laying Bricks using Profile Posts Method

Fig 2

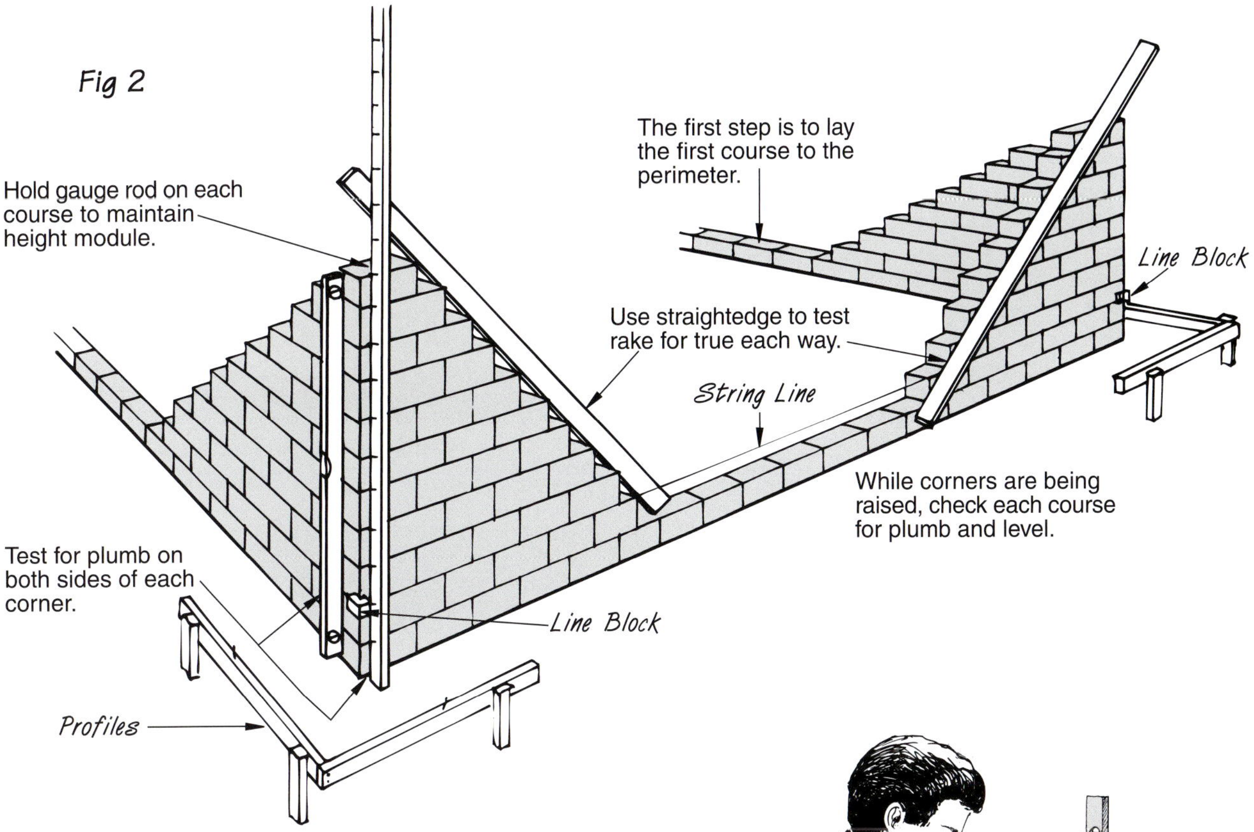

Constructing Walls using the Level & String Line Method

Lay one course around the perimeter of proposed brickwork. Construct corners by laying the corner bricks first. Establish the heights of these bricks using the gauge rod. Then level and plumb them as in figs 4 & 5. A string line is then stretched between using corner blocks. The infill course is then laid. To ensure each raking brick is true, use the straightedge on the face and edge of the rake as in fig 2 above.

Fig 4

When care is taken to lay the corner bricks accurately, the infill course is very easy to keep in alignment.

Fig 3

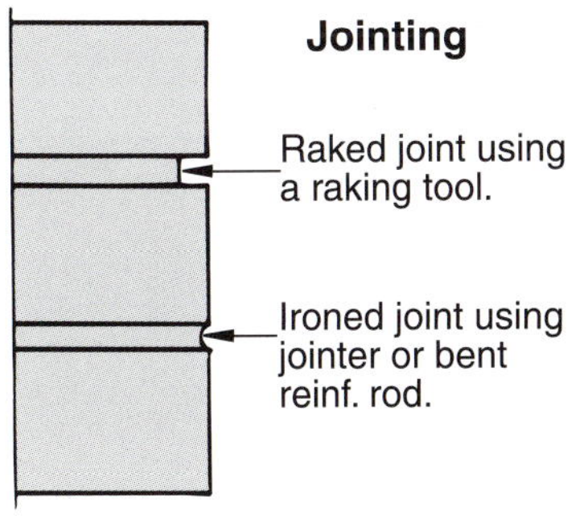

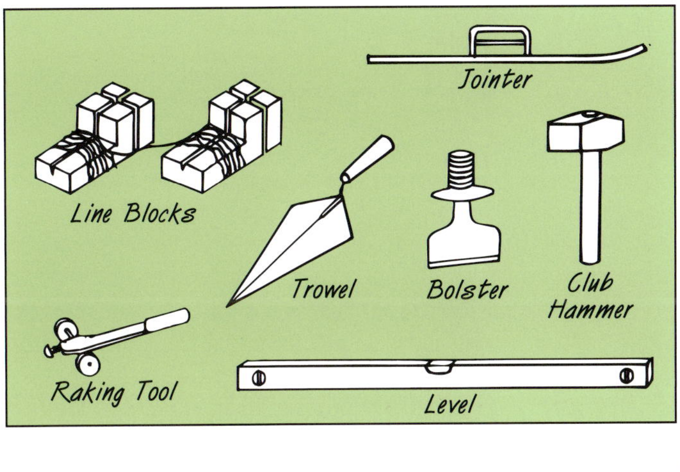

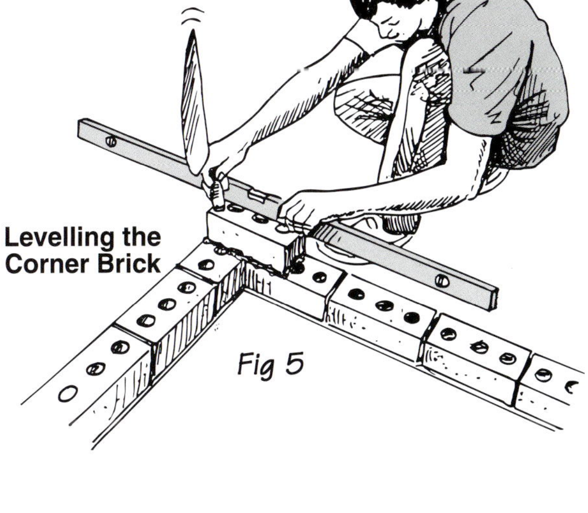

Fig 5

How to Lay Bricks

Step 1 Test mortar for correct consistency (see Page 136) and the HBM for correct mortar mixtures.

Step 2 Lay the mortar bed.

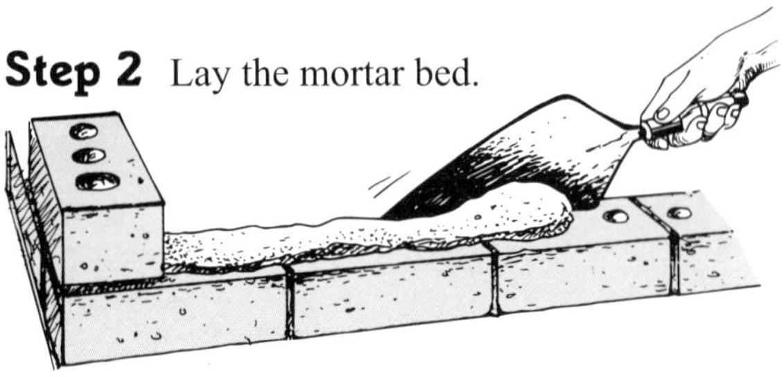

Step 3 Furrow the mortar bed.

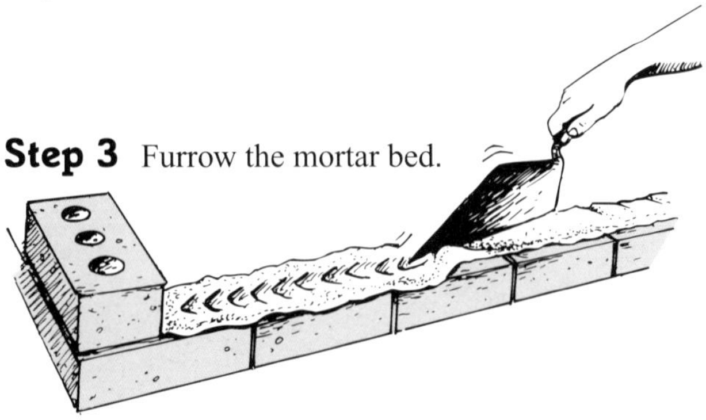

Step 4 Salvage the spread mortar from each side of wall.

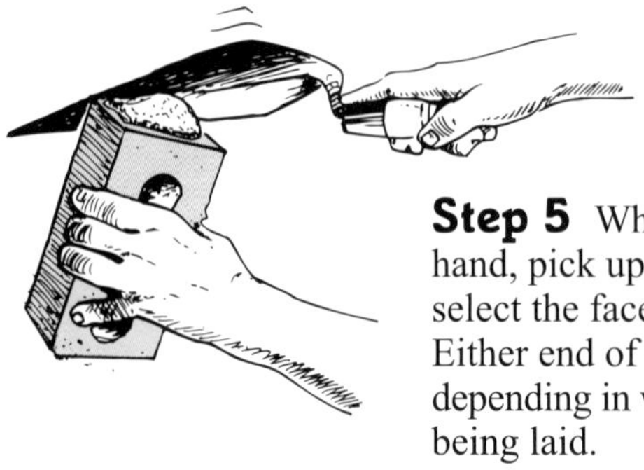

Step 5 While retaining the trowel in one hand, pick up a brick with the other and select the face. Then butter the perpend. Either end of the perpend can be buttered depending in which direction the bricks are being laid.

Bricks can be laid in either direction.

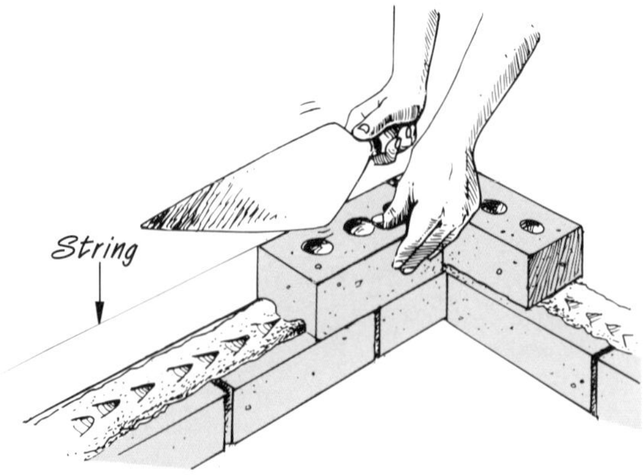

Step 6 Place the brick into the mortar bed and firm down with hand and fingers and gentle taps with the edge of the trowel to align bricks with the string line.

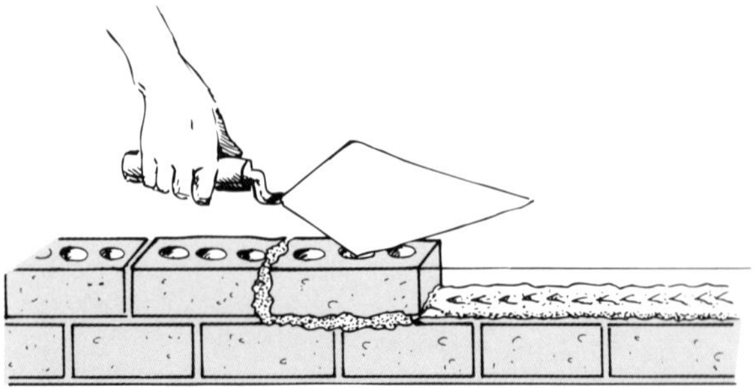

Step 7 Continue to lay the course tapping each brick down to the string line.

Step 8 Remove mortar that has squeezed out of joint.

Step 9 Jointing should be performed as soon as mortar has firmed sufficiently. This is followed by brushing the bricks down. Where mortar has overspread the surface, you may need to clean off with a damp sponge to prevent mortar stains.

Kitchen Cupboard Construction

Constructing kitchen cabinets is not beyond the capabilities of the handyperson. Pre-made doors and drawers are available. Doors can either be overlapping (most common method) or flush fitting.

For overlapping doors the doors close on either mullions or the edges of partitions concealing the cabinet carcass. Doors are hung to hide the end grain of the bottom shelf. Flush fitting doors are hinged inside and flush with the face of the cabinet exposing the mullions (rarely used).

Constructing Cupboards (for overlapping doors)

Step 1 Construct kickboard and floor using 16mm particle board. Kickboards are usually 100mm deep and can be from 150-200mm high. Cut supports for the centre and the back edges of the floor (called floor supports in the illustration) and same height as the kickboard. Glue and nail the floor to kickboard and floor supports. Floor supports are indicated by dashed lines.

Step 2 Cut gable ends out of 16mm particle board. Allow extra depth for kickboard to run past the end edge of gables. The floor will butt into the gable ends.

Step 3 Attach gable ends to floor and kickboard, gluing and nailing.

Step 4 Attach shelf supports to gable ends and erect 42x19mm perpendicular mullions with 42x19mm benchtop blades to support mullions or use strips of laminated material. Bottom ends of mullions are rebated into cupboard floor and spaced to suit doors.

Step 5 Fit cross runners to support intermediate shelf and attach shelf. Shelf can fit inside mullions.

Step 6 Fit benchtop pre-laminated or 18mm particle board can be used. Benchtops usually overlap cabinets and the overlap thickened with particle board or dressed wood. Surface and edge is then laminated.

Step 7 Fit and hang doors using appropriate hinges.

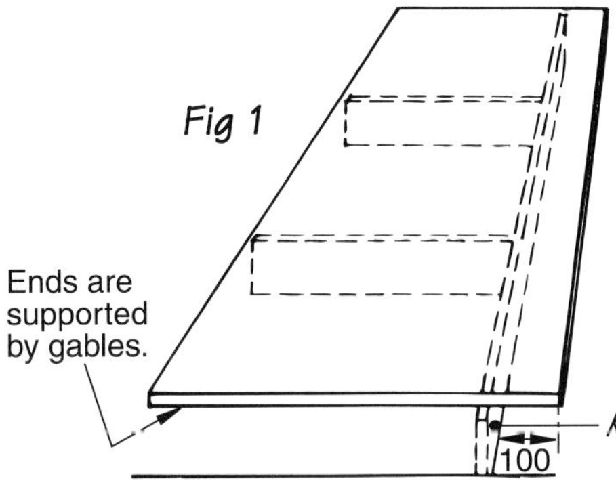

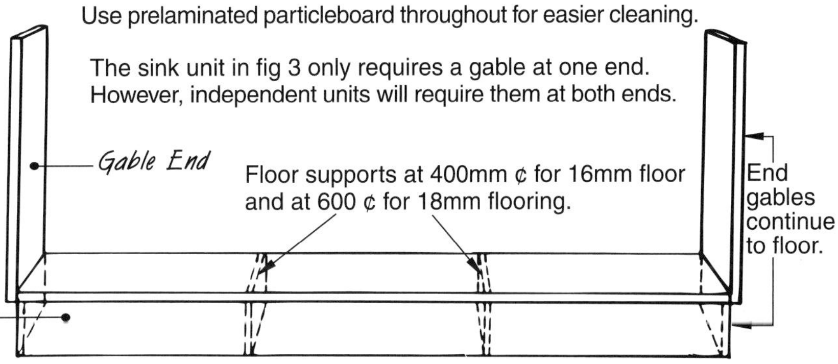

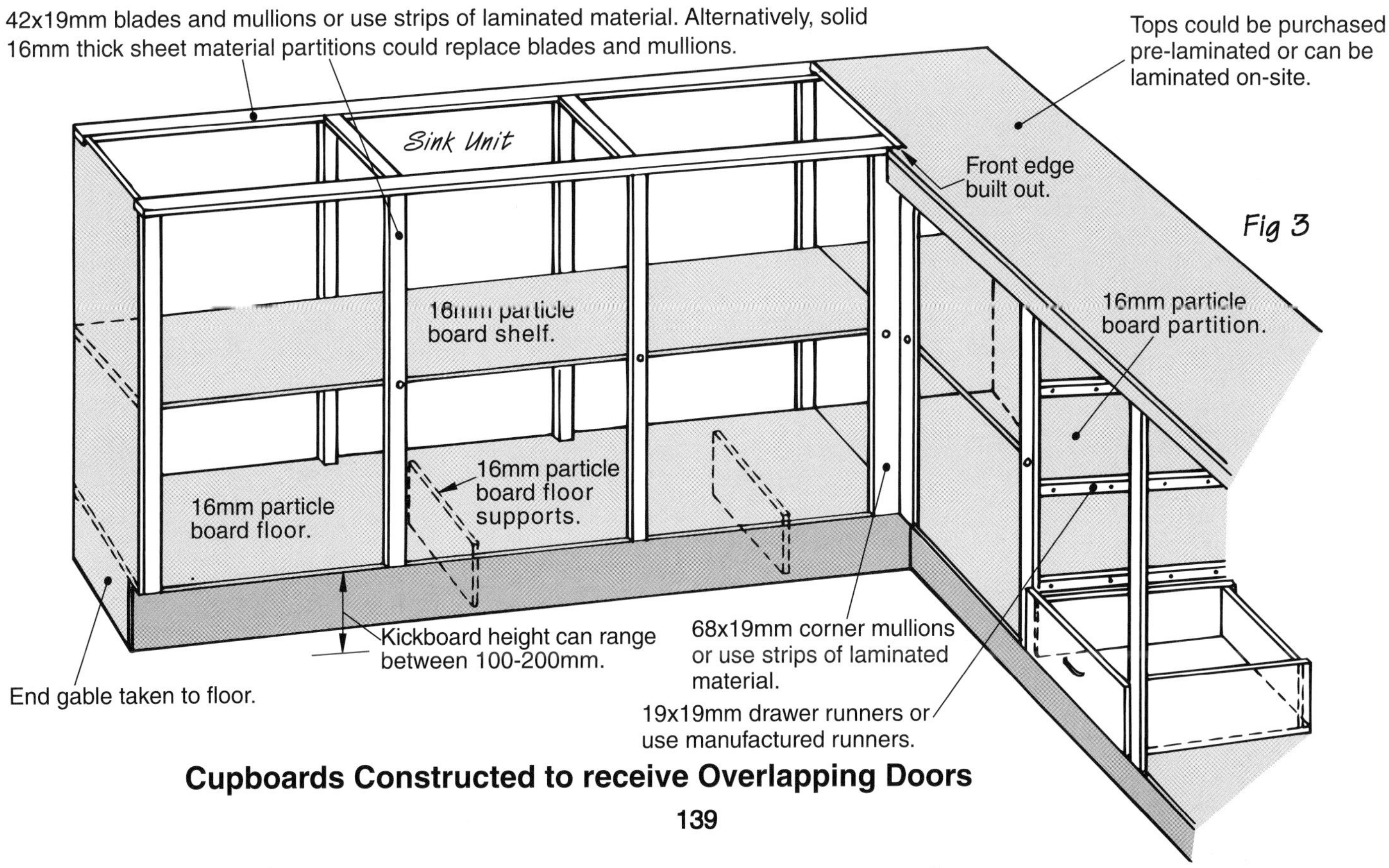

Cupboards Constructed to receive Overlapping Doors

Cont.

Fig 4

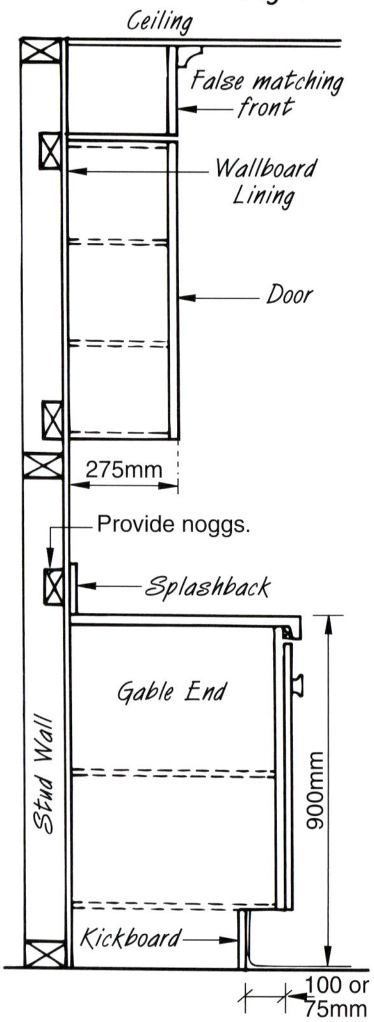

Fig 5

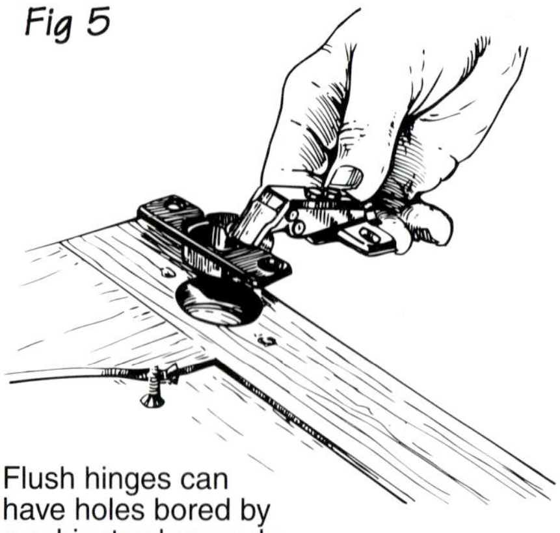

Flush hinges can have holes bored by a cabinetmaker ready for you to fit.

Fig 6

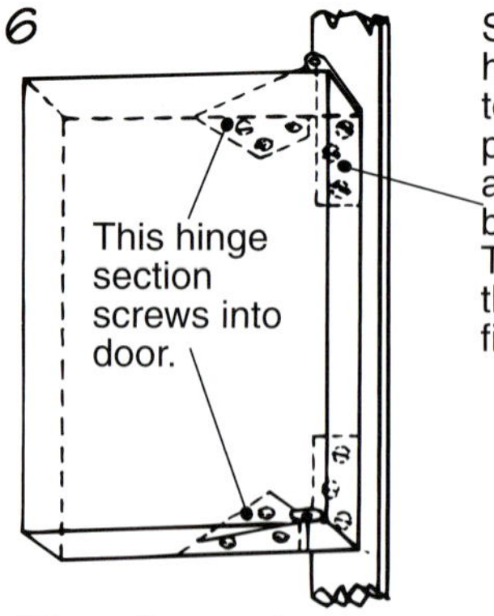

Semi concealed hinges enable doors to be hung in close proximity to one another and not bind on opening. The same applies to the flush hinges in fig 5.

Alternative semi concealed flush hinges which can be easily fitted by the home builder.

Fig 7

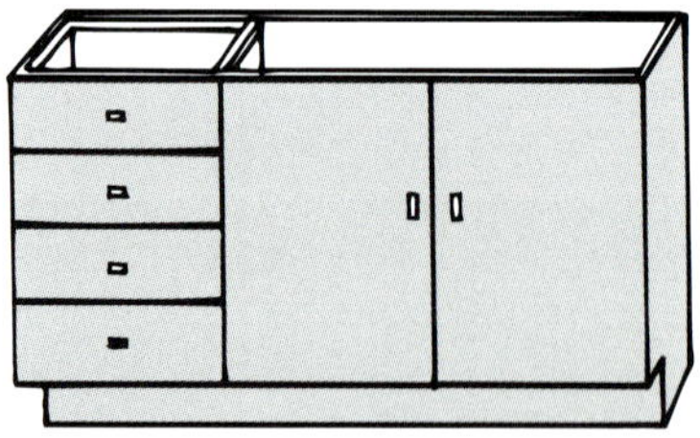

Fig 10

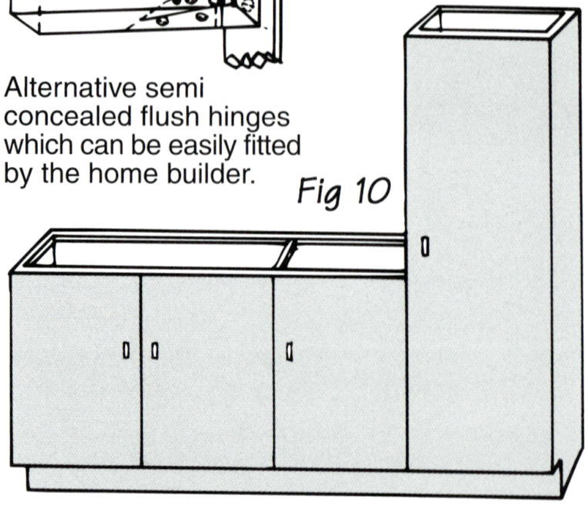

Fig 8

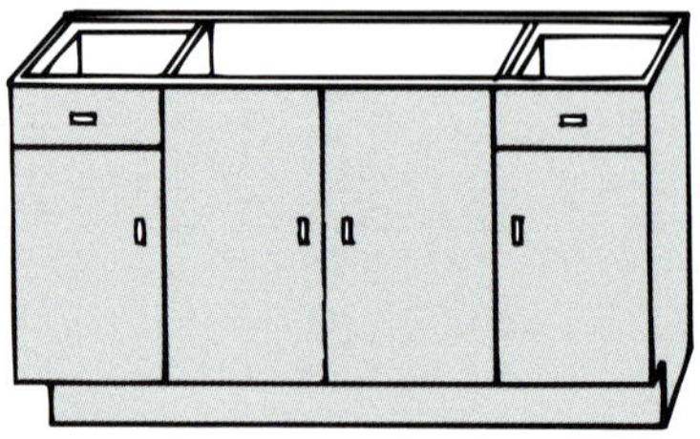

Fig 11

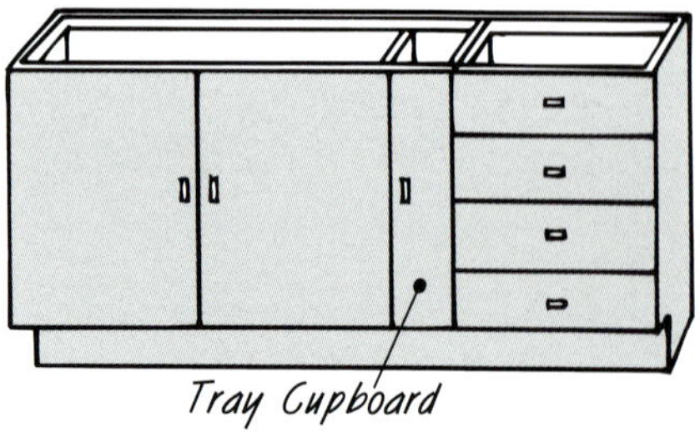

Fig 9

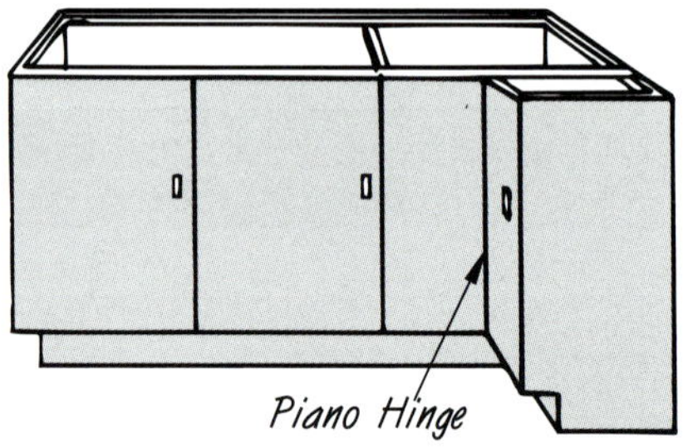

Fig 12

All the above suggested unit designs will accept a sink.

Constructing Drawers

Step 1 Measure and divide opening height up into drawer spacings. Mark position of drawer spacings. Work from the top making allowance for the overlapping of drawer faces. If the bottom drawer is not required, a false front and handle can be attached to the cabinet.

Step 2 Drawer sides and fronts are squared and cut to length and given a groove or slot to house the bottom, usually 4mm hardboard or melamine board. Sides of drawers have a slot across the back end to house the back leaf (see fig 13).

Step 3 Cut back leaf and the bottom to size. Assemble the draw using glue and nails.

Step 4 Drawer face is then cut and attached. Glue and screw from the inside.

Step 5 Runners are then attached at the appropriate spacings. Blocks are fitted to prevent drawers from falling out when fully extended.

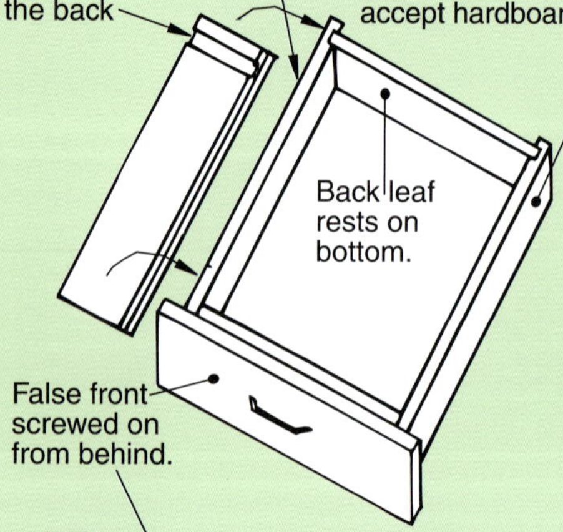

Fig 13

Fig 14

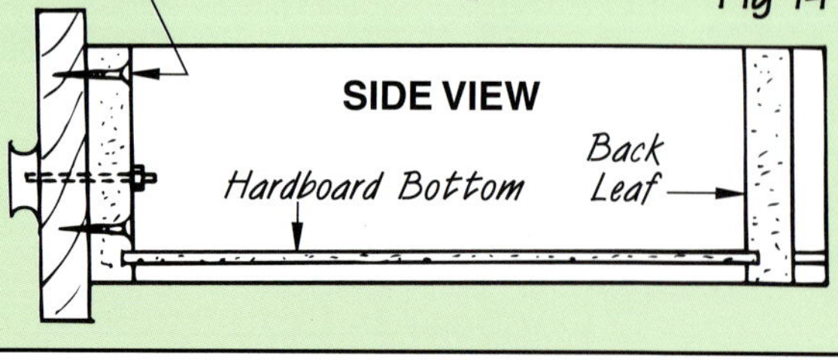

Building Interior Arches using Gyprock Plasterboard

Use the manufactured arch beading and apply as described below.

Step 1 Measure the opening width and cut 13mm thick particle board arch centres as described in fig 1.

Step 2 Construct archway framework using timber of the required thickness to space apart the 13mm particle board arch centres out to existing wall framing thickness (see fig 2). Then nail the centres in place.

Step 3 Hold plasterboard over the proposed archway and mark the arch profile on the back of the sheet allowing an extra 10mm below the particle board centres for fitting the soffit. Then, using a knife or keyhole saw, cut out the plasterboard arch. After carrying out this operation on both sides, nail the plasterboard arches in place ensuring they finish 10mm below the particleboard centres all round the curves.

Step 4 Cut the plasterboard soffit strip to fit between the face sheets and attach this soffit by first applying beads of cornice adhesive to the back edges of the particle board centres. Then press the soffit into place ensuring that continuous contact has been made. The soffit should be nailed each side of the arch 150mm MIN. below the springing line.

Step 5 Take the archway beading supplied and preform it to the shape of the constructed arch by moulding it by hand around the 13mm particle board waste from which the arch was cut. Then holding it to the constructed arch, cut it to the correct length allowing 150mm below the springing line.

Step 6 Fit archway bead to arch with perforated edge on the soffit side of the arch. Nail to studs no closer than 50mm below the springing line. Now using pressure on the opposite side, force the bead to fit tightly around the arch contour and nail again below the springing line on the opposite side.

Step 7 Fit perforated corner beading to vertical corners below the arch. The arch is then ready for finishing compounds.

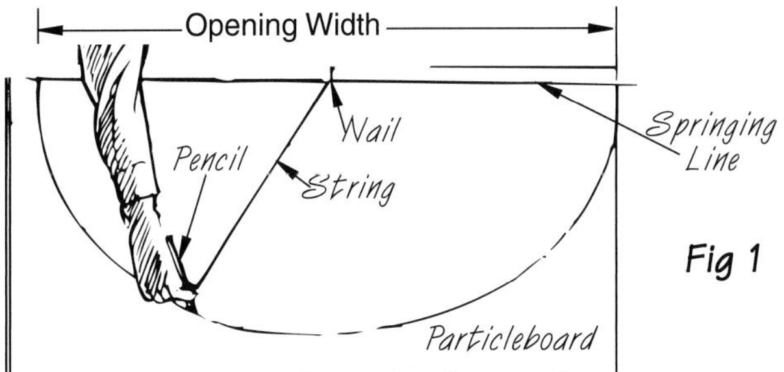

Fig 1

Makeshift compass with a string line attached to a nail at one end and a pencil at the other to form a half circle arch.

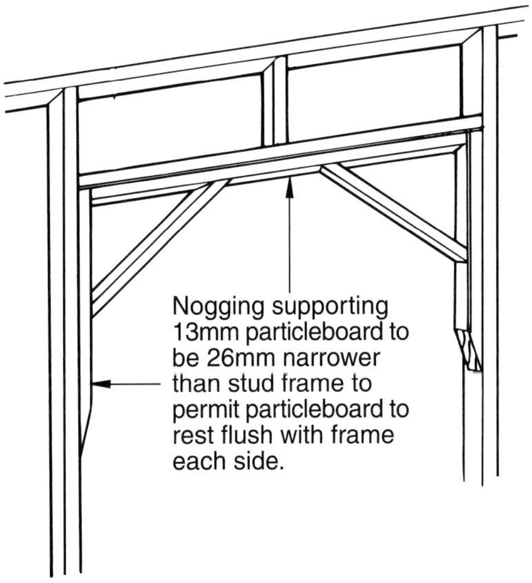

Fig 2

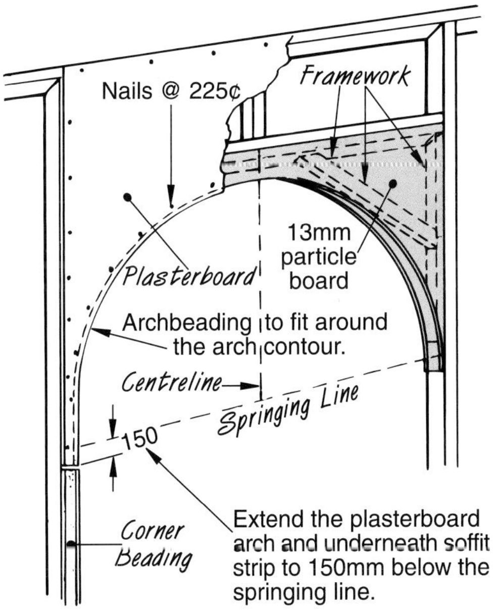

Fig 3

Index

House Builders Series

This entirely Australian manual is thoroughly researched in co-operation with the Australian timber, brick and concrete associations. It is written in Allan Staines usual easy to comprehend style.

It has literally hundreds of clear and technically accurate drawings covering each stage of construction. The text and drawings correlate well. The manual covers the carpentry aspect in detail as well as brick veneer, cavity brick and concrete block systems.

The manual provides current trade practices and hints that help bridge the gap between theory and practice. For these reasons it is an essential class room text.

This all Australian title has large scale drawings to make it easy to understand how the various stages and components fit together. The Owner Builder is shown how to plan the house to suit the chosen allotment and the most economical methods of owner building.

You will learn how to identify and correct faulty building practices, the correct trade terms to use and how to order building products.

This manual will provide you with confidence to build a typical Australian home in weatherboard, brick veneer, cavity brick or concrete block. The manual is cross referenced with 'The Australian House Building Manual' which provides further in-depth construction information.

This step by step guide is full of easy to follow instructions. An indispensible aid for teaching Apprentices, plus quick and easy to use tables and bevels for all roof pitches from 5 degrees to 75 degrees. Bevels drawn on the page ready to transfer directly to the bevel tool. A Builder's dream.

Contents of Manuals

Australian House Building Manual

Understanding:
Timber Frame Weatherboard Construction
Brick Veneer Construction
Cavity Brick Construction
Concrete Block Construction
Setting out the Site
Foundations & Footings
Footing & Slab Floors
Timber Floor Framing
Timber Wall Framing
Truss Roof Construction
The installation of fittings such as: windows, doors, weatherboards, baths, shower recesses and mouldings.
Wet Areas
Flashings, Stair & Handrail construction
Plan Reading
Estimating Quantities
Termite Proofing
Building in Bushfire Areas
Retaining Walls
Adhesives & Sealants
Safety & More

How to be a Successful Owner Builder & Renovator

Understanding House Construction
Designing the House
Weatherboard Houses
Brick Veneer Houses
2 Storey Brick Veneer & Weatherboard
Split Level Houses
Double Brick
Concrete Block Masonry
Extensions & Renovations
Extending Brick Veneer Houses
Extending a Weatherboard House
Adding a Verandah or Carport
How to Supervise the Site
Positioning & Raising an Existing House or a Removal House
Identifying & Correcting Common Problems
Trade Skills for Owner Builders & Apprentices
How to Use Tools

The Roof Building Manual

Roofing Basics
Roof Designs
Roofing Members & Where They Fit
Roofing Terms
The Triangle Makes it Easy
The Rafter Length
Marking Out Top Plates & Ridges
Marking Out Rafters
Cutting Out Rafters
Erecting the Roof
Miscellaneous Details
Easy to Follow Rafter Lengths, Tables & Bevels

ORDERING COUPON OVER PAGE

This book is specifically designed to deal with problems confronted when renovating or altering an existing dwelling. It also shows step-by-step how to accomplish popular renovation projects.

It solves problems such as rising damp, floor and wall cracking, rot in members, small kitchens and bathrooms, leaking shower recesses, and termites. It also describes how to support the roof when making openings in walls.

How to build attic rooms. Installing skylights, guttering, shelving. Replacing existing floor joists, flooring. Fixing sagging roof rafters. Installing french doors. Building carports, enclosing patios and verandahs, installing sliding patio doors, enlarging window openings. Applying Gyprock, restumping, cooling a hot house, attaching laminate and fixing laminate panelling to shower recesses. Wall and floor tiling. Painting. Gives the correct adhesives, sealants and fillers to use and much much more.

This book will teach you how to successfully decorate your home and achieve that professional decor look. Step-by-step it will show you how to avoid costly mistakes by understanding the key principles of decorating and their relevant application. It will be just like having a professional decorator on-hand to help you with much needed advice.

Chapters cover: How to discover your own decorating style, the principles of design, colour, tonal values, using neutrals, colour combinations to achieve a specific image or atmosphere. How to use pattern and texture, furniture and its placement, using decorator materials, environmentally friendly options, hands-on decorating and decorating to re-sell.

An easy to follow, well illustrated manual.

This all Australian manual is packed with ideas and know how and will suit the Builder, Architect or Home DIY'er. It provides many fresh ideas in colour and easy to follow step-by-step instructions cover every procedure. From designing and drawing an acceptable plan for Councils to constructing the post supports, attaching decks or pergolas to the house, methods of handrailing and lots more. All using proper trade procedures. The easy to follow tables included have been prepared by the Timber Associations - TDA in Sydney and Timber Queensland in Brisbane. These cover footing sizes, posts, bearers, joists, deck fastening, handrailing, pergola bearers, rafters and battens. The manual is an indispensible tool in the hands of Designers and Architects.

(All Prices include GST)

Take a photocopy of this page and indicate your requirements on the order form. Books are normally return mailed within three days of receiving order.

Quantity	Title	Cost	Total	*I have enclosed a cheque/money order with this coupon.*
	Decks & Pergolas Construction Manual	$ 22.00		Name:
	The Australian House Building Manual	$ 39.50		Address:
	Successful Owner Builder & Renovator	$ 37.00		
	The Roof Building Manual	$ 29.00		Postcode:
	The Australian Renovators Manual	$ 27.50		Phone Number:
	A Practical Guide to Interior Decorating	$ 22.00		Please send to:
Special Offer 1.	Any Four of the above books for	$113.00		Pinedale Press 2 Lethbridge Court CALOUNDRA QLD 4551
Special Offer 2.	Buy Six - One of each title for	$150.00		Fax Number: (07) 5491 9219
	Plus Postage and Packaging		$ 7.00	*Special Rates for Colleges.*
	Payment Enclosed			*Contact the Publisher for Reseller Price Fax as above.*